Advance Praise for Educating O

"What a delight to find this wonderful volume. It does something that I've long contemplated, offering specific and detailed examples of how people actually create those Natural Critical Learning Environments that I wrote about more generally in *What the Best College Teachers Do*. Here you will find the voices of both teachers and students analyzing their work together across the liberal arts curriculum on problems that are authentic, challenging, and consequential. One of the leitmotifs of the book is the trust that is established between teacher and student, taking each other seriously as learners on an intellectual journey that is at once highly collaborative and highly individualized. Beyond the exploration of pedagogical strategies and experiences, this book thus conveys a sense of the ethos and spirit that characterizes a vibrant and unique learning community. Bard College at Simon's Rock exemplifies the power and reach of the early college idea, and this collection has much to say to both traditional and non-traditional institutions of higher education."

—*Ken Bain, Author of* What the Best College Teachers Do;
*Vice Provost for University Learning and Teaching, and Director,
Research Academy for University Learning, Montclair State University*

"In an age in which, arguably, the art of conversation is dead, preconceived notions are more important than learning, and either-or thinking triumphs over deliberative reflection, *Educating Outside the Lines* offers a simple, yet brilliant antidote. Mining decades of alternative and imaginative college pedagogy at Bard College at Simon's Rock, each chapter presents a distinctive approach to college instruction that finds meaning in that which the university-level establishment dismisses. This volume cultivates the 'spaces in-between'—the gaps in traditional approaches to education— and lends them meaning and pedagogical force. It is the space between academic disciplines (interdisciplinarity), age (adolescent-adult), experience (novice-expert) and power (subordinate-dominant) that triumphs. Bravo for a book that liberates undergraduate education from stifling polarity. Professors and students are free to engage a twenty-first century where ambiguity and uncertainty are dominant, and where answers to our queries about how to improve our pedagogies may lie precisely in these unexplored spaces."

—*William G. Durden, President of Dickinson College; and former Executive Director
of the Center for Talented Youth at Johns Hopkins University*

"American education can only be as great as is our willingness to experiment outside of the conventions, and in that Bard and Simon's Rock have long been inspiring leaders. We all have much to learn from their efforts and analysis, for which we are all grateful."

—*Anthony W. Marx, President, Amherst College and President-Designate,
The New York Public Library*

"This exquisitely crafted set of essays illuminates the rich gifts that a humanistic design for learning extends to everyone—to students themselves, to a thoughtful democracy, and to our entire society's capacity to explore, *in community*, far-reaching questions about our responsibilities to one another and to our shared and vulnerable planet."

—*Carol Geary Schneider, President, Association of American Colleges and Universities*

Educating Outside the Lines

This book is part of the Peter Lang Education list.
Every volume is peer reviewed and meets
the highest quality standards for content and production.

PETER LANG
New York • Washington, D.C./Baltimore • Bern
Frankfurt • Berlin • Brussels • Vienna • Oxford

Educating Outside the Lines

Bard College at Simon's Rock on a
"New Pedagogy" for the Twenty-First Century

Edited by Nancy Yanoshak

PETER LANG
New York • Washington, D.C./Baltimore • Bern
Frankfurt • Berlin • Brussels • Vienna • Oxford

Library of Congress Cataloging-in-Publication Data

Educating outside the lines: Bard College at Simon's Rock on a "new pedagogy"
for the twenty-first century / edited by Nancy Yanoshak.
p. cm.
Includes bibliographical references and index.
1. Education, Humanistic—United States. 2. Education, Higher—Curricula—
United States. 3. Education—United States—Experimental methods.
4. College student orientation—United States. 5. Bard College. Simon's Rock.
I. Yanoshak, Nancy.
LC1011.E39   378'.012—dc22   2010014272
ISBN 978-1-4331-0947-8 (hardcover)
ISBN 978-1-4331-0946-1 (paperback)

Bibliographic information published by **Die Deutsche Nationalbibliothek.**
Die Deutsche Nationalbibliothek lists this publication in the "Deutsche
Nationalbibliografie"; detailed bibliographic data is available
on the Internet at http://dnb.d-nb.de/.

FSC
Mixed Sources
Product group from well-managed
forests, controlled sources and
recycled wood or fiber
Cert no. SCS-COC-002464
www.fsc.org
©1996 Forest Stewardship Council

Cover design by Chase Simmering

The paper in this book meets the guidelines for permanence and durability
of the Committee on Production Guidelines for Book Longevity
of the Council of Library Resources.

© 2011 Peter Lang Publishing, Inc., New York
29 Broadway, 18th floor, New York, NY 10006
www.peterlang.com

Printed in the United States of America

Writing as the editor of this book, I would like to dedicate it to my family, defined broadly as loved ones who live primarily, but not exclusively, in Massachusetts and Pennsylvania.

First and foremost, it is dedicated to my beloved spouse, Sandra Smith. I am in awe of Sandie's wisdom, her generosity to all whom she meets, and her incredible capacity for love. I am grateful for every minute of every day that we share.

It is dedicated to my Simon's Rock family, the friends and colleagues (faculty, staff, and administrators), and the students whom I have been so fortunate to know since coming to Simon's Rock in 1982. It is also dedicated to the memory of our founder, Elizabeth Blodgett Hall, whose vision made Simon's Rock possible, and whose fortitude and dedication maintained it for so many years.

It is dedicated to my family of origin, the Yanoshaks and the Kulmatiskis in Pennsylvania, and now also in many other parts of the country. Finally, it is dedicated to the memory of my parents Stephen and Mary, and of my Aunt Helen Markford.

—NANCY YANOSHAK

Contents

List of Figures

Foreword

MARY B. MARCY

To understand the educational innovation embodied by Bard College at Simon's Rock, it is essential to first understand its heritage. Founded in 1966 by Elizabeth Blodgett Hall, the former headmistress of Concord Academy and the daughter of a distinguished New England family, Simon's Rock from its inception held innovative and classical education in creative tension. It thrives today because it continues to meld the classical and progressive, egalitarian principles alongside meritocratic ideals. This book captures not the how, but the why of the college's success.

The founding date of 1966 is not incidental to the story. The 1960s, of course, were defined by experimentation and disruption, idealism and iconoclasm, and higher education was no exception. Just as the student movement challenged the war in Vietnam and questioned established hierarchies, students and faculty in higher education also began to reconsider conventional methods of teaching and learning. The result was the creation of over three hundred new colleges and universities in the United States in the late 1960s and early 1970s. To be sure, some were little more than glorified encounter groups. Some had compelling ideals, but lacked the physical or human resources to endure. But some were innovative, intriguing, and wholly necessary to the evolution of American higher education.

As the spirit of experimentation of the 1960s gave way to different priorities in the succeeding decades, so, too, did educational innovations. Most significantly, of those three-hundred-plus new colleges and universities, fewer than thirty still exist today. Those that remain tend to have an intellectual ambition and academic currency that fills a fundamental need in our system of higher education.

Bard College at Simon's Rock is one such institution. Simon's Rock was founded on the deceptively simple notion that not all young people mature, socially or intellectually, at the same rate. Simple in concept perhaps, but not a notion that is supported by the traditional structure of American education, nor one that leads to a straightforward educational response.

The great strength of American higher education is its diversity—not only of students, although that is important—but diversity of opportunity. The American system of higher education is rightly considered the best in the world because students can find the education that matches their skills, interests, and passions, whether it involves a technical training program, a path to a professional degree, or a rigorous liberal arts education. To be sure, access to these pathways is not always equitable, but the quality of the opportunity is real.

The great challenge of American basic education is a relative lack of diversity— again, not of students, but of opportunity. Despite recognition that students develop at different rates with different affinities, it is the rare college-bound student who does not go through high school on an age- (rather than ability- or interest-) defined progression. Yet we know this kind of rigidity does not serve students well.

Elizabeth Blodgett Hall's founding vision, then, was to create a means of greater opportunity for young students who were ready for the challenge of college at an earlier age than the norm. She believed that when young people's intellectual curiosity was ascendant, but before they viewed their educational plans primarily as a pathway to a profession, was the ideal time to engage them in a rigorous liberal arts education. And she recognized that few, if any, institutions of education were offering such an opportunity to young scholars.

Yet what is profound about the institution that Mrs. Hall established, as you will find in reading these pages, is not the age of the students. It is the educational approach that has been created to respond to their distinctive blend of intellectual ambition and social development. And it bears consideration for education well beyond the confines of early college conventions.

Central to education at Bard College at Simon's Rock is an ability to manage diverse ideas in creative tension. The college's approach to the liberal arts is anchored in the classical model of a common core seminar for students that tends to the traditional: close reading of primary sources, analysis of major intellectual events in history (particularly Western history), and an integration of arts, humanities, and the sciences. At the same time, the classical approach is leavened by elements that are often considered progressive: a strong emphasis on interdisciplinarity at the upper as well as the lower division, rigorous cultural perspective and language requirements, and an understanding of difference, conveyed through pedagogies that nurture student initiative, and link the classroom to the world beyond.

Faculty and students work and learn in an educational community that assumes that learning is a collaborative experience and a personal journey, and that ultimately the standard for excellence is found in each individual's capacity. Inherent in all activity is an assumption that critical thinking and problem solving are at the core of liberal education.

Within these pages you will find specific examples of this elegant, complex, resilient, and enduring notion of education. While this educational model grew out of an idiosyncratic idea, the lessons learned have a far broader application, one that has an essential place in discussions of the future of higher education.

Acknowledgments

This project began as an invitation to my colleagues at Bard College at Simon's Rock to "write a book together." It constituted the core activity during my tenure as our Emily H. Fisher Faculty Fellow in 2007–2009, when we drafted the substantial part of the work, and secured Peter Lang as our publisher.

I am grateful to the family of Emily H. Fisher, Chairman of our Board of Overseers, for establishing the Faculty Fellowship in her name to honor Emily, a leader who has cared so well and for so long about Bard College at Simon's Rock. I thank our Provost and Vice President, Mary B. Marcy, who selected me to serve the college in this capacity. I also thank Mary for her unwavering enthusiasm for the book project, and for all of the resources, both personal and institutional, that she put at our disposal to advance it.

Now that the project has come to fruition, it is my great pleasure to acknowledge the many and varied forms of support that have made this work possible.

In first instance, I would like to acknowledge the vision of Leon Botstein, President of Bard and of Simon's Rock, who set standards of excellence that enabled us to realize our potential as the nation's pioneer early college. Leon believed in us, and in early college as a viable educational alternative, when few others did, and has worked in myriad capacities to make believers out of others across the country.

Patricia Sharpe, our Academic Dean in the nineties and early 2000s, and one of our contributing authors, offered wise counsel that helped to shape the project both in its early stages, and at its end. I particularly want to thank Pat for her incisive comments on the introductory and concluding chapters of this volume, and for her willingness to consult about matters great and small regarding the project as a whole. Bernard F. Rodgers, Jr., who served as Vice President of Bard and Dean of Simon's Rock for many years before returning to the faculty in 2004 as Emily H. Fisher Chair in Literature, provided timely help in making our project known to others in the field of higher education, and securing their support of our work. Bernie also kindly dug deep into his files to supply important information on the history of the college in the 1980s. I am grateful to Steven Coleman, our Director of Admission, who first brought to my attention the significant connections of Bard College at Simon's Rock to the history of progressive education, and generously shared the work he has done on this topic. Moira Buhr, Associate Registrar, and Karen Advokaat, Assistant to the Dean of Academic Affairs, spent much time and effort cheerfully and quickly answering my many questions about alumni and current students, faculty, staff, and administrators. Chase Simmering, our Art Director and Publications Manager, designed a wonderful cover that captures the spirit of our students, ever willing to go "outside the lines" that define education in the United States today. I thank Alejandro de Onis as well, who took the original photographs of these students for Simon's Rock, and, I thank the students themselves and their parents, for granting us permission to include these images.

Simon's Rock provided substantial institutional support for the book in the form of Strategic Initiative Grants in the summer of 2008, which gave us authors the opportunity to develop our conceptualization of the collection, to write early versions of our chapters, and to provide critical feedback on each other's work.

Simon's Rock also awarded six Faculty Development Grants that enabled several of us to present our ideas as papers at professional conferences, and supported the completion of the index, and the typesetting of the book.

Grateful acknowledgment is made to Hampton Press for permission to reprint Pat Sharpe's "Early College: What and Why?" which she has updated for inclusion in this collection. The original version appeared in *Time For Change: New Visions for High School*, edited by Robert W. Smith (Cresskill, New Jersey: Hampton Press, Inc., 2006), 121–134.

I wish to thank Christopher S. Myers, Managing Director of Peter Lang, for his resolute advocacy of our book, and his patience with the inevitable delays we encountered in completing it; Sophie Appel, our Production Supervisor at Peter Lang, for overseeing the production process with great skill and understanding; and Oliver Sharpe for the superb job that he did as our typesetter.

Speaking on behalf of my fellow authors, I want to express our gratitude to the many members (and former members) of the Simon's Rock community, too numerous to name here, whom we consulted as we prepared our chapters. These friends, colleagues, students, and alumni answered our myriad questions about their experiences with great insight, patience, frankness, and generosity.

As have my fellow authors, I have attempted to acknowledge specific intellectual debts in the notes to my own chapters, but there are some people whom I would like to thank here for support that bridges the distinction between the intellectual and the personal.

My spouse Sandra Smith was an avid and ever optimistic supporter of the project. Even on those days when, after long hours of writing, I could muster only a few sentences, she would not let me forget that they were *good* sentences. And if by chance they were not, she was always willing to read them with me, and suggest changes that made them better.

Joan DelPlato, who contributed one of our chapters, has been my best friend, best critic, and staunchest advocate during the quarter century we have worked together at Simon's Rock. She brings a prodigious intellect and a heart to match to every task she attempts, and I have long been the beneficiary of both.

Deepest thanks go as well to Simon's Rock colleagues Wendy Shifrin, also a contributing author, and Barbara Resnik, and their spouses, respectively, Steven Moritz and Sol Resnik. I thank these dear and wise friends for their counsel on matters of common concern at the college and outside of it, their constant and generous friendship in good times and difficult ones, and for all that we have shared since I came to Simon's Rock.

Last, and far from least, I want to extend heartfelt thanks to my fellow authors, whose erudition and dedication will be evident on every page of this work.

NANCY YANOSHAK
Great Barrington, Massachusetts
March 13, 2011

1

INTRODUCTION

1

"For Nothing Was Simply One Thing"

An Introduction to Simon's Rock
and to Our Book[1]

NANCY YANOSHAK

ABOUT SIMON'S ROCK

In the 1980s, when Simon's Rock College was roughly sixteen years old, its founder, Elizabeth (Betty) Blodgett Hall, would tool around the unpaved roads in her golf cart, asking the students, also about age sixteen, what they thought of the world and of her educational experiment. They would tell her, cheerfully, and in no uncertain terms. Chief custodian Stan Farnum cared for a small group of buildings whose architecture students described as "early Pizza Hut," and wrote poetry on the side. And, inspired by his native Burma, Dean of Students Ba Win cooked celebratory meals that you could eat with your fingers for students and faculty. Everyone in this intimate college community of less than 400 seemed to know everyone else, and all of us, from Betty to Ba Win to Stan, were on a first-name basis.

In 2011, Betty is no longer with us, Stan has retired from the college (but continues with his poetry), and we are now Bard College at Simon's Rock. The roads are paved, and the "Pizza Huts" are dwarfed by a number of impressive Centers, buildings dedicated to the Sciences, the Performing Arts, and to Athletics. U Ba Win, now a Vice President at Bard College, has helped to found two Early College High Schools, where students also start college work before the traditional age, but he still comes back to campus to cook his legendary curries.[2] Most importantly, our students still speak their minds. As a visitor to a recent Board of Overseers meeting told me, she was astonished at how readily senior Timothy R. Meyers (B.A., 2008) and junior Isaac (Gabriel) Salgado (B.A., 2009) entered into a discussion

*about campus transportation problems, and "told Emily {Fisher, Chairman of the Board},
what's what."[3] She was no less astonished at how intently Emily listened. And everyone, from
Emily to Tim and Gabe, is still on a first-name basis, a ritual of campus culture, which helps
to enact the crossing of conventional boundaries of age and status that it symbolizes.*

Mrs. Hall founded what was initially known as Simon's Rock in 1966,[4] in
part as a response to a crisis in the relationship of the nation's youth and its elders.
As she saw it, the sixties mantra "never trust anyone over thirty," was understandable: Many adolescents, idealistic, physically mature, and yearning for the privileges
and responsibilities of adulthood were treated like children wholly unready for any
meaningful contact with the world outside. No wonder alienation and nihilism
were rampant on college campuses.[5] Mrs. Hall's solution was to create an institution
where sixteen-year-olds who had left high school early would simultaneously be
challenged to assume the adult responsibilities they craved, and nurtured with the
institutional and pedagogical support necessary for them to succeed.

The nature of the problems confronting American education from the sixties
onward, as well as the proposed remedies, are still contested, and some would identify the reputed permissiveness of the decade of "sex, drugs, and rock and roll," as
one of the causes of these problems, rather than their symptom. Nevertheless, Mrs.
Hall's insight that adults must keep faith with the younger generation, and keep up
with what is actually happening in their lives, if they are to engage adolescents in
learning that is important, meaningful, and consequential, have proved valid long
after the protests of the sixties became history. Our own history, particularly in the
early decades, has itself been one of struggle to persuade students and their parents
that not only was Simon's Rock a "real college," but one that was worth the risk of
attending, despite its lack of name recognition and its unusual mission. We have
been fortunate to have had strong leadership, from Mrs. Hall's time forward, and
emerged in the 1980s after our merger with Bard strong enough to withstand the
uncertainties of a fluctuating economy, and the pain and trauma of the nationally
reported shootings on campus in 1992.[6] Despite such vicissitudes, Bard College at
Simon's Rock has grown and thrived as a testimony to Mrs. Hall's vision, and in this
collection past and current members of our community would like to contribute to
the project that she began by sharing what we have learned about college teaching
through our work with younger students.

Virginia Woolf's *To the Lighthouse* has for many years been a core text in our
general education curriculum. The passage from the novel that inspired the title of
this introduction, "For nothing was simply one thing," captures the unique position
of Simon's Rock within contemporary higher education. Neither simply "college,"
nor "early college," we are both at once. Despite our growth over the past forty-five

years, we remain an intimate, egalitarian academic community, now of about 650, including 400 students, a core faculty of about fifty, plus administrators, staff, and adjunct instructors. The sense of being an important part of a collaborative enterprise that nurtures individual development and active community involvement is palpable, felt even by first-year students who have been here but a few weeks. Classes are small, most are conducted seminar style, and a strong advising system ensures that faculty and staff develop close connections to incoming students, with whom they meet regularly and frequently, particularly during their initial term. As they grow in experience, students assume increasing responsibility for their academic and social lives. They participate in college governance via a student-led community council, and sit on academic and student-life committees as full voting members. Roughly half of our students transfer, often to prestigious, and certainly larger, institutions after earning their A.A. degrees. Those who stay on for the B.A. create an individualized Program of Study that combines a concentration established by the faculty with a student-designed concentration, which complements the former. Tutorials, internships, and the like, encourage independent work on projects initiated by the student. Additionally the college offers Signature Programs, including articulation agreements with Oxford University, Columbia University, and Dartmouth College, which provide juniors with a number of options for studying away or for participating in select in-house programs. B.A. requirements culminate in a capstone interdisciplinary seminar, and a year-long senior thesis.

Our current curriculum was inspired by the distinctive synthesis of the classical tradition of general education with educational progressivism that Leon Botstein, President of both Bard College in Annandale and Simon's Rock, developed at Bard in the 1970s.[7] We are "classical" in the sense that all students in their first two years take a series of interdisciplinary core seminars with common syllabi, focused on discussions of important primary texts spanning ancient times to the present. And we are like the progressive colleges established in the 1930s in that we seek to reconfigure the traditional classroom as both a less hierarchical and a more flexible space wherein student initiative is nurtured and valued and where the boundary between the academy and the larger world is blurred in productive ways.[8] While a number of other selective liberal arts colleges now promote a more student-centered pedagogy through their own variants of such practices, we are unique in that our students are, on the average, two years younger than those at other institutions, and may earn their B.A. here before they are twenty.

Further, Bard College at Simon's Rock stands now as one of the leaders of a growing early college movement. In 2011 the institutions most associated with the term "early college" are the Early College High Schools, of which Bard High School Early College (BHSEC), now with campuses in Manhattan and Queens, is a particularly successful exemplar.[9] These combine an accelerated high school curriculum with the first two years of college, and lead to an A.A. degree. BHSEC's academic program was modeled on ours, and we have conducted an Institute for Early College Pedagogy that shares our teaching techniques with secondary school and college educators from around the country.[10] Nevertheless, our program is entirely at the collegiate level,[11] and we remain the only residential "early college" designed expressly for younger scholars to offer the B.A. Thus, in significant ways, Simon's Rock stands apart, even from the very category of higher education that it has helped to create. In this collection we will explore what this unique vantage point has taught us about effective college pedagogy.

The heart of our enterprise is what we are calling a "new pedagogy,"[12] grounded in the meaningful intellectual connection of students and faculty, which in its closeness and in the mutual respect that it entails, resembles the types of relationships which can obtain between graduate students and their mentors. Lest this sound grandiose, we hasten to add that we are certainly cognizant of the ways that our mentorial relationships must differ from those at the postgraduate level, given the obvious fact that most of our students have not yet even reached the age of first-year undergraduates at other institutions. Indeed these students are atypical, less because of any intellectual precociousness, than because of their determination to begin higher education at sixteen. They leave the comforts of home, family, and the familiar, because they do not "fit" in their old educational environments, where, they tell us, they were not challenged intellectually, and were not allowed to challenge much of anything themselves. They are at once idealistic and worldly, playful, often irreverent, and yet in deadly earnest about the life of the mind, their academic and professional futures, and about doing good in the world they will inherit. As they move, sometimes with breathtaking speed, between adult and adolescent, and back again, the faculty moves with them, enjoying their exuberance, their feistiness, and above all, taking them seriously as learners on the brink of beginning their adult lives. Finally, although our mission of educating this population has entailed the creation of distinctive pedagogies, we also note that our students are in fact like most others at their stage in life— curious about the world, impatient for the privileges of adulthood, and both anxious and hopeful about what the future might bring. We do not offer ourselves as *the* model of higher education for every college, or even every early college, but we think we have learned something about engaging students of both high school and college age, and about moving them quickly from one level to the other, and in many cases beyond, to the brink of postgraduate work. Thus we hope in this book to enter into a dialogue with educational professionals, with parents, and with students themselves, who care about adolescents, about learning, and about teaching, and want to think through the ways to meet the challenges of a new century.

ABOUT OUR BOOK:
EDUCATING (INSIDE AND) OUTSIDE THE LINES

Our book is the collaborative effort of twenty-nine authors, all of whom are, or have been, associated with the college. Virtually all of the "generations" of faculty and students who have been part of the institution from its beginnings to the present are represented, as are all four of the academic divisions. In addition to the Foreword by our Provost and Vice President, Mary B. Marcy, and my introduction (Part I of the book) and conclusion (Part VI), there are fifteen core chapters on aspects of teaching and learning at the college. Thirteen are written or co-written by faculty, one is by a faculty member and her students, and another is co-written by two alumni.

Whatever our place within the nearly half-century history of Simon's Rock, the pieces we have written reflect our shared commitment to an academic experience that respects but is not limited by the categories that overtly or covertly have organized higher education, whether they be professional, intellectual, social, or institutional. We have been inspired, provoked, enlightened, and delighted by the ways theses "lines" can be redrawn and reinvented. These reinventions constitute the basis for the organizational schema of the book. The fifteen core chapters are grouped into four thematically related sections (Parts II–V of the book), each of which problematizes aspects of the conventions of contemporary academia.

Entitled "Big Questions from Small Classes: Engaging Students in Consequential Dialogues in the Arts and Humanities," the first section (Part II) addresses what might be called the "Art of the Discussion Class," the format which is the norm for most courses at the college. The chief pedagogical issues considered concern the creation of a de-centered classroom, where learning is driven by collaborative problem solving of substantive issues of interest to all participants. How do expert and novice (teacher and student) learn to work together in an open situation in which the former is not the font of all knowledge, and in which the latter must figure out what to say about material that he may hardly know at all?

These questions are pursued in three articles. In "Intellectual Warm-Ups: How 'Writing and Thinking' Prepares Students for College Study," John B. Weinstein focuses on our "Writing and Thinking Workshop," an intensive five-and-a-half-day academic orientation for in-coming students, which must be completed in order to earn a Simon's Rock degree. John directs the Workshop, and here he discusses the ways in which this highly structured program prepares new students for the responsibilities of collaborative and self-directed work in the more free-wheeling atmosphere they will encounter in their regular classes. He describes workshop techniques designed to build the skills of active learning that our classes require, and, to illustrate his points, invites us to participate in an interactive experience using these techniques. Thus, we learn (or re-learn), firsthand how writing becomes a way of discovering one's thoughts; how reading another's thoughts becomes practice for truly listening to that person; and how such activities become the basis for intellectual collaboration in a classroom space genuinely shared by teacher and students.

In the second piece, entitled "Generations Y and Z Drash Alpha and Omega: Young Scholars Encounter Sacred Texts," Rebecca Fiske focuses on the ways that younger students, despite being steeped in the ephemera of a largely secular culture, can become engaged with very old, sacred texts through the practice of Midrash. Rebecca argues that the latter, as hermeneutic mode derived from the ways in which early rabbinic thinkers aggressively questioned sacred texts and generated layers of commentary, is congruent with our Writing and Thinking techniques, in that both help to explore multiple meanings. She analyzes the process by which her students (both believers and non-believers) use their own versions of "drashing" to move from awed, but often little-informed, respect for the Bible and the Qur'an as authoritative texts with fixed meanings, to respectful but creative (and sometimes playful) exegesis.

Lastly, in "Finding the Bridge: Integrating Music Theory and Composition," Laurence D. Wallach, considers the ways in which he and his students have worked together to break down the barriers between music theory and composition, which have traditionally been viewed as discrete fields by academic and non-academic musicians alike. In the collaborative atmosphere of his classes, which may mix upper-division students well-acquainted with music theory, and beginning students with strong performing skills but no "theory," composing becomes a learning activity that is crucial to the understanding of musical structures. Insights gained about structure, in turn, inform the creative effort of composition, as new pieces are "workshopped," i.e., subjected to critical feedback by the group. Larry's piece thus highlights the ways that a music program developed in an intimate setting where the input of colleagues and instructors is available as a resource rather than an authoritative source, permits each student to construct a bridge from theory to composition in a way that nurtures the integrity of his or her creative impulse.

Part III is entitled "The Virtues of Cross-Disciplinary Pedagogy: Integrating Knowledge from the Sciences, Humanities, Social Sciences, and the Arts." Its three chapters explore the connections their authors have made between their own disciplines and others, through participation in the intellectual life of a learning community that features interactive pedagogies and encourages cross-disciplinary collaborations. Whereas the first cluster of articles focused on the establishment of a classroom where the teacher was not the sole authoritative voice, this one problematizes authoritative discourses of the traditional disciplines, as its authors describe their efforts to use these discourses in conjunction with each other in the classroom.

The pedagogical implications of blurring the distinction between novice and expert, which figured in Part II as that between teacher and student, reappear here in Part III in a new key, as a teacher from one field works in the field of another.

First, in "Modeling Plato's Heaven and God's Green Earth," Samuel Ruhmkorff proposes interdisciplinary and interactive teaching models for mathematics and science. In place of disciplinary courses that emphasize the acquisition of extensive factual knowledge, Sam recommends a focus on teaching scientific and mathematical methodologies, informed by wise choices as to the content that will support them. The key to bridging the gap between novice and expert in courses that integrate science and mathematics is Sam's insight that at their core both fields are sophisticated forms of everyday critical thinking. Thus he advocates team-taught courses that explore compelling issues (e.g., climate change), and mix students with different levels of expertise. Taught by teachers who address math and science anxiety by conveying the reality that these disciplines utilize cognitive abilities that everyone has, these courses can be structured to allow all students to work at a pace that challenges them. Additionally, Sam underlines the value of a general education that appropriately integrates mathematics and science with the humanities. Here he argues that in crossing disciplinary boundaries, teachers must trust that they will find not a defender of epistemic exclusivity, but a colleague who offers help with an unfamiliar topic.

Next, Allen B. Altman and John E. Myers provide a concrete example of an interdisciplinary offering that links the humanities and the sciences, and that exemplifies both the kind of trust between experts that Sam advocates as well as the larger collaborative spirit that thrives at Simon's Rock. Their piece, "Intelligence and Consciousness, Artificial and Otherwise: An Interdisciplinary Seminar on *Gödel, Escher, Bach*," describes their experiences teaching a BA Seminar (our required capstone course) named for Douglas Hofstadter's interdisciplinary exploration of the nature of cognition. Mathematician Allen, musician John, and their students, employ all disciplinary perspectives at their disposal in their collective attempt to understand the fundamental questions about thought, intelligence, and the relationship of human and machine posed in Hofstadter's book. Their efforts bridge the differences between the disciplines in no small part because each participant feels that his or her expertise is valued by the others in the class, and because each recognizes that no one disciplinary lens is adequate to the questions they want to answer.

In the third article, " 'So What If You're a French Major, You Should Totally Be in the Dance Concert': 'Effective Interdisciplinarity' at Simon's Rock," I analyze the ways that interdisciplinarity informs our mission and permeates our learning culture. I compare the views of colleagues and alumni on these issues to the scholarly literature on interdisciplinarity, and, indebted to Michel Foucault's concept of "effective history," I propose the idea of "Effective Interdisciplinarity," to describe the processes by which we accomplish this key curricular goal. "Effective history" attempts to recover "subjugated knowledges," i.e., the voices of those marginalized in mainstream discourses, and I argue that adolescents, often silenced in the discourses of adults, can be viewed in this way. Simon's Rock students, who are encouraged, but also expected, to express their views in our classes, often use "Effective Interdisciplinarity" to do so, by bringing ideas encountered in one course to bear in another. Thus, through an analysis of the ways students integrate their experiences in a range of disciplines to empower themselves in our classrooms, I explore the relationship that can obtain between interactive pedagogies that disperse authoritative voices throughout a group and interdisciplinarity, which disperses epistemological authority among various disciplinary terrains.

The title of Part IV is "College Teaching and 'Post-Identity Politics': Collaborations across the Boundaries of Age, Status, and Place." Whereas Part II highlighted several disciplinary iterations of de-centered pedagogical authority, and Part III considered ways to rethink the epistemological authority of the disciplines, the chapters in this section problematize the authority of society and culture as determinants of our identities as learners both inside the classroom and outside of it.

Several of these pieces explicitly claim a politics, and others do not. Be that as it may, they all reflect an awareness that the "identity politics" espoused by marginalized groups in an earlier generation tended to reify boundaries that separated one group from another, ironically replicating the divisive practices of those from whom these groups sought liberation. Instead, these pieces imply a more fluid conception of how identity is constituted, recognizing it as a function of one's relationship to an "Other." They explore ways to re-conceive the nature of the classroom experience so that it enhances individual agency through participation in flexible, egalitarian learning situations that valorize difference at the same time that they promote a richer, more positive connection to that "Other."

In "Arabic at Simon's Rock: Spanning Two Wars and Counting," Gabriel V. Asfar describes an approach to teaching this language that incorporates materials disseminated by the U.S. military in Iraq, all of which have been sent to him by Simon's Rock alumni. As supplements to more traditional textbook content, these materials bring a "real-life" context that engages students more deeply in their language learning. Their use also allows Gabriel to add cultural and sociological dimensions to his language courses, which may fulfill the "Cultural Perspectives" requirement of the college. The latter is intended to expand students' understandings of other cultures, many of which have been marginalized by the West. In the unique learning communities he has created, past and present students are brought together to develop their understandings of contemporary political and cultural configurations in the Middle East. We are at once heartened by the intellectual collaborations that Gabriel fosters, and disturbed by the ignorance of, and condescension toward, "the Other" reflected in the texts on which he focuses.

Jennifer Browdy de Hernandez' piece, "The Politics and Poetics of Global Feminist Alliance, or Why I Teach Such Depressing Books," is also concerned with the establishment of mutually respectful connections of the United States with peoples beyond its borders. Her focus is on her course on the writing of Latin American and Caribbean women, wherein students enter into dialogues with a series of disquieting tales of exploitation and heroic resistance. Faced with evidence about the economic and political relationships with the United States that have contributed to such conditions, students are moved to what psychologist Kaethe Weingarten terms a "compassionate witnessing" of the pain these women have endured, and thence to search for ways to form "ethical alliances" with them, grounded in the recognition of our responsibilities to "the Other." To understand the multi-stage process of developing an activist political awareness that she and many of her students have experienced through these encounters, Jenny creatively deploys post-colonial feminist Gloria Anzaldúa's conceptualization of *conocimiento* ("knowledge," "consciousness").

In "Visual Learning: Female Students, Women Artists, and Mothers," Joan DelPlato explores psychological and intellectual processes at the heart of teaching and learning her primary discipline. Like Jenny, she looks toward the creation of mutuality between the dominant and subordinate, focusing in particular on the relationships between mothers and daughters. Extending concepts from feminist film theory and Lacanian psychology, Joan constructs an original tri-partite schema to understand how students in her "Women Artists" course move from an initial silent encounter with an image to the articulation of an informed art historical analysis. She notes that the coming to voice that her students, especially the females, experience in studying art history can be part of their larger processes of intellectual maturation. And she seeks to understand the relationship of her identity as both teacher and mother to this process. Thus Joan combines roles usually kept separate in the lives of professional academics, and offers an example of "transgressive" teaching that can empower both students and professor.

In "The Simon's Rock Dance Concert: Reflecting, Defining, and Creating Community," Wendy Shifrin discusses this event as an exemplar of "community" at Simon's Rock that gives concrete expression to deeply held values of our educational philosophy. In these semiannual productions, which Wendy directs, we may find a venerable mathematician, a staff member, and several dance majors choreographing a piece together, while a group of neophytes learn Maori, Native American, Flamenco, and Indian dancing from community members versed in these dance forms. Students take on new responsibilities, from organizing their own rehearsal sessions to handling the technical aspects of mounting a large public production.

Moreover the connection between performers and audience is palpable in our small community, as not only students, but faculty, staff, and administrators, all make a point of attending. In bringing together representatives of virtually all campus constituencies, and nurturing the skills, aesthetic sensibilities, and confidence of all participants, whatever their background, the concert thus embodies an egalitarian learning culture premised on initiative, creativity, collaboration, and respect for diversity.

"At Home with Uncanny Labors: A Case of Working and Thinking the Social Sciences," is co-written by Asma Abbas and her students (Nuola Akinde, Noah Appelbaum, Els Baum, Laura Cheung, Brendan Flynn, Dara Levy-Bernstein, Dylan Neely, Anastasia Rodionova, and Emanuel Stults) in one of our signature programs, the Proseminar in Social Scientific Inquiry. The piece focuses on "Home and the Haunts of Modernity," the core course for the pilot year of the program. One of the chief goals was to re-imagine a social science classroom. This was accomplished by exploring the connections between modes of inquiry and modes of relating to others in a shared space that problematized assumptions about social science inquiry as the simple acquisition of knowledge by an a priori, fixed subject. Thus this multi-vocalic piece does not tell us what the group discovered about "home" as an object of social science inquiry. Rather it documents their labors to create the democratic intellectual community that provided the home for these inquiries, and that effected important changes, professionally and personally, for all concerned. This work recalls the collaboration across boundaries of age and status that is sometimes found in postgraduate research projects. Here it is carried out by a college teacher and junior and senior undergraduates who are two years younger than those at any other institution of higher education.

Lastly, in "Bringing Our 'Best Selves' to the Table: Awakening Critical Compassion in the Classroom," Linda Anderson and Anne O'Dwyer also explore the classroom as an emotionally and intellectually charged space, and challenge traditional views of what is possible and appropriate to attempt within it. They focus on "pedagogies of compassion," which deepen self-knowledge and appreciation of "the Other" through a recognition that human existence cannot adequately be grasped in purely impersonal terms, divorced from social and personal contexts. Linda and Anne conceptualize their version of such a pedagogy as "critical compassion," to underscore both the cognitive and affective domains of the type of teaching and learning that they advocate. By invoking the skills of critical reason and empathy together, they develop pedagogical strategies that advance participants' understanding of the processes by which we are distanced from each other, and of how we may bridge this distance. With learning grounded in a recognition of the full-blown humanity of each individual, students are inspired to create new ways of problem solving as they chart their complex paths toward maturity.

With Part V, "Early College from Margin to Center: Transforming Higher Education by Rethinking 'the Spaces In-Between,'" we enter into a discussion of the implications of the early college idea, which forthrightly challenges traditional views of higher education in the United States. Seemingly grounded in the experience and wisdom of the past, these views are found in significant ways to be based on a misreading of that past, as well as of the capabilities of the youth of today. As the works in this section imply, in establishing unnecessary and arbitrary boundaries between middle and late adolescence, such traditions can impede young people from realizing their full potential. Exploring the meanings of the educational spaces between adolescence and adulthood, these articles combine historical inquiry with reflections on personal experiences to problematize unquestioned assumptions that underlie our educational traditions, and to look toward a better educational future.

In "Early College: What and Why?" Patricia Sharpe explicates the philosophy that underlies early college, and explores its conceptual and institutional history since the founding of Simon's Rock. She documents the importance of the latter as a model for several Early College High Schools, and brings to bear research on adolescent development and her own experiences as a teacher and administrator to elaborate the core insight informing the early college movement: At sixteen, young people are not only ready, but at the ideal age to begin college work. It is at that point, before they have begun any professional training, and have yet to find a clear direction in life, that they are most open to the range of human inquiry. At the same time, because intellectual capacities at this age outstrip capacities for well-reasoned decisions, young people need structures specifically designed to provide the combination of affirmation and support that characterizes Simon's Rock and the institutions that have followed in its footsteps.

The components of the early college idea synthesized in Pat's article—a challenging academic experience offered in a nurturing intellectual and social environment to students whose capabilities are respected—are touched on many times in this collection, but principally from the point of view of faculty. In the second piece in this section, "Early Ever After: Alumni Reflect on Life After Simon's Rock," we see their iteration from the point of view of former students. Michael Lawrence and Loren L. AliKhan draw on their own recollections, and those of other alumni, to reflect on what their education "outside the lines" has meant as they engage "life after Simon's Rock." They note that the age gap that separated them from their peers at other colleges becomes virtually irrelevant as graduates embark on their careers. Thus, they problematize the very factor that on its face would seem to define early college, and engage more fundamental aspects of an educational experience that developed their self-confidence, powers of mind, and willingness to take risks, intellectually and creatively. To Mike, Loren, and their fellow "Rockers,"[13] going to college "early" has made a difference in their lives because it meant going to college "deliberately," through their conscious choice of an alternative path, and, because at Simon's Rock, it entailed going to college "differently."

Finally, in "'We Work the Black Seam Together': Ritual Politics and the Educative Ethic of Tending Delirium," Philip Mabry and Chris Coggins interpret college matriculation as a ritual process through which today's adolescents attain adult status. The first layer of this process is the consciously pursued "micro-rituals" of academic life—exams, deadlines—which mark advancement through a program, and which are grounded in the same logic of accumulation that animates modern economic life. The individual accumulates truths as she accumulates credits, so that she may accumulate the markers of worldly success. This commodified knowledge, however, remains external to her being. The second layer is the "historical unconscious" of modern academia, the remnant of a pre-Enlightenment eremitic tradition of retreating from the world to seek sacred truths. Rather than possess these sorts of truths, the individual is possessed—purified and transformed—by them. Youngsters leave their old lives behind to study at campuses separated from their environs, and emerge to claim their new status by participating in the grand ritual of Commencement, replete with the symbols of higher powers invoked in an earlier era. Philip and Chris conclude with an appeal for pedagogies that support students' desire for insight and growth, rather than for the simple accumulation of skills and credits.

Our rich, but complex, experiences with a unique student body in an unusual learning community have placed us both inside the educational mainstream and outside of it, and it is from that position that we speak in this collection. Our aim is not to answer again the question which Mrs. Hall had to face from skeptics in the sixties and seventies: are sixteen-year-olds ready for college? Our history of nearly a half century, and the growing success of the early college movement already offer ample testimony that they are. Rather, in sharing what we have learned about effective and imaginative college pedagogy, working with these students in this setting, what we wish to offer our readers is an invitation to re-imagine what college itself could be.

NOTES

1. A number of colleagues and friends have helped in the preparation of this chapter. I want particularly to thank Joan DelPlato, Sandra Smith, Patricia Sharpe, and Mary B. Marcy for their close readings of several of its drafts, and for suggestions that have greatly improved the final product. Also, many thanks to Wendy Shifrin, Michael Lawrence, John E. Myers, and Allen B. Altman for their helpful comments.

2. Through initiatives begun by Bard and Simon's Rock President Leon Botstein, Bard High School Early College (BHSEC) was established as a collaboration of Bard Col-

lege and the New York City Board of Education, in 2001. U Ba Win and Dr. Patricia Sharpe, then Academic Dean at Simon's Rock, worked with Principal Raymond Peterson to found the initial campus in Manhattan, and then together with Principal Valeri Thomson established a second campus in Queens which opened its doors in 2008.

3. Ellen Condliffe Lagemann, personal communication, Spring, 2008. Ellen currently teaches at the main campus of Bard College in Annandale-on-Hudson, New York, where she is Levy Institute Research Professor and Senior Scholar at the Levy Economics Institute. Cited with permission in an e-mail message to the author, October 21, 2010.

4. "The Evolution of an Educational Innovation," Bard College at Simon's Rock website, accessed November 1, 2010, http://www.simons-rock.edu/about/story.

5. Elizabeth B. Hall, *The House of Education Needs Overhaul: The Theory Behind Simon's Rock* (National Association of Independent Schools, 1967; reprint, Great Barrington, MA: Simon's Rock College, 1973, 1994), 4–5.

6. In order to maintain Simon's Rock in the midst of financial difficulties, in 1979 Mrs. Hall turned to Bard President Leon Botstein, who embraced the idea of early college. We became part of Bard in that year, and our B.A. degree is granted by the latter, although we retain our distinct identity and mission. In 1992, student Wayne Lo obtained an assault rifle and murdered student Galen Gibson and Professor of Spanish Ñacuñan Sáez. He also wounded security guard Teresa Beavers, and three students (Thomas MacElderry, Joshua A. Faber, and Matthew Lee David). Our sorrow about these irreparable losses is only deepened by the recognition that so many other schools have suffered from similarly tragic events. Our own story has been written from a number of points of view. For example see the book by Galen's father, Gregory Gibson (*Gone Boy: A Walkabout: A Father's Search for the Truth in His Son's Murder* [New York: Anchor Books, 2000]), and the article by former student Rachel Hope Cleves ("On the Writing of the History of Violence," *Journal of the Early Republic* 24 [Winter 2004]: 641–665.)

7. "About Bard/History of Bard," accessed October 2, 2010, http://www.bard.edu/about/history/.

8. Steven R. Coleman, "Dangerous Outposts: Progressive Experiments in Higher Education in the 1920s and 1930s," in *Reinventing Ourselves: Interdisciplinary Education, Collaborative Learning, and Experimentation in Higher Education,* ed. Barbara Leigh Smith and John McCann (Boston, MA: Anker Publishing Company, Inc., 2001), 8. See also Steven R. Coleman, "To Promote Creativity, Community, and Democracy: The Progressive Colleges of the 1920s and the 1930s" (PhD diss., Columbia University, 2000) for an analysis of the histories of Antioch, Sarah Lawrence, Bard, Bennington, and Goddard, five "experimental" colleges of the twenties and thirties that were grounded in the principles of progressive education.

9. For information on the BHSEC campuses in Manhattan and Queens, see "Bard High School Early College," accessed October 2, 2010, *http://www.bard.edu/bhsec/.*

10. The Institute for Early College Pedagogy grew out of a series of Early College Teaching Seminars taught at Simon's Rock in 2005 and 2006, and funded by the Gates Foun-

dation and then the Fund for the Improvement of Postsecondary Education (FIPSE). ("Bard College at Simon's Rock Hosts Early College Teaching Seminars," iBerkshires. com: Your Guide to the Berkshire Community, accessed October 2, 2010, *http://www. iberkshires.com/story/24154/Bard-College-At-Simon-s-Rock-Hosts-Early-College-Teaching-Seminars.html*.) In subsequent years, the Institutes' activities have included Early College Consultancies in Alaska, Texas, and New York.

11. In other words, we do not blend a high school and a college curriculum; our entering students begin college work in their first semester here.

12. As I explain in the conclusion to the present work, this "new pedagogy" is also in many ways an old one, which is connected to other progressive approaches to education, and has deep roots in the educational traditions of the West.

13. "Rocker" is the nickname for a Simon's Rock student. It is used by everyone on campus, including the students themselves. On occasion faculty and other community members will also refer to themselves as Rockers.

WORKS CITED

"Bard College at Simon's Rock Hosts Early College Teaching Seminars," iBerkshires.com: Your Guide to the Berkshire Community. Accessed Ocrober 2, 2010. *http://www.iberkshires.com/story/24154/Bard-College-At-Simon-s-Rock-Hosts-Early-College-Teaching-Seminars.html*.

"Bard High School Early College," accessed October 2, 2010, *http://www.bard.edu/bhsec/*.

Cleves, Rachel Hope. "On the Writing of the History of Violence." *Journal of the Early Republic* 24 (winter 2004): 641–665.

Coleman, Steven R. "Dangerous Outposts: Progressive Experiments in Higher Education in the 1920s and 1930s." In *Reinventing Ourselves: Interdisciplinary Education, Collaborative Learning, and Experimentation in Higher Education,* edited by Barbara Leigh Smith and John McCann, 6–18. Boston, MA: Anker Publishing Company, Inc., 2001.

———. "To Promote Creativity, Community, and Democracy: The Progressive Colleges of the 1920s and the 1930s." PhD diss., Columbia University, 2000.

Gibson, Gregory. *Gone Boy: A Walkabout: A Father's Search for the Truth in His Son's Murder.* New York: Anchor Books, 2000.

Hall, Elizabeth B. *The House of Education Needs Overhaul: The Theory Behind Simon's Rock.* National Association of Independent Schools, 1967; reprint, Great Barrington, MA: Simon's Rock College, 1973, 1994.

"The Evolution of an Educational Innovation," Bard College at Simon's Rock website. Accessed November 1, 2010. http://www.simons-rock.edu/about/story.

II

BIG QUESTIONS
FROM SMALL CLASSES

*Engaging Students in Consequential
Dialogues in the Arts and Humanities*

2

Intellectual Warm-Ups

How "Writing and Thinking" Prepares Students for College Study

JOHN B. WEINSTEIN

Take out a piece of paper. Now, taking pen in hand, begin to write. Write about anything—whatever comes to mind. After five minutes, finish the sentence or the thought you are on, and put down your pen.

If you have actually done what I just asked, and I certainly hope that you have, then you have just completed the first step in a Simon's Rock education. This step is universal for all students who attend the college. It is not, technically speaking, exactly the first thing that happens—they have already, that morning, picked up dorm room keys, moved in at least some possessions, had lunch in the dining hall, and listened to opening speeches in a brief ceremony—but it is their first moment of actual academic work as college students. After that opening ceremony, each student, along with eleven or so of his or her newfound peers, goes to an assigned classroom where a teacher tells the student to take out a piece of paper and write. Anything.

Now, the second step may begin. The parameters are somewhat narrowed, for now I ask that you again take your paper and pen, but this time I will pose a topic upon which to write. For the students I might say, "Write about a specific person instrumental to your being here today in this classroom." They may end up writing about a favorite teacher, one of their parents, or even themselves. For you, the reader, I need to modify the question somewhat, as you are not necessarily in a classroom at the moment. So instead, as my prompt for your writing, I will offer, "Write about a specific person instrumental in your reading this book today." Take five minutes and write. And write.

Read aloud what you have just written. I realize that you are likely alone, and this may feel foolish. Our students would not, at this point, be alone, and each would read his or her writing aloud, beginning with a brave volunteer and proceeding in a circle from there. While I cannot physically transport you to a classroom, I can at least offer you some classmates. The students have, of course, answered a slightly different question, but they should nonetheless offer some companionship for you. If you are the brave volunteer, read your work first, and then those below. If you are feeling less brave, you might wait until the end to insert your writing. And if you are feeling that I am out of my mind, then you might not read yours at all. But I hope you will choose otherwise.

> Throughout my childhood I had several idols. These were people I wanted to be like when I grew up. Sometimes they were authors, sometimes my parents. Sometimes I just wanted to be cool like my older sister. Through all of this, however, one man was always there in my life, not every day, but always when it mattered. My grandfather was special to me beyond words. I enjoyed nothing more than going to a museum on a rainy afternoon and stopping at every sign to read about the exhibits. My sisters could not comprehend how we could spend so much time in a boring museum because they lacked the necessary patience. Those afternoons with my grandfather really taught me that there is nothing better than learning. I want to learn and keep learning in his memory, and that is why I am here at Simon's Rock.
>
> —J. C.[1]

> A person who was instrumental in me being here was my Great Uncle Dennis. He's paying the difference between my financial aid and tuition. More than my parents could possibly afford. I got accepted after tenth grade, but was unable to attend due to lack of funds. I've only met him a few times. He used to work high up in the government for many years. I'm not sure exactly what he did, but as my dad put it, if the government knows about aliens, so does he. But all that influence, those accomplishments and progress, it only means so much. The true measure of a man is not the life he lives himself but rather the life he helps others to live.
>
> —R. H. S.

I'm here because of me. Because I'm ready to be selfish and ready to have my life be about what I want and what is best for me.

—L. A.

*   *   *

Early college pedagogy knows well the need to teach students how to engage with the material, how to interact with instructors and classmates, and how to configure study time—in short, how to learn. At Bard College at Simon's Rock, we spend significant time in the early phases of our entire curriculum teaching students the skills they will need to be productive members of a college classroom. For us, orientation is not only about adjusting to daily life in college residences, though that does play a major role. Orientation also has an academic component, for a student studying in college for the first time is no more automatically prepared for that than a student doing his or her own laundry for the first time would be. Learning at any level requires certain approaches, and these too must be taught. This is not time wasted by any means. By investing more time at the outset on basic approaches, we later reap the benefits of an elevated learning experience.

The "Writing and Thinking Workshop," the academic component of the orientation week and the first step toward a degree from Simon's Rock, actualizes this theoretical idea through specific exercises. In this intensive class, of roughly one week in length, students explore ideas through writing and share their thoughts with their classmates in a variety of highly structured formats. Free discussion is very rarely part of the class. Instead, students might simply read responses in a circle, or, more complexly, build upon a previous classmate's comments by repeating them and then adding their own views in a "thought chain." Such exercises teach students that listening is as important a component in a discussion as speaking; talking frequently in class is not necessarily the same as truly engaging in a discussion. Workshop exercises also teach students to interact with one another, instead of always speaking directly to the instructor. Such decentering of power in the classroom is another key component of our approach. Only after students have learned the abstract skills of class discussion are they ready to engage in content-specific discussions in their regular courses.

Students in Workshop also learn techniques of peer evaluation and revision of written work. Again, this is a decentered process, in which the students take an active role in determining the direction of their own writing, not just responding to comments from a teacher. Initially, this process is highly time-intensive, but students benefit by gaining a true understanding of the techniques and the value of revision. All of the Workshop exercises are clearly bounded, and in their way a bit repetitive, but that is intentional. Like a musician practicing scales, a ballet dancer at the barre, or an athlete stretching before a workout, the student in Writing and Thinking warms up his or her mind through specific techniques that teach listening, analysis, and expression.

PART I. CONSTRUCTED MAGIC

My goal for Workshop is for each group to have a magic moment, one which raises the group to a higher level, with each person an integral part of that experience. The moments are simultaneously collective and private, shared by all members of the group, but likely indescribable to those outside of it. Like the funny joke that just isn't funny to those who weren't there, that magic moment is magic only to those in the Workshop group. Now, classroom magic may seem a lofty goal, or at least one difficult to attain in a planned way. Moreover, we strive for a decentered classroom, one in which the teacher is not at the center of the focus and attention, but in which the center shifts from student to student. This may make planning itself seem impossible, further reducing the likelihood of any magic, or indeed of any effective instruction at all. On the contrary, the techniques of Writing and Thinking offer a series of steps that, taken as a whole, are likely to build toward those magic moments. Each exercise offers one or more essential building blocks for this constructed magic.

Throughout their years at Simon's Rock, I hope that students will also experience magic through great class discussions. Effective class discussion is a key element in the Simon's Rock curriculum, and Writing and Thinking offers students and teachers concrete tools for fostering it. These tools, taught in their simplest forms during Writing and Thinking, enable students to build a discussion as a group, during Writing and Thinking and in the courses that follow. During the five and a half days of Writing and Thinking, participants may feel that little free discussion occurs at all, and consequently wonder how this prepares students at all for a heavily discussion-based curriculum. However, this is in fact one of many cases where the warm-up does not look all that much like the actual event that will follow it. Through an intentional series of simple activities that steadily build in complexity, Writing and Thinking builds the discussion one step at a time. In the end, the students will learn how to discuss effectively. In the process, they may realize that an effective discussion is not particularly "free." This is a valuable lesson for the instructors as well, for they must offer a strong, if largely invisible, guiding hand in all classrooms, even decentered ones.

Writing may not seem a logical starting point for class discussion, a primarily oral activity. However, when the relationship between writing and thinking is considered, the primacy of writing begins to make more sense. Writing and Thinking is based on the principle that writing is as much a means toward thinking as it is a result of it. These ideas are not unique to Simon's Rock, but instead have evolved from the work of others, including the teachings of Peter Elbow, Professor Emeritus of English and former Director of the Writing Program at the University of Massachusetts, Amherst.[2] On the main campus of Bard College in Annandale-on-Hudson, the Institute for Writing and Thinking has offered a three-work workshop for incoming Bard students since 1981 (with Elbow serving as director of the 1981 workshop), and has been offering workshops for college and high school faculty since 1982.[3] That same year, the "Writing and Thinking Workshop" was offered to Simon's Rock students for the first time, initially under the direction of John Paskus, and subsequently, in order, of Natalie Harper, Pat Sharpe and Jamie Hutchinson, and Joan DelPlato.[4] Now, it is my responsibility to lead the "Writing and Thinking Workshop" and pass on its techniques to teachers and students. Students often arrive at Workshop believing that writing is an end point only, and that you cannot put pen to paper until you know what you wish to say. The result is a lot of angst over the blank page. Nowadays, a blank computer screen is more frequent, but the principle is the same. (That being said, during the actual Workshop, students are expected to do their writing by hand on actual paper, even if they never do so again after that.) You will note that in my earliest instructions to you, I did not state that you must think. But you did think. Through the act of writing, you thought about the topics, and, indeed, at times even discovered the topics. And you have a record of your thoughts. Had I asked you to merely think about a topic for five minutes, you would now find it hard to recall the exact wanderings of your mind. Your writing records your thoughts. You are thinking through writing. And your page is not blank.

The Writing and Thinking curriculum is replete with terminology, and while the ideas are more important than the terms, the terms do enable us to acquire a common language. With my students, I always do the activity before I name it. After doing that first piece of writing, the one about anything at all, I would tell them that this is called a "Free Write," which I would then abbreviate on the blackboard as "FW." The second piece, the one written to a specific prompt, is called a "Focused Free Write," or "FFW." The prompt may be one that I pose in my own wording, as was the case in our exercise above, or it may come from a text. The "Writing and Thinking Workshop" includes a Reader, a selection of short texts developed over the years and gradually evolving. Located as we are in Great Barrington, Massachusetts, the birthplace of W. E. B. Du Bois, we have long included a selection from his autobiography in our Reader. Take five minutes to write in response to this excerpt:

> I was born by a golden river and in the shadow of two great hills, five years after the Emancipation Proclamation, which began the freeing of American Negro slaves. The valley was wreathed in grass and trees and crowned to the eastward by the huge bulk of East Mountain, with crag and cave and dark forests. Westward the hill was gentler, rolling up to gorgeous sunsets and cloudswept storms.[5]

After you have finished writing, and not during, read through your piece and see where your thoughts have taken you. See what new ideas you have discovered through the act of writing.

Homework during Writing and Thinking often takes the form of what we call the "Response Journal" entry, or "RJ." A homework assignment might be to read the full Du Bois selection, thirteen pages in our current Reader, and then select, for example, three passages from it. For each passage, the student is asked to first copy out the entire passage in one column. Copying out the quote is not just a convenience for later reading aloud in class, but instead an active part of the process. This act of writing, like all acts of writing, may reveal new discoveries for the student, words and meanings previously unseen through the act of reading. In a second column, the student writes a response to the passage, in effect an FFW with Du Bois' words as the prompt. This "2-column RJ" is only one possible format; a 3-column version might include the author's exact words, a restating of the points in the student's own words, and then the student's opinion on those points. Students may previously have thought that doing the reading was all they needed to do to prepare for a discussion class, but there is far more to it. Thinking about the reading is also a necessity. Writing, as the means through which thinking is executed and recorded, also becomes essential. Whether done as homework, or as an in-class activity just prior to discussion, students use writing as private brainstorming that develops their own ideas before sharing them in a group setting.

The first act of sharing during the Workshop week is accomplished through a "Read-Around." Simply put, a student volunteers to share his or her piece, and then, proceeding in either a clockwise or counter-clockwise direction around the seminar table, the other students each share theirs. For example, if the prompt were the Du Bois quote to which you responded earlier, one of your classmates might share,

> This quote is testament to how Du Bois faced adversity and uncertainty in his early years, but chose the "gentler" hill to education and information. Bullied in a homogeneously white town by some of his neighbors, the biracial Du Bois did not allow himself to fall into the darkness of returning his tormentors' hate, but rather avoided them and constructively advocated equality.
>
> —M. G.

When the Read-Around made its way around the table to you, you would likewise read your piece aloud. Pieces are read exactly as written, without editing, prefacing, or apologizing. No judgment is offered; at most, the teacher might offer a simple "thank you." This act of sharing, equal for all participants, allows each person to reveal his or her thought process to the others. The primacy of writing as a means toward thinking, and ultimately to speaking, is affirmed, for you can only speak if you have already written, and, in the process, thought. After everyone has shared, the Read-Around is complete, and the class moves on to the next activity.

This class discussion may seem an odd one, for thus far no has responded directly to anyone else. There has, you may feel, been no "discussion" at all. That is true. But essential steps have occurred. Through the "read-around," all of the students have experienced the act of sharing their words—and ideas—with their classmates. Students need not have any anxiety as to when to speak, since they all speak in turn, or as to what to say, since each reads exactly what s/he has already written. This is not to say that the process is entirely without anxiety; indeed, some students who wish to say more than they have written may find the restrictions disconcerting. A naturally talkative student may find the notion that everyone participates equally to be unexpected or even alarming. He or she will even have opportunities to vent such frustrations, but not during the "discussion" itself.

That opportunity is called "Process" writing. Process writing is done periodically, not after every single step, but after a few activities have been done. The Process piece might just recount what has happened, or offer opinions on it, perhaps with reference to one's own sense of success, satisfaction, or otherwise. This kind of writing once again offers a chance to use writing to think and to record thoughts; instead of discussing how the class went on the way to lunch after class has ended, we use actual class time to "discuss" (such as discussions are at this stage) how the class went. Having used FW, FFW, and sharing through Read-Around, you should have much upon which to comment. If you wish, take a moment to engage in Process writing yourself.

*   *   *

PART II. HEARING WRITTEN WORDS

A great class discussion, replete with magical moments, is the amalgam of exciting material and skills of thinking, listening, and speaking. I place them in that order with intent, in order of importance. For the talkative student, used to judging quality of participation via quantity of speaking, my order may seem rather odd. But without continual thinking about the material and attentive listening to the words of others, speaking in itself has little use. After numerous Read-Arounds, students become accustomed to speaking in class and listening to the words of others, and doing much more of the latter than the former. However, they have to demonstrate if they are truly *hearing* their classmates, or even paying attention to them at all. Through Writing and Thinking exercises, they can now warm up their hearing.

One technique can do this, oddly enough, without any speaking at all. I might ask students to do a "3-column RJ" assignment for homework, filling the first two with quotes and responses, but leaving the third column blank. On the following day, they might trade notebooks, and each student will read a classmate's response and then offer an additional response to that response. For example, a student might be handed the following quote by Henry Louis Gates, Jr. along with a classmate's response:

QUOTE: "But even when I published a review in, say, the *New York Times*, my brother and his friends, who belonged to book clubs and were lawyers and doctors and dentists, couldn't understand what I meant. ... When are you going to write a book that Mama and Daddy can read?"[6]

RESPONSE: The concept of accessibility of thought troubles me. I discovered this early on, before I could give it a name. I wanted everyone to understand things the way I did. I wanted to be able to share what went on in my head. But somewhere between my brain and mouth the words got tangled and my thought, mangled. It has left me with something to prove. I *need* people to understand my motives, my logic, my process. But they never have. There are so many things I want to discuss that instead find their way spinning through my head like underwear spinning through a washing machine, nearing the end of legitimate usability. How desperately I want to hang them out to dry on a clothesline, for the world to see. The few times I've felt truly understood have been the greatest of my life. The rest leave a sour feeling of being stuck backwards on a speeding escalator, descending into insanity.

—Z. G.

The student then responds in turn, in effect a response to a response. The notebooks might then go back to their owners, or they might be passed to yet another voice, in either case writing a response to a response to a response—which is, in its way, a discussion. By sharing their writing with others, students can reveal their thought processes to them. And by responding to the writing, and thinking, with some more writing and thinking of their own, they begin to engage their viewpoints in dialogue with one another. They begin to truly discuss.

In its way, using reading as "listening" initially eases the task, for recalling someone's written words is usually less daunting than recalling what has been said orally, particularly when preoccupied with trying to jump into the discussion. Students do also have to use true listening, however. The exercise begins with a student sharing an FFW. Following that, someone whose own FFW either supports or negates what everyone has just heard, will say: "I hear you saying ..." followed by a summary of what the first student has read aloud. Then, the student must choose to say either "and" or "but," whichever is more appropriate, and finally reads his or her own response. This "Thought Chain," as it is called, continues in that manner until everyone has formed a link. There is certainly motivation to join in early, for the linkages can get rather distant for the final few participants. While "but" may predominate toward the end, that is not always the case; students may find resonance in places they would not have seen it, had they not been forced to look. Or, more accurately, to hear. In a Thought Chain, if you do not listen, you have no way to speak.

The phrase "I hear you saying ..." is key to the process, and both the phrase itself and the ideas it embodies become part of our campus culture. Beyond mere hearing, the phrase insists upon hearing as an act of engagement between two people. There is "I," and also "you." The ellipsis is also essential, standing in for the ideas ultimately spoken by one person and heard by another. Sometimes, students initially mishear the phrase, instead substituting, "I hear what you're saying," followed by "and" or "but." By replacing the ellipsis with "what" instead of an actual idea, the student eludes restating, and with it validating, the other's ideas. Neither the person who has just spoken, nor the other people in the room, have any way of knowing if the speaker really did hear what the person is saying or not. If the speaker has misheard, then he or she is not positioned to forge a valid link in the chain.

Ideally, the ideas expressed will be forever connected to whoever has first voiced them. During the "Writing and Thinking Workshop," I often let the discussion continue orally after every single student has linked the initial written response into the chain. What follows in the continuation has not used writing as inspiration, but students are still required to use the "I hear you saying ... and/but" mechanism each time they add a new point to the discussion. I might, at some point, begin to allow them to refer back to points earlier in the discussion, indicating that they previously heard someone saying a given point—ideally using the classmate's actual name—and now they wish to respond by linking with either "and" or "but." While "I hear you saying ... and/but" is the catch phrase, it is the classmates' names that are in fact the most important words uttered during the discussion. Students in our classes often recall earlier comments, either from that day or previous days, and they give their classmates ownership over the ideas that they have expressed. This sense of respect and ownership develops naturally from the Thought Chain, long after it is used in its pure form.

PART III. REVISING WITH PEERS

Now that students have "warmed up" their skills of thinking through writing, and of hearing and remembering, they are ready to proceed to a longer written piece as well as a longer process of listening and sharing. The "Writing and Thinking Workshop" culminates in each student reading aloud one revised, edited piece of writing, fancifully termed the "Polished Piece of Prose," or "PPP." Although the final piece serves as a vehicle for celebrating the Workshop's successful completion, it is the actual revision process that is the true lesson of the PPP. The process guides students as they listen to their classmates' work and respond to the words of the writer. The listening is key; each piece is read aloud a minimum of three times, often more. The repeated reading aloud is itself instructive. In an age when students may never have reread their writing before submitting it to their teachers, the chance to slow down and really hear a piece of writing, either one's own or someone else's, is a rarity.

The first round of "Small Group Critique" (SGC) involves three distinct steps, each offering the writer feedback on a certain quality. The first step, "Positive Pointing," celebrates the pleasures of individual words. While the writer is reading aloud, listeners jot down specific words or phrases that strike them. After the reading, each listener says "I liked ..." or "I noticed ..." followed by the jotted list. The writer underlines the words in the piece each time a listener notes them. No explanation is offered as to what about the words was striking; the listener is not required to even know the reason why. The writer simply learns which words seem to have a special impact. The second step moves from words and phrases to larger concepts by seeking the "Main Idea." The language "I hear you saying ..." returns here. The listeners, each in turn, state what they consider the Main Idea of the piece, using their own words, not quoting the writer's words. Listeners should write this down before saying it aloud. Now, these pieces have usually been developed simply by building upon an FFW, which means they most likely do not have a clear thesis or even topic. That can be preferable, in fact, for the writer has the chance to hear what listeners *think* the writer wants to write about. The writer may realize that even with one topic in mind, a different topic might be bubbling beneath the surface. The third step, "Active Listening," casts the net even wider. Listeners ask specific questions of the writer concerning ideas in the piece, ideas that might merit clarification or expansion at some point in the revision process. Useful phrases for beginning these questions include "Have you considered ..." and "I'd like to know more about ..."

There should be no argument, defense, or even conversation between the writer and the listener. The writer is under no pressure to decide which suggestions to implement, and it is best not to make quick judgments that might later be over-turned. Moreover, a suggestion has no inherent "quality." A listener may truly wish to know more about something that the writer has no interest in developing in the written piece. There is no need for the writer to say, "Well, I don't want to do that, because ..." and offer some sort of polite reason. The writer has the right to write what s/he pleases, and the writer's ultimate "response" to the comments is made through the revision of the piece. Just as we have used "thank you" as a response elsewhere in the Workshop, the writer can simply say "thank you" to all of the lis-teners' comments. They have taken the time to listen, and that is worthy of thanks. By not permitting any debate over the comments, the focus remains on the writer, and more specifically, on his or her written words.

Beyond the benefit of offering feedback that the students will use as they revise their pieces, this technique also demonstrates how much the students already know about evaluating writing. There may still be some areas where the teacher has par-ticular understanding, but on the whole, peers can determine if a piece has a point, if it follows an effective order, and, most importantly, if the piece is interesting to the reader. We continue to use peer evaluation, in various forms, in the general education Seminar sequence.[7] At that stage, with more developed, more analytical papers, I ask different questions than those of the three steps of Small Group Cri-tique: I ask more directly about interest, thesis, proof, organization, and evidence. However, the students still use peers as integral parts of the revision process. After reading the students' final drafts of their Seminar papers, I always look to see what their peer evaluators wrote, and I rarely find a problem in the paper that the peer evaluators had not noticed. Through this work, beginning in Workshop and con-tinuing in Seminar, students see that their peers already know a great deal about writing. And if their peers do, then so do they.

IN CONCLUSION: VARIATIONS AND EXTENSIONS

Following the Workshop week, the exercises of Writing and Thinking are only infrequently carried out in their purest forms. Certain courses and instructors may use them, perhaps doing so with freer variations. Though the Seminar sequence utilizes peer review of essay drafts, the specific procedures used by the Seminar instructor likely diverge from the strictness of the three-part structure of Small Group Critique, just as mine do. Seminar often involves Response Journals, though they might become longer and less guided exercises than the more restricted Writ-ing and Thinking exercise of the two-column author's quote with student response. That is not to say that the pure forms of the exercises will never appear. A Seminar instructor may very well use the techniques to generate class discussion. And free writing might occur in a foreign language class, following the same general principles, just in another language.

Variations mark the natural extensions of the exercises of Writing and Thinking. Instructors may appear not to use the exercises at all, but that is to be expected. Indeed, to teach an entire curriculum only through pure Writing and Thinking exercises would be as odd as attending a concert in Carnegie Hall where the pianist played nothing but scales. However, the principles taught through each exercise inform students' work throughout the four-year curriculum. Our students attain high levels of achievement because they, and we, take the time to properly warm up before jumping into the intellectual engagement that is college study.

NOTES

1. All students quoted in this chapter granted me permission via e-mail to include their comments and responses. In order to protect their privacy, I have used their initials, rather than their full names.

2. Joan DelPlato, *Writing and Thinking Workshop: A Teacher Guidebook* (typescript, 2008), 7.

3. Bard Institute for Writing and Thinking, accessed October 4, 2010, *http://www.bard.edu/iwt/about/history/*.

4. DelPlato, *Writing and Thinking Workshop*, 6–7.

5. W. E. B. Du Bois, *The Autobiography of W. E. B. Du Bois: A Soliloquy on Viewing My Life from the Last Decade of Its First Century* (New York: International Publishers, 1968), 61.

6. Henry Louis Gates, Jr., "Lifting the Veil," *Inventing the Truth: The Art and Craft of Memoir*, ed. William Zinzer. (Boston: Houghton Mifflin, 1995), 141–159.

7. The sequence currently consists of "First Year Seminar I and II: The Examined Life," and "Sophomore Seminar: Voices Against the Chorus." In 2011 the faculty was in the process of reviewing and revising these three courses.

WORKS CITED

Bard Institute for Writing and Thinking. Accessed October 4, 2010. *http://www.bard.edu/iwt/about/history/*

DelPlato, Joan. *Writing and Thinking Workshop: A Teacher Guidebook*. Typescript, 2008.

Du Bois, W. E B. *The Autobiography of W. E. B. Du Bois: A Soliloquy on Viewing My Life from the Last Decade of Its First Century.* New York: International Publishers, 1968.

Gates, Henry Louis Jr. "Lifting the Veil." In *Inventing the Truth: The Art and Craft of Memoir*, edited by William Zinzer, 141–159. Boston: Houghton Mifflin, 1995.

3

Generations Y and Z Drash Alpha and Omega

Young Scholars Encounter Sacred Texts

REBECCA FISKE

> Whenever a portion of Holy Writ was read, a Drash—
> a searching inquiry—into the meaning of every sentence
> was made, with explanations drawn therefrom, based on
> the Oral law. (Rapaport, 1)

> Only be careful, and watch yourselves closely so that
> you do not forget the things your eyes have seen or let
> them slip from your heart as long as you live. Teach
> them to your children and to their children after them.
> (Deut. 4:9)

It is commonly held that the Torah, the Bible, and the Koran are written versions of the spoken word of G-d. Further, the manner in which G-d's language is expressed in the sentences of these sacred texts is often understood as complex and even mysterious. Thus, when students embark on a study of these books, the issue of textual meaning is foregrounded. How should one read a holy book?

The 2003 Robert Alter translation of *The Five Books of Moses* comes with a sewed, hard cover binding held in a sturdy, glossy outer sleeve, emblazoned with Guido Reni's seventeenth-century Italian Baroque masterpiece—*Moses with the Tablets of the Law. The New Oxford Annotated Bible with Apocrypha* is leather bound with gold page edges and two red ribbon markers. A. J. Arberry's translation, *The Koran Interpreted* boasts a cover of delicate Arabic calligraphy. Of course, we should never judge books by their covers, but these books come covered with such elegance and pomp that students often feel some trepidation on the first day of a religion and literature class. Indeed, introducing these sacred texts to highly motivated young scholars is both challenging and exhilarating. The ways in which students explore; the assumptions they bring; the questions they ask; the intellectual, emotional and even spiritual changes they experience all join to make this pedagogical endeavor highly rewarding.

The Torah, The Bible, and The Koran, are the main texts in three courses I have developed and taught over the last fifteen years at Bard College at Simon's Rock. "Hermeneutics and the Hebrew Bible," "The Bible as Literature," and "Religion and Literature" ask students to read sacred texts closely for their artistic expression and for the ways in which they address issues of religious belief and experience. The students explore classic and contemporary art, music and literature that spring from these primary sources, even as they consider historical and political context. Finally, they write creatively and theoretically about such themes as salvation, sin, creation, holy war, mysticism, law, and retribution. None of these three courses is required, yet there has been a waiting list after every registration. The students take them for a variety of reasons, and they enter into the study of sacred texts with a variety of backgrounds. One or two may be devout; most are not. Except for a rare few, the students have never read these texts. Many have popular conceptions of them, and they recall some images and stories from attending services or from secular sources such as video games; cartoons; films; and famous works of art, music, and literature. Still, without exception, they file in to our first class, sit in their places around the table, and look up at me with expressions and with demeanors unlike any other Rockers in any of my other classes.

Kira is dressed in ripped jeans, a Michael Starr tee, and black flip-flops.[1] Her dirty blond hair is long and dreaded, and her silver hoop earrings and tiny ruby nose ring catch the midday light, twinkling, as she enters my class. She has an 80% recycled green laptop bag over her right shoulder. Cradled in her arms, is Robert Alter's *The Five Books of Moses*, all 1,064 pages, still in its sleeve, Guido Reni's Moses glaring. She surveys the room, being the last to arrive, smiles at me, perhaps for reassurance, and finds her place between Rob and Shayna. Letting her bag hang from the back of her chair, Kira places Moses' book gently on the table. It is time to begin: day one, "Hermeneutics and the Hebrew Bible." Before I open my worn, dog-eared copy, and before I hand out the syllabus, I take a moment to survey my students. Fifteen very bright seventeen-or-so-year-olds, all shapes, sizes and hues, sit, sacred texts poised. Many have unconsciously folded their hands, as if in prayer. Some are stroking their Torahs, touching Guido's handiwork. Not one has freed the text from its sleeve. Later, after a few weeks, I will watch as they slowly become more and more comfortable with their books, but for now, even the thought of writing in the margins, highlighting, or simply popping Moses in their backpacks along with good old *Calculus, Microeconomics,* and *The Oedipus Cycle* seems madness. Something about taking a class on sacred texts is, well, just different.

One of the first assignments in each of these three courses is to write a short paper explaining the reasons for taking the class. The answers are often similar. Students report that they think of the texts as foundational, as mysterious and uncanny, as being familiar yet foreign, as offering intellectual cachet. Often, students connect these texts and their study to their relationships to family and community. "My parents are atheists and never let me read the Bible. Now I can, and they can't say a thing," wrote one "Bible as Literature" student. "I went to Hebrew school, and I had my Bat Mitzvah, but I'd like to study this stuff outside of all that … " and "My dad is a believer. He is shocked I am reading the Koran in English. He's really angry. I told him it is the only way I am going to learn," wrote two students in "Religion and Literature."

Another preliminary question I ask students involves authorial intent. Born in the early nineties, the World Wide Web awaited their use. Bill Clinton led their nation. The Oklahoma City bombing, Columbine shooting, and September 11 colored their earliest memories. Postmodernity's race-, class-, gender-identity politics, Obama's presidency, the war on terror and global environmental anxieties mold their psyches. These students have ambivalent and sometimes surprising attitudes toward authority. Cell phone chatting, twittering, text messaging, blogging, IM'ing, myspacing, facebooking, Wikipedia researching, they are awash in information and opinions and endless, global chatter. Finding textual Meaning or Truth—even believing there is such a thing—seems dizzyingly complex. I wonder how they read any text for meaning. I wonder how they will read these sacred texts as well. Will there be a difference? Should there be a difference?

So I ask, "When you read anything, how do you decide what it means? Do you want to find out what the author intended to say? Do you want to know about his life? Do you want to see how it makes you feel or think?" To these basic questions, students will offer a variety of ideas. Ultimately, most will settle on some form of Reader Response Theory as their answer. For example, many decide that the meaning of a text needs to be a combination of authorial intent and the readers' interpretations. Students declare it is a creative process: reading and meaning can be fluid. Most do not think any critic can offer the True interpretation, even if the critic is also the actual author. Perhaps this way of viewing the meaning of a text is unique to Generations Y and Z; it is difficult to say. Perhaps it is a function of adolescence to question authority. What I can say is that their view changes when I ask the next question.

"When you read a sacred text, say *The Five Books of Moses*, how do you decide what it means?" Immediately, students begin to struggle with the question. "Wait," said one student, "who wrote this, G-d, right?" They believe that if God, or G-d, or Allah wrote the text, it must be that finding the True Meaning is possible since the author is divine. In fact, in the case of "Religion and Literature," where we read the Torah, the Bible, and the Koran, students point out that the same divinity authored all the texts and that the three should tell a consistent narrative. However, most students have a hunch that they do not, at least on the surface. "Otherwise, what is all the fighting about?" asks one student.

Often, the next concern centers around one sticky fact: all three texts are translations. Alter, the Joint Committee and its chair Donald Ebor, and Arberry translated these books. The students wonder if they translated correctly. What if God, G-d, and Allah's Authorial Intentions were misunderstood? When I remind them that we read many books in translation, the struggling intensifies. They claim that mortals who create texts don't know their own minds so all they create is open to interpretation. Inevitably, a few students will bring up the notion of the unconscious, citing that as proof. "When people write, they end up expressing all kinds of unconscious things they didn't expect or plan," explained one student. However, these sacred texts, spoken originally by a (The) Deity, must, by definition, be consistent and must be correctly read, many students demand. Meaning here is not a matter of Reader Response. Meaning is fixed in the text. Interestingly, many students who identify themselves as atheists maintain this stance.

Of course, as I present the sentiments of many classes here, I am oversimplifying. Each class is multivocal, and the above ideas represent a large, but not total, part. Some students simply dismiss the idea of a divine author and suggest we read the texts as cultural constructs or as "just really important books." Others become agitated by the questions, not knowing what to think. For the first few classes, Kira, for example, didn't say a word. Still, it is clear the majority enter into the study of sacred texts with some trepidation, a measure of respect, a belief that they should read in a different way, and a great deal of curiosity about just what this Author might say. Many, even if they profess to be atheists, seem to expect (or hope) that these texts will be fundamentally different from other books, will hold the Mysteries somehow. "I want to find out what G-d really said. Then I can decide for myself what to believe," Kira finally confided.

As a teacher, these first classes make me pause. I know that I am about to give my students many tools with which to explore and begin to answer their questions. But I also know that there is one assumption nearly all make: the author will speak in one voice, will be consistent, and will mete out His meaning. Students expect that, unlike human authors, G-d spoke being fully conscious, with intent, and in possession of Meaning. Indeed, one of the most disconcerting aspects of teaching sacred texts in a secular setting is, at least for me, watching this core assumption crumble as students become more and more acquainted with the actual language of the texts.

Oddly, this crumbling of the assumption is essential, and it sometimes leads to astonishing changes in the students' attitudes toward spirituality. We often talk about the special qualities of our Simon's Rock students: intelligence, courage, diversity, creativity, and promise. While these qualities are true, my bet is that our demographics regarding social, political, and spiritual habits match national averages. The Pew Research Center's recent study *How Young People View Their Lives, Futures, and Politics*, points out that this age group is the least likely to attend religious services regularly, with many—20%—claiming no religious affiliation or claiming agnosticism or atheism. This is nearly double the proportion of young adults who expressed this sentiment in the 1980's. Sixty-three percent believe in the theory of evolution, and only 4% express a primary wish to become more spiritual. Further, even as this survey shows a flight from traditional religion, it indicates significantly closer familial ties, especially to mothers. Nearly 80% talk to their parents daily, 75% see them once a week, and 50% see them daily. Finally, they are more likely than any other generation to turn to their parents for advice and among the least likely to turn to "religious advisors, religious scriptures or some higher power" (Pew, 19). According to the study, these students are on a quest for wealth and fame, not spirituality. They look to their mothers when they are in need, not G-d and certainly not sacred texts. If my guess is correct, and Rockers hold these traits in common with their peers, why do they enter into the study of sacred texts with such ideals? Why do they handle them with such care; hope for such revelation of Meaning; express such thirst for textual truth? And why, when G-d does not live up to their expectations, when He is not omniscient, just, loving, and consistent in the text, do they become so disconcerted?

> And it happened as humankind began to multiply over the earth and daughters were born to them, that the sons of G-d saw that the daughters of the men were comely, and they took themselves wives howsoever they chose ... The Nephilim were then on the earth, and afterwards as well, the sons of G-d having come to bed with the daughters of man who bore them children ... (Gen. 6:1–4)

> And it happened when a long time had passed that the king of Egypt died, and the Israelites groaned from the bondage and cried out, and their plea from the bondage went up to G-d. And G-d heard their moaning, and G-d remembered His covenant with Abraham, with Isaac, and with Jacob. And G-d saw the Israelites, and G-d knew. (Ex. 2:23–25)

> "I am the LORD your G-d ... But if you do not heed Me and do not do all these commands ... I will come against you with wrathful encounter ... and you shall eat the flesh of your sons, and the flesh of your daughters you shall eat ... and I will put your corpses on top of the corpses of your fetishes, and I will loathe you." (Lev. 26:14–31)

These three quotations from the Torah are some of the earliest passages to disconcert. Perhaps it is because they sneak up on the students just as they are reading cozy, familiar stories. The first is right before Noah's Ark. The second is right after the sweet baby Moses is found in the rushes. The third is at the end of the Commandments. All three stories have been depicted by Disney and by countless other artists. Students feel they know perfectly well how G-d had no choice and had to send a flood. They recall the boat, Noah's happy family, and the cute animals: elephants, giraffes, and lambs. And they know Moses, both as a baby (chubby, swaddled and sailing gently down the Nile) and then all grown and strong—holding the sacred stone tablets. There is even Guido Reni to prove it. The idea that the text says G-d had sons who came down from heaven and had sexual encounters with human women because they were "comely," and that the resulting offspring were the evil ones, dismays students. That when the Israelites, the good ones, were groaning and suffering, G-d had forgotten them and had to be reminded of his promise worries students. That G-d will loathe us, even make us eat our children, that He will pile our corpses on top of the corpses of fetishes, shocks students. The demand for G-d to be omniscient, just, loving, and consistent becomes quite strong, and students debate fervently, write passionately, and create complex and astonishing Midrashim in an attempt to come to terms with what they are reading.

Midrash is one extraordinary tool students employ in order to interpret sacred texts, especially when those texts dismay, worry or even shock. When used together with more traditional assignments such as essays and exams, Midrashim provide students with an alternative way to embrace and enjoy the challenge of sacred study. The term Midrash originates from the Hebrew letters d-r and sh, meaning "to search out." Midrash is an ancient form of hermeneutics: a way to study the interpretation of texts, particularly sacred texts, in a manner that accepts multiple meanings, meanings between the lines, under and above the lines. When I asked my students where meaning could be found in books, they wanted secular texts to have fluid meanings and chose Reader Response Theory; however, when it came to sacred texts, most students preferred fixed meaning. At first, they assumed it was just a matter of reading the words. Once done, G-d's intent would be clear enough to any educated sort. Unfortunately, as soon as the students encountered passages such as the three above, their assurance in Meaning began to crumble faster than Lot's wife looking back at Sodom and Gomorra. Through the use of Midrashim, students can explore multiple ideas about what the author might have intended by a confusing passage.

Sometimes, things seem simple enough and can be understood literally. "I am the LORD your G-d," for example. Sometimes, passages seem to hint at a deeper meaning. "And G-d heard their moaning, and G-d remembered His covenant with Abraham, with Isaac, and with Jacob. And G-d saw the Israelites, and G-d knew," for example. Sometimes, passages could even have multiple meanings, expressing the author's complexity of thought. "I am the LORD your G-d ... and I will loathe you," for example. Finally, sometimes, passages appear to hold secrets, mysteries. "... you shall eat the flesh of your sons," for example. To the ancient scholars, Midrash worked best for exploring deep meaning and especially for multiple meanings. Why does G-d need to remember His covenant? Did He forget it? Why did He have to see the slaves in order to know? Can't He see everything? Further, what if "you shall eat the flesh of your sons" holds a secret message? What might it be—a reference to the Gospels, a gesture toward the House of Atreus, a stab at the Egyptians? Our contemporary Midrashim seek ways to answer these questions through creating interpretive essays, stories, poetry, paintings, and music. By "drashing"— doing Midrash—students discover multiple possibilities even as they play with the text. In this manner, they can explore. They can struggle with the meanings, wrestle with the text, reckon with their understanding, as Jacob did at the Jabbok. Drashing is one fallible, mortal way of following the myriad paths (sometimes hidden, often undiscovered) within our sacred texts.

For Simon's Rock students, drashing is similar to a variety of writing and thinking exercises they are introduced to during New Student Orientation. Focused free writing, loop writing, poetry play, and—certainly—response journal writing all ask readers to explore multiple meanings through a variety of workshop techniques. These techniques are used consistently in "First Year Seminar" and "Sophomore Seminar," [2] as well as in many other courses. Consequently, students in my religion and literature courses quickly embrace this aspect of textual interpretation. They have written plays with titles such as "In the Apartment of Eden" and "Wild and Waste" exploring concepts of sin and creation. They have composed imagined diaries of G-d where He agonizes over actions and struggles to make decisions. They have rendered Moses' victory song in multiple musical genres; crafted slaughter sites; sewn priestly garments; designed tents of appointment, golden calves, and even the disguise Jacob used to trick Isaac out of the birthright. Students have found many gaps in the texts, places of confusion, silence, even repression. Midrash has given them a way to add their voices to the texts and enrich their sacred textual study.

Perhaps because Midrashim is an accepted part of the study of The Torah, this method seems ideal, and students seem to flourish. Indeed, one insightful student pointed out that the great patriarch Abraham even drashed in a way when he argued and made deals with G-d: "'Here, pray, I have presumed to speak to my Lord when I am but dust and ashes. Perhaps the fifty innocent will lack five. Would you destroy the whole city for five?' And He said "I would not destroy if I find there forty-five ...'" (Gen. 18:28).

While close reading combined with this Midrashic technique can be both a highly creative process and an invaluable method of textual analysis, placing the texts in a historical and cultural context is essential. For example, Eliot Friedman's *Who Wrote the Bible?* provides students with powerful information regarding the political and cultural climate that may have led to the writing of the Hebrew Bible. It even suggests possible identities of the human authors. With this text as an additional tool, students' Midrashim can expand. They can write debates among these possible authors; they can explore reasons for the treatment of certain characters such as Ishmael, Hagar and Aaron; they can analyze doublets (stories told twice in different ways). Jack Miles' two texts, *G-d: A Biography* and *Christ: A Crisis in the Life of G-d* allow students to consider further the character of G-d within the Bible. How does He change? How does He relate to his creations? Howard Kee's *Understanding the New Testament* makes visible such essentials as the political climate during the life of Jesus; the timing of the writing of the Gospels; the agenda of Paul; the relationship between the early Christians and the Roman world; the use of the Jewish canon in the formation of the Christian canonical text. Ibn Warraq''s *The Origins of the Koran* is a collection of pioneering studies regarding theories of the sources of the Koran and of Muhammad's revelation. *Www.islam.tc/ali/#Audio* is an online Islamic Audio Library where students can listen to Koranic recitation from many popular reciters. Given these texts as models, students begin to feel free to question and to explore from myriad perspectives, depending on individual interests. This sort of freedom becomes very important the deeper students wander into these complex texts. While they were disconcerted to watch their initial assumptions regarding fixed meaning crumble, once they have read the Torah and the New Testament and begin the Koran, students often gravitate toward particular, personally evocative issues.

Again, these issues have common themes, and each of the three sacred texts seems to call forth certain concepts and questions. Without a doubt, however, one powerful theme all the texts seem to foster in our students is the nature of faith. Students often ask the following questions. What does it take to be a believer? Can I even read these texts if I am not a believer? Do I have the right?

> Read the Bible as though it were something entirely unfamiliar, as though it had not been set before you ready-made. . . . Face the book with a new attitude as something new. . . . Let whatever may happen occur between yourself and it. You do not know which of its sayings and images will overwhelm and mold you. . . . But hold yourself open. Do not believe anything a priori; do not disbelieve anything a priori. Read aloud the words written in the book in front of you; hear the word you utter and let it reach you. (Buber, 5)

> I warn anyone who hears the prophecy of this book: if anyone adds to them, G-d will add to that person the plagues described in this book; if anyone takes away from the words of the book of this prophecy, G-d will take away that person's share in the tree of life and in the holy city, which are described in this book. (Rev. 22:18–19)

It may be reasonably claimed that no Holy Scripture can be fairly presented by one who disbelieves in its inspiration and its message. ... The Koran can not be translated. ... The Book is here rendered ... but the result is not the Glorious Koran, that inimitable symphony, the very sounds of which move men to tears and ecstasy. (Arberry, 21)

Those to whom We have given the Book and who recite it with true recitation, they believe in it; and whoso disbelieves in it, they shall be the losers. (Koran, The Cow: 115)

Martin Buber, John of Patmos, A. J. Arberry, and Muhammad all have different, conflicting answers with which students must contend. Clearly, Buber's response is soothing; what is Midrashim if not facing the book? But, when students read John's warning, even as they are crafting multiple meanings from The Book of Revelation, their jaws drop. "What is the difference between drashing and altering a text?" they ask. It is clear John decries adding or subtracting anything from his book. Still so much in art reflects the ideas it puts forth. From Michaelangelo's Sistine Chapel to tarot cards and video games, much has been added and much taken away. Indeed our culture abounds in such plunder. Still, such a warning seems to demand (even as it denies) discussion, exploration, consideration. Ultimately, The Book of Revelation is one of the most drashed by the students. Perhaps because it is so rich in imagery, so laden with guilt, punishment and reward, so charged with poetics, students tend to find ways to legitimize not heeding John's warning. Often, the quotation is understood literally. "Don't change my actual words!" is what John means, wrote one "Bible as Literature" student. "This quote can be interpreted in millions of ways; he could mean his book or even the whole Bible. But, wait; when John wrote this, the Bible wasn't even canonized, so really, we can't know what book he means. In fact, all the scholars who finally did set the canonical text, and all the translators even, didn't listen to John," wrote another student.

Translation as addition and subtraction becomes an essential aspect of faith, especially when students read *The Koran Interpreted*. Arberry's quote is highly charged, and students find the concepts fascinating and—surely—difficult. *The Koran Interpreted* is not the Glorious Koran. It is an "essay in imitation" (Arberry). Indeed, it is generally accepted that the original language—Arabic—is the only language that can carry the true meaning of this sacred text. Thus, even when it is translated well, it must come, line by line, with the original Arabic, a highly poetic and complex language. *Www.islam.tc/ali/#Audio* is immensely useful to illustrate this concept. Indeed the elusive, even melodic, rhythmic, and perhaps contradictory qualities of The Koran underscore the very nature of drashing. Of all three sacred texts, The Koran perhaps best expresses the multivocal, nonlinear poetics of the spoken word of G-d.

A few years ago, I had a student, Amir, who studied The Koran daily for most of his young life. Interestingly, he embraced drashing easily, explaining that every Sura (section) of The Koran had many, many stories behind it and that the whole was much more than the linear sum of its parts. He composed a play in which two long estranged brothers—the Hebrew G-d and Allah, the Beneficent, the Merciful—reunite beneath the tree of knowledge of good and evil in Eden. The two discussed their shared sorrow at the state of the Israeli–Palestinian conflict. The play evoked many emotions, from despair to hope, and the class exploded in discussion after the performance.

I had another student, Tatyana, a Baptist from Alabama who understood our drashing as "hearing the Spirit." Once, she asked if she could address the class regarding the concept of the Spirit for one of her Midrashim. I agreed. She started by reading a passage from The Koran: "These are the verses of the Glorious Book. In all truth We shall recount to you the tale of Moses and Pharaoh for the instruction of the faithful. Now Pharaoh made himself a tyrant in the land. He divided his people into castes, one group of which he persecuted, putting their sons to death and sparing only their daughters. Truly, he was an evil-doer" (28:1). Then she simply began to sing a capella. Her voice was powerful and resonant, and the song, "Go Down Moses," had a haunting and surprising effect. When she finished, she explained that she believed the Spirit of G-d was with her as she sang.

Drashing was a way for her to enliven sacred texts and to bring the ancient past into the present. To me, her combining of a Koranic passage, a Christian spiritual, and a Hebrew, Muslim and Christian patriarch offered a perfect example of the spirit of Midrashim. She played in and among the texts. She explored spaces as yet unexplored. She used her unique voice to open herself and the whole class to a new way of reading the sacred. Amir's drashing helped him to articulate some of the confusion he had regarding the nature of the Diety. An agnostic, he believed that G-d and Allah, the Beneficent, the Merciful are one in the same character, and he struggled with the apparent contradictions in the texts. By bringing the two together in Eden and having them discuss the conflict that had so plagued his life and the lives of many, he could begin to contend with those contradictions. Both students believed that their drashing neither added to nor subtracted from the texts. Rather it honored them, trusting in the integrity of the texts themselves. "The books are bigger than me," Tatyana explained.

This integrity can be understood as the whole landscape of meaning which sacred texts chart with language and which readers explore. Of course there are differences among the three religions regarding exploring textual meaning and integrity. Christian Biblical exegesis generally looks for the one true meaning. Tafsir, Islamic exegesis, generally explores hidden depths and esoteric meanings. Pardes, Jewish exegesis, generally searches for literal, deep, comparative, and hidden, secret meaning. All use a variety of techniques in their search, and none declares the search complete. Further, the best method for mapping the landscape of the sacred text, of revealing meaning, has been the subject of endless debates, both sacred and secular, from Aristotle to Hans-Georg Gadamer, Aziel of Gerona to Harold Bloom, Ali ibn Abi Talib to Jacques Derrida. How should one read a sacred text? How should one read a secular text? Should the two differ?

> But the shared necessity of exegesis, the interpretive imperative, is interpreted differently by the rabbi and the poet. The difference between the horizon of the original text and exegetic writing makes the difference between the rabbi and the poet irreducible. Forever unable to reunite with each other, yet so close to each other. ... (Derrida, 67)

Here, Jacques Derrida expresses a common idea: the religious reader seeks a "final truth, which sees interpretation as the unfortunately necessary road back to an original truth." The poet-reader "does not seek truth or origin but affirms the play of interpretation" (Derrida, 311). The two ways are contradictory, irreducible. Or are they? Within our classroom, students can do both—they can drash as a way to understand the original word of G-d, and they can drash to explore and play with the ideas. The space of the classroom can hold these two, seemingly contradictory methods. Further, the concern with the nature of the drashing can be suspended. As students, they don't need to decide whether their drashing will result in uncovering the original truth or affirming the play of interpretation. In fact, they really can't be sure how they will think and feel about the texts for a long time. They are students, scholars, explorers. They are in the journey together, learning from one another. Even the most ardent "poet-readers" recognized the power of Tatyana's spiritual. Even the most devout "religious readers" were moved by the sorrow of Amir's characters. Indeed, the space of the classroom can be liminal, allowing and encouraging seemingly contradictory ideas the freedom to flourish and interact.

Kira's pristine *Five Books of Moses* is now well worn. "I never really thought I'd read this whole thing," she confessed at semester's end. Like many students, the idea of having read these texts is much more appealing than actually reading every word. Numbers can be slow going, for example. The very act of reading such an important text has changed her in many ways. She has a sense of real accomplishment, knowing she has a strong foundation upon which to build further study. Indeed, the simple fact of students having read the Torah, Bible, and *Koran Interpreted* means something. Drashing these texts with a classroom full of other creative, curious, and diverse people is an excellent way of experiencing the rich, multilayered world of the sacred text. Kira now knows the contents of her book even as she realizes the infinite ways it can be explored. She has a portfolio of her own Midrashim and the memory of hundreds of others' drashing. If the goal of teaching sacred texts to our students is for them to have a strong foundation upon which to build continued study both in and out of the classroom, drashing works beautifully. If students can accept that as a group they can be both poet-readers and religious-readers and that they can honor and accept the contradictions inherent in this way of reading, they are well situated to continue their work. Tatyana's simple statement, "The book is bigger than me" expresses this concept clearly. If, as a group, students can accept opposing ways of reading, can suspend judgment, trusting in the integrity of the text and the importance of the work of textual exploration, perhaps they can do the same as individuals. Perhaps, they can begin to explore any text, sacred or secular, with a different vision of their place within the landscape. Drashing need not be just a way to read sacred texts. It can be a way to read the world.

NOTES

1. This article is based on classes that occurred over a number of years. The anecdotes recounted all actually occurred, but in order to protect students' privacy, I refer to them by pseudonyms. Quotes of class comments by students, or from their written work, given in the text are accurate according to my recollections, but, for obvious reasons, should not be understood to represent direct citations from any materials provided by these students.

2. Our general education core in the humanities currently consists of "First Year Seminar I," "First Year Seminar II," and "Sophomore Seminar."

WORKS CITED

Alter, Robert, trans. *The Five Books of Moses*. New York: W. W. Norton, 2004.

Arberry, A. J., trans. *The Koran Interpreted*. New York: Touchstone, 1955.

Buber, Martin. *On the Bible: Eighteen Studies*. Edited by Nahum Glatzer. New York: Schocken Books, 1968.

Derrida, Jacques. *Writing and Difference*. Translated by Allan Bass. Chicago: University of Chicago Press, 1978.

Friedman, Richard E. *Who Wrote the Bible?* New York: Harper Collins, 1997.

Kee, Howard. *Understanding the New Testament*. Engelwood, NJ: Prentice Hall, 1998

Metzger, Bruce, and Roland Murphy. *The New Oxford Annotated Bible with the Apocrypha*. New York: Oxford University Press, 1994.

Miles, Jack. *Christ: A Crisis in the Life of G-d*. London: Vintage, 2001

——. *G-d: A Biography*. London: Vintage, 1996.

Pew Research Center for the People and the Press, *A Portrait of "Generation Next" How Young People View Their Lives, Futures and Politics*. 2007.

Rapaport, Samuel. *Tales and Maxims from the Midrash*. New York: BiblioLife, 2008.

Warraq, Ibn. *The Origins of the Koran*. Amherst, MA, and New York: Prometheus, 1998.

4

Finding the Bridge

Integrating Music Theory and Composition

LAURENCE D. WALLACH

INTRODUCTION

In the spring semester of 2008, as part of a class in the analysis of tonal music,[1] I assigned an exercise from the textbook[2] in which the students were given a condensed musical progression (a kind of musical skeleton) and asked to expand upon it to create an actual piece of music (including characteristic elements of rhythm, harmony, and melody) about four times as long as the original. My expectation was that students would use a number of techniques (known as "prolongation techniques") that they had discovered in their analyses of the classical literature we had already studied.[3] One student, Z. A., produced an expansion as requested, but the techniques were imaginative extensions and recombinations of those studied such that the piece gained an original "sound," closer to Stravinsky than to Mozart. Most importantly, his piece was judged by class consensus to be beautiful and expressive.

Z. A. was at that time also enrolled in my composition class,[4] where the students were working on an assignment to compose something for three instruments. I had no expectations about idiom, harmonic style, or "correctness" of any kind; those were creative matters to be decided upon by the composers themselves. When I canvassed the class to discover their intentions for this assignment, Z. A. announced that he was planning to continue to work on his "theory exercise," which had metamorphosed into a string trio. This he proceeded to do over the next several weeks. The process of expansion now graduated to a larger dimension, and the composer found his way to a form that came, finally, to fill 155 bars of mostly slow tempo, or seven and a half minutes of music, more beautiful and expressive than the original exercise.

I recount this story not to portray a "typical" way in which the subjects of theory and composition dovetail; there is no "typical" way. Rather it demonstrates one powerful way that the character of the students, the approach to teaching, and the nature of the curriculum at Simon's Rock enable this type of synergy to occur. It is significant in this situation that a faculty member is teaching both theory and composition with the same student in both classes at the same time. In an institution that takes the term "interdisciplinary" seriously in its many dimensions, both teacher and student are predisposed to interrogate the boundaries that define and, too often, compartmentalize those subjects. Under these circumstances, there can be a constant interchange between the activities of theory and composition, each feeding the other, and doing so with an abundance of structure as well as, simultaneously, a healthy absence of structure.

The music-learning environment at Simon's Rock is characterized by: small seminar-style classes with an average of ten students about one and a half years younger than their peers elsewhere; two full-time music faculty sharing a five-semester theory sequence who also teach courses in composition, improvisation, and music literature (Western and non-Western); and an active performing program supported by a group of adjunct faculty who are working professional musicians. The college's curriculum stresses interdisciplinarity, and faculty often teach both out of field, and, within their field, out of specialization.

A significant strength of the learning environment is that younger college students take little for granted. The authoritarianism implicit in the categories of traditional academic disciplines may be readily challenged by the students or by the instructors. The intimacy of the music program and its connections to other disciplines in the college (such as science, philosophy, or critical theory), combined with the openness of the students to new creative and intellectual experiences, have conspired to break down the barriers between composition and theory in unexpected and, I will contend, very productive ways.

In the following paper, I first examine aspects of the theory curriculum and indicate the ways it incorporates composing as a learning activity crucial to the proper understanding of musical structures and the proper role of theory in accounting for the way such structures work. I then look at some of the strategies used in teaching composition, with examples of how theory can enter in spontaneous and contingent ways that depend on the nature of the individual composer and composing project. Along the way, I explore a variety of encounters students have had with the combination of classes, and some of the ways their responses have shaped my understanding of the relationship between theory and composition. I would like to thank two former students currently active as teachers and composers, Robert Hasegawa (B.A., 1996) and Gabriel Gould (A.A., 1992; B.A., Bard College, 1995), for generously sharing their thoughts about their experiences in my classes and in others'. Their words are woven into this article, and provide valuable supplementary perspectives on the subject.[5] If there is a lesson here that can be transplanted to a more typical college situation, I think it is simply to call attention to the real utility of what is learned in these classes. Since such uses are fundamentally creative, they suggest that applications of theory for composing, performing, analyzing, and understanding in historical context are continuously being discovered or invented by the students themselves, and we are obliged to maintain an open dialogue with them concerning the transmission and reception of theoretical concepts and creative processes.

PART I. THEORY

The discipline of music theory, although ancient, has evolved through a constant process of self-redefinition. Debates about its ontological status have grown more heated in the past century as developments in complex systems of music theory grew stronger especially in the United States during the 1960s and continuing today, as seen in publications such as *Journal of Music Theory* and *Music Theory Spectrum*.[6] Many of these approaches to thinking about music have been and remain within the academic mainstream. Composers have voiced reservations, however, pointing out that the presentation of musical materials in complex systematic ways has its dangers, a primary one being that students may experience abstract constructs as irrelevant distractions in relation to the working out of their own creative impulses through their aural imagination. Theoretical a prioris may inspire creative work in some students, but may stifle it in others. For this reason, careful distinctions need to be made in approaching the pedagogy of these two subjects, as well as among the students to whom it is presented.

Despite ambiguities about its purview and ambivalences about its utility, theory remains a universal requirement for musicians at conservatories and universities. Musicians-in-training also have mixed feelings about it; some find it very useful while others are relieved to have it over and try not to think of it once they have entered professional activity.

One group of music students that tends to have a particularly polarized view of the subject is would-be composers. In a typical teaching situation, composers will study theory with a teacher who self-identifies as a "theorist" and composition with one who self-identifies as a "composer." Former student and active composer Gabriel Gould writes: "... all of my coursework in theory at Simon's Rock College and at Bard College had been taught by the same faculty members who taught my composition classes and/or studio. I suppose that I had come to think of composers and theorists as one and the same, essentially interchangeable. Thus the idea that there were indeed separate (but not necessarily equal) faculty in composition and theory intrigued me, and it took some time to come to terms with the way each was taught in what I took to be a typical conservatory setting. Only one member of the theory faculty at [the] U[niversity of] M[ichigan Graduate School of Music] actively identified himself as a 'composer' as well as a theorist, although it was immediately clear that most of the theory faculty either composed (on the side, as it were), performed, or both."

A result of this separation may be that little conscious effort is made by instructors to explore the relationships between the subjects. Two questions often left unanswered are (1) what students do with theory once they have learned it, and (2) what methods and materials are to be used in teaching composition. Composers report that they either avoid theory altogether as being too abstract and generalized to have relevance to the specific creative impulse of a given student in a given piece; or that they teach special methods that they have devised for their own work, which may or may not derive from techniques taught in theory classes.[7]

Given these concerns, fundamental challenges arise within the classroom almost immediately:

What are the students' common-sense understandings of the subject? (after all, they did sign up for the course)
What is the relation between music theory and musical practice?
In what way does the word "theory" apply to this subject?
Is there one or more than one theory about music?
What are the historical roots of the subject?
In what ways does music theory resemble other kinds of theory, particularly scientific theory?[8]
How will the study of music theory help me to play, improvise, and compose my own music?

Although each question can lead to a lengthy and fruitful discussion, this last, about the role of theory in composition, is the most important from the perspective of this article. It is one instance of a complex intellectual problem encountered across the curriculum that has attracted the attention of many bright Simon's Rock students: whether a theory is descriptive or prescriptive, and whether a theory possesses absolute or only contingent authority. It is also the most emotionally potent question about music theory for creative musicians, going to the core of what motivates such students to pursue this subject. As a result, it is a question that requires from the instructor the most personalized kind of response. Having the same student in both theory and composition classes equips the instructor with significant information for crafting such a response.

It seems to me that there are two fundamental benefits of thinking systematically about the structures of music: it suggests some of the (often complex) ways that music can achieve coherence; and it can indicate a model for the sequential presentation of musical materials, a theory curriculum that can move students from simple and basic structures to complex and multilevel ones through acts of composing with guidelines. One such model can be found in the pedagogical system of species counterpoint, taught in the third semester.[9]

As a student, theorist, and composer Robert Hasegawa responded positively to the systematic qualities of music theoretically presented.[10] He has written:

> I'm not sure whether it's my own personality or something coming from my classes at Simon's Rock, but I feel that I mix theory and composition more than most of my colleagues, who tend to be either "theorist" or "composer" but not both. To me, a big part of what composition is about is inventing a certain language, and then exploring how music written in that language might sound. My recent composition and theory both examine similar ideas—for me, one informs and inspires the other.[11]

The relationship between music theory and practice has been interdependent throughout history, never more so than in the twentieth century. Of the multiple systematic approaches to the study of music currently available, the two largest and most influential categories are Schenkerian theory, and "pitch-class set analysis." The former, based on the works of Heinrich Schenker (1865–1935), addresses systematic characteristics of a canonical repertory of European music which achieved dominance and remained recognizable from about 1670 until 1900 (the so-called "common practice" period). Fundamental innovations in twentieth-century music brought about a "break up" in the use of a harmonic common-practice,[12] one side-effect of which was the development of modern theories of music. The latter was developed in the wake of the introduction of "atonal" and twelve-tone composition methods employed by Schoenberg, his students, and his more distant acolytes in the United States, most notably composer Milton Babbitt. In the Simon's Rock theory sequence, Schenkerian theory informs the first four semesters. The fifth semester, "Twentieth Century Theory" engages in powerful alternatives to the Schenkerian perspective such as "pitch-class set theory,"[13] and explores the question: at which point (historically or phenomenologically) does tonal theory lose its analytic usefulness?

SCHENKERIAN THEORY IN THE CLASSROOM

Schenker viewed common-practice music (also referred to as "tonal," making systematic use of major or minor triads and scales[14]) as being predicated on the physical characteristics of tone and therefore grounded in nature. He viewed a successful tonal work as having a progressively unfolding temporal-harmonic structure which integrates meaningful traits within and across its various temporal dimensions, from foreground to middleground to background. He concluded that this was the most powerful and artistically fruitful way to compose.

Schenker's "system" has been refined and modified by generations of theorists and has almost assumed the status of orthodoxy; but it has generated much controversy and has been rejected by others. It can be seen as a brief against music that deviates from the practices on which it is based (i.e., post-tonal music of the twentieth and twenty-first centuries) but it has also been argued that its principles can be extended to include music of widely different idioms. The value of including it as a backbone of the Simon's Rock theory curriculum may seem contradictory to our interest in questioning authority and fostering our students' individualism, but that would take too simple a view of the matter. Rather than insisting on a single vision of tonal practice, "tonality" may be seen as a collection of characteristics of musical behaviors that work together to create tonal architecture across long expanses of musical time, experienced in a predominantly unconscious way by listeners. As such, some characteristics may be modified without damaging the overall coherence of the practice; in fact, such modifications are necessary for the practice to adapt to cultural and artistic evolutions. It is this view of tonality that underlies theory at Simon's Rock, and that Z. A. discovered in his creative interpretation of Schenker's ideas.

The degree to which normative and deviant characteristics appear in tonal music is often considered an issue peripheral to theory, its discussion relegated to musicology or cultural studies. But it goes to the heart of the challenges mentioned above, and is central to an understanding of contemporary compositional styles. The selection of normative repertories and paradigmatic works has powerful pedagogic value, but it possesses liabilities that at least must be open to discussion, and at most may throw doubt on the entire enterprise: why these works, selected according to which criteria? In a small class of inquiring minds predisposed to interrogate authority, the strengths and weaknesses of any pedagogic approach generate important conversations. Tonal theory engages in the study of the normative qualities of tonal music, particularly as exemplified by the chorale settings of J. S. Bach. Students whose musical experiences emanate from vastly different cultural milieux may respond strongly to the perceived shift that they are being asked to make in order to be part of the music theory conversation.

This is particularly true of students who have been outside the normative track of classical training, and who may not be particularly interested in the intellectual questions surrounding systematic or quasi-linguistic aspects of musical structures.[15] The confrontation between the curriculum and the typically anti-authoritarian impulse of a rock musician or of a student whose primary experience has been acquired through playing by ear and improvisation is too often suppressed in conventional teaching situations by the defined limits of the subject, but it can function as an ongoing source of energy that reminds us that the subject is actually posed as a series of questions and oppositions. Typically, such questions include: why is smooth flow a desirable quality for melodies? Why should I avoid complex rhythms in my first melody-writing exercises? Why are major and minor scales given preference to other modes? Why is consonance considered more basic than dissonance? Conversation around these (and other) questions generates energy which illuminates both the strengths and weaknesses of the normative approach.

At Simon's Rock, the ongoing development of a composition-based approach to tonality has demoted Schenkerian theory from an ultimate source of authority to a useful way of integrating individual experiences into a large-scale systematic perspective. This is carried out through a series of guided composition exercises building on each other with increasing complexity until a series of well-formed short tonal compositions in three or four voices is achieved.

Such an approach has different impacts on different students. The improvising musician who can spontaneously and intuitively develop a structure of satisfying length and complexity is most likely employing some systematic approach to materials that is aurally generated, based on repeated exposure to and use of an idiom that has become familiar. The musically literate, classically trained musician easily makes use of tonal structures because her musical experiences correspond more closely to the practices she is learning about, but may need to work harder to find ways to enliven these exercises with bold and original elements. A balance between unifying and diversifying processes (referred to below as "concentration" and "dispersion") is intrinsic to musical entities; the predilection of students toward one or the other may find its balance-point in the classroom.

The moment that questions about "the rules" arise might be viewed as a parting of the ways between theory and composition. In fact, such questions are integral to any serious discourse about musical structure and language, and categorizing them as appropriate to "theory" or "composition" is usually an act of pedagogical convenience. It is worth examining such a moment more closely.

The very first composition exercise (at the start of the first semester) may be posed in the following way: using the notes of a scale (major or minor), create a linear sequence of notes (between ten and twenty) of the same rhythmic value that corresponds to your sense of what constitutes a "melody" in a more or less satisfactory way. Responses to the exercise fall roughly into three categories: the student will (1) come up with something rather traditional-sounding and feel fairly confident in the results; (2) create a line with many jumps, either apparently random or showing a back-and-forth pattern, and will say that her purpose was to experiment or reproduce an "interesting" or "exciting" experience similar to one she has enjoyed in existing music; or (3) express frustration and dissatisfaction at being unable to achieve some result that she was aiming for. In any of these categories, some aspect of the instructions may have been (or commonly is) ignored: there may be notes that do not belong to the scale, but were included "because they sounded right/good," or the maximum limit of twenty notes might be violated for the same reason or because once started, the student forgot about that "rule."

At this point the new melodies are "workshopped," that is, shared with the entire class for feedback. The terms in which feedback is given are always personal, and each student bases his evaluation on his own criteria. One goal of this conversation (and others subsequent to it) is to explore the systematic potential within the prescribed musical format, most crucially the structural character of the tones of the scale; in other words, one goal is to discover the potential of the material itself. The principal discovery that will be obvious to some and inaudible to others is the hierarchical character of the scale. This emerges dramatically when suggestions are offered for substitutions, often by notes adjacent to those originally present. Group listening becomes quite intense, including shared evaluation of the results.

The process thus far is indistinguishable from what might occur in a composition class; however, two kinds of hierarchy emerge in this simple exercise, conventionally referred to as "time" and "space."[16] The awareness of this begins to establish a theoretical lens through which students can start to view their own work. It is relatively easy to establish that the temporal hierarchy can be generalized as "beginning-middle-end." The spatial hierarchy is more controversial, and splits into a "high-low" possibility, a "pattern" or "motive" one, and a (more sophisticated) "stable-unstable" one. It is usually the more "classically" oriented students (category 1) who identify these qualities. Other students (category 3) who could not identify or articulate these distinctions are now in a position to evaluate the usefulness of the stable/unstable distinction. Typically, there is immediate interest, especially in category 2, in the disruptive potential of unstable tones. It may also become clear to this group that their intuitive generation of an "interesting" pattern will need some systematic basis in order to "go anywhere," i.e., to develop further in some way.

A set of normative conclusions can emerge: that linear connections (i.e., using adjacent notes adjacently) bind the elements together more clearly than jumps, while jumps create excitement and interest; that the varying degrees of stability divide into two categories (relatively stable/relatively unstable); and that the tonic is the most stable endpoint. Approaching this endpoint by descending steps creates the most palpable sense of a stable conclusion.

These conclusions form the basis for subsequent exercises that explicitly intend to explore further aspects of tonality by building upon the results of the ones already established. The ongoing discussion about the value and usefulness of such normative practice leaves the door open to a variety of different conclusions that might take subsequent exercises in different directions. There may be a reference to the possibility of individual explorations of idiosyncratic characteristics as well as of alternate theories. This falls under the headings of "composition" or more advanced levels of theoretical study (which will be taken up again in the last section of this essay.) At this early stage, however, normative conclusions are consistent with basic elements of Schenkerian theory. Hasegawa writes, "Having certain theorists presented in a compositional context made them much more exciting to me. Schenker for example was introduced in an early melody writing exercise—to me, this emphasized the most interesting aspects of his thought, and I still am more fond of Schenker than were many of my fellow students ... "

The systematic details of tonality are explored through the first and into the second semester of this curriculum through a process of composing with materials that become increasingly more complex. The effort is made to present each exercise in the form of a complete musical entity, one which possesses a beginning, middle, and end. In this way, the structural functions of musical-syntactic elements are not lost sight of, and the structural consequences of compositional choices can be perceived. This process poses two kinds of challenges. First, it requires many students to enhance aural skills in relation to the increasingly complex demands for recognition, particularly of intervals, chords, and eventually harmonic regions. Second, it requires awareness that as each systematic aspect of tonality is introduced, alternate methods, approaches, and materials might be available and integrated into a modified or expanded system.

Such a process reflects the historical reality of the final phase of the tonal era, when composers began to explore such possibilities. While the (linear) curriculum excludes the possibility of making use of these alternatives within the earlier stages of this subject (i.e., within the preliminary series of exercises), there is a clear indication of a means of doing so, through original composition. The composition class begins after the first semester of theory, and presents students with the possibility of continuing in both subjects. In this way, two messages are simultaneously delivered: that composition can involve nonstandard or individualized approaches to using theory, and that more open and intuitively evolved approaches to composition are appropriate.

PART II. COMPOSITION

Most students choosing the composition course have had some amount of theory; one semester is a formal prerequisite which is treated flexibly, since previous exposure to theoretical concepts can translate into a wide range of abilities in actually utilizing musical materials.[17] This liberal approach to admitting students means that the course can take on radically different profiles from one iteration to the next, sometimes characterized by students with classical training on an instrument and a working knowledge of the basic materials covered in first semester theory, at other times dominated by autodidacts who have been in bands or who self-identify as singer-songwriters with varying degrees of experience. Students typically describe their motivation in taking the class as "wanting to learn how to write" either a song or a piece; but this statement has a wide spectrum of meanings, from simple notation of musical ideas to discovering techniques for organizing them into larger entities.[18]

On the overlap between theory and composition, Hasegawa writes: "Just having a shared vocabulary when talking to your 'theory teacher' and 'composition teacher' (at SR, of course, the same person) is very helpful—I've had many situations since where it was difficult to convey my ideas to a composition teacher because of a lack of this vocabulary. . . . [E]specially at early stages of learning, having the same terms is a big help."

In the composition class, the first assignment is, once again, to produce a "short melody." No restrictions are placed on the material; the only specifications are that the melody be either single-line or accompanied in some way. No idiom or set of materials is mentioned or recommended. Parallel to the theory exercises, this is envisioned as the first in a series in which the initial material is expanded into a short composition, usually gaining a degree of complexity as it expands. First melodic exercises frequently exhibit a variety of modal characteristics and motivic structures, which the class usually is able to discover and describe in response to the question "What are the characteristics of this melody? What holds it together?" The choice of terms at this stage of the discussion is comparable to the activity of the *bricoleur* who picks up whatever is lying at hand in order to complete the task. Students will identify scale-materials and tonal centers, repeated rhythmic-melodic patterns, and overall contours using a variety of existing or improvised terminology without privileging the language of tonal theory. This may be due either to a recognition that systematic tonal theory does not apply, or to a desire to do justice to the unique characteristics rather than the general properties of the creative utterance. The intention here is to remain "theory-neutral," to validate the students' conceptualization of materials insofar as it serves the project of constructing the musical object; after-the-fact analysis of the composition may later be helpful in revealing the identity of those materials in the context of tonal theory. Students are mainly supportive with their critical feedback; this can even take a form of defensiveness against the potential critique that the musical idea lacks "correctness" in some academic-theoretical sense. From a historical point of view, new compositions are created in a post-tonal era, one characterized by diversity of compositional methods and materials.

A useful characteristic of peer feedback is that it can point to characteristics that the composer herself may not be aware of. Given the lack of strict prescriptive guidelines, such feedback often carries great authority; the instructor's role is then to mediate this by reminding composers that the feedback simply represents other individuals' observations and opinions, as well as reminding colleagues to restrain their own prescriptive impulses. Such mediations continue throughout the course. Supplementing and counterbalancing peer feedback is the composer's own statement of intention. Students offering critical suggestions gradually learn that what sounds good to them may not correspond to the intentions of the composer. This dialogue is crucial in helping composers identify or define what is central and what is peripheral to their artistic goal, and to validate the challenging task of adhering to it through a process of experimentation and discovery.

Increased awareness of the characteristics of a musical impulse sets the stage for the expansion of that impulse into a short composition. Once again, the way this takes place is highly diverse: the intuitive impulse that generated the original sketch may be strong enough to continue adding material to what was initially established. In the process, the awareness of significant characteristics, augmented by group discussion, can provide a degree of technical support for the development of the material. A variety of developmental techniques might be introduced at this point, but it is important not to allow the initial impulse to get lost in what could easily turn into a technical exercise.

One optimal scenario would establish the technique for which the composer feels the most compelling need to support the intentional characteristics already present. However, here again there is a branching of possibilities. An intuitive composer with a strong initial impulse can push forward with little need for technical information. A student who has produced eight bars and gets stuck can benefit from thinking about what the motivic elements of her sketch are, and how they can be used to construct one or more new phrases. And a student who believes there may be a logical consequence to what is already composed may be eager to absorb a more thorough technical explanation of motivic development. In the last case, the activity may in fact turn into a technical exercise, but one which speaks to the creative impulse of that particular composer.

There is no prescribed sequence of exercises, nor is there a clearly defined model for content in the composition semester. The model of the *bricoleur* persists for each student and for the class as a whole. The through-line is the continuing exploration by each student of his or her individual compositional impulse, fed by an expanding awareness of compositional possibilities and the use of theory-as-needed.

Gabriel Gould refers to this approach as integrative, and comments: "It is clear that the type of theory training I received [at Simon's Rock] helped to shape my approach as a composer. I routinely think of basic theoretical concepts (e.g., intervals, scales, meter, subdivision, voice-leading, etc.) when working on a piece, and often will push myself to think in these terms when 'stuck.' It is in many ways quite difficult to comment on how my development as a composer might have been different with a more 'traditional' (i.e., academic) and less fluid approach to theory, since that is not my background. Although the graduate work was rigorous and important in terms of filling in some holes in my knowledge of theory, as a composer I believe I am most deeply affected by the undergraduate training I received. I also have the feeling (although it is difficult to state this empirically) that I actually retained more from my undergraduate theory training than from my graduate work."

CONCENTRATION AND DISPERSION

Students present their work to the class as a whole and receive feedback from all of their colleagues, which ensures that what they receive is diverse enough to permit them to accept or reject it comfortably. There are two large categories of feedback, which I am calling here "concentration" and "dispersion." These are convenient general categories of responses to students' compositions; they are not technical terms, nor do I ever use them in conversation with composition students. Feedback calling for "concentration" implies that the music needs greater focus, i.e., it needs to be more tightly constructed, its elements need to relate more audibly to each other, there needs to be the equivalent of a narrative "through-line," there needs to be some audible unifying principle in evidence. This feedback may point to the usefulness of some theoretical concepts. "Dispersion" feedback indicates that the music is too tightly organized, seems excessively uniform, and needs more audible variety, a stronger sense of moving from one state to another, a greater diversity of surfaces, a stronger sense of drama. It implies that a freer exercise of imagination, using a wider variety of materials, would benefit the music.

Observations by classmates are often supplemented by direct comments from the instructor which may include theoretically familiar concepts to critique details and recommend revisions, especially if greater concentration is needed. The most common of these concepts, applicable to exercises in bringing two or three instruments together, are those regarding voice-leading.[19] Invocation of the "rules" of voice-leading makes a direct connection between formal theory and compositional activity; it provides an occasion for helping students to discover the utility of what they have learned in a theory class (which was perceived as "a different subject"). Typically, this depends on an awareness that the composer has successfully understood and applied voice-leading techniques in a previous course, and on marking the composition as if it were a theory exercise, i.e., using the same symbols and abbreviations, as well as suggesting alternatives that would resolve problems. Unlike a theory class, here the composer is free to reject such suggestions as contrary to the artistic aims of the composition, which the instructor may not fully comprehend.

On the other hand, students can be encouraged to consider more creative options within the material. Here, theoretical language can point students to greater dispersion of ideas, as opposed to bringing elements together into a system of similarities. Dispersion can call for stronger shaping of musical ideas through the use of wider range, variety of dynamics, greater use of rhythmic gestures, and awareness of the role phrasing and articulation can play.

Dispersion of musical materials aims to enhance expressiveness and interest. This is often articulated in colleagues' comments, based on a first hearing, and is likely to be what my own composition teacher Otto Luening termed "impressionistic," meaning based on generalized characteristics rather than a clear understanding of the fully articulated structure. Feedback based on impressions can be valuable in characterizing the overall expression or color; it can be particularly useful in describing the degree of impact or intensity of character possessed by a musical idea. The class as a whole accrues a vocabulary of expressive parameters (mentioned above), and becomes articulate in applying it to particular pieces. It is less common for colleague feedback to diagnose (much less recommend a cure for) a need for greater internal coherence, but students who have had more exposure to theory or who are taking composition for the second time gain skill in doing so. Sometimes students get carried away with giving advice, and have to be reminded who the composer actually is.

Concrete examples can demonstrate the application of feedback aimed at achieving concentration on the one hand and dispersion on the other.

Example 1: Concentration

When E. D. took composition for the first time, he had not taken theory before, but had extensive experience as a rap singer-songwriter with skill as guitar and bass-guitar player. His songs were highly satirical, and made humorous use of exaggerated musical gestures, uniquely presented in his own performances. In response to an assignment to create a composition for an instrument he didn't play, he asked if he could compose for a "found object," a small electric keyboard he had retrieved from a dump. The instrument functioned unpredictably, sometimes generating its own series of pitches semi-randomly. The composer's strategy was to improvise, accompanying the instrument's (somewhat random) output with a variety of nonverbal vocal sounds produced by himself and a collaborator. The results were recorded into the computer program "Garage Band" which can control and edit sound files. The five minute recording was shared with the class.

Supportive feedback applauded the originality of the chosen medium, pointing to moments of high contrast and dramatic surprise. The dispersion of elements achieved both by accident and in spontaneous but deliberate response to accidents was judged to be the fundamental characteristic of the piece. Critical feedback centered on long stretches which dissipated the musical-dramatic energy through lack of incident. To the listeners, they seemed psychological "dead zones." Emerging from both forms of feedback was the recommendation to use the capacities of "Garage Band" to re-edit the material and to overdub with new material. These recommendations were essentially seeking concentration by identifying and developing tension and release in such a way as to enhance the unity of the musical experience. The result was a work that was just as long, but with a clearer sense of form. It was included as a pre-recorded "prelude" to the concert of student works at the end of the semester.

Example 2: Dispersion

O. V. is an experienced clarinetist immersed in classical literature; in the winter of 2008, he took "Composition" and second-semester theory simultaneously. His response to the first assignment was an accompanied melody scored for string trio that assumed the form of a Viennese dance in a completely tonal idiom. The accompaniment intended to supply full harmonic support. The conventional idiom implied a classical dance form, which O. V. created by adding parallel phrases to the initial short melody. Feedback supported the unified character and idiom of the music, but criticized the apparently rambling nature of the subsequently added phrases.

The listening group recommended revision with attention to clearer and stronger melodic contour, in order to pull the sequence of phrases together into a larger shape, making use of tonal movement and a variety of cadence types (the equivalent of varied punctuation). Although the student was inexperienced as a composer, the technique being recommended was a highly sophisticated one that forms the focus of both second and fourth-semester theory classes, namely, tonicization and modulation.[20] Given this student's aural familiarity with relevant models, the suggestion to aim for tonal variety was an ambitious gamble. Through further consultation, a simplified process was arrived at where a previous section could be transposed and varied. The composer was pleased with the results, and he chose this composition for performance at the conclusion of the course.

INTRODUCTION OF EXAMPLES
FROM ESTABLISHED REPERTORY

Introducing both theory and established repertory into the composition class is a delicate operation. The implicit message should not be "this is what your music should be like," but rather "here are some ideas you might want to consider" and "here are some techniques and materials you might want to use in your own way, or in your own context." Keeping the message implicit is important; it is easy to intimidate fledgling composers with an example from Beethoven if the pedagogic point is too obvious. It is better to look at and/or listen to a piece and see what conclusions the students themselves can draw from it. Use of examples best emerges spontaneously in the classroom from a conversation about a student's work. In such a situation, the presence of a laptop computer loaded with sound-files is a great help in providing an immediate, spontaneously chosen illustration. Nonprescriptive illustrations are best drawn from two (or more) contrasting sources, for example, the "Petit concert" from Stravinsky's *Histoire du soldat* and a well-produced Afro-Cuban dance piece can both illustrate clear texture among complex rhythmic layers. At some point in the semester (close to the middle) it is useful to present an analysis (and therefore a more comprehensive theoretical discussion) to demonstrate how coherence can be achieved with idiosyncratic or non-standard materials. Excellent choices are available from the Debussy *Préludes* or from Bartók's *Mikrokosmos*. These works often make use of an original harmonic language which departs from familiar idioms and forms of continuity. The examples can be used to encourage a more intensive exploration of harmonic materials (in order to create a unique "sound") or to open up possibilities for imaginative ways to use gestures and rhythms as the basis for a compositional structure.

Introduction of more systematic or coherent theoretical ideas into the composition curriculum needs to be balanced by attention to compositional process. While I have characterized students as being either more intuitively inclined or more likely to be stimulated by systematic perspectives, fostering creativity requires acknowledgment that these are both necessary functions that can be integrated for each student without a sacrifice of individuality. As the theory sequence progresses, the notion of a single source of authority (Schenker, Schoenberg) gives way to multiple perspectives; in its extreme form, there would potentially be as many theories as there are pieces. Practically speaking, the main theoretical approaches would be adapted to account for the methods and artistic purposes of individual composers and compositions. In the composition class, this translates into a growing recognition of the value of applying selected analytic and generative techniques to a composition project only after its characteristic materials have had a chance to show themselves.

Creative application and modification of theoretical approaches characterizes the final semester of the theory sequence ("Theory V"), converging with more advanced approaches to composition. Hasegawa writes:

> Some of the things I remember well from your classes at Simon's Rock [include] exploring particular techniques learned from analysis (in "Theory V," I think) in brief composition experiments. I remember doing a little composition with

inversionally symmetrical harmonies right after a discussion of inversion in
Bartok … [;] doing this made certain abstract ideas like the difference between
inverting around a single pitch or a pair of pitches (e.g., C#/D) very clear. I think
I also got a better sense of the limits of the technique; some of the invertibility
didn't seem to be as audible as I thought it would be, and that put the analytical
claims of some theorists in perspective.

CONVERGENCE OF THEORY AND COMPOSITION

There are many paths by which composition students experience the bridge between
their original music and theory. The particular one depends on the individual student's willingness or desire to view his or her music in less concrete terms; generally
the less experienced students prefer to focus on tangible qualities such as rhythmic detail, gesture, range, and instrumental effects. Experience generates a greater
ease in dealing with more abstract issues such as mode, interval, motive, harmonic
region, and over-all structure. Eventually, students are able to start thinking in systematic terms in relation to their original pieces, and in some cases (e.g., Hasegawa's
example cited above) they may be able to take a theoretical a priori as a starting
point for a compositional exercise.

Using an abstract premise to generate a piece can be attempted through exercises in highly restricted materials. As an example, I often propose an exercise in
composing with only three or four pitch-classes. The latter is a kind of primitive
but fruitful experience of pitch-class set thinking (mentioned above as a major
alternative to tonal theory). Students are asked to choose three pitch classes, for
example, C, F, and G, and use them to compose a short piece using only those notes.
The immediate discussion centers on the larger consequences of choice. It becomes
immediately apparent that the micro-characteristics of the relationships among the
three notes will be projected onto the larger characteristics of the piece as a whole
(one of the fundamental characteristics of tonal music described by Schenker). A
choice of C, F, and D-flat will create a radically different piece from C, F, and G.
The discussion then focuses on how it is possible to create even a short piece with
such limited resources, which leads to an intensive exploration of the other available
parameters (rhythm, dynamics, compass, texture). Once this process begins, the
apparent limitation is perceived to be no limitation at all; sketches for these pieces
can almost always be expanded to greater lengths than could have been initially
imagined. One talented student, A. H., expanded his three notes (F, G-flat, and C)
into a six-minute showcase for the composer's virtuosic piano skills, modeled after a
Liszt Hungarian Rhapsody. This experience, along with Robert Hasegawa's, offers a
window into the question of the ways in which theory functions both descriptively
and prescriptively; the two are not mutually exclusive.

MULTIPLE THEORIES AND THE USE OF THEORY IN COMPOSITION

An informal introduction to pitch-class set theory may take place after such an exercise; students like Robert Hasegawa find creative inspiration in systematic approaches to material, while others continue to prefer an intuitive impulse, a literary or dramatic idea, or a colorful combination of instruments as starting points. By the time students arrive at "Theory V," they usually have taken at least one semester of "Composition" and have had practical experience with this way of thinking. The fifth theory semester is concerned with music written since 1900, but its actual subject matter is the notion of multiple music theories. It is prepared in the fourth semester by the use of a Schenkerian-based but flexible approach to tonal analysis, allowing students to personalize the process of reduction and graphic analysis to reflect their own understanding of a score once they have studied it intensively. The structure of the five semesters is comparable to curricula in larger schools. The strict course sequence provides for an intellectual rigor which many students find compelling, while the small classes and repeated contact with teachers builds familiarity with each student's musical predilections. The result is a flexibly individualized experience.

By looking at a range of contemporary analytic approaches and applying several of them to the same piece, students in "Theory V" are exposed once again to the question of whether what analysis reveals is "scientific or hermeneutic." In itself, this question will appeal to students with a philosophical bent, but it will also have a practical impact on composers. By looking at the theoretical systems explicitly advocated by composers like Schoenberg, Hindemith, and Harry Partch, or implicitly revealed through analysis of works by Stravinsky, Bartok, or Messiaen, it becomes apparent that systematic thinking is both intrinsic to tonal innovation, and contingent upon an individual quality of creative impulse.

That does not prevent composers from believing, and often convincing some followers, that there is an objective basis for the principles of choice and organization of materials that they have discovered. Such a belief often strengthens the creative enterprise of the believer; but an awareness of the practical and contingent nature of such a choice is useful for students who have yet to commit to any one system, and yet who have come to recognize the necessity for some principle of organization, even if such a principle remains nameless and is administered through the powerful offices of the intuition.

CONCLUSION

Individual artistic expression originates by a mysterious process unknowable to the conscious intellect. An academic institution can seem a paradoxical setting for fostering such a process, but a small, intimate setting in which the input of colleagues and instructors is available as a resource rather than an authoritative source may prove to be the appropriate one. Academic institutions are often the incubators of theoretical systems; critique of theory often refers to its remoteness from practical application ("the ivory tower"). An educational environment where the theoretical idea and its practical application can be closely juxtaposed provides a beneficial context for balancing theory tempered by practice, liberally nourished by contingent disciplines such as critical studies, philosophy, and of course the other arts. Simon's Rock provides one such environment, where the bridge from theory to composition can be constructed by each student in such a way that the integrity of his or her creative impulse can be preserved and fostered.

NOTES

1. The fourth semester of a five-semester theory sequence.
2. Carl Schachter and Felix Salzer, *Counterpoint in Composition* (New York: Columbia University Press, 1989).
3. This had included works by Bach, Mendelssohn, Beethoven, and Chopin. Techniques included arpeggiation, register transfers, rhythmic displacement, "composing out" harmonic areas, ornamentation and embellishment, often used in combinations with each other.
4. I teach one composition class that can be taken repeatedly, with higher expectations for each iteration.
5. Comments from these former students were solicited by e-mail, and are cited with their permission. Robert Hasegawa is an instructor in theory and composition at Harvard University, and Gabriel Gould is a freelance composer living in Bryn Mawr, Pennsylvania.
6. The controversy about the ontological status of theoretical percepts is exemplified by the following article: Douglas Dempster and Matthew Brown, "Evaluating Musical Analyses and Theories: Five Perspectives," *Journal of Music Theory* 34, no. 2 (autumn 1990): 247–279. One subheading sums up the matter: "Music Theory: Scientific or Hermeneutic?"
7. See for example, Charles Wuorinen, *Simple Composition* (NY: Longman, 1979, reissued by C. F. Peters, 1994). Here he proposes a specific approach to using twelve-tone rows as an objectively valid method of composing, which nevertheless stems from techniques developed in his own music.
8. Matthew Brown, *Explaining Tonality: Schenkerian Theory and Beyond* (University of Rochester Press, 2005) proposes general criteria for theories of all kinds, including: accuracy, scope, fruitfulness, consistency, simplicity, and coherence (p. 18). He later adds to this predictive power.

9. The method was created by J. J. Fux in his classic text *Gradus ad Parnassum* of 1710.

10. Robert Hasegawa, "At the Limit of Fertile Ground," Senior Thesis, Bard College at Simon's Rock, 1996.

11. Above, Hasegawa illustrates the process by citing a composition exercise based on the theoretical concept of axial symmetry, discovered to be operative in the works of Webern and Bartok among others. In such a case, composition suggests new theoretical thinking, which in turn gives rise to further composition.

12. The concept of early twentieth century "break up" belongs to Katharine Kuh, who described it as applying to all the visual arts in her 1965 book, *Break Up: the Core of Modern Art* (New York: New York Graphic Arts Society).

13. A text used in "Theory V" is John Rahn, *Basic Atonal Theory* (Macmillan, 1980).

14. "Tonality" has been defined as: "Key, meaning particularly observance of a single tonic key as basis of comp., thus, *bitonality*, use of 2 keys at once; *polytonality*, use of several keys at once; *atonality*, loyalty to no key." "Tonality," *The Oxford Dictionary of Music*, 2nd ed. rev., ed. Michael Kennedy, *Oxford Music Online*, accessed August 6, 2008, *http://www.oxfordmusiconline.com/subscriber/article/opr/t237/e10323*. There is a discussion about whether scales or triads constitute the fundamental material of tonality.

15. The linguistic approach to discovering a systematic basis for musical structure was explored in a senior thesis, based on the work of R. Jackendorff and F. Lehrdahl: Rashad J. Ullah, "Music as Language: A Study of Meaning, Grammar, and Mind," 2000. Other Simon's Rock theses that explore "systematicity" in restricted musical vocabularies are those by Daniel Neilson ("Method: Theory and Practice in Three Disciplines," 2001), Zoe Sherman ("A Mere Formality: Axiomatic Systems in Counterpoint and Geometry," 1999) and Brenda Mathisen ("Music of the Mind: A Study of Musical Perception and Meaning," 2006).

16. "Space" here refers to the metaphorical sense in which we commonly distinguish "high" tones from "low" ones. The physical reality is that of higher versus lower rates of frequency.

17. One semester of theory ("Theory I" or equivalent) is the normal prerequisite for "Composition"; some students claim enough prior familiarity to be exempted. The composition class is multilevel, and students can take it twice, the second time for more credit with heightened expectations. The class population therefore represents a broad range of theoretical background, from zero semesters up to five.

18. With the increasing availability of notation software there has developed a significant emphasis on learning to use it as both a helpful adjunct and a direct medium for creative work. The ease with which revisions and alternate versions can be made has proven a positive element to encouraging students to write multiple drafts and to respond to critical feedback.

19. "Voice-leading" in theoretical terminology refers to the way voices, stacked vertically, move horizontally from moment to moment in a coordinated way. A normative premise of multivoiced music is that each layer has its own integrity, or independence, and that

listeners will notice and be disturbed by changes in the number of layers. Voice-leading rules ensure that a musical texture will retain its integrity, and can be adapted to various musical practices. Most of these are discovered in the first two semesters of theory.

20. Even the names for these techniques are controversial, and mean different things in different text-books. For example, in *An Introduction to Tonal Theory* (Norton, 1975), Peter Westergaard opts exclusively for the term "tonicization" (p. 355, especially Footnote 2). On the other hand, Robert Gauldin, *Harmonic Practice in Tonal Music* (Norton, 1997), p. 258, distinguishes the two terms based on smaller or larger scales of operation. The text used for our theory classes, Stefan Kostka and Dorothy Payne, *Tonal Harmony* (McGraw-Hill, 2009) blurs the distinction as subjective (pp. 303–304). These terms generally indicate varying degrees of key-change, from fleeting to well-established. The technique for achieving and controlling this smoothly is advanced, and requires the ability to think in terms of several scales at once, as well as a grasp of larger structural dimensions.

WORKS CITED

Brown, Matthew. *Explaining Tonality: Schenkerian Theory and Beyond.* Rochester, NY: University of Rochester Press, 2005.

Dempster, Douglas, and Matthew Brown. "Evaluating Musical Analyses and Theories: Five Perspectives." *Journal of Music Theory* 34, no. 2 (autumn 1990): 247–279.

Fux, J. J. *Gradus ad Parnassum* of 1710.

Gauldin, Robert. *Harmonic Practice in Tonal Music.* New York: Norton, 1997.

Hasegawa, Robert. "At the Limit of Fertile Ground." Senior Thesis, Bard College at Simon's Rock, 1996.

Kostka, Stefan and Dorthy Payne. *Tonal Harmony.* New York: McGraw-Hill, 2009.

Kuh, Katharine. *Break Up: the Core of Modern Art.* New York: New York Graphic Arts Society, 1965.

Mathisen, Brenda. "Music of the Mind: A Study of Musical Perception and Meaning," Senior Thesis, Bard College at Simon's Rock, 2006.

Neilson, Daniel. "Method: Theory and Practice in Three Disciplines." Senior Thesis, Bard College at Simon's Rock, 2001.

Rahn, John. *Basic Atonal Theory.* New York: Macmillan, 1980.

Schachter, Carl, and Felix Salzer. *Counterpoint in Composition.* New York: Columbia University Press, 1989.

Sherman, Zoe. "A Mere Formality: Axiomatic Systems in Counterpoint and Geometry." Senior Thesis, Bard College at Simon's Rock, 1999.

"Tonality." *The Oxford Dictionary of Music.* 2nd ed. rev. Edited by Michael Kennedy. *Oxford Music Online.* Accessed August 6, 2008. http://www.oxfordmusiconline.com/subscriber/article/opr/t237/e10323.

Ullah, Rashad J., "Music as Language: A Study of Meaning, Grammar, and Mind," Senior Thesis, Bard College at Simon's Rock, 2000.

Westergaard, Peter. *An Introduction to Tonal Theory.* New York: Norton, 1975.

Wuorinen, Charles. *Simple Composition.* New York: Longman, 1979, reissued by C. F. Peters, 1994.

III

THE VIRTUES OF CROSS-DISCIPLINARY PEDAGOGY

Integrating Knowledge from the Sciences, Humanities, Social Sciences, and the Arts

5

Modeling Plato's Heaven and God's Green Earth

SAMUEL RUHMKORFF

There is something wrong with mathematics and science education in the United States. All colleges are forced to confront this. Simon's Rock's necessity is greater, as, whatever the value of secondary education in science and mathematics, our students are missing a year or two of it. The Simon's Rock science and mathematics faculty has endeavored to address this through attention both to teaching the methodology of science and mathematics at the level of general education and to positioning these disciplines in a broader, interdisciplinary context. In what follows, I share my perspective on these efforts. I write as a philosopher of science (and non-mathematician and non-scientist) who has thought about what general education might look like for the messy reality of the natural world and the formal systems modeling some of the necessary truths of Plato's heaven; I quote extensively from the science and mathematics faculty at Simon's Rock.[1]

The teaching of science and mathematics[2] at the level of general education poses a range of difficulties. Some students arrive at college with a limited understanding of these subjects, and with a great deal of anxiety and fear. Achievement in these subjects requires a good deal of information that must be conveyed quickly. This leaves less room for the give-and-take of an interactive classroom familiar to the study of literature, history, philosophy, et al. Modeling the process of discovery can be helpful, but only to a point: undergraduates seem to have a limited patience for simply retracing the steps of others, and rightly so. This also separates them from the essence of what scientists actually do: trying to discover *new* things about the way the world works.

The amount of material a scholar of science needs to know, namely, the baseline knowledge, skills, and abilities, is quite extensive. A student who invests in this scholarship will endure many basics courses before being able to go into a field of choice.

—Patty Dooley

Additionally, it is hard to know how to balance ensuring that students have an understanding of scientific and mathematical methodology with providing some of the basic outlines of current scientific understandings and mathematical discoveries.

In section I, I discuss some of the methodologies involved in these disciplines and give a perspective on the learning goals of general education requirements, including the proper balance between content and methodology and the role played by integrating the humanities with the sciences in general education. In section II, I share some of the ways that Simon's Rock faculty members have addressed common challenges to the achievement of these learning goals.

I. UNDERSTANDING WHAT IS DISTINCTIVE: THE GOALS OF SCIENCE AND MATHEMATICS GENERAL EDUCATION

I maintain that a main goal of general education in the sciences and mathematics is achieving student understanding of the distinctiveness of scientific and mathematical methodology.[3] In this section, I discuss the scientific method, the aspects of scientific inquiry that make it distinctive, and the aspects of mathematical inquiry that make it distinctive. I also discuss the role of content areas and the relation of the humanities to the sciences.

a. The Nature of Science, Part I: The Myth of the Scientific Method

We may, perhaps, all remember the version of the scientific method we learned in middle school. It runs something like the following:

Step 1: Form a hypothesis.
Step 2: Devise an experiment to test the hypothesis.
Step 3: Perform the experiment.
Step 4: Make observations.
Step 5: Use the observations to determine whether the hypothesis is true or false.

As far as middle school education goes, this is not an entirely inappropriate approximation of the activities of many scientists. It communicates something about the importance of data, experimentation, and testability in scientific theory evaluation. But the reality is that there is no such thing as the scientific method. The variety of subject matter, evidence bases, and inferences is too broad and nuanced to be reduced to any simple formula. Theoretical cosmology has methods that more closely resemble those of mathematics than those of analytical chemistry; the passivity of historical astronomical observation is quite removed from the interventions of modern genetics research; the inferences made by geologists are quite different from those of field biologists. Lacunae and infelicities abound in the above statement of the scientific method, e.g.:

- An essential aspect of the work of scientists lies in generating hypotheses in the first place; we are not given guidance on this process at all.
- It does not appear possible to design an experiment to test a hypothesis in isolation from a general theoretical background, including claims about the nature of the instruments used, relevant laws of nature at work, and auxiliary assumptions. An apparently disconfirming experiment may be rejected by defenders of the apparently disconfirmed hypothesis on the grounds that a part of the general theoretical background is false.[4]
- Similarly, the idea of the results of the experiment as observations with a privileged epistemic status has been questioned due to the role that one's theoretical commitments play in one's observations or statements thereof.[5]
- The implicit notion that an experiment may prove a hypothesis true or false does disservice by artificially inflating the power of scientific evidence. Science is not in the business of proof.
- There is much more to science than experimentation. The longest established physical science, astronomy, was successful for more than 2,000 years before scientists were able to conduct a single experiment. Observation, logic, analogy, and symmetry also play crucial roles in scientific inquiry.

Philosophers of science have made many observations about scientific methodology, including the above reflections. Since the nineteenth century, working scientists have not in general been involved in philosophical discussions of scientific methodology. The demands of specialization in both science and philosophy have made doing both well an extraordinary task. For these reasons, contemporary philosophy of science is farther removed from the practice of science that it ever has been before.[6]

Perhaps it is for this reason that methods of scientific inquiry are not generally well understood. It would be a good thing for college students to have a more sophisticated, contemporary understanding of the methods of science. The separation of philosophical reflection on scientific methodology from the day-to-day activities of working scientists has created a situation in which it is less likely that students will achieve such an understanding. Yet the widespread influence and implications of scientific reasoning are making this understanding ever more imperative.

b. The Nature of Science, Part II:
The Myth of the Myth of the Scientific Method

In the decades since Thomas Kuhn's *The Structure of Scientific Revolutions*,[7] there has been a strong current of criticism of science, especially from the fields of philosophy, social theory, critical theory, and gender studies. The critiques leveled have often been inspired by (sometimes what is arguably a misreading of) Kuhn's critique of scientific rationality, as well as the idea that science is not as distinctive as the mythology surrounding it suggests. Scientists are humans. The institutions of science are troubled by human failings, including oppression (racism, sexism, homophobia), resistance to change, entrenchment of the ideas of the powerful, and dependence on language and conceptual schemes. According to the critiques, science's claim to speak with a special authority is window-dressing on what is in reality a subjective process fueled by something not unlike religious faith.[8] These criticisms have been joined by a revival of empiricist critiques of scientific knowledge[9] inspired by the theoretical quandaries of quantum mechanics and the surprising replacement of Newtonian mechanics by general and special relativity.[10] These critiques tend to argue that scientific inference is truth-conducive in certain domains where the evidence is sufficiently direct; yet it is frequently and perhaps most paradigmatically applied in domains beyond the proper bounds of its use, especially in the postulation of entities and forces not directly observable.

At the same time, there have been numerous advances in the nuanced understanding of scientific practice, including detailed sociological studies.[11] Additionally, it has been argued that some of the very features that form the basis of critiques of science may in fact be elements that are central to its epistemic credentials. For example, Helen Longino argues that the subjective perspective of individual scientists can lead to objective judgments through the lively exchange of ideas, arguments, and data among diverse groups of scientists;[12] and Richard Boyd argues that the dependence of scientific theorizing on the background theories of the scientists is an essential component of the objective confirmation of these background theories.[13]

The recent critiques of science deserve examination and response. In particular, scientists and science students would do well to reflect on the structure and diversity of the profession, the role of financial, political, and government interests, and the mechanisms of publication and grant funding. At the same time, students need to have an understanding of the extent of the empirical success of scientific theories and some of the methods used to arrive at this success. There is no denying that scientists in general know what they are about.[14] The most potent of scientific methods is the extensive mutual critique of the peer review process. Indeed, among the harshest critics of individual scientists are other scientists. Research that survives this process has generated a wealth of information and predictive power. For example, the theory of quantum mechanics, for all of its conceptual puzzles, has attained an extraordinary level of precision.

Science may be thought of as a *techne*, a craft in the ancient Greek sense, like music. Whatever critiques there are to be made of the epistemological and social credentials of science, it consists of a set of practices that are well-defined and followed by its practitioners, just as in world traditions of music. It is important that students have an understanding of scientific methods and the things that have been achieved by them, whatever they intend to do with this knowledge in the future.

c. What Is Distinctive about Science?

In analyzing a creature, Aristotle was interested in its *ergon*: its distinctive property or set of properties. A plant's *ergon* is nutrition and growth; an animal's, reproduction; a human's, reason. In thinking about the practice of science we might ask, what is its *ergon* as opposed to other human activities? The primary source in the philosophy of science literature for this sort of question is the debate about the demarcation between science and pseudo-science (e.g., astrology). It is puzzling that this is the case, as it may seem even more interesting to consider what makes science distinctive from human activities that do not purport to be science.

I cannot give a fully explicit account of the nature of science here. Indeed, as discussed, the variety of scientific methodologies makes such a task a difficult one in general. However, I will list some features that together appear to be distinctive about science.

Observation. In general, scientists aim to evaluate the theories they consider by means of a set of systematic observations. These observations are conducted in such a way as to control for as many relevant variables as possible. Note that scientists do not simply attempt to maximize the number of observations, as there are diminishing returns. Rather, they attempt to maximize the number up to the level of significance, as well as practicality, variety (according to established or plausibly relevant variables), and interest. The body of observations to which scientific theories are expected to be faithful becomes more robust and detailed over time.

> As time goes by, experimental methodologies improve and scientific theories must also stand up to those improved methodologies. ... Nothing is ever fully proven. This fact is what drives scientists to propose new hypotheses and experiments. To those who look for absolute proof, the sciences are maddeningly frustrating, as the only "proof" is the test of time and the number of experiments which support the idea.
>
> —DAVID MYERS

Objective Reasoning. Scientists hold each other to the norm of reasoning in an objective manner, and scientific understandings of the world have developed out of a concerted, systematic effort to understand the processes of nature in an objective way. In scientific practice, the norm of objectivity prescribes:

- Reasons have to be publically accessible
- Experiments have to be replicable
- Proper controls need to be in place to ensure that there are not confounding variables
- Investigators' methodology can have no identifiable bias

> I believe in an external reality. That does not mean that we can know all nor that the questions we ask aren't influenced by our times, but it does mean that there is a physical and biological world that exists separate from our own imaginations, and this world can be observed and measured, within certain theoretical and experimental limits. I do believe this world is so complex that in practice, we are likely to know only a very small piece of it.
>
> —MICHAEL BERGMAN

The Attraction of Destruction. While everyone is human, scientists put a remarkable amount of effort into undermining their life's work, or at least the current theories they are investigating. This, of course, is not entirely self-defeating, as making unlikely predictions can generate the highest levels of confirmation, as demonstrated by the discovery of Neptune.

Categorization and Measurable Properties. Science carries with it some fundamental methodological assumptions.

1. The world can be usefully divided into types of things that have some similar properties which result in their behaving similarly in important ways. These types can include biological species, chemical elements, geological features, etc.
2. The properties of things can be measured according to their dimensions, intensity, etc.

Measurement. Scientists identify natural kinds and qualities that can be measured through observation in repeatable ways. This can include qualitative measurements (specimen x is a juvenile anemone) or quantitative measurement (specimen x weighs 153 grams). Measurement is important in that it provides the data for determining relationships among objects and properties.

> The tools of inquiry in science are rooted in relentless, scrupulous adherence to the scientific method informed by impartiality and integrity—if the instrument reads 565 nm, I record 565 nm, not some other value. If I disagree with what I observe, I cannot persuade the substance to emit light at a different wavelength. Other disciplines could provide cogent arguments for a person to change his mind about a perspective or opinion, but 565 nm light is 565 nm light.
>
> -—PATTY DOOLEY

Starting Where They Are. Scientific activity is grounded in a tradition and a research program. While it is important to try to consider the possibility of fundamentally different explanations for new data, doing this exclusively would make progress impossible. One looks to the history of one's field and the specific area under consideration for guidance regarding, e.g., what variables might be relevant or irrelevant. A biologist examining the molting of geese may consider age, temperature, and latitude, but not the day of the week or the position of Saturn.

Modeling. A model is a theoretical construct (residing in Plato's heaven, if you will) attempting to represent an aspect of reality. Many scientists' activities can be described as attempting to model relevant aspects of reality (e.g., the movements of the planets, the activities of subatomic particles). Modeling involves simplification for the sake of progress.

A Language of Its Own. There is a strong tendency for scientists to employ mathematics in their modeling of aspects of the world. This is related to the importance of measurement and of natural kinds. Once the world is divided in certain ways, things can be counted!

Natural Laws. Science tends to be interested in what is general and applicable to other situations. The object of discovery is regularities of nature, not the specifics of individuals. The other aspects of scientific methodology may have developed because they have proven to be the most effective way to investigate natural laws. In other words, content may be driving methodology. If you take as your subject matter something such as how wolves reproduce, you will discover that the best way to approach this involves the activities and values above. If this is correct, then science is, first, a kind of question; and second, a set of methodologies that have been shown to be effective at answering that kind of question.[15]

Critical Thinking. Behind all of its achievements, science is simply critical thinking. The use of mathematics, modeling, and technical language may obscure this to some. Scientists have developed highly sophisticated forms of inference, analysis, and testing; but these have been built step-wise from commonsense principles.

Collaboration. Science is collaborative, by necessity. Moreover, it is becoming more collaborative over time as the complexity of experiments grows. The questions asked by scientists demand extensive reliance on the findings and thinking of others. As fields of expertise become narrower, scientists defer to each other's judgments more and more frequently. Thus the collaboration is not merely practical, as in carrying out an experiment. It is epistemic, in that scientists' beliefs are based strongly on those of their colleagues.[16] Thus in science we see an intriguing blend of a critical appraisal of peers' work and a strong trust in peers' expertise.

d. Tour Guide of Plato's Heaven

> Mathematicians do not study the human condition per se, although their discoveries are either interesting or useful to other human beings.
> —WILLIAM DUNBAR

The discussion so far has concerned only science. According to Plato, we have been neglecting what is most important. For Plato, the most fully real things are those that are timeless, eternal, unchanging, and necessarily true, such as the essences of kinds of objects and logical and mathematical truths. A necessary truth is one that could not have been otherwise; for example, no matter how things might have gone in the world, it would still be true that A=A. The ontological status of mathematical entities and the nature of mathematical truth are hotly disputed, if not among the general populace, at least among the small subset of philosophers of mathematics. Whatever the result of these debates, it is agreed that mathematicians have succeeded in exploring (or constructing) some of an infinite domain of necessary truths (however "necessary" is understood).

To teach mathematics is to be a tour guide of Plato's heaven. This is a hard job. It's a big place! The record of human mathematical achievement is not infinite, but the subject matter is. An important goal of mathematics education, especially at the level of general education, should be to convey understanding of what is distinctive about mathematics, and to give students some familiarity with the variety of its methods.

Necessary Truth. Mathematics has the privilege of being the discipline with the most certain grasp on truth. As I've said, the underpinnings of this kind of truth are debated. Nevertheless, there is a reason that philosophers from Plato to Descartes to Russell to Wittgenstein have sought to emulate the methods of mathematics. A correct mathematical demonstration brings with it the certainty that not only is the proven proposition true, but it could not possibly be false, no matter what the nature of the universe. In many theologies, even God cannot break or alter the truths of mathematics!

Proof Based on Objective Reasons. The most distinctive method of mathematics is that of proof. Proof can range from deduction from axioms to proof by contradiction to mathematical induction. Other disciplines utilize logical inference, but from premises that are not as explicit and univocal as those of mathematics.

> Mathematics assumes that any two people (who try hard enough) will agree
> as to the soundness or unsoundness of any given proof.
>
> —WILLIAM DUNBAR

Assumptions. Mathematics has an elegant structure of proof; it does make assumptions, striving to generate as much as it can from as little as possible. Axioms (such as those of Euclidean geometry) are most familiar.

Modeling. Remarkably, all manners of natural and human phenomena can be modeled mathematically. Plato's heaven has a strong connection to the material world! The complexities of the world's financial markets, the behavior of quarks and stars, and the spread of viruses are subject to representation in the language of mathematics. Even more striking is that many complicated physical phenomena, e.g., gravitation, waves, and electromagnetic radiation, seem to be able to be represented in surprisingly simple mathematical terms (relatively speaking). There is something to be said for the claim that mathematics is the language of nature.

Critical Thinking. Behind all of its achievements, the truth is that mathematics is simply critical thinking with formal representation. Its abstractness, capacity for complexity, and formality may be daunting. Yet fundamentally, its method is the same we use when we read a mystery. The symbols of mathematics can confuse the uninitiated; but a natural language is also a representative structure highly confusing to those who aren't familiar with it.

Collaboration. As with science, mathematics is becoming more collaborative as the complexity of proofs grow and communication becomes easier.

In thinking about teaching mathematics and science at the level of general education, a number of issues arise related to the relative priority of the two. Math is the language of science, but is not simply handmaiden to it. Mathematical understanding is an important goal of general education in its own right. However, teaching mathematics is also importantly linked to whatever one wants to accomplish in science general education. Moreover, a science course is an opportunity to reinforce key mathematical understandings, as it provides an elegant context for applications. At Simon's Rock, we have discovered that one cannot venture to do anything ambitiously different in the teaching of science without thinking carefully about the role of mathematics in the curriculum.

e. Method versus Subject Matter

The learning goals I have endorsed do not refer to any content areas. They entail some content—for example, understanding measurement would entail knowing about significant digits—but not much. What do we think of this? Is it essential for college students to have an understanding, for example, of the theory of evolution, or the concept of a normal distribution?

Part of studying for a bachelor's degree is being oriented to humanity's understandings of and expressions about the world. It's the map in the airport with the "you are here" marker. It follows that a college graduate should have general insight into humanity's current best take on the large- and small-scale structure and physical laws of the universe, and thus that there are some specific scientific and mathematical principles and content areas that should be understood by B.A. graduates. Which ones should be up to each college's science and mathematics faculty.

f. The Integration of the Sciences and the Humanities

It might seem that we have more than enough goals concerning general education in mathematics and science. It is already a lot to accomplish. Yet I think it is important to add a further dimension to the discussion: the connection of the sciences[17] to disciplines outside of these fields, specifically, the humanities. Students who end up in humanities fields will in some cases have to be able to reconcile what they do with scientific pictures of the world, and students in the sciences will have to work with people in the humanities. Climate change experts have to be able to communicate with politicians; therapists dealing with boundary-of-life issues have to understand something about biology.

At Simon's Rock, we think a lot about interdisciplinary work, for practical reasons (because the small size of our faculty forces us to), and principled reasons (because there is a lot that can be usefully done by combining the methods of different disciplines). Not surprisingly, there are significantly different kinds of interdisciplinary study. First, there is interdisciplinary study that applies one discipline to another. This, when done well, involves use of—or at least awareness of—the methodologies of both disciplines, but is primarily contained within one discipline: sociology of science is sociology, although frequently, it involves detailed knowledge of scientific methodology. Thus one way to connect the sciences and the humanities is through the study of the history of science, philosophy of science, sociology of science, other social scientific critique of scientific authority, etc.

Another kind of interdisciplinary study is using the methods of more than one discipline to explore and gain understanding of a common problem not easily solved by the methods of a single discipline. To explore this kind of integration at the level of general education would involve the identification of areas of study where progress is best made by a combination of the methods of disciplines within and without the sciences. These areas might include:

- The story of human migration and conquest, mating behavior, and social structures.
- The history of scientific discovery.
- Anthropogenic climate change (or any environmental issue) and solutions thereto.

- The spread and containment of disease.
- Public health policy in general, including that related to health disparities.
- Altruism and cooperation in humans and other animals (including their evolutionary history, neuroscience, psychology, and conscious and unconscious rationales).
- Sustainable agriculture.
- Cognitive science and education policy.

The history of scientific discovery is an intriguing item on this list. History of science may seem to fall under the category of other disciplines' study of science. However, there is a good deal of history of science that attempts to document and elucidate the process of scientific discovery. Doing this requires knowing about historical and contemporary methods of science and scientific understandings of the world—and so the methodology employed is as scientific as it is historical.

> It seems to me that one cannot study scientific and mathematic breakthroughs
> without putting these in historical and sociological context.
>
> —DAVID MYERS

Should general education include the integration of science and the humanities? Answering this kind of question involves having a sense of the trajectory of human inquiry. The abundance of data touching on almost all areas of human concern; the ready attainability of information; and the growing applicability of methods of the sciences to other areas of inquiry mean that current liberal arts students will be expected in their lives to be able to use the methods of different fields and to think across the sciences and humanities. Yet I am always reluctant to think of the goal of a liberal arts education as an attempt to keep students "current," as if we were teaching them the latest management theory. Rather, our goal should be to help our students achieve excellence in thinking. One of the things we have learned at the end of the twentieth century and beginning of the twenty-first is that approaching problems from the standpoint of a single discipline can be limiting. The world isn't always neatly partitioned for exploration by traditional academic disciplines in their respective domains. (Indeed, the history of the academic disciplines conceived as distinct from each other is surprisingly brief.) The rise in importance of fields such as biophysics, biochemistry, cultural studies, gender studies, medical anthropology, and statistics, as well as collaborative work between scholars in different fields, illustrates that the excellence in thinking we want our students to achieve often involves the integration of disciplines.

II. OVERCOMING OBSTACLES IN THE TEACHING OF SCIENCE AND MATHEMATICS

In the last section, I outlined what I take to be some of the important goals of general education in the sciences and mathematics. Liberal arts students should have, at minimum, a practiced understanding of science's emphasis on observation; an objective, systematic approach; measurement; the priority of testing challenging cases; working within a research tradition; modeling of physical phenomena; applied use of mathematics; interest in natural kinds and natural laws; reliance on principles of everyday critical thinking; and collaborative investigation. They should have, at minimum, an understanding of mathematics' relation to necessary truth; reliance on proof; use of assumptions; ability to model phenomena; reliance on principles of everyday critical thinking; and collaborative method. Finally, they should have a general understanding of the basic outlines of scientific and mathematical understandings of the world, and some of the ways that the sciences can be used in partnership with the humanities to expand human knowledge. In this section, I outline some pedagogical approaches for achieving these goals in the face of some common obstacles: self-doubt and fear; teaching students of different levels of interest and preparation; and teaching outside of expertise.

a. Teaching against Self-Doubt and Fear

Let's begin with a central feature that I claim science and mathematics have in common: both are, at bottom, highly sophisticated and technical forms of familiar, everyday critical thinking. A goal of general education in these subjects is to attain student appreciation of this. Every college student has the capacity to do science, to do mathematics, and to understand that what she or he is doing is simply using her or his capacity for critical thinking (albeit in ways less comfortable for some).

There are two major obstacles to this process. One is a false belief in scientific and mathematical exceptionalism. The idea is that science and math are somehow mysterious processes that some people are fundamentally unable to fathom, and that other people can execute effortlessly. We hear, for example, the phrases "I can't do science," or "I'm not a math person." This can be combined with the erroneous idea that science and math "people" are able simply to intuit the right answer without work or risk of error.

In the previous section, I discussed ways in which science and mathematics *are* exceptional, mainly in their descriptive and predictive accuracy. However, exceptional outcomes do not translate to extraordinary processes. Science and mathematics utilize normal human cognitive abilities that everyone has in systematic and formal ways so that our world and Plato's can be better understood. Normal human cognitive abilities—period.

The second obstacle to understanding the commonality between scientific and mathematics methods and critical thinking (and, a fortiori, methods in other liberal arts disciplines) is fear. Students arrive at college with a set of experiences studying science and mathematics beginning at least in kindergarten. For many, these experiences may have involved humiliation (problems at the blackboard); being told that they have or do not have the ability to succeed; or simply having had someone assume that they do or do not have the ability to succeed. The emotional associations many students have with science and mathematics have absolutely nothing to do with the subjects, but rather the messages they have received. (Note that even the students who were told they could do well in these subjects may have been harmed by the message—implicit or otherwise—that other students could not.) Part of the work of general education in these subjects is to overcome this fear and demonstrate that it does not have a basis in reality. To repeat, every single college student has the ability to do science and mathematics, by virtue of being a human with a functioning brain.

Overcoming self-doubt and fear that prevent student understanding is an interesting problem for educators, because we are not usually trained formally to address such fundamentally emotional issues. Here are some suggestions:

Assert Reality Happily and Incessantly. The first step, I submit, is to hold out the reality of the students' competence (contrasted with the false belief of inadequacy) frequently, cheerfully, and non-judgmentally. One can say "you can do this" in a tone faulting someone for not having done it yet, or you can say it with boundless optimism. The latter is more helpful.

Fear often leads to defensiveness, which can take the form of apathy and disinterest. This is also important to combat. Part of asserting reality happily and incessantly is never wavering from the idea that the subject matter is interesting. Science and math are totally and completely intriguing! There are no non-interesting parts. Yes, even significant digits.

One of the challenges in my mind for college faculty in the sciences and mathematics in adopting this approach is that students come to college with preconceptions of their own aptitude, the inherent interest of the subject, and the quality of instructors in these disciplines. (There is something a bit easier in teaching a subject that is seldom taught at earlier levels of education.) These preconceptions can be positive or negative. When they are negative, faculty members can be pushed towards a defensive attitude about their subject. It is hard to assert reality cheerfully when one feels besieged! It is important to persevere, to remember that students' negative thinking about sciences and mathematics when they arrive at college has nothing to do with one's subject or oneself, but rather, negative experiences they have had previously that have given them a false picture of reality. So keep giving them the true picture, which is that science and mathematics are doable, completely interesting, and taught by fantastic people dedicated to their education.

> I haven't found any strategy or combination of strategies that reliably removes these obstacles. I just try to be very clear about two things:
>
> > (a) I believe that every student is capable of doing the coursework.
> > (b) I'm willing to spend the time to help anyone who asks.
>
> (I also make an effort to be sure I'm giving positive feedback to those who are trying hard.)
>
> —WILLIAM DUNBAR

Learning Disabilities? By law and by right, students with documented learning disabilities need to be given reasonable accommodations for completing their work. It is good to keep one's eye on other students who may have similar struggles but who have not been given this diagnosis. They might also benefit from accommodations such as more time on tests.

A learning disability does not mean that a student is unable to do science or mathematics. This is merely an indication that more patience or one-on-one work may be required in his or her education. Such students should not be exempted from math and science requirements, and we should never be tempted to think that they are anything less than fully capable of success.

Black Tie? Self-doubt and fear are exacerbated in formal situations. Here, this means unfamiliar symbols and technical language, which abound in science and mathematics. It is important not to let some students' fear or confusion about symbols and technical language drive one to the idea that they should be avoided. On the contrary, discomfort here is a sign that these things should be discussed more. Some students' brains will turn off, so to speak, when a symbol or equation is written on the board. Perfect! You have discovered an area in which they need some help.

Now, saying that formalism and technical language should not be avoided is not saying that we should go full-steam ahead. Patience is required. Students speak at least one language already. Therefore, we know they are completely capable of understanding a system of abstract representation. (See above.) The standbys of having students take the lead in problem solving; one-on-one tutoring; repeated, varied explanations; and of group work on problems are helpful ways to slow things down.

Humor. Laughing is the ultimate antidote to fear. Silliness is in order. This goes well with asserting reality happily and incessantly, as enthusiasm and silliness are complementary, strangely.

> Whenever I present bonding models to my classes, I try to get them physically to visualize how the bonds actually look. (There are two kinds of bonds we usually address in chemistry: sigma [s] and pi [p].) Inadvertently, I used my arms to illustrate this point. I pointed my fists at each other and said "sigma"; I then placed my arms vertically parallel and said "pi" then horizontally parallel and said "pi" again. This became the chemistry cheer—sigma, pi, pi. The whole class laughed and that was that—or so I thought. On the next exam, I see many members of the class, using their fingers to do "sigma-pi-pi." I've now incorporated this into my classes and it appears to have worked.
>
> —DAVID MYERS

Small Successes. Breaking things down into very small steps, and celebrating each accomplishment along the way, is a great way to communicate to students their ability to do math and science.

> I carefully encourage students to use what they already know to synthesize a solution to the issue. Often they *do* know how to approach the issue and just need a little "hand-holding" to get to it; as they improve in ability, this "hand-holding" lessens.
>
> —DAVID MYERS

Analogies. As part of the goal is to convey the continuity of scientific and mathematical reasoning with everyday reasoning, counteracting the unfamiliarity of these methods, it can be useful to make analogies to everyday, non-scientific and non-mathematical situations and reasoning. This is quite compatible with silliness, too. When I discuss predicate logic in my formal logic classes, I use examples such as 'Every plump hedgehog dates a plump hedgehog' to keep things light $(\forall x((Hx\&Px)\supset(\exists y((Hy\&Py)\&Dxy))))$, in case you are curious).

A Sense of Community. The vast majority of students' lives are not spent in one's classroom. Fostering class identity and relationships among the students will facilitate their ability to use each other as resources. This can take the form of group work in or out of class. Francie Chew reports that paired listening in science classes results in higher learning outcomes.[18] Having a chance to listen to each other and be heard by other students about their anxieties or accomplishments is a great way to promote class bonding and to relieve anxiety. As Chew observes, undergraduate classroom science education often omits the very kind of collaboration that is central to scientific methodology; allowing collaborative work in the classroom addresses this lacuna.[19]

b. Managing Differences in Interest Level and Preparation

In the sciences and mathematics, distribution requirements create a situation in which some classes are composed primarily of students who are interested in science and have already developed strong skills, while others are composed primarily of students who have less preparation and interest and are taking the course only because it is required. Students not majoring in the sciences are often not exposed to those who are enthusiastic about the material.

At Simon's Rock, we have found that it benefits students to be in classes containing a range of levels of expertise and interest. For example, incoming students are placed together into our general education humanities seminars regardless of their preparation and enthusiasm for textual analysis and essay writing. This allows less-prepared and interested students to see the enthusiasm of other students, to have informal discussions with peers with stronger backgrounds, and to be effectively tutored by these peers. The result is a much higher level of discussion and accomplishment than would occur were we to separate students into sections of basic composition and advanced seminars.

To achieve this effect in the sciences at Simon's Rock, we have developed a series of courses that appeal to science students as well as those who are seeking to fulfill a distribution requirement. These classes cover subjects not included in basic science sequence classes but which are central to ongoing areas of scientific inquiry, for example: "Global Climate Change," "Paleontology," and "Dynamic Earth." As a small college, we do not offer many high-level science courses in climate science, paleontology, or geology. This makes these courses attractive to students already interested in science and allows us to have a variety of levels of preparation and interest in the same class.

It is more difficult to manage different levels of preparation and interest in a science classroom than in a humanities classroom. First, the language of science is mathematics. Some students enter college without being able to speak this language sufficiently well. In the humanities seminars, students have more or less facility with language and writing, but at least everyone is basically familiar with the language of instruction. Second, science is cumulative, building on prior research and ideas. It is helpful to know some Aquinas before reading Dante's *Inferno*, but you can still read the *Inferno* without that knowledge. One cannot do most chemistry experiments without knowing about molarity. Finally, the benefit of having students of all levels in the classroom is magnified by teaching in the seminar style, with extensive class discussion. It is more difficult to have an interactive classroom when the material is less open to debate or interpretation, and when the instructor must communicate a large quantity of information to students.

In order to overcome these challenges, both the curriculum and the style of teaching must be carefully calibrated. There are several desiderata for an appropriate curriculum for students of varying levels of interest and skills. First, the subject matter should minimize the need for preparation. Columbia University's Frontiers of Science program is based on the principle of "inverting the pyramid." This refers to teaching what would normally be an advanced subject matter with a host of prerequisites (e.g., neuroscience) without the prerequisites, with background information being given on a "just in time" basis. Second, in order to maximize the interest of students with better preparation and skills, it is useful to teach a subject matter that is not typically covered in secondary education. Third, the subject matter should be thematically unified, interdisciplinary among the sciences, and interesting to the student population. Finally, the subject matter should be expandable. By this, I mean that there should be many different paths down which more advanced students can explore issues at a more complex level, without rendering the course opaque to other students. For example, when I teach formal logic, I use a book that has additional chapters dealing with the proofs of the soundness and completeness of the logical systems we use. These chapters are skipped in the normal run of class, but advanced students can do additional assignments regarding them, including making presentations to the remainder of the class on these topics.

The appropriate subject matter is necessary for a successful general education science course, but it must be approached carefully. It is challenging to teach students who lack sufficient preparation or interest in the sciences. While it is of great potential benefit to teach these students in a class with other, more prepared or interested students, doing so successfully is an art. For example, at Simon's Rock, the ability level of students in formal logic courses typically ranges from the top mathematics and computer science students at the college to students who test into the most basic mathematics course. One strategy with which I have found success in this course (and other courses) is not to teach only to the middle of the class. Instead, I partition the class and create periods that are just for some groups of students or others. For example, I may take five minutes, make it explicit to everyone that the material we are discussing is not something they are responsible for understanding, and go over ideas that I think it's likely only more advanced students will understand. At other times, when it is called for by a lack of understanding by a few students, I will review material that I know most students grasp, varying my explanations and asking students in the class for other ways of conceptualizing the material. It is helpful for more advanced students to consider how a particular point might be explained to someone who has not yet grasped it. In general, it makes sense for most of the class time to be accessible, but it is useful for students to have some class time spent on material that stretches or surpasses their understanding, and some class time spent on review material.

Another important strategy for dealing with different levels in the classroom is to have the class be as interactive as possible. This allows the enthusiasm and skills of the more advanced students to be evident to those who may be less interested or prepared. The challenge of doing this in the sciences is that the subjects are content heavy. When I teach philosophy of religion, we can have great, far-ranging debates about a particular proof of the existence of God. When I teach logic, it is harder to have a useful debate about, say, modus ponens, the argument form: If A, then B; A; Therefore, B. There is a lot of material to convey to students, and it is generally not as open to interpretation or questioning as topics in the humanities. A strategy I have found useful here is to find *all* of the spaces and creases for discussion and debate. It is not productive to argue the topic "modus ponens: pro or con?" for long. But the justification for modus ponens is arguably circular, as Lewis Carroll has pointed out.[20] That's interesting! This raises questions about the foundations of deductive inference and the role of assumptions in logic and mathematics. We might also discuss why modus ponens has the prominence that it has; whether natural language formulations of this form of argumentation are equivalent to the formal language formulations; which other forms of inference it is equivalent to; etc.

This strategy extends to foundational issues, definition of terms and variables, experimental setup, units used, etc. For example, instead of telling students how variance is defined, we might ask them to come up with different possible ways of measuring it, evaluating each one. They are more likely to understand and remember why variance is measured by taking the average of the square distances of data points to their mean if they evaluate other conceivable ways of measuring variance and discover their strengths and shortcomings. Not only do they have the potential to engage student discussion, but these foundational questions should be of interest and importance to students of all levels.

A shortcoming of an interactive classroom is that less material is covered. If we take methodology to be what is most important, this is just fine. Interactive discussion of aspects of scientific methodology and processes is precisely what students should be doing. The amount of content should be scaled to allow for such discussion.

c. Teaching Outside of Expertise in Science and the Humanities

In order to achieve the goal of integrating the sciences and the humanities, one must venture into unfamiliar and sometimes uncomfortable territory. Very few people have a deep expertise in multiple academic disciplines. For most of us, it is hard to know on our own how to proceed either in discussing another discipline from the standpoint of our own, or in investigating complex problems which require using the methods of multiple disciplines to address.

To gain some traction on this difficulty, it is instructive to turn to what we have noted about the methodology of the sciences. As discussed in I.c, science involves placing trust in other scientists. Eric Barnes outlines several kinds of trust in expertise involved in the scientific enterprise.[21] Not only is there the trust that non-experts place in scientific experts; there is the trust scientific experts place (i) in experts in different fields during interdisciplinary inquiry; (ii) in other experts in the same field who have different subspecialties, (iii) in other experts in the same field and subspecialty because of their own epistemic humility, and (iv) in past experts in their field who contributed to the knowledge that forms the foundation of their inquiries. Richard Foley has argued that this trust is well grounded as an extension of our trust in ourselves: because our beliefs are deeply dependent on information from others, to the extent that we trust our own thinking, we should trust the thinking of our peers, *ceteris paribus*.[22]

I propose that trust is as important to the project of integrating the sciences and humanities as it is to the workings of interdisciplinary and disciplinary science. In order to integrate the sciences and humanities, which almost always will involve thinking and teaching outside of one's expertise, one simply has to involve oneself with—and trust—experts in fields outside of one's own.

At Simon's Rock, we have informal and formal ways of doing this. As a small college, each faculty member knows every other, which is helpful. Informally, we often invite each other to each other's classes for discussion of relevant topics. I have been invited to discuss philosophy in a biology class, and have myself invited physicists and biologists to my philosophy of science courses to discuss, e.g., the nature of evidence in cosmology and the use of gendered language in the biology of reproduction. These interactions are invaluable. Having someone else with a different expertise in the classroom achieves much more than simply providing the information would be, even if we had it ourselves. Students get to see how people with different training and methodologies approach similar problems and questions.

Collaboration is supported formally through the college's BA Seminar courses, interdisciplinary, team-taught courses required for the B.A. degree. Many BA Seminars have paired together science and mathematics faculty with humanities faculty. We offer, e.g., courses on the mathematics and philosophy of infinity co-taught by a philosopher and computer scientist; on Douglas Hofstadter's book *Gödel, Escher, Bach* by a musician and a mathematician; on the development of the atom bomb by a physicist and a political scientist; and on science fiction taught by a physicist and a literature faculty member.

In working on integrating the sciences and humanities, it is important—as with all good teaching—not to hide ignorance. If we are to model to students the importance of collaboration in the pursuit of knowledge, we must articulate when we know something and when we don't. They need to see us run up against the bounds of our expertise and ask for help beyond it. They need to see us double-checking our thinking against that of others. In other words, they need to see us explicitly employing a collaborative approach, both with our colleagues and with themselves. The model of education in which the teacher has all the answers and shares these with the students is belied by the irreducibly social nature of inquiry and knowledge.

NOTES

1. Quotations are from a survey completed among the faculty in the Division of Science, Mathematics, and Computing during the summer of 2009, and are used with permission. Many thanks for helpful information from: Michael Bergman, Physics; William Dunbar, Mathematics; Patty Dooley, Chemistry; David Myers, Chemistry; Bob Schmidt, Biology; and Brian Wynne, Mathematics.

2. The Division of Science, Mathematics, and Computing at Simon's Rock includes biology, chemistry, physics, computer science, and mathematics. I include all of these disciplines in my discussion.

3. The importance of this approach has been emphasized to me by Brian Wynne.

4. Pierre Duhem, *The Aims and Structure of Physical Theory*, trans. P. Wiener (Princeton, NJ: Princeton University Press, 1951); W. V. Quine, "Two Dogmas of Empiricism," *Philosophical Review* 60 (1951): 20–43.

5. N. R. Hanson, *Patterns of Discovery* (Cambridge: Cambridge University Press, 1958).

6. Gary Gutting, "Scientific Methodology," in *A Companion to the Philosophy of Science*, ed. W. H. Newton-Smith (Oxford: Blackwell, 2000), 430.

7. Thomas Kuhn, *The Structure of Scientific Revolutions* (Chicago: University of Chicago Press, 1970).

8. See, e.g., Paul Feyerabend, *Against Method* (London: Verso, 1975).

9. See, e.g., Bas van Fraassen, *The Scientific Image* (Oxford: Oxford University Press, 1980).

10. Lawrence Sklar, *Space, Time, and Spacetime* (Berkeley: Berkeley University Press, 1974), 17.

11. See, e.g., David Bloor, *Knowledge and Social Imagery* (London: Routledge & Kegan Paul, 1976); Bruno Latour and Steve Woolgar, *Laboratory Life: The Construction of Scientific Facts* (Beverly Hills, CA: Sage Publications, 1979); Steven Shapin and Simon Schaffer, *Leviathan and the Air-Pump: Hobbes, Boyle, and the Experimental Life* (Princeton, NJ: Princeton University Press, 1985).

12. Helen E. Longino, *Science as Social Knowledge: Values and Objectivity in Scientific Inquiry* (Princeton, NJ: Princeton University Press, 1990).

13. Richard Boyd, "Observations, Explanatory Power, and Simplicity: Toward a Non-Humean Account," in *The Philosophy of Science*, ed. Richard Boyd, Philip Gasper, and J. D. Trout (Cambridge, MA: MIT Press, 1991), 349–377.

14. Gutting, "Scientific Methodology," 431.

15. One may ask about pseudoscience: don't, e.g., astrologers take regularities in nature as their object of study? On this account, one could do astrology scientifically for a while, but once it is established that the regularities one is looking for are not there, then one is no longer doing science. Those regularities are absent, and one is ignoring the fact; in other words, one is no longer actually studying them.

16. Eric Barnes, *The Paradox of Predictivism* (Cambridge: Cambridge University Press, 2008).

17. For brevity, I will use "the sciences" in this section to include mathematics.

18. F. S. Chew, "Peer Interaction Boosts Science Learning," in *A View From the Academy: Liberal Arts Professors on Excellent Teaching*, ed. Thomas Warren (Lanham, MD: University Press of America, 1992), 156–65.

19. Chew, "Peer Interaction Boosts Science Learning," 161–62.

20. Carroll argues that there is a suppressed premise: If, if A, then B, and A, then B. But if *this* premise is introduced there is another suppressed premise: If, if, if A, then B, and A, then B, then B. Etc. (Lewis Carroll, "What the Tortoise Said to Achilles," *Mind* 4 [1895]: 278–80; reprinted in Mind 104 [1995]: 691–93.)

21. Barnes, *The Paradox of Predictivism*, 31–59.

22. Richard Foley, *Intellectual Trust in Oneself and Others* (Cambridge: Cambridge University Press, 2001).

WORKS CITED

Barnes, Eric. *The Paradox of Predictivism*. Cambridge: Cambridge University Press, 2008.
Bloor, David. *Knowledge and Social Imagery*. London: Routledge & Kegan Paul, 1976.
Boyd, Richard. "Observations, Explanatory Power, and Simplicity: Toward a Non-Humean Account."

In *The Philosophy of Science*, edited by Richard Boyd, Philip Gasper, and J. D. Trout, 349–377. Cambridge, MA: MIT Press, 1991.

Carroll, Lewis. "What the Tortoise Said to Achilles." *Mind* 4 (1895): 278–80. Reprinted in *Mind* 104 (1995): 691–93.

Chew, F. S. "Peer Interaction Boosts Science Learning." In *A View From the Academy: Liberal Arts Professors on Excellent Teaching*, edited by Thomas Warren, 156–65. Lanham, MD: University Press of America, 1992.

Duhem, Pierre. *The Aims and Structure of Physical Theory*. Translated by P. Wiener. Princeton, NJ: Princeton University Press, 1951.

Feyerabend, Paul. *Against Method*. London: Verso, 1975.

Foley, Richard. *Intellectual Trust in Oneself and Others*. Cambridge: Cambridge University Press, 2001.

Gutting, Gary. "Scientific Methodology." In *A Companion to the Philosophy of Science*, edited by W. H. Newton-Smith, 423–432. Oxford: Blackwell, 2000.

Hanson, N. R. *Patterns of Discovery*. Cambridge: Cambridge University Press, 1958.

Kuhn, Thomas. *The Structure of Scientific Revolutions*. Chicago: University of Chicago Press, 1970.

Latour, Bruno, and Steve Woolgar. *Laboratory Life: The Construction of Scientific Facts*. Beverly Hills, CA: Sage Publications, 1979.

Longino, Helen E. *Science as Social Knowledge: Values and Objectivity in Scientific Inquiry*. Princeton, NJ: Princeton University Press, 1990.

Quine, W. V. "Two Dogmas of Empiricism." *Philosophical Review* 60 (1951): 20–43.

Shapin, Steven, and Simon Schaffer. *Leviathan and the Air-Pump: Hobbes, Boyle, and the Experimental Life*. Princeton, NJ: Princeton University Press, 1985.

Sklar, Lawrence. *Space, Time, and Spacetime*. Berkeley, CA: Berkeley University Press, 1974.

van Fraassen, Bas. *The Scientific Image*. Oxford: Oxford University Press, 1980.

6

Intelligence and Consciousness, Artificial and Otherwise

An Interdisciplinary Seminar on Gödel, Escher, Bach

ALLEN B. ALTMAN *and* JOHN E. MYERS

What is thought, and are machines capable of it? This question is at the heart of the text *Gödel, Escher, Bach: An Eternal Golden Braid* by Douglas Hofstadter. This Pulitzer Prize–winning book delves into an astounding array of topics usually considered the province of a number of discrete academic disciplines. Among these are fugues and canons, logic and truth, brain and mind, recursion, syntactic structures, visual patterning, Zen Buddhism, paradoxes, DNA and genetic code, artificial intelligence, the nature of meaning, and the question of "what is proof." Given our respective expertises in mathematics (Allen) and music (John), it intrigued and challenged us, and thus seemed an ideal text to choose as the center of our co-taught interdisciplinary BA seminar. First offered in Fall 2001, and later offered at intervals of two or three years, the seminar consistently attracted interested groups of students pursuing concentrations in all four of the college's academic divisions (Arts; Languages and Literature; Science, Mathematics, and Computing; Social Studies). The focus on a single work provided a basis for organization as well as the chance for a serious exploration from the perspectives of several disciplines, including (but not limited to): mathematics, music, computer sciences, visual art, linguistics, biology, and literature. In this article, we first explore the basic themes and style of the book, and then describe how we used it in the seminar.

The creation of artificial intelligence and its impact on our rapidly-evolving relationship with computers is one of the fundamental issues of our time. With Raymond Kurzweil and other experts predicting that computers will exceed human "intelligence" (more on this later) by 2030, there is an increased incentive to explore this issue, even if definitive answers are elusive. At the very least, *Gödel, Escher, Bach* presents an interesting variation on the fundamental anthropological question "what does it mean to be human?" which is interwoven with another question "what does it mean to be intelligent?" The three people whose names form the title were fine examples of intelligent human beings.

Born in 1765, J. S. Bach looked forward to the eighteenth century Enlightenment in his embrace of reason, and in his enthusiasm for scientific advances in instrument construction and tuning. At the same time, he also looked back to the past in terms of his deep religious mysticism and his integration of musical traditions from earlier periods. M. C. Escher is highly regarded in the visual arts world as an intriguing graphic designer and illustrator of the early twentieth century, but has not yet achieved the canonic status of contemporaries such as Picasso, Dali and others. Kurt Gödel, a friend of Albert Einstein, was the most important mathematical logician of his time. By showing that no sufficiently powerful formal system can be complete, his work dashed the hopes of mathematicians to be able to derive all of mathematics from simple logic without internal contradictions.

So why did Hofstadter bring these three disparate personalities together? Although their intellectual vocabulary differed greatly, as might be expected considering their disciplines, all three of these spectacularly gifted people are united by the presence of explicit and implicit self-reference in their work. Self-reference is found in Bach's musical themes that twist and turn on themselves to become their own accompaniment; in Escher's hands that draw each other, and landscapes that wrap around themselves; and in Gödel's numbering system in which statements of mathematical logic can address their own validity. Hofstadter went beyond a simple juxtaposition of the work of three people, and highlighted these shared qualities of self-reference, which he worked into the design of the book itself. Aside from the three central figures, there are many references to the mathematician and writer Lewis Carroll. Two of Carroll's characters, Tortoise and Achilles, whom Carroll had borrowed from Zeno of Elea (fifth century B.C.E.), appear at several points in the work. Hofstadter also utilizes Carroll's playful literary style in the introductory dialogues which precede each of the chapters. The underlying shared characteristic of self-reference, while occasionally made explicit by Hofstadter, is more often than not just hinted at, especially in the earlier chapters of his book. An atmosphere of adventure, discovery and wonder is maintained throughout. We tried to leave space for the students to find their individual connections with the work, which is why the class meetings were so important. For the overall shape of the course, we used the text, which gradually introduces increasingly complex modes of self-reference in various fields. The first chapter introduces Bach and Escher, and Kurt Gödel, who showed that Bertrand Russell's attempt to axiomatize mathematics was futile. The phenomena of self-reference and recursion are explored in the work of all three of these men, and are also abundantly present in Hofstadter's own fictional and expository writing. The reader encounters the musical compositions of Bach, and the enigmatic images of M. C. Escher, along with special numerical codes created by Gödel to allow a formal system to talk about itself through typographical number theory. As the seminar progressed, students could see that the various examples involved a similar kind of thinking, building a whole which is larger than its parts. No description can be both complete and consistent. Starting with simple formal logic puzzles, Hofstadter gradually builds up to more and more sophisticated systems so that by the middle of the book, readers can reach an appreciation of Gödel's revolutionary but formidable self-referencing string.

Usually, class meetings started with music. Recordings of selections from Bach's "Musical Offering" or other pieces were played, and copies of scores were provided for members able to read music notation. Some of these pieces were directly discussed in the text, and others were chosen on the basis of the musical puns with which Hofstadter often titled his dialogues. For example, one of his dialogue titles, "Air on G's String" (A reference to a critical string in Gödel's proof that allowed for self-reference), is obviously taken from Bach's "Air on the G String," so we listened to this piece before that day's discussions. Sometimes we discussed musical features of the pieces as they related to the topics. The listening experiences provided a meditative and stimulating introduction to each class. We would then proceed to our discussions. As with many of the courses in our general education program, the students read a substantial text in increments, and offered their individual and collective interpretations of it. Required written responses to each of the book's twenty chapters were used as a starting point for class discussions. Each class was devoted to a single chapter. We asked the students to submit these responses a day before each meeting so that we could read them ahead of time. At the beginning of each discussion period, we randomly distributed copies of the responses, and provided some time so that each student could read at least one of their classmates' commentaries and responses. In the ensuing discussions, we sometimes mentioned comments and insights that various students had offered, using this to help maximize the number of student voices, and to cover as much of the material as possible. Occasionally, we asked the students in advance to include certain elements in their responses. The book included many puzzles written in code that could be translated into statements of logic or descriptive mathematics. For example, near the beginning of the semester, a series of symbols might be used to make a statement such as "two is not a square." While this seems like a blatantly obvious assertion, expressing it in code takes a great deal of careful thinking. Taking the time to work through these puzzles gave the students practice so that they could work though increasingly complex layers of logic. Fortunately, Hofstadter's presentation of typographical number theory does not require a background in calculus or other higher mathematics. Thus the material was accessible to all of the students.

As we made our way through the book together, the seminars explored many of *Gödel, Escher, Bach*'s internal loops as recurring themes, some of which are connected to classical philosophical problems. For example, Zeno's paradox of the impossibility of motion appears in Hofstadter's very first dialogue between Achilles, the Tortoise, and Zeno himself. Achilles and the Tortoise reappear in most of the subsequent dialogues, and interact with new characters and concepts. Hofstadter's connection with literature reminds us of the pre-disciplinary roots of our academic traditions, and similar methods could be applied to the works of ancient thinkers such as Aristotle. Philosophy serves as a kind of bridge that unites the disciplines represented in the work. Since we created this course to serve Simon's Rock B.A. students, we encouraged them to make connections between the themes of our wide-ranging discussions and their own work.

Throughout the semester, whenever possible, we encouraged students to bring their individual strengths and backgrounds to bear in addressing various topics. A student with expertise in computer science, for example, would have been invited to explain how nested structures work in programming, while another with a background in visual arts would have given a presentation on the three-point perspective that Escher subverted so disturbingly. Musical performances were sometimes prepared and presented by members of the class. The two written exams were structured around the same goal of disciplinary balance, and required that each student be able to work with Hofstadter's typographical system as well as provide more interpretive answers in prose form. The book includes so many different disciplines that each of the participants in the seminar was able to bring a unique and useful perspective to the course. At the end of the semester, all students presented special individual projects related to the book. These projects reflected their diverse interests and skills, and, along with research papers, included computer programs, musical compositions, and other kinds of creative output accompanied by essays explaining their work. Occasionally, the disciplinary perspectives represented in the classroom were broadened and deepened even more by the presence of eminent faculty colleagues, including neuropsychologist/musician David LaBerge and novelist/chemist Emmanuel Dongala. With their participation, the meetings became more like those of an interdisciplinary graduate seminar, and rather than being intimidated by these guests, the students participated even more enthusiastically.

One of our most fascinating discussions happened in the spring of 2006, and involved an update on the physical structure and function of human brain cells. In the text, Hofstadter describes how linkages between large networks of very primitive mechanical switching programs such as those in logic circuits of computers could form extremely complex patterns, and compared these to the brain's neurons, which are unaware of themselves as individual units. In his introductory literary dialogue to this chapter, Hofstadter illustrates this by introducing a new character, Aunt Hillary, who, although she represents the consciousness of an ant colony ("ant hill," a typical Hofstadterian pun), is not mindful of her individual constituents. Similarly, modern computer operating systems consist of parts written by hundreds of individual programmers, most of whom do not need to concern themselves with other parts in the overall structure, and even if they do have a sense of the other components, such knowledge is usually not required.

Dr. LaBerge pointed out that the drawing of the human neuron included in Hofstadter's book was actually based on the simple motor neuron, and that since the time of *Gödel, Escher, Bach*'s first publication, scientists have discovered that the relatively more plentiful and complex neuron with very long, further-reaching dendrites is of key importance in human memory and attention. In discussions, we realized that rather than refuting Hofstadter's essential points, the newer findings actually support his concept of a "tangled hierarchy" by suggesting that the looping across levels of structure occurs on a much deeper level in humans. Ray Kurzweil has described modeling human brain function in terms of massively parallel processing, in which the synaptic connections between neurons could be represented by connections among separate processors (which are becoming increasingly inexpensive, faster, and physically smaller). Without the limitation of the relatively slow speeds at which biological neurons function, a new "brain," made up of millions of parallel processors and/or complex software threads, would have certain advantages over human brains.

Each of the four times we offered the class, we became more aware of the fact that rapid developments in technology have made the insights within this book, first published in 1979, even more relevant in the twenty-first century. For example, computer chess programs, which are mentioned in *Gödel, Escher, Bach,* have already beaten human grand masters so consistently that attention is now turned to other games. These developments have in some ways reinforced Hofstadter's identification of self-reference, which transcends redundancy while maintaining a coherent structure, as a key element in consciousness and intelligence. In pattern recognition, for example, which is a key element in artificial intelligence, lower-level patterns formed of redundant elements are massed together to form larger patterns and lower-level systems are "broken out of" or transcended as higher level systems emerge. Chess programs are now dismissed as "narrow" AI (artificial intelligence), while "broad" AI remains an elusive but compelling goal, to be verified by language-based methods such as the Turing test. In this test, first proposed by computing pioneer Alan Turing in 1950, one person, designated as the judge uses text to "talk" with two other parties in an imitation game, one party being another human being, and the other party a computer. If the judge cannot tell which of the parties is human, and which the machine, the machine is regarded as having won the game. When we discussed this, Hannah Finley[1] and other students pointed out that they had encountered interesting "Chat-bots" on the internet. Visitors to websites or virtual environments in which these programs are embedded can entertain themselves by exchanging text messages with the programs, much like what was done with the computer entity in the Turing test. Of course in most of these modern cases, the game-playing subject knows ahead of time that he or she is "talking" with a computer, but often continues, especially if the program is sophisticated and well-designed. Once the domain of advanced research institutions, AI programs have already become part of popular culture. Self-modifying programs, which can learn based on experience and interaction with humans, are becoming more commonplace. In our 2008 seminar, Gabriel Fortunato Stocco, pointed out that this self-modification is now happening on the hardware level, in the area of automated circuit design; the chip-designing software and associated hardware is able to generate and test patterns much more rapidly than human researchers.

Another aspect of AI that our classes discussed, usually near the end of the semester, is the issue of agency (whether computer-driven entities would, or should, be able to act independently), and connections between agency and consciousness. Hofstadter stresses the importance of recognition, transcription, and translation as stages in which the potential meaning of a structure, a meaning which is embedded in its code (such as the text you are reading, genetic code, or computer programs), is waiting to be set into motion, and turns into active meaning through emergent processes. Hofstadter uses the metaphor of records (the message bearer), record-players (the interpreter) and music (the message itself). This often led our classes to discussions of causality. Without the biologically driven imperatives of self-preservation and procreation characteristic of organic intelligence, and without human beings to turn them on to begin with, why would even the most sophisticated programs bother to function at all without human intervention, much less prevent themselves from terminating? Would the introduction of Darwinian imperatives to mechanical intelligence eventually lead to the nightmare oppositional conditions dramatized in science fiction, or instead to a blending of organic and mechanical intelligence based on a shared recognition of consciousness, or at least shared interests? One might find some comfort in the fact that our own intelligence is woven into the data structures and logic patterns that are being used as the building blocks of artificial intelligence. Aside from burgeoning military applications, much of the physical impact of computer-driven devices has been very constructive, ranging from applications in medicine, machine-aided learning, devices for the physically challenged, new forms of communication, and so on.

Related to the issue of agency, another dimension of the anthropological question as it relates to our rapidly evolving relationship with computers is consciousness itself. While it is possible to provide a consistent description of life itself in biological terms, the *experience* of being alive is paradoxical. Hofstadter often expresses paradox in humorous terms, and points out that the very delight the reader takes in finding the many puns and acrostics of his book is a profound symptom of both intelligence and consciousness, a phenomenon he calls "jumping out of the system." In all of our classrooms, even when (and perhaps especially when) the most rigorous topics are being explored, humor may permit the leaps of insight that more direct methods inhibit. Perhaps humor will become an essential part of the Turing test; the humorless android has already become the quintessential "straight man" in fiction, with the android needing to break out of this ultimate limitation.

Along with humor and other emotions, creativity is often thought of as the domain for particularly human modes of intelligence. As with all of our technologies, we have used computers and peripherals as means of extending our bodies and minds. Emotional intelligence may be the last frontier of artificial intelligence. If they need one, perhaps we have provided computers with a reason for existence even as we continue to explore our own. At the very least, and especially for the purposes of our seminar, we have found that "The Magic Mirror," a phrase used by author Bruno Ernst to describe the work of M. C. Escher, might apply as well to how the study of artificial intelligence reveals and reflects human intelligence. In terms of its role in our general curriculum, this particular BA seminar completes a circle, or perhaps a spiral, moving from pre-disciplinary to interdisciplinary, and finally to transdisciplinary. Because we (Allen and John) share interests in many of the topics within the central text, we were able to leverage our own disciplinary backgrounds in mathematics and music, respectively, to create an environment in which to explore Hofstadter's book in some depth. Hofstadter's embrace of diverse expressions of intelligence resonates well with Liberal Arts pedagogic values. In our BA Seminars, we continue to ask questions that our students, and others whom they encounter in their lives beyond Simon's Rock, might find to be meaningful for quite some time to come.

Brenda Mathisen, who studied both mathematics and music in her B.A. course work at Simon's Rock, described the course in this way:

> The material connected us straight into the heart of life, focusing a wide range of disciplines into a study of the human mind, intelligence, and the pursuit of universal truth. The study of patterns and induction, levels and

meta levels, infinite loops, and how a set of simple functions can combine into something we recognize as intelligence absolutely fascinated me. It is something I still reference constantly.

NOTE

1. To prepare this article, we e-mailed several former students in *"Gödel, Escher, Bach,"* asking them to reminisce about their experiences. All e-mailed us back with permission to quote or paraphrase their views in our text. We are grateful to Hannah Finley (B.A., 2008), Gabriel Fortunato Stocco (B.A., 2009), and Brenda Mathisen (B.A., 2006) for their input.

WORKS CITED

Ernst, Bruno. *The Magic Mirror of M. C. Escher.* Köln and London: Taschen, 2007.

Gainer, James. *Evening in the Palace of Reason: Bach Meets Frederick the Great in the Age of Enlightenment.* New York: Fourth Estate, 2005.

Hofstadter, Douglas R. *Gödel, Escher, Bach: An Eternal Golden Braid.* New York: Basic Books, 1979, 2nd ed. 1999.

Kurzweil, Raymond. *The Singularity Is Near.* New York: Penguin, 2006.

LaBerge, David. *Attentional Processing: The Brain's Art of Mindfulness.* Cambridge, MA: Harvard University Press, 1999.

Turing, Alan. "Computing Machinery and Intelligence." *Mind, A Quarterly Review of Psychology and Philosophy* 59, no. 236 (October 1950): 433–460.

7

"So What If You're a French Major, You Should Totally Be in the Dance Concert"

"Effective Interdisciplinarity" at Simon's Rock[1]

NANCY YANOSHAK

"SWIMMING IN INTERDISCIPLINARITY"

A commitment to interdisciplinarity is central to the institutional ethos and pedagogical practices of Simon's Rock, and it permeates our learning culture. The faculty
is organized into four multidisciplinary divisions (Arts; Languages and Literature;
Science, Mathematics, and Computing; Social Studies), and the academic program
has a place also for "Interdivisional Studies" (e.g., Asian Studies), which cut across
divisional as well as disciplinary boundaries. Incoming students' first assignment,
Book One, is to read a work that promotes "interdisciplinary conversations" about
diverse cultures;[2] and course descriptions, and the college catalogue frequently use
the term "interdisciplinary" to describe educational objectives. Our general education program at the A.A. level features three interdisciplinary seminars with common readings of important primary texts spanning ancient times to the present.
Students who stay on for the B.A. develop interdisciplinary competences by taking
a required interdisciplinary BA Seminar and completing both a primary concentration (many of these incorporate several disciplines) and a complement, a substantial
group of courses meaningfully related to the primary field, but explicitly oriented
toward giving "evidence of interdisciplinary breadth."[3] The third major component
of the B.A. is the required senior thesis, and it, too, frequently attests to students'
success in integrating several disciplinary perspectives.

Although we are interdisciplinary by design, at least to an extent, we are so of necessity. As has been noted earlier in this volume, we are a small community of about 400 students and fifty regular faculty, plus administrators, staff, and adjunct instructors. Rarely are there more than two representatives of any one academic discipline on the permanent (full-time and part-time) faculty, and there are never more than five or six students on campus concentrating in any field in any given year. Everyone here constantly interacts with people with different specialties, inside the classroom and out of it. As alumnus Michael Lawrence (B.A., 2002) put it:

> Any time three members of the Simon's Rock community were gathered in a room, we were swimming in interdisciplinarity . . . . [U]nlike other college communities I've been a part of, there was never a sense at Simon's Rock that a student could create an intellectual and social life composed mostly of other folks who shared a major. When we sat around the seminar table or the dining hall table and talked ideas, we couldn't help but hear the voices of faculty and students whose disciplinary identification differed from our own.[4]

Interdisciplinarity, in other words, is virtually inescapable at Simon's Rock, and, by and large, we like it that way. In this article I explore our understandings of what has become a crucial aspect not only of our educational mission, but of higher education more generally in the United States. My contribution to the discussion is a concept I term "Effective Interdisciplinarity," which is informed by critical theorist Michel Foucault's ideas on "genealogy," "subjugated knowledges," "power," and "effective history." I argue that this concept provides a useful way to describe the process by which our students (and not only they) become "interdisciplinary." I will first contextualize my discussion with remarks about the scholarly literature on interdisciplinarity, and the views expressed by Simon's Rock faculty and alumni. I will then explicate the idea of Effective Interdisciplinarity, and illustrate it in action in my own classes and in those mentioned by past Simon's Rock students.

INTERDISCIPLINARITY IN RECENT SCHOLARLY LITERATURE

Some researchers locate the pre-history of interdisciplinarity in alternating tendencies toward unification and specialization in the pursuit of knowledge that have characterized Western intellectual development since classical times,[5] but the term itself does not appear in scholarly literature until after the establishment of the disciplines in their modern forms. It has been in use at least since the 1920s, and interest in it continues unabated in the present. As a description of reconfigurations in the organization of knowledge, new trends in research, and reorientations in college curricula, interdisciplinarity has been the object of numerous monographic and shorter works. Entire journals are currently devoted to it (e.g., *The Journal of Interdisciplinary History*), as are professional conferences, and federal funding agencies offer support for projects that advance it.[6]

Not surprisingly, given the varied constituencies that have been interested in interdisciplinarity, what it means has occasioned lively debate and, despite myriad attempts to pin it down, each new understanding seems to provoke several more. Related terms such as multidisciplinary, cross-disciplinary, transdisciplinary and post-disciplinary, have proliferated without any noticeable consensus, beyond what is the most general and therefore perhaps the least useful for analytical purposes: "Interdisciplinarity" is about making connections between two recognized academic disciplines to solve a problem or answer a question for which each is inadequate.[7] As the literature related to interdisciplinarity grew in the second half of the twentieth century, scholars mounted exceptional efforts to make sense of it by creating several typologies, grouped variously according to the goals of the research involved, the methods employed to attain them, or, in recognition of the inherent complexity of the topic, according to emphases placed on sets of interrelated goals or methods.

From Julie Thompson Klein's pioneering studies of interdisciplinary schol-arship, it is possible to discern two more or less distinct orientations, a synoptic approach which harks back to the quest for the unity of knowledge that began in classical times, and reflects a concern about the consequences of its fragmentation, and an instrumental approach which focuses on solving particular research prob-lems.[8] Additionally, already visible in the last decades of the twentieth century, was what Klein termed a "general form of 'critical interdisciplinarity' that challenged the existing structure of knowledge and education."[9] Klein's work implies that we might thus constitute a third major type of interdisciplinarity developing from the 1960s onward, inspired both by the emancipatory social and political movements of that decade, and by the new theorizations of the relationship of language, power, culture, the material world, and the construction of identity, associated with post-structuralism, deconstruction, cultural studies, and contemporary critical theory.[10] Since the concept of Effective Interdisciplinarity that I propose has significant con-nections to some understandings of "critical interdisciplinarity," I will complete this survey of the scholarly literature with a brief exploration of what seems to be this latest phase of thinking about the topic.

Klein credits Canadian Studies scholar Arthur Kroker with inventing the term "critical interdisciplinarity," which to him involved " 'an active migration beyond the disciplines to a critical encounter with different perspectives on the Canadian situation,' " and was to be distinguished from a *"vacant interdisciplinarity,"* which supports mechanisms of normalization.[11] The term has gained some traction, but, as with every other variant of interdisciplinarity, no definitive common understand-ing has been established.

In a 2002 discussion of themes articulated in his interdisciplinary study group at University College London, Stephen Rowland compared an instrumental to a critical variety of the phenomenon. Like Klein's, his instrumental interdisciplinarity is about solving discrete problems, and he particularly underlines its role in the management of intellectual resources by research institutions to provide for the needs of the economy. He believes this emphasis on utilitarian concerns can lead to a dissolution of the disciplines themselves as knowledge increasingly comes to be organized as a commodity.[12] In contrast, Rowland's "critical interdisciplinarity" presupposes a strong sense of the disciplines, whose boundaries become sites of contestation that challenge and politicize the "dominant disciplinary packaging of knowledge."[13]

Robert Frodeman and Carl Mitcham in 2007 developed a concept of "critical interdisciplinarity" meant to address the exponential increases of information in the internet age, as well as the separation of much scientific research from the ethical and practical problems, from "social anomie to climate change," facing us in the current historical moment. In contrast to Rowland, they contend that most interdisciplinary work leads not to the dissolution of disciplines, but to the creation of new ones.[14] They advocate a "critical interdisciplinarity" conceived as a controlled pursuit of knowledge that will integrate perspectives of the humanities with those of the sciences in order to address crucial public policy issues.[15]

In 2003 Jennifer Sumner foregrounded an oppositional political stance in her advocacy of the infusion of interdisciplinary work with the critical theory of the Frankfurt School of the 1920s–1930s, which critiqued contemporary capitalism and imagined better, post-capitalist lives for all human beings.[16] Sumner draws parallels between this theory and interdisciplinarity (with no qualifier): both promote intellectual synthesis and encourage reflexivity, and both have had to struggle to get respect in the academy. However, she contends, "while critical theory accepts its outcast status, interdisciplinarity struggles for mainstream acceptance."[17] As such, it runs the risk of "reinforcing the status quo," rather than contributing to "progressive change" by genuinely helping to address pressing contemporary issues such as globalization.[18] In order thus to avoid "becoming just one more form of narrow-minded investigation that merely dilutes established disciplines," Sumner proposes that scholars use critical theory to open up "relations of suspicion"[19] with work done in all disciplines. Such work would call into question claims that research can be "apolitical, objective and value neutral,"[20] seek to reveal what interests particular projects may serve,[21] and challenge the disciplinary hierarchies that such claims have supported, e.g., the presumed preeminence of "neo-liberal" economics within the social sciences.[22]

These advocates of critical interdisciplinarity do not mention each other's work, and it is unclear if they would see that they have a great deal in common.[23] However, it might be argued that what they do share is a disquiet with the status quo inside academia, and a desire to integrate knowledge gained from a sometimes confrontational interaction between disciplines. This sort of interaction would entail rethinking the boundaries between disciplines, and may displace commonly perceived intellectual hierarchies. Additionally, all three scholars' conception of critical interdisciplinarity implies some degree of dissatisfaction with the status quo outside of academia. Both Fordeman and Mitcham, and Sumner (albeit in all likelihood from different political stances), are explicitly interested in the connections between academia and the world beyond, and are clear about their desire to use the knowledge produced by critical interdisciplinarity to better people's lives.

INTERDISCIPLINARITY AT SIMON'S ROCK: FACULTY AND ALUMNI PERSPECTIVES

In the winter of 2010, I e-mailed forty-four Simon's Rock colleagues (regular faculty, part-time teachers familiar with the institution, and several administrators who also teach), and thirty-two alumni whom I knew well, to solicit their views on interdisciplinarity. I asked five questions: How did each person understand "interdiciplinarity" as it related to his or her field; how did the teachers attempt to make their courses interdisciplinary, or how did students feel that they "became" interdisciplinary at Simon's Rock; what educational value did each find in interdisciplinarity; whether we have moved beyond interdisciplinarity to a post-disciplinary world; and, to what extent did each see a congruence between Simon's Rock as a place that challenges traditional views about the nature of higher education, and interdisciplinary pedagogy as a way to challenge the epistemological "authority" of particular disciplines?

I indicated that "Focused Free Writes"[24] on any or all of these questions would be welcome, and that no question was obligatory. This survey functioned, in other words, as an informal exploration of what we thought and did about interdisciplinarity at Simon's Rock. While its results are not definitive, it is an interesting snapshot of opinion, in that it incorporates the views of interested current faculty and a cross-section of recent and older alumni at a small institution which foregrounds interdisciplinarity in its mission. One alumna is also a faculty member, and both the faculty and alumni groups include representatives of all of the academic divisions at the college.

Eleven colleagues (one-fourth) and eleven alumni (roughly one-third) responded, several in some detail. With one exception,[25] all are credentialed professionals, active in fields inside academia and out of it. However, none had made a study of interdisciplinarity *qua* interdisciplinarity, and not surprisingly, no one brought up any of the three broad typologies (synoptic, instrumental, critical) discussed above.

Nevertheless, their understandings of the term, and their practices clearly manifest some of the salient characteristics of each of these categories.

Many mention that they regularly make connections between their own disciplines and others in order to address research questions and/or classroom topics, which would benefit from exploration from more than one disciplinary perspective. Thus they provide instances of an "instrumental" interdisciplinarity. For example, Livingston Hall Chair in Music Laurence D. Wallach has adapted concepts originally used to analyze films to discuss the elements of musical compositions, and Victor Mateas, a 2009 graduate in biomedical engineering notes that to solve the problem he had set for himself in his senior thesis, he had to bring his mathematics education, and his knowledge of the pure sciences into contact "with other fields such as public health."[26]

As indicated above, "critical interdisciplinarity" implies some dissatisfaction with the status quo both inside academia and outside of it, and can involve an active desire to alter not only traditional power relations perceived between the disciplines, but also those perceived to exist in the larger world. All of these aspects of the developing category of "critical interdisciplinarity," again unnamed as such, appeared in remarks made by my respondents.

Languages and Literature professor Jennifer Browdy de Hernandez who also heads our Gender Studies Concentration, does not explicitly seek confrontation between the disciplines, but she does define the term "interdisciplinarity" primarily in terms of "boundary crossings," and thinks these boundaries have become "increasingly. ... blurred and unstable." She freely crosses them in her research, and encourages her students to do the same in her courses. And, in comments that resonate with Sumner's on the relationship between academia and the larger world, Jenny argues that "The whole idea of dividing knowledge up into disciplines has grown increasingly archaic in our speeded-up web-based world. Global problems demand solutions that move across boundaries, and responsible global citizens need to be fluent not only in several languages, but also in a variety of epistemologies."[27] Playwright and actor Richard P. Vaden also highlights the artificiality of the boundaries between the disciplines, but more openly underlines the idea of contestation between them. Rich is a 2008 graduate whose senior thesis project consisted of a play that he wrote and produced at the college. Based on interviews conducted with young gay men, it blended sociology, psychology, and theatre. To Rich, the healthy tensions that interdisciplinary encounters produce are key ways to inspire innovation. Beyond that, like Jenny, he believes that interdisciplinarity can be employed to "challenge the status quo" outside of academia, and he takes pride in the ways that he and other alumni have attempted to make their world "more inclusive."[28] Finally, in discussing the issue of the permeability of boundaries between the disciplines, some of my respondents did clearly critique disciplinary hierarchies. Languages and Literature professor James W. Hutchinson thought that talking of a "post-disciplinary" era was premature, because "there is still a good deal of entrenched disciplinary thinking going on in the world." Noting that "poetry may say meaningful things not merely (subjectively) about oneself but (objectively) about the world," Jamie called for mutual respect across the humanities and the sciences. And he was hopeful that increased effort at "cross-disciplinary conversations" would help to address such issues.[29]

These last sentiments, about the desirability for ever more conversations across the disciplines, capture the predominant attitude of my respondents toward the topic: all saw great value in interdisciplinarity, and felt that it coexisted with "disciplinarity" in productive ways at Simon's Rock both in terms of research projects and classroom activities. Also, with the broaching of ideas of connection and cross-disciplinary cooperation, we come to what links these members of the Simon's Rock community most clearly to that synoptic interdisciplinarity which other scholars have found to be the earliest variety to appear.

Only one colleague posited a kind of original unity for knowledge,[30] and no one explicitly mentioned a quest to reunify it, but as noted above, many spoke of the artificiality of disciplinary divisions. Moreover they expressed other views about integration, unity, and synthesis that call to mind a synoptic approach. Dance Professor Wendy Shifrin sees the value of interdisciplinarity precisely in the fact that it is about "relationship." It underlines the interconnectedness of the knowledge produced by all the disciplines, and helps one to perceive "the world in a more complex way," and therefore to act in a more ethical manner.[31] A similarly holistic perspective is articulated by Professor of French and Arabic Gabriel V. Asfar. He too emphasizes the "interrelatedness of disciplines," and recalls that early on in his time at Simon's Rock, the Dean, who was a physicist, encouraged him to make connections among his various fields, and with colleagues in other fields. Invited to teach "as a whole person," Gabriel thinks of interdisciplinarity as a way of helping students turn "into more whole human beings—that is, human beings with fewer holes."[32]

A third link to a synoptic or holistic perspective on interdisciplinarity was the use by several colleagues of the term "predisciplinary" as a way to think about the organization of knowledge, and perhaps most distinctively, to think about our students' approaches to it. Professor of Music, Interactive Arts, and Asian Studies John E. Myers sees our first-year students, two years younger than their peers at other colleges, as "pre-disciplinary," in the sense that they have not yet been fully socialized into the traditions, values, and approaches that characterize the academic disciplines. He notes that in our three A.A. general education seminars, much material is encountered without being filtered through the disciplinary and interdisciplinary lenses which students will only acquire later as they move to advanced work for the B.A.[33] John B. Weinstein, Professor of Chinese, Asian Studies and Theater, also observes a progression from pre- to disciplinary states, and, like John M., believes the concept is particularly useful for thinking about our A.A. students. He argues that even in an academic world as specialized as ours is, there are elements of any topic that exist on a pre-disciplinary level, and that can be approached with general non-specialized skills. For example "Novels exist prior to literary analysis of them, [and] a piece of music moves its listeners even if they know nothing of its construction." And he too underlines the relevance of pre-disciplinarity to teaching our general education seminars. It is in these courses in particular that students and professors can meet each other on somewhat equal grounds, as non-experts on many issues, since no teacher has mastered all of the interdisciplinary materials that they will cover together.[34]

FOUCAULT, GENEALOGY, EFFECTIVE HISTORY, AND SUBJUGATED KNOWLEDGES: EFFECTIVE INTERDISCIPLINARITY CONCEPTUALIZED

As indicated earlier, my term for the ways that ideas from several disciplines are productively integrated at Simon's Rock is Effective Interdisciplinarity. This concept has significant connections to the critical interdisciplinarity discussed above, if the latter is understood as a critique of the status quo in the academy and "on the street," and as a recognition that the two are intimately related. It implies some challenge to disciplinary hierarchies in academia, and a desire to use the knowledge gained to work for a just and equitable global society.

Despite these commitments, in elaborating on Effective Interdisciplinarity as it relates to pedagogy, which is the prime focus of my discussion, I want to emphasize that I do not advance political agendas in my courses. Rather, I affirm the value of both traditional and newer understandings of the humanities and the sciences, and work to acquaint students with the range of ideological orientations and disciplinary methodologies that these entail. Additionally, in contrast to the adversarial posture implied in some of the work on critical interdisciplinarity here surveyed, like my Simon's Rock colleagues, I seek conversations, not confrontations with those espousing other points of view. In what follows, I will first discuss the Foucauldian background to the view of interdisciplinarity I am proposing, and then, contextualized with testimony from colleagues and alumni, discuss how I have encountered it at Simon's Rock.

Effective Interdisciplinarity is related in the first instance to Foucault's analysis of the discourses of modern historical study, and is grounded in four interrelated Foucauldian concepts: "genealogy," "*wirkliche Historie*" ("effective history"), "subjugated knowledges," and "power."

"Genealogy" in Foucault's idiom is an approach to studying the past that is meant to undermine what we have assumed is self-evident, eternal, natural, immutable, or pre-determined about the human condition. It begins with a "diagnosis" of what ails us in the present, with the aim of using what we find about its history to enhance our lives now, and, in the future, to create "possibilities for no longer being, doing, thinking what we are, do, think."[35]

Foucault's first major discussion of genealogy was in "Nietzsche, Genealogy, History," originally published in 1971. Here, he critiqued historical writing common in the West from the nineteenth century onward, for assuming a "suprahistorical perspective,"[36] that found its justification in something beyond, beneath, above, or outside of the world in which we live (viz., the class struggle, Reason, a national spirit, an innate human drive toward freedom). Whether in its theological, Marxist, or liberal guises, this approach tends to posit an identity between favored elements in the present, past, and a pre-determined future, and creates a narrative wherein historical events are given meaning as they fit into the story, and discarded or ignored as insignificant or anomalous if they do not.[37] Pretending to base its judgments on an "apocalyptic objectivity,"[38] in reality this sort of history creates a past in its own image that it then "discovers." In more mundane terms, it is subject to committing what historians know as the presentist fallacy of reading contemporary values, ideas, and phenomena into the past, and of "false cause" (*post hoc ergo propter hoc*), assuming that temporal sequence implies historical causation.

The "privileged instrument" of genealogy was what Foucault called *wirkliche* or "effective" history,[39] which provided an alternative to the type of historical writing described above. Effective history avoids the metaphysical postulates of the latter by refusing the stability and "the certainty of absolutes."[40] Thus, it puts everything in motion,[41] assuming not an a priori fixed human nature forever identical to itself, and animated by a soul existing outside of history, or a body eternally bound by the dictates of its physicality and biology, but a human subject and a human history that is constantly subject to change.[42] Rather than "dissolving an event into an ideal continuity—as a teleological movement or a natural process," effective history "deals with events in their most unique characteristics."[43] Rather than draw an arbitrary line between occurrences, and name one as cause, one as consequence, it looks at events in their particularities. Influenced by Nietzschean ideas on the history of moral systems as the product of the conflict of various wills to power, Foucault thinks of "events" not in the usual terms as treaties and reigns, but as reversals of the "relationship of forces, the usurpation of power, the appropriation of a vocabulary turned against those who had once used it."[44] To Foucault, there is no power that directs human destiny from the beyond, there are only haphazard conflicts. Also, in contrast to the grand narratives of traditional history, the conflicts on which effective history focuses may be mundane, apparently insignificant, sometimes almost unnoticed, and frequently ignoble. Foucault argues that the world we know and live in is messy. Not always simple, understandable and ordered, "on the contrary it is a profusion of entangled events."[45] Patient, detailed, and meticulous, effective history honors the unique qualities of this profusion of occurrences, even as it seeks to make sense of them. Finally effective history eschews the mask of objectivity, acknowledging that the researcher has a point of view on the material being considered, and is explicit about the perspectives he or she adopts toward this material.

Foucault developed his ideas on genealogy further in a lecture given in 1976. Here he refers to it as the union of two types of "subjugated knowledges": The first is scholarship that has unearthed information that questions dominant political, institutional, legal and moral structures, and the second is this information itself, i.e., the "naïve," popular knowledge that these structures have disqualified and excluded.[46] Both types of "subjugated knowledges" have participated in a promising "insurrection" that can further the struggle for emancipation from the hierarchical systems that have marginalized them.[47] The genealogical research Foucault has in mind is first and foremost his own, on the constitution of subjectivities in modern discourses that discipline us by defining and then cordoning off what is "normal" or "healthy," from what must be feared as deviant. And, by naïve, disqualified knowledges, he means primarily, what may be said by the "abnormal" or "unhealthy" person herself, who lacks the requisite expertise to pronounce authoritatively about normality and deviance in the discourses in question.[48] Foucault notes that the aim of his work is to entertain the claims of these "illegitimate" knowledges against the claims of any "unitary body of theory which would filter, hierarchize and order them in the name of ... some arbitrary idea of what constitutes a science and its objects." He then goes on to characterize his genealogies as "anti-sciences."[49] One of his key targets here is what he sees as "the effects of the centralizing powers which are linked to the institution and functioning of an organized scientific discourse,"[50] which, despite their benefits to our modern societies, have regularly diminished and disempowered speaking subjects in the past and present.[51] Thus in this discussion, Foucault links genealogy with the political scene of his time, and expands its reach as critique from history to the social sciences and the sciences. Ultimately his project is to deploy it to reactivate "subjugated knowledges" in opposition to the institutionalized discourses of the sciences and related disciplines, inside and outside of academia.[52]

The final component of Effective Interdisciplinarity is the famous Foucauldian idea of power. This concept has been embedded in all of the above discussions, but it would be useful before proceeding to elaborate it more directly. Most simply put, in contrast to common ways of thinking about power in the West, Foucault does not see it as a commodity or quality that a person or an institution can possess. In his pioneering work on the history of sexuality, Foucault argued that "power" is a relationship, or series of relationships, a "multiplicity of force relations immanent in the sphere in which they operate." These force relations are unstable, and constantly moving, engendering states of power and resistance, actions and reactions that produce new relationships.[53] Moreover, rather than operating simply in a negative fashion, i.e., as a dominant power repressing a weaker one, these power relationships are mutually constitutive, i.e., they form and re-form the subjectivities involved, as they are continually acting on, and hence changing, each other. Indeed, for Foucault, where there is no resistance, no mutual interaction, there is no power, or, more precisely, no power relationship. He elaborated on the implications of this possibility of resistance in his later work, when he defined power as the governing of the actions of another, and explicitly acknowledged that it entails freedom.[54] Finally, he argued that analyses of power that focus on its centralized apparatuses, miss the core of shifting power relationships, which occur at the local level, where power is most intimately operationalized. In other words, rather than focus on the formal political institutions of the state, we might more productively look at the "local" relationships of warden and prisoner, physician and patient, . . . or teacher and student.

In the discussion which follows, I explain the ways that I have extended and adapted these Foucauldian concepts to formulate the idea of Effective Interdisciplinarity. It should be noted at the outset that I do not attempt to be "true" to everything Foucault has written about power, agency, and the like.[55] As a historian of Russia and Europe familiar with the tremendous coercive power vested in centralized state apparatuses, I find Foucault's insistence on an almost exclusively "local" view of power problematical. And, as an educator, I remain an inveterate "liberal humanist," convinced that subjects are not merely "relations of power," but individuals who may be persuaded by reason, evidence, empathy, and good will, and that they can empower themselves to take actions that will be efficacious in their world.

These caveats aside, I maintain that Effective Interdisciplinarity, grounded in the Foucauldian ideas I have outlined, provides a way to think about research, teaching, and learning activities involving several disciplines, as "process," i.e., as ongoing, open-ended intellectual exchanges that can result in new understandings of whatever topic or task is at hand.

Effective Interdisciplinarity shares with Foucault's idea of genealogy a discomfort with the positing of absolutes, a suspicion of claims of objectivity, a rejection of teleological schemata, and an emancipatory aim. It thus entails contesting ideas about hierarchical relationships between disciplines. Similarly to other conceptions of the topic, including those of my Simon's Rock colleagues, it emphasizes the permeability of the boundaries between them.[56] Also, like genealogy it problematizes the hierarchical relationship between disciplinary practitioners and the objects of their inquiries, when these are living persons who might be marginalized or inappropriately silenced. In other words, again, like the approaches of my Simon's Rock colleagues articulated throughout this collection, it entertains and takes seriously the voice of the lay person or non-expert.

I have named Effective Interdisciplinarity after "effective history," because the latter encompasses both Foucault's critical attitude toward traditional modes of disciplinary inquiry, and his alternate methodology. In effect it describes the activity of conducting a genealogical inquiry. Just as effective history is about history in motion, documenting power shifts and reversals, and positing instability, change, and discontinuities in place of assumptions about constants, stability, or destination, so is Effective Interdisciplinarity, "interdisciplinarity in motion." Just as effective history attends to testimony often not considered significant in traditional historical approaches, i.e., the ideas and attitudes of the marginalized and disempowered, the fleeting ideas and actions not considered historically worthy, so does Effective Interdisciplinarity. Thus it describes a fluid situation where changes in the relations between the dominant and the disempowered might occur, enacting the insurrection of subjugated knowledges that Foucault addressed in his discussion of genealogy as an expanded critique of hierarchies across the disciplines of the humanities, social sciences and sciences.

Effective Interdisciplinarity is thus not meant as still another variety or type of interdisciplinarity to be added to those already proposed by other scholars. I do not prescribe it as a research methodology or strategy, although its concerns could inform the approaches scholars might take to their interdisciplinary activities. Rather, in a sense it does nothing more than describe interdisciplinary activity *qua* activity. As an aspect of pedagogical process, in particular, it concerns the ways that specific, albeit sometimes fleeting, intellectual encounters and interactions can involve the disruption of hierarchies, and challenges to received wisdom, and can thus produce new knowledge. Uncertain in outcome, their ultimate significance in relation to any grand schema far from clear, these sorts of encounters also describe the goings on in many a Simon's Rock classroom.

EFFECTIVE INTERDISCIPLINARITY IN ACTION AT "THE ROCK"

In this section I elaborate on Effective Interdisciplinarity, conceived as an aspect of Simon's Rock pedagogy, and then offer examples of how it works "in action," by exploring what has transpired in my classes and others. This discussion is based on my recollections, and on what former students have told me of their experiences with, and attitudes toward, interdisciplinarity, and is informed as well by my colleagues' comments on the topic.

As an aspect of pedagogy, at its core Effective Interdisciplinarity is about intellectual exchanges that can bring to the fore the subjugated knowledges, i.e., the voices of those marginalized in dominant academic and professional discourses. I would argue that adolescents in many ways are members of such disempowered groups. Chafing under what seems a double standard of liberties for adults and restrictions for them, certainly they often view themselves that way. A sense of mar-ginalization is easily deepened for our younger scholars at Simon's Rock, who often forego even the credentialization of a high school diploma, and face adult intellec-tual expectations earlier than do their peers in other colleges. Newly separated from home and hometown, frequently alienated from the main stream of secondary edu-cation, they arrive here to enter small classes where most everybody had also been a star in high school, no one can hide, and they are asked to say what they think about the likes of Plato, Dante, Marx, and Nietzsche.

Becoming conscious, perhaps for the first time, that received knowledge might be questioned, that many of one's views may have been based on such knowledge, obtained from parents, teachers, or the larger culture, how does such a student advance an informed opinion that is not derivative of these sources? How does she resist the temptation to insist on the familiar (what is "natural" or "what everybody knows"), to defer to yet another authority (the teacher, another, perhaps older, stu-dent), or to retreat to a safe but ultimately unproductive relativism ("everybody has a right to his or her opinion")? How in other words, does she authorize herself to speak in a new situation, on an unfamiliar topic?

This is one of the central concerns for our first-year "pre-disciplinary" students, both in their general education seminars and in other classes, which almost always include some upper-division students. And, it does not disappear as they develop disciplinary expertise and acquire interdisciplinary facility as well. Classes become more challenging, and one's peers, met frequently in a number of shared courses, may have become just as advanced.

The positive side, of course is that in our de-centered classrooms, students are not only expected, but encouraged to give voice to their views, and, as has oft been noted in this volume, nurturing their skills at doing so is one of the prime goals of their teachers. In the ebb and flow of a class discussion, as in most any conversation between peers, everyone is potentially empowered to speak, and in both classes and written assignments, students may be praised for disagreeing with their teachers, and with authoritative texts. Traditional pedagogical relationships based princi-pally on age, knowledge, and power differentials can thus be disrupted, overturned, reconfigured, and resisted.

We strongly believe that students at all levels will have worthy and original ideas to contribute to any discussion topic under consideration, based on what they already know, on their thoughtful engagement with the texts, and with what they are hearing in class. My contention here is that Effective Interdisciplinarity is a significant dimension of how these students (and indeed any college student), as the subjects of subjugated knowledges, empower themselves by bringing to bear information, concepts, and methodologies that they encounter in one course into another. This information may be used to critique their texts and to respond to the views of their classmates and teachers. Not incidentally, a student's ability to use such information and such concepts in a new venue, can be a good test of her growing mastery of what they entail. In other words, Effective Interdisciplinarity as a pedagogical phenomenon is something that students use to establish their niche in class, to enrich our conversations there, to develop arguments made in their written work, and, overall, to gauge their own intellectual progress.

To begin the discussion of how this has worked with my own classes, it would be helpful first to consider the ways that "interdisciplinarity from above," i.e., from the point of view of the teacher, may manifest itself. Originally trained as a specialist in medieval Russia, I now teach courses in Russian, European, World, and Women's history; gender studies; the social sciences; and in our general education program. I also offer several BA Seminars, either alone, or with a colleague. All of these courses are structured as seminars, premised on active student participation and initiative, and, in addition to making sure that they consider varied ideological, cultural, and political points of view, I attempt to make all of them interdisciplinary, as appropriate to the subject matter under consideration.

Interdisciplinarity is an explicit objective in many of these courses, particularly in the upper division; it is required by virtue of the reading lists; and invited and implied in a number of writing assignments and in-class projects at all levels. Moreover, all of these courses on some level address the "big questions" about the human condition (e.g., Does "human nature" change over time? To what extent do humans have agency, and therefore responsibility, for their actions?), for which no discipline, in the humanities or the sciences, provides adequate answers. I make it a practice to raise these questions, and invariably they provoke responses from many disciplinary points of view.

Opportunities for interdisciplinarity are built into many specific classes, in disciplinary as well as interdisciplinary offerings. I regularly juxtapose texts from varied genres, and draw on scholarly interpretations that may explicitly include methodologies and approaches from several disciplines. For example, sessions on World War I in "The Tricks We Play on the Dead," an introductory topical survey of World History, include poetry, film, and a scholarly article by a feminist literary critic on the literary misogyny apparently spawned by the gender role reversals of the era;[57] those on the Nazi Holocaust have considered works by a psychologist and a professor of religious studies.[58]

In sessions such as these, the "big questions" noted above, about who or what we are, and what motivates us, certainly come to the fore, and these are often occasions for moments of Effective Interdisciplinarity. Regarding the causes of the Holocaust in the class mentioned above, and in discussions of subsequent genocides, students frequently bring up material from their psychology courses, in particular the Milgram experiment in which subjects' willingness to obey authority figures apparently trumped their ethical objections to inflicting pain on innocent people. Such comments elicit discussions of inherited predispositions in human behavior, initiated by students familiar with evolutionary biology, which may in turn be countered by gender studies students who note feminist anthropologists' arguments on the primacy of culture and nurture over biology. As facilitator, I intervene when appropriate, to suggest how the comments have advanced our understanding of the historiographic issues at hand. Although I have frequently described conflict and resistance as aspects of Effective Interdisciplinarity, I want to emphasize that when it occurs in the midst of a class conversation, all involved have an interest in maintaining amicable relations, and we regularly remind each other that our goal is to deepen our knowledge of a complex topic. As I often say in classes to illustrate Foucault's famous statement, "power is everywhere," [59] no one has power definitively in a Simon's Rock classroom. It flows from one of us to another at any given moment, and my comments as teacher, as well as any other participant's views, may be contested, ignored, accepted, or modified. In other words, rarely does anyone (either particular students, or the teacher) actually "win" the argument. The point is that in these fleeting moments, students have been listened to, as representative experts on various dimensions of a difficult and important issue to which all have contributed useful perspectives, and they can feel that they have moved us in productive directions.

Effective Interdisciplinarity also happens in my classes through the ways that some students carry out writing assignments. In history courses, the principal goal of the term paper is to emulate the procedures of a working historian (critical analysis of sources; evaluation of historiographic debates) in exploring a topic of the student's choice. Here students often use the occasion to research a historical aspect of a topic that interested them in another class, and so incorporate concepts from the latter to help formulate their arguments. Sometimes this leads a student somewhat "outside the lines," to focus almost exclusively on readings that typically would not be considered in a history course. For example, some years ago a beginning student wrote a paper that critically analyzed scholarly studies of bi-racial identity, all written by sociologists. The student mounted a judicious critique, did consider some aspects of the history of the topic, and received a good grade. Although she did not fully follow my guidelines for the project, I decided to validate her creativity, her interest in the topic, and, what was, perhaps, her will to resist giving the teacher full authority to determine what the paper would be about.

All of my classes, history or otherwise, include in-class collaborations. Teams of two-to-four students take responsibility for part of a class session, and, with my guidance, devise a topic, assign readings, and conduct the class itself. Here again, history course collaborations provide occasions for Effective Interdisciplinarity. Teams in Russian History have written and performed historical plays on Catherine the Great, and composed and performed music to emulate the egalitarian "conductorless orchestras" of the Soviet 1920s, and teams in "Tricks" have devised sessions on sociological and psychological perspectives on the Cold War.

Our general education seminars at the A.A. level, also interdisciplinary by design, provide many occasions for the spontaneous, Effective Interdisciplinarity seen in other classes. Commenting on the value of interdisciplinarity, alumnus Matthew Christian said that

> it would be impossible to write a ["First Year" or "Sophomore Seminar"] paper without other classes—where would our best ideas come from? ... [Such a] Seminar . . . functions as a space where the thinking of various disciplines can converge on a certain text or spot in a text, both as an exploration of collective difference and as a development of personal thinking.[60]

The examples I have mentioned thus far apply to what my colleagues would describe as the pre-disciplinarity of our beginning students. I will now turn to some instances of effective interdisciplinarity as exemplified by our advanced students, well versed in both the disciplinary and interdisciplinary aspects of our B.A. Program.

Abigail E. Edber, our 2010 B.A. Commencement speaker, captures one of the key aspects of the maturing interdisciplinarity that I think characterizes these students.

> Over the course of ... [my senior] year, I thought I was simply being disorganized when I had a difficult time keeping track of what assignments were due for which of my classes. Apparently this is what "interdisciplinary" means: when the act of unpacking and repacking your book bag every night is rendered unnecessary. Books I read for my BA Seminar class were totally appropriate for use in a response journal for my comic acting class, which in turn motivated discoveries I made while rehearsing for my thesis production. No longer were my individual classes separate entities; each supported and inspired the others in the most fulfilling, satisfying way."[61]

Thus, like our first- and second-year students, Abby is able to use what she is learning in one class to inform what she does in another, but, in addition, displays a strong awareness of the interconnectedness of what she encounters in all of her courses, and thinks deliberately and productively across several disciplines at once.

Another aspect of what connects our beginning and advanced students, but also of what distinguishes the two groups, has to do with what I like to term their intellectual feistiness, a descriptor meant as a compliment. Despite the uncertainties and anxieties to which I allude above, our pre-disciplinary students quickly become willing to abandon many of the "self evident truths" they had been taught, to ask outrageous questions (again, a compliment) about virtually everything, and to ignore the conventions of disciplinary boundaries. Michael Lawrence, reflecting on his Simon's Rock experiences (early and late), captures the sense of intellectual adventure embedded in this attitude when he says:

> At Simon's Rock, the idea of disciplinarity had very little, if anything, to do with my understanding of how intellectual life worked. ... If a smart person was interested in a topic and had read a lot about it, why should it matter what her degree was in? ... At Simon's Rock, we saw ourselves in conversation with Marx and Foucault . . . [rather than simply with what later authors had told us about them.][62]

Both our beginning and our advanced students readily engage with and make judgments on venerable texts and complicated contemporary issues. For the beginners, the freedom they feel to do so is a function of both their lack of familiarity with academic conventions and disciplinary boundaries, and their intellectual exuberance and curiosity. In the case of advanced students, the exuberance and the curiosity do not disappear; however, their willingness to weigh in on complex issues, leavened by personal experiences, and informed by disciplinary and interdisciplinary knowledge, has evolved into a more confident and nuanced Effective Interdisciplinarity.

"In the Beginning. ... The Pursuit of the Chimera of the Origin," a course I taught recently as both a BA Seminar, and as a Proseminar in our Social Science signature program,[63] provides some interesting examples of this sort of informed Effective Interdisciplinarity. Like many other BA Seminars, this one covered readings across the social sciences and the humanities. As a Proseminar it also included master classes and public lectures by several visiting scholars.

Two interrelated instances of Effective Interdisciplinarity stand out from this experience. The first occurred during a master class given by one of our visitors. Several female members of the class disagreed with some of this scholar's views about female adolescents, drawing on their own experiences, and their knowledge of gender studies, political thought, cultural studies, and post-structuralist theory. Their perception was that their ideas were not given due consideration, a concern which they voiced in several ways. Importantly, in a later class, another visitor presided over a discussion that sharply veered from the proposed topic to pursue extended exchanges between males in the class on the merits of video war games and "robotology." In our first meeting after this occurred, female students mounted a sophisticated and pointed critique of the gender dynamics in the sessions in question. Our exchanges were civil, the males ended by agreeing with the critique, and the teacher (yours truly), apologized for not intervening sooner in the classes in question. In this instance, in other words, we find at once virtually all of the elements associated with Effective Interdisciplinarity: resistance, reversals of power differentials that compel a new interpretation of the issues at hand, the voicing of traditionally subjugated knowledge of marginalized groups (in this case, female adolescents), and the employment of knowledge gained from both disciplinary and interdisciplinary experiences for empowerment. This resolution of the problem was made possible by the character, courage, and maturity of the students (male and female) involved, and, above all, by their confidence in their own intellectual powers, and right to speak their minds.

Finally, Del Slane (B.A., 2009), a computer science major now pursuing a career in software development, provides several examples of an informed Effective Interdisciplinarity, understood as Abby did, as the ability to connect what he was learning in a number of disciplines in meaningful ways. In answer to the questionnaire I sent to alumni about their views on interidsiciplinarity, Del offered the following:

> In an experience that it seems could only happen at Simon's Rock, I combined visual arts with technology in a way that was never offered to me before through [ethnomusicologist] John Meyer's "Interactive Arts Workshop" class. . . . My final project used a piece of software called Unity to combine my original 3-D objects and other works with my technical software knowledge to create an environment where one could walk through a forest, hop in an airplane and fly away.[64]

In addition to using his computer science skills to do his own work, in this class, Del also employed his knowledge of physics modeling to help a classmate with a project that involved creating realistic images in motion and flight.[65] More, Del's ventures outside of the sciences did not stop at the interactive arts. He also took photography and ballet classes,[66] and the latter experience culminated in a *pas de deux* performed at our biannual Dance Concert. Thus, like the Promseminar students, for Del, interdisciplinarity was not only related to career and academic interests. He saw it as an "opportunity for personal growth." Noting that interdisciplinarity must be balanced with disciplinary expertise, he nevertheless affirmed that it "is crucial to happiness."[67]

CONCLUSIONS:
"SO WHAT IF YOU'RE A FRENCH MAJOR. . . ."

As much as we, faculty and administrators, endorse interdisciplinarity as an important goal of our academic program, and work systematically and consciously to make it a meaningful part of our curriculum, there is no set of requirements and assignments that can fully determine how this goal is accomplished. And, while we have significant commonalities in our understandings of the term and its educational value, in the end there is no definitive statement that can be made about what it means for us or our students. Nevertheless, it will continue simply to "happen," in discussions in our classrooms and our offices, in chance conversations at lunch and in the dorms, and in those solitary moments when individuals think through the thorny scholarly and creative tasks they have set for themselves.

In this regard, it is worth returning to the passage from Margaret Dunlap's response to my alumni questionnaire which gave me the title of this article. In its entirety, it reads:

> Going to a college where there was an attitude of, "So what if you're a French major, you should totally be in the dance concert," I think gives me the confidence that I can at least try something different than what I thought I was focused on.[68]

Margaret, a 1999 graduate, wrote an interdisciplinary senior thesis that combined historical research with feminist critique and creative writing. Now a professional writer for film and television, Margaret concentrated in both Creative Writing and French and Francophone Studies, and like Del and so many other Rockers, went well out of her disciplinary comfort zones to explore what interdisciplinarity meant both personally and academically.

Interdisciplinarity is thus an integral part of the learning culture at Simon's Rock, prized for the intellectual stimulation it provides and for the ways it can change how one looks at the world and one's academic work, and how one thinks about one's friends and colleagues, and oneself. Ultimately, as an aspect of our pedagogies, it can best be understood as both the product of deliberate effort on the part of students and teachers alike, and as an expression of an academic environment that nurtures a spirit of intellectual adventure, and a recognition that the complexities of our world cannot be understood, or its richness appreciated, when compartmentalized within traditional ways of organizing our knowledge about it.

NOTES

1. I am indebted to many colleagues and former students who, named or unnamed in this article, have helped to make it possible. I extend particular thanks to Joan DelPlato, Sandra Smith, and Michael Lawrence, for their intelligence, erudition and patience in reading drafts of this chapter, and suggesting emendations that have made it far more intelligible than it might have been.

2. *Bard College at Simon's Rock Catalogue 2009–2010*, 11, accessed and downloaded June

25, 2010, *http://www.simons-rock.edu/campus-resources/college-offices/registrar/catalogs/0910_coursecatalogue_072809.pdf/view?searchterm=Catalogue.*

3. *Bard College at Simon's Rock Catalogue 2009–2010,* 16–17.

4. Michael Lawrence, e-mail message to the author, March 11, 2010. All alumni and Simon's Rock faculty members named in this text, including Mike, have given me permission to quote or paraphrase comments that they have sent to me by e-mail. I am very grateful for this, and for the many contributions their ideas have made to my own thinking on the topics at hand.

5. Julie Thompson Klein, *Interdisciplinarity: History, Theory, and Practice* (Detroit: Wayne State University Press, 1990), 19.

6. Klein, *Interdisciplinarity,* 1990, 33, 35.

7. Cf. Klein, *Interdisciplinarity,* 1990, 196.

8. Klein, *Interdisciplinarity,* 1990, 196, cf. 28, 37–38, 41–42.

9. Julie Thompson Klein, *Humanities, Culture, and Interdisciplinarity: The Changing American Academy* (Albany: State University of New York Press, 2005), 5.

10. Klein, *Humanities, Culture, and Interdisciplinarity,* 2005, 4–5, 34–54, 176–202.

11. Arthur A. Kroker, "Migration from the Disciplines," *Journal of Canadian Studies* 15, no. 3 (1980): 3–10, cited in Klein, *Interdisciplinarity,* 1990, 96. Italicized words are in Klein's original.

12. Stephen Rowland, "Interdisciplinarity as a Site of Contestation" (Draft paper presented at the annual conference of the British Education Research Association, University of Exeter, 12–14 September 2002), 3, accessed October 7, 2010, *http://webcache.googleusercontent.com/search?q=cache:iD7OSChJhFoJ:www.ucl.ac.uk/cishe/seminars/interdisciplinarity/contestation_paper.doc+Rowland+Interdisciplinarity+as+a+site+of+contestation&cd=1&hl=en&ct=clnk&gl=us&client=firefox-a).*

13. Rowland, "Interdisciplinarity."

14. Robert Frodeman and Carl Mitcham, "New Directions in Interdisciplinarity: Broad, Deep, and Critical," *Bulletin of Science, Technology & Society,* forthcoming, accessed by Google search and downloaded, October 7, 2010, 2, cf. 6, 7. The published article in the *Bulletin of Science, Technology & Society* 27, no. 6 (2007): 506–514, was not available to me when I was writing the present chapter.

15. Frodeman & Mitcham, 10, 11.

16. Jennifer Sumner, "Relations of Suspicion: Critical Theory and Interdisciplinary Research," *History of Intellectual Culture* 3, no. 1 (2003), ISSN 1492-7810, accessed October 7, 2010, *http://www.ucalgary.ca/hic/issues/vol3/7,* 3–4. Page number references taken from the pdf file downloaded from this site.

17. Sumner, "Relations of Suspicion," 6.

18. Sumner, "Relations of Suspicion," 10, 7.

19. Sumner, "Relations of Suspicion," 10–11.

20. Sumner, "Relations of Suspicion," 4.

21. Sumner, "Relations of Suspicion," 4, 11.

22. Sumner, "Relations of Suspicion," 8.

23. Sumner writing in 2003 does not seem aware of Rowland, whose work appeared in 2002, and Fordeman and Mitcham in 2007 cite neither of those two authors. Only Sumner (p. 11, Note 1) mentions Kroker as a pioneer of "critical interdisciplinarity." This would seem to be testimony, again, to the indeterminacy of the term "critical interdisciplinarity" and the growing amount of literature devoted to it. As a further example of the increase in scholarly interest on this topic, I note the following reference: Esperanza Brizuela-Garcia, "Towards a Critical Interdisciplinarity? African History and the Reconstuction of Historical Narratives," *Rethinking History* 12, no. 3 (September 2008): 299–316. Despite a great deal of searching, I encountered this title only recently, and, unfortunately was not able to obtain the text in time to consider it in this article.

24. See the chapter by John B. Weinstein in the present volume for a discussion of the "Free Write," "Focused Freewrite," and other techniques of our "Writing and Thinking Workshop" for first-year students.

25. Matthew Christian (A.A., 2009) in 2011 was a senior at our main campus, Bard College in Annandale-on-Hudson in New York. Six faculty respondents (Gabriel V. Asfar, Jennifer Browdy de Hernadez, John E. Myers, Wendy Shifrin, Laurence D. Wallach, John B. Weinstein), and one alumnus respondent (Michael Lawrence) have written, or co-written articles for this collection. Jenny is, in addition, an alumna (B.A., 1982).

26. Laurence D. Wallach, e-mail message to the author, January 26, 2010; Victor Mateas, e-mail message to the author, March 16, 2010.

27. All comments quoted or paraphrased from Jennifer Browdy de Hernandez, e-mail message to the author, February 16, 2010.

28. All comments quoted or paraphrased from Richard P. Vaden, e-mail messages to the author, March 10, 2010, and March 27, 2010.

29. All comments quoted or paraphrased from Jamie Hutchinson, e-mail message to the author, February 1, 2010.

30. Mark J. Vecchio (Faculty in Interdivisional Studies), e-mail message to the author, January 26, 2010.

31. All comments quoted or paraphrased from Wendy Shifrin, e-mail message to the author, January 24, 2010.

32. All comments quoted or paraphrased from Gabriel V. Asfar, e-mail message to the author, January 31, 2010.

33. John E. Myers, e-mail message to the author, February 2, 2010. Frodeman and Mitcham, p. 4, use the term "predisciplinarity" in an historical context to describe a premodern approach to learning.

34. John B. Weinstein "What is Pre-Disciplinary?" 2–3. Shared with the author by e-mail, January 16, 2010. Cited with permission. Several other Simon's Rock colleagues (Larry

Wallach, Mark Vecchio) also endorsed the idea of "pre-disciplinarity" as a dimension of our pedagogical approaches.

35. Michael Mahon, *Foucault's Nietzschean Genealogy* (Albany: State University of New York Press, 1992), 125.

36. Michel Foucault, "Nietzsche, Genealogy, History," in *The Foucault Reader*, ed. Paul Rabinow (New York: Pantheon Books, 1984), 86.

37. Foucault, "Nietzsche," 77–78.

38. Foucault, "Nietzsche,"87.

39. Foucault, "Nietzsche," 86.

40. Foucault, "Nietzsche," 90.

41. This point is indebted to Hubert L. Dreyfus and Paul Rabinow, *Michel Foucault: Beyond Structuralism and Hermeneutics*, 2nd ed. (Chicago: The University of Chicago Press, 1983), 110, who discuss effective history as an attempt to put "everything in historical motion."

42. Foucault, "Nietzsche," 87–88.

43. Foucault, "Nietzsche," 88.

44. Foucault "Nietzsche," 88.

45. Foucault, "Nietzsche," 89.

46. Michel Foucault, "Two Lectures," in *Power/Knowledge: Selected Interviews and Other Writings 1972–1977*, ed. Colin Gordon, trans. Colin Gordon, Leo Marshall, John Mepham, Kate Soper (New York: Pantheon Books, 1980), 81–82, cf. 83.

47. Foucault, "Two Lectures," 81–82. To be sure, in contrast to those who espouse a traditional liberal position, Fouault does not expect some final denouement for the political struggles he discusses in this article. Although he is clearly here interested in emancipation, his work taken as a whole implies that any change for the better might be followed by something else.

48. Foucault, "Two Lectures, 82.

49. Foucault, "Two Lectures," 83.

50. Foucault, "Two Lectures," 84.

51. Foucault, "Two Lectures," 85.

52. Foucault, "Two Lectures," 84–85.

53. Michel Foucault, *The History of Sexuality*, vol. 1, *An Introduction*, trans. Robert Hurley (New York: Vintage Books, a Division of Random House, Inc., 1978), 92.

54. Michel Foucault, "Afterword: The Subject and Power," in *Michel Foucault: Beyond Structuralism and Hermeneutics*, 2nd ed. With an Afterword by and an Interview with Michel Foucault. (Chicago: The University of Chicago Press, 1982), 220–221.

55. Interestingly Foucault was not always "true" to himself. While he critiqued notions of the a priori subject, and master narratives about its liberation, at times, like the Marxist and liberal thinkers who espoused these conceptions, Foucault too implied the

existence of agents (individual or collective) who, in effect, did "possess" power, and the existence of an abstract realm of freedom prior to history. Moreover, he actively and hopefully participated in the liberation struggles of his time. (cf. Nancy Fraser, *Unruly Practices: Power, Discourse, and Gender in Contemporary Social Theory* [Minneapolis: University of Minnesota Press, 1989]; and Judith Butler, *Gender Trouble: Feminism and the Subversion of Identity* [New York: Routledge, 1990], 93–111). Thus, in Foucault we find a kind of tension between the critique and the espousal of the normative values and epistemic assumptions of Western narratives of human liberation. My thanks to Michael Lawrence for pointing out that my own work expresses a similar sort of tension. (E-mail message to the author, 10/26/10.)

56. At the same time, in terms of research methodology, Effective Interdisciplinarity may go further in emphasizing the instability of any configuration of knowledge, and thus challenge the permanence of any disciplinary or interdisciplinary domain. Thus, in contrast to the conceptualizations of interdisciplinarity advanced or implied by many of my colleagues and former students, this concept entertains the idea of post-disciplinarity, implying that disciplines may at some point disappear.

57. Sandra M. Gilbert, "Soldier's Heart: Literary Men, Literary Women, and the Great War," in *Connecting Spheres*, ed. Marilyn J. Boxer and Jean H. Quataert, 2nd ed. (New York and Oxford: Oxford University Press, 2000), 275–288.

58. Respectively: Ervin Staub, *The Roots of Evil: The Origins of Genocide and Other Group Violence* (Cambridge: Cambridge University Press, 1989); and Darrell J. Fasching, *The Ethical Challenge of Auschwitz and Hiroshima: Apocalypse or Utopia?* (Albany: State University of New York Press, 1993).

59. Michel Foucault, *The History of Sexuality*, 1: 93.

60. Matthew Christian, e-mail message to the author, March 3, 2010. As Matthew's teacher in "Sophomore Seminar," the third course in our sequence, in Fall 2008, I can certainly attest to his success in this endeavor. His class contributions, as well as his papers were sophisticated and articulate, and clearly informed by what he had learned of literary theory, in particular its post-structuralist varieties, in his other courses.

61. Abigail E. Edber, "Edber BA Speech 2010," 3. Address of the B.A. Class Speaker, given at the Commencement Exercises, Bard College at Simon's Rock, May 15, 2010. Cited with permission.

62. Michael Lawrence, e-mail message to the author, March 10, 2010.

63. See the article by Asma Abbas and her students in this volume for an analysis of their experiences in our inaugural Proseminar in Social Scientific Inquiry.

64. Del Slane, e-mail message to the author, March 3, 2010.

65. Del Slane, e-mail message to the author, March 3, 2010.

66. Del Slane, e-mail message to the author, March 3, 2010.

67. Del Slane, e-mail message to the author, March 3, 2010.

68. Margaret Dunlap, e-mail message to the author, March 26, 2010.

WORKS CITED

Bard College at Simon's Rock Catalogue 2009–2010. Accessed and downloaded, June 25, 2010. *http:// www.simons-rock.edu/campus-resources/college-offices/registrar/catalogs/0910_coursecatalogue_072809. pdf/view?searchterm=Catalogue.*

Butler, Judith. *Gender Trouble: Feminism and the Subversion of Identity.* New York: Routledge, 1990.

Dreyfus, Hubert L. and Paul Rabinow. *Michel Foucault: Beyond Structuralism and Hermeneutics.* 2nd ed. Chicago: The University of Chicago Press, 1983.

Fasching, Darrell J. *The Ethical Challenge of Auschwitz and Hiroshima: Apocalypse or Utopia?* Albany, NY: State University of New York Press, 1993.

Foucault, Michel. *The History of Sexuality.* Vol. 1. *An Introduction.* Translated by Robert Hurley. New York: Vintage Books, a Division of Random House, Inc., 1978.

——. "Nietzsche, Genealogy, History." In *The Foucault Reader,* edited by Paul Rabinow, 76–100. New York: Pantheon Books, 1984.

——."The Subject and Power." In *Michel Foucault: Beyond Structuralism and Hermeneutics,* 2nd ed. Edited by Hubert L. Dreyfus and Paul Rabinow. With an Afterword by and an Interview with Michel Foucault, 208–226. Chicago: The University of Chicago Press, 1982.

——. "Two Lectures." In *Power/Knowledge: Selected Interviews and Other Writings 1972–1977,* edited by Colin Gordon. Translated by Colin Gordon, Leo Marshall, John Mepham, Kate Soper, 78–108. New York: Pantheon Books, 1980.

Fraser, Nancy. *Unruly Practices: Power, Discourse, and Gender in Contemporary Social Theory.* Minneapolis: University of Minnesota Press, 1989.

Frodeman, Robert and Carl Mitcham. "New Directions in Interdisciplinarity: Broad, Deep, and Critical." *Bulletin of Science, Technology & Society,* forthcoming. Accessed by Google search and downloaded, October 7, 2010.

Gilbert, Sandra M. "Soldier's Heart: Literary Men, Literary Women, and the Great War." In *Connecting Spheres,* edited by Marilyn J. Boxer and Jean H. Quataert, 2nd ed. 275–288. New York and Oxford: Oxford University Press, 2000.

Klein, Julie Thompson. *Interdisciplinarity: History, Theory, and Practice.* Detroit: Wayne State University Press, 1990.

——. *Humanities, Culture, and Interdisciplinarity: The Changing American Academy.* Albany: State University of New York Press, 2005.

Mahon, Michael. *Foucault's Nietzschean Genealogy.* Albany, New York: State University of New York Press, 1992.

Rowland, Stephen. "Interdisciplinarity as a Site of Contestation." Draft paper presented at the annual conference of the British Education Research Association, University of Exeter, 12–14 September 2002. Accessed October 7, 2010. *http://webcache.googleusercontent.com/ search?q=cache:iD7OSChJhFoJ:www.ucl.ac.uk/cishe/seminars/interdisciplinarity/contestation_paper.doc +Rowland+Interdisciplinarity+as+a+site+of+contestation&cd=1&hl=en&ct=clnk&gl=us&client=firefox -a).*

Sumner, Jennifer. "Relations of Suspicion: Critical Theory and Interdisciplinary Research," *History of Intellectual Culture* 3, no. 1 (2003). ISSN 1492-7810. Accessed October 7, 2010, *http://www. ucalgary.ca/hic/issues/vol3/7,* 3–4. Page number references taken from the pdf file downloaded from this site.

Staub, Ervin. *The Roots of Evil: The Origins of Genocide and Other Group Violence.* Cambridge: Cambridge University Press, 1989.

IV

COLLEGE TEACHING AND "POST-IDENTITY POLITICS"

*Collaborations across the Boundaries
of Age, Status, and Place*

8

Arabic at Simon's Rock

Spanning Two Wars and Counting

GABRIEL V. ASFAR

The limits of my language are the limits of my world.
—WITTGENSTEIN

In July 2005, a Johns Hopkins University survey estimated that approximately 2.5% of the population of Iraq (where I was born and raised before becoming a U.S. citizen)—some 655,000 people—had died as a direct result of the U.S. invasion of 2003, with three million Iraqis wounded and fourteen million Iraqis displaced from their homes.[1] That same month I received in the mail from one of my former students of Arabic and at the time a U.S. Marine stationed in Baghdad, a packet of printed materials and a note referring to them as "some of the propaganda ... er, I mean—INFORMATIONAL FLYERS we hand out here." He adds, in idiomatic Arabic, the phrase "Until we meet again."[2]

The first such flyer, printed in color on glossy card stock, features an image of the earth flanked by two hovering white doves. The text in Arabic reads: "The security forces of Iraq are working to bring peace and security to your families and neighborhoods. ... Please assist us." The Arabic text, while ironically underscoring the gap between such publications and the reality of Iraqi suffering, also provided an authentic context for the teaching of Arabic grammar: the nominative case, the implied verb "to be," the use of plurals, prepositional phrases, the genitive case, and the polite use of the imperative.

On the back of this particular leaflet, against a photo of a bomb blast showing a turbaned Iraqi holding a dead child in his arms, is the caption: "Innocent Iraqis have suffered enough from bombings. Help rid your country of explosives and their makers. Think of your children's future." Another line adds: "Report bombs to the Allied Information Services (AIS)." A space at the bottom provides the handwritten phone number of the local AIS office. The language here once again provided interesting variations of several grammatical and syntactical forms useful in basic conversation.

My former student's mailing—timely as it was in underscoring the collateral damage that I had just read about in the Johns Hopkins survey—was not the first time I had received such documents from a former student of Arabic. For over eighteen years since the first Gulf War, in 1991 (referred to by our government as "Operation Desert Storm"), former students of my courses in Arabic have been sending me materials disseminated by the U.S. military in Iraq. From the first such mailing, I have found various ways of using these in my classes: The most obvious was to supplement the more traditional, textbook-based language content of my courses with the language from these publications, which has a "real-life" context— material especially appropriate for beginners, given the fairly simple syntax and clearly legible type.

While cultural context is necessarily a part of all foreign-language teaching, it is recognized at Simon's Rock as especially important for the non-Western language courses offered (Arabic and Chinese), in that these courses help to broaden the students' cultural perspectives. Among the college's other requirements for graduation with the Associate in Arts Degree—requirements such as mathematics, foreign language, science, and the arts—there is the requirement that students take one course designated Cultural Perspectives (CP). One purpose of such courses is to introduce students to non-Western societies and cultures, particularly in light of an increasingly interconnected global community of nations. To quote from the 2010–2011 college catalogue (p. 13): "By focusing in depth on one culture or subculture, or on one topic analyzed and compared across a number of differing cultural traditions, these [CP courses] build on the other core courses in the general education sequence, expanding students' understanding of the ideas, perspectives, values, and activities of cultures often marginalized by the West."

The accelerated beginning Arabic course I teach (Arabic 100–101CP)—a two-semester sequence, meeting five hours per week, for a total of twenty-eight weeks (140 class hours)—can satisfy either the college's foreign language requirement or the CP requirement; an appreciable number of students over the years, having satisfied the language requirement with one of the more commonly taught European languages (French, Spanish, German), have chosen to take Arabic in order to fulfill the CP requirement. While the course seeks to establish a solid foundation in Modern Standard Arabic (MSA) in preparation for further study of the language at the intermediate level, I have built into it almost weekly presentations that seek to inform students about the historical, religious, cultural, and political under-pinnings of Arabic-speaking and predominantly Muslim countries of the Middle East.

Anyone who proposes to teach Arabic in an American college or university must decide what type of Arabic to teach. Unlike the more commonly taught European languages, Arabic is characterized by a sharp division, within linguistic groups, between the more formal, written forms and the colloquial, spoken forms of the language—a phenomenon known as diglossia, and described by Bakhtin and Ferguson.[3] Thus a teacher of Arabic must choose: There is classical Arabic, the lan-guage of Muslim holy scripture and of most Arabic literary forms. There is MSA, the language (mostly written) of educated native speakers and printed media. And then there is spoken Arabic: Levantine, Palestinian, Saudi, Gulf, Lebanese, and so on—sometimes two or three or more spoken idioms within each political entity.

My courses in the Arabic language are devoted largely to the study of MSA, because it is the language with widest currency in the Arabic-speaking world, but I also devote several hours to basic conversation in some of the more widely spoken dialects. Including some colloquial language practice also allows me to introduce my students to the concept of diglossia and to the cultural and historical context in which linguistic divisions among Arabic-speakers developed.

Having taught various levels of Arabic at Simon's Rock for some twenty-five years, I had already developed a culturally contextualized approach—one which introduces perspectives touching on various aspects of the history of the modern Middle East—long before the start of the first Gulf War. I had also established a correspondence network with many of my former students, encouraging them to stay in touch with me, to let me know whether they continue their Arabic studies, and to send me any relevant printed materials, should they travel to Arabic-speak-ing countries, as well as cartoons from Western publications depicting Arabs, for a cartoon collection I began in the early 1970s.

Most courses in modern languages incorporate "realia"—printed, contemporary documents, intended for native speakers—to give a current, culturally authentic context; realia are especially important in the teaching of Arabic, where such docu-ments often include printed messages in the spoken idiom of the region. Although I had begun collecting cartoons of Arabs as a student, out of personal interest, I have since found that my collection sparks much fruitful discussion among my students of Arabic, as we study evolving Western perspectives on the Middle East. Thus, thanks to my network of former students, I have enhanced my collection of cartoons and realia concerning the Middle East, and have made good use of them in reinforc-ing linguistic and cultural aspects of my courses.

At the start of the first Gulf War, I was eager to incorporate into my teaching any materials our military forces might use in their attempts to communicate with Iraqis in Arabic or to assist our troops in understanding the people of Iraq. Such materials would assist me in teaching the language in a specific historical context, as well as in the context of the CP component of my course—that is, to explore what value their study might have in broadening the students' understanding of how the U.S. military perceives and represents Iraq. It made pedagogical sense for my students to gain an understanding of the nature of such communications, and to have the opportunity to assess their accuracy and usefulness. Furthermore, such materials would have the linguistic value of containing Iraqi-spoken Arabic as well as MSA.

But these materials proved difficult to find. Thus it was a happy day when, shortly after the start of the Gulf War of 1991, another former student, at the time serving with the Marines in Iraq, wrote to me and enclosed copies of several leaflets distributed in Iraq by the U.S. military. I lost no time turning these into lessons in language and culture. Not long thereafter, another former student, now serving as a "communications specialist" in the U.S. Army, sent me copies of additional leaflets and other printed materials intended for Iraqis "on the ground."

Here again, I was eager to study these with my classes, both for their language content and for their implications for cultural understanding. Indeed, over the years spanning the two U.S. invasions of Iraq, I have received a good number of documents (some marked "For Official Use Only") from former students who have gone on to serve in the U.S. military; these documents include: public notices issued to Iraqi civilians by U.S. forces; printed materials intended to acquaint U.S. soldiers with local customs and cultural practices (so-called "Culture Smart Cards"); and—most valuable of all for my purposes as a teacher of language—phrase-books intended to enable military personnel to communicate with Iraqis in transliterated Arabic (so-called "Arabic Language Survival Guides" produced by the Marine Corps). Due to the continued U.S. military involvement in Iraq, and the understandable attraction of Arabic students such as mine to career paths in the Middle East, my collection of such Arabic materials grew.

In early 1992, I received some interesting items from a former student of Arabic whose boyfriend was a Marine. He had been stationed in Saudi Arabia following Operation Desert Storm and the liberation of Kuwait from the invading Iraqi army of Saddam Hussein. The student sent me a copy of the September 1991 issue of *Army Magazine* that she had received from her boyfriend. The magazine featured an article about leaflets that had been distributed across the Arabian Peninsula and Iraq. It described these items as examples of "psychological operations leaflets" purporting to depict "U.S. Army capabilities." One of the leaflets ("cartoons" would be a more appropriate description) is described in the article as a depiction of "an

AH-64 Apache helicopter and an M1A1 Abrams tank attacking an Iraqi tank." The drawing is so stylized as to make such a precise description farfetched.

Somewhat less implausible is the article's assertion that "other leaflets contain messages declaring Arab partnership in confronting Saddam Hussein"—less implausible, that is, until one notes the copyright on all four cartoons in the article: "Department of Defense." This would suggest that such leaflets may be no more than U.S. propaganda, created to exaggerate the extent of Iraqi partnership with the United States, in an attempt to foment anti-Saddam sentiments and to justify its own agenda.

Another cartoon, entirely wordless, is of a smiling Saudi King Fahd, with a thought-bubble from his mouth showing three Arab soldiers holding hands; beneath is an angry Saddam Hussein, whose thought-bubble depicts weapons and dead soldiers.

The most substantial of these cartoons, from the perspective of a teacher of Arabic, depicts a blood-spattered Iraqi flag with Saddam superimposed and one definitive assertion—an excellent example of a simple declarative sentence containing subject, predicate, pronoun, adjective, preposition, verb, gerund, and direct object: "Saddam is the only reason for the bombing of Iraq!" (In discussing how else to translate the leaflet's caption, students found several words under the same verb root [*qasafa*: bomb] in the dictionary: oppress, break, smash, shatter, and destroy.)

Cartoon-like leaflets such as these have lent themselves not only to the politically charged cultural dimension of teaching Arabic, but also to the nuts-and-bolts teaching of the language in a living context. Rather than practice vocabulary, syntax, and sentence structure taken from standard textbooks in beginning Arabic ("I am a butterfly with velvet wings; I fly among the doves and sparrows"), I could introduce students to more clearly relevant material with a current context: "Awe-inspiring long-range weaponry" and "Devastating firepower."

These leaflets also gave me the opportunity to broach the thorny subject of plurals in Arabic, using illustrations drawn from authentic current materials. For students of the more-commonly taught European languages, where the formation of plurals involves few and fairly regular rules, the numerous distinct types of Arabic plurals, each with its own set of rules, are among the few egregious difficulties of the Arabic language. As I remind my students, in the words of T. E. Lawrence, quoted in one of my grammar books, "The whole question of plurals in Arabic is jolly complicated." In one or two simple leaflets, students could discover that the plurals for "airplane," "fire," "terrorist," and "improvised explosive device" represent four distinct types.

My students have benefited for years from these leaflets by studying the Arabic, imitating the grammatical and syntactical patterns, and substituting new vocabulary introduced in class to create original phrases and sentences.

In addition to learning from the Arabic-language content of these leaflets, my students have also commented thoughtfully about the effects such publications can have on the civilian population for which they are intended. In an assignment in which students were asked to write a brief response to the leaflets, one summarized the feelings of many:

> I am not sure we could tolerate these 'informational handouts' in our own country if we were occupied by a foreign army. These signs, which either would promise us paradise, or instruct us not to live in fear of terrorists who are killing innocent people every day, or even a sign telling us that we are the key to our own government, would be a bit offensive in our country. I can see how someone would interpret these signs as a questioning of the intelligence of Iraqis. The communications from these [leaflets] don't seem to come from eye-level. What they remind me of is how someone glorious and godly would speak.

Thus for the past fifteen years or so, as more and more materials were sent to me by former students with access to them (leaflets, public notices, so-called "Culture Smart Cards", and Arabic phrase-books), I have incorporated them into my curriculum in beginning and intermediate Arabic; the lessons I have based upon them have been useful in teaching the language, as well as in illustrating and exploring the CP designation of courses at Simon's Rock. This CP component, furthermore, has allowed my students to take the measure of America's standing in the Arab world.

As I have adapted the language content of these materials for use in classroom teaching of the language, I have also sought to engage my students in considering what that content suggests about our military's perspectives on the country and people it sought to deliver from a repressive regime.

There are no references in any of these materials to the allegations that the government of Saddam Hussein had been engaged in the production of weapons of mass destruction—perhaps a tacit recognition that none had ever been found. Nor are there direct references to the other allegation (now discredited) of the U.S. government: that the Iraqi government had supported the activities of, and served as a haven for, members of Al-Qaeda. But there are abundant references to the dangers posed by the so-called "Insurgency" that had grown since 2003 in the wake of our poorly planned and culturally misguided efforts to bring democratic institutions, peace, and stability to a country we invaded.

By all accounts, the two invasions of Iraq have caused the country to fall into a state of disorder bordering on the dysfunctional. "Collateral damage," in the phrase used by our military, may have by now, in 2010, caused the deaths of some three-quarters of a million Iraqi civilians, including tens of thousands of children who have died of water-borne diseases. The embargo imposed upon Iraq by the administration of President George H. W. Bush following the liberation of Kuwait banned the importation of chlorine, for instance, because it was considered a "strategic material"; this prevented the restoration of water-treatment plants. (Millions of gallons of raw sewage flow into the Tigris River every hour—a blight observed from space by U.S. satellites in February 2008 as a dark spot in the heart of Baghdad.[4]) Though the cost of repairs would amount to twenty billion dollars—roughly one month's worth of war—Baghdad still has no reliable supply of clean drinking water. The current war, which has reportedly cost us some 750 million dollars a day, has also destroyed the electric grid in Iraq's major cities.[5] Over 200 years ago, Goethe, reflecting on the effects of European wars, recognized that disorder is worse than injustice.[6] Little wonder that ordinary citizens of Iraq today might look back with longing on the regime of Saddam Hussein.

In addition to their usefulness in teaching Arabic and in introducing the topic of our military engagements in Iraq, the Arabic-language materials produced by and for the U.S. military have proven useful in encouraging students to reflect on the process of language-learning itself, as well as on the assumptions that may underlie a particular approach to teaching a language.

After one semester's study of MSA, for example, I asked my beginning Arabic students to examine and comment upon the contents of a booklet produced for the U.S. military by the Defense Language Institute Foreign Language Center (DLIFLC) of Monterey, California, titled "Surviving in Arabic" and distributed to U.S. troops in Iraq in February 2003. A brief prefatory note to this booklet states, "This language guide is intended to provide survival-level language skills to members of any contingency force deployed to an area where the target language is spoken."

We are also informed that DLIFLC "packages this guide with a quick-reference, two-sided, laminated 'Command and Control' (C2) card that contains the most critical words and phrases for contingency operations." The preface adds, "Previous users have found the C2 card to be extremely useful in tactical situations where there is not sufficient time to thumb through even a short phrase book." (I shall return to this "Command and Control" card presently.) The material in the phrase book is arranged in three columns: English on the left; Arabic in the middle; and a transliteration (i.e., phonetic transcription) of the Arabic on the right.

My students' most consistent observations about this material were that the U.S. troops, who are not expected to have any skills in reading the phrases in the Arabic column, would be entirely dependent on the transliterations, which—students were quick to point out with numerous examples—are frequently faulty and do not correspond accurately to the Arabic column. Indeed, many noted that it would be far easier, and more efficient, to teach someone to read the Arabic—better yet, to actually say the phrases in Arabic, according to a systematic approach to learning the language. I have ascertained repeatedly, during decades of teaching this language, that the average student in a beginning Arabic course can learn to read and write basic phrases after less than one month (i.e., approximately twenty hours) of formal instruction.

In one CP writing assignment, a student observed that the transliteration in the phrase book "limits communication," because body language, facial expressions, gesticulation, eye contact, all are part of oral communication as well. The student found it "disheartening" that the phrase book seems to encourage U.S. soldiers to abandon "these natural methods of communication." Since "they can't sound out the phrases for themselves," not being able to read Arabic, "they stumble through the transliterations as best they can, and point at pictures or words." The student concludes: "Because the transliterations are already so terrible, and extremely difficult for an Iraqi to understand, especially with the American accent further muddling it, [Iraqis] now have no hope of gleaning the soldiers' intentions from their body language or natural tone of voice. This makes the already unclear communication almost impossible."

Students were quick to note two types of errors typical of the Arabic phrase book: inaccuracy in the written Arabic, and phonetic transliterations which, for an English-speaker, do not correspond to the Arabic sounds. One wrote: "A glaring example of the second type can be found on the first page, where '*huna*' ("here") is transliterated as '*ihna*.' Interestingly, a different but equally incorrect transliteration of '*huna*' appears further down the first page." This student concludes: "Ultimately, the differences among these languages are going to make any transliteration inadequate." Calling for more thorough and systematic Arabic language instruction for U.S. troops, the student notes: "If we spend billions of dollars occupying the country, surely we can manage this."

Many students noted the frequent conflation, in the military phrase book, of MSA and Iraqi spoken Arabic—a problem for anyone learning Arabic who lacks an adequate understanding of the pitfalls of diglossia. (One student wrote: "It is important to understand that most American soldiers are neither Ph.D. holders nor linguists.")

Such comments are quite typical of my students' reactions. They easily recognize that these materials, while intended to facilitate communication, in fact have the effect of hindering it.

Similarly, students noted that, by its very nature, an alleged guide for communication whose theme is "Command and Control" is going to be replete with phrases virtually guaranteeing suspicion and animosity from those for whom they are intended ("Stop or I will shoot," "Do not move," "Do not resist," "Surrender," "Lie on your stomach," "You are a prisoner").

In another CP writing assignment, when I asked students to think of other useful expressions our soldiers might use in attempting to communicate with Iraqi civilians, their suggestions were immensely heartening to me, for they confirmed my belief that learning another language is a reliable way of understanding another culture, another way of thinking about the world. For example, the phrases "God willing" ("*Insha-allah*"), and "In God's name" ("*Bismillah*"), and "Praise God" ("*Al-hamdu-lillah*") are some of the most common markers of simple everyday discourse among native speakers of Arabic in predominantly Muslim countries—perhaps reflecting how cultures in thrall to the language of faith cope with lives that are arbitrary and fraught with daily setbacks. Simple conversation that includes such locutions would go far in establishing humane rapport between a foreigner and an Arab. It is a credit to students for having understood this in coming up with the sort of phrase book they might have substituted for the one provided by the U.S. military.

Indeed, many of the students' suggestions for phrases to be included in such a language guide were also practical and down-to-earth: "Do you understand me?" "How are you?" "Where are your children/parents?" "What do you need?" "We can help you." "We will not hurt you." "Americans are your friends."

My students were no less perceptive in their reactions to the U.S. military's limited and misguided notions of cultural awareness and its inadequate attempts to promote cultural understanding among the troops.

The "Iraq Culture Smart Card," which I received from yet another former student, is a publication distributed to U.S. troops by the Marine Corps Intelligence Activity Quality and Dissemination Branch (MCIAQDB) in 2004; it is intended as a "Guide for Communication and Cultural Awareness." Handsomely printed (entirely in English) and illustrated in color, laminated in some sixteen accordion-panels in a pocket-size booklet, this item purports to help a U.S. soldier to "quickly learn operationally significant aspects of Iraqi culture." Indeed, the "smart card" does contain some reasonably accurate information, including: a map of Iraq's provinces; a brief description of the "Five Pillars of Islam" (although the fast of Ramadan, "*Sawm*," is misspelled); a statistical breakdown of the five principal Iraqi ethnic groups; and key Muslim religious dates.

Virtually all the other sections of this document, however, are of questionable value as reliable guides to the cultures of Iraq.

The panels in question have titles such as "Do This," "Don't Do This," "Cultural Customs," "Cultural Attitudes," "Clothes/Gestures," and "Cultural History." These categories include topics that I have addressed throughout my courses in Arabic, since they fit squarely within the purview of the Cultural Perspectives component of my courses. Thus students had little difficulty questioning numerous assertions in the "Smart Card," including the following: From the panel titled "Don't Do This":

- "Don't ask for a single opinion on an issue, *as Iraqis often first reply with the answer they think you want to hear, rather than an honest response.*" [emphasis mine]
- "Don't praise an Iraqi's possessions too much. He may give them to you *and expect something of equal value in return.*" [emphasis mine]

From: "Cultural Customs":

- "Admitting 'I Don't Know' is shameful for an Iraqi."
- "Constructive criticism can be taken as an insult."
- "Iraqis do not share an American concept of 'personal space' in public situations, and in private meetings or conversation. It is considered offensive to step or lean away from an Iraqi."

From "Cultural Attitudes":

- "Arabs view Kurds as separatists within Iraq and are wary of their desire for autonomy."
- "Arabs look down upon the Turkomen because Arabs generally view Turkish culture as inferior."
- "Sunnis blame Shia for undermining the mythical unity of Islam and they view them as less loyal to Iraq."
- "As a religious and ethnic minority, the Chaldeans distrust both Kurdish and Arab intentions."

Invited to study this "Smart Card" and write an essay about it, students responded with fair-minded observations and criticism.

One wrote: "The card's purpose is to have soldiers 'quickly learn operationally significant aspects of Iraqi culture.' The term 'operationally significant' is subjective and allows one to use the pamphlet as a way of judging what exactly was the purpose of Operation Iraqi Freedom." And: "I wonder how Americans would react to a similar culture card depicting American ethnicities." And: "The worst is the phrase 'Don't ask for a single opinion on an issue, as Iraqis often first reply with the answer they think you want to hear, rather than an honest response,' which seems [to suggest] Iraqis lie."

Another student observed: "Character traits vary from person to person, and it is foolish to be telling soldiers that every Iraqi they meet will carry this disposition." And: "It's really necessary for our soldiers to understand the people they are in contact with every day, but this pamphlet is so juvenile and even a bit rude."

"All [this pamphlet] can cause," wrote another student, "is stereotypes and prejudice."

Another wrote: "Perhaps the most amusing instance of linguistic bias occurs in the Cultural History section, where the writers proudly claim that 'The British forged modern Iraq.' I suspect most Iraqis wouldn't see it the same way. Nowhere does it mention that these outsiders divided up the Middle East with borders drawn across ethnic lines, in effect setting up the instability that plagued the country." And: "Judging from this booklet, it's more 'significant' for our soldiers to simply get by in this alien country than to understand the religious and cultural history that has made it the way it is. In the end, I believe that this attitude toward cultural education is what does the 'Smart Card' in, and perhaps the war as well."

And finally, from another student: "This document does not do the cultural history of the region justice, devoting a total of eleven bullet points to cover 4,000 years of history."

From the many years of my students' comments about the array of materials produced by and for the U.S. military, three persistent criticisms of their content emerge:

1. Flyers and public notices in Arabic are often simplistic and puerile, seeming to treat the people to whom they are addressed as illiterates with little sense of citizenship or civic responsibility.

2. Phrase-books and language guides provided to our military forces are often in transliterated Arabic, but the numerous mis-transliterations make it virtually impossible for American soldiers, were they to attempt to read these poor transliterations from a phrase-book, to be understood by an Iraqi.

3. So-called "Culture Smart Cards" are replete with stereotypes, unsubstantiated generalizations, and false information about a complex, multilayered Iraqi population, which is religiously, ethnically, and culturally diverse.

Incorporating these materials into the curriculum has served, in some ways, to transform my classroom into a multi-generational community. Students from my classes, over time, have become members of a larger community of students of Arabic: many have become beneficiaries of some who went before, enhancing their understanding of the language in specific contexts (historical, political, cultural) and gaining an awareness of America's standing in the Arab world; and, for as long as our military engagements in the Middle East continue, many will add to my ever-growing collection of U.S. military publications, thus benefiting the next generation of students.

In commenting on the Iraq war in February 2009, one of my students wrote: "Now that President Obama has set a time-table for withdrawal [of U.S. troops from Iraq], perhaps we should issue apologies? Maybe we should admit, in a non-condescending way, that we could have handled things much better and that we went into the war for the wrong reasons? It could be time for America to swallow its pride and apologize. Moving on involves genuine apologies and forgiveness. Let us start to treat others as we would have them treat us. If a country invaded our country for selfish reasons and helped throw it into absolute chaos, at least an apology would be nice. Then we could move on, and rebuild."

Exploring the content and context of these materials in Arabic language courses has helped my students to assess what is arguably the single greatest factor in the U.S. failure to achieve acceptable goals in Iraq: Ignorance of the language and cultures of the people of Iraq. The cycle of pedagogical cross-pollination that has occurred over the years has enabled my students to deepen their sense of the shortcomings of United States efforts to understand and communicate with a people and country who have become the objects of what can at best be termed a form of benevolent belligerence.

NOTES

1. Gilbert Burnham, et al. "Mortality after the 2003 Invasion of Iraq: A Cross-Sectional Cluster Sample Survey." *The Lancet*, 368 (2006): 1421–1428. "An excess mortality of nearly 100,000 deaths was reported in Iraq for the period March 2003–September 2004, attributed to the invasion of Iraq. Our aim was to update this estimate." (p. 1421) "We estimate that, as a consequence of the coalition invasion of March 18, 2003, about 655,000 Iraqis have died above the number that would be expected in a non-conflict situation, which is equivalent to about 2.5% of the population in the study area. About 601,000 of these excess deaths were due to violent causes. Our estimate of the post-invasion crude mortality rate represents a doubling of the baseline mortality rate, which [...] constitutes a humanitarian emergency." (p. 1426) Estimates of the number of Iraqi "excess deaths" caused by the U.S. occupation since March 2003 vary widely, ranging from a December 2005 estimate by then-President George W. Bush of 30,000 deaths to an estimate in September 2007 by Opinion Research Business, an independent polling agency based in Britain, of 1,220,580 deaths.

2. This article is informed by communications with my students over a number of years, and by my recollections of what they have said in class and in written assignments.

In some cases I have copies of the assignments and quote directly from them, but was unable to contact the author. Materials sent me by former students, who remain anonymous for obvious reasons, are all cited with permission.

3. M. M. Bakhtin, *The Dialogic Imagination: Four Essays*, ed. M. Holquist; trans. C. Emerson and M. Holquist (Austin: University of Texas Press, 1981), 263. "Diglossia is a relatively stable language situation in which, in addition to the primary dialects of the language, there is a very divergent, highly codified superposed variety ... which is learned largely by formal education and is used for most written and formal spoken purposes." See also Charles A. Ferguson, "Diglossia," *Word* 15 (1959): 325–340.

4. "Baghdad drowning in sewage: Iraqi official (AFP)—Feb 3, 2008 BAGHDAD (AFP) Baghdad is drowning in sewage, thirsty for water and largely powerless, an Iraqi official said ... sewage is forming a foul lake so large it can be seen 'as a big black spot on Google Earth,' said Tahseen Sheikhly, civilian spokesman for the Baghdad security plan." Accessed September 12, 2010, http://afp.google.com/article/ALeqM5jam-lrcdX-uQLtrYRSz43-tYNO7fQ.

5. Linda Bilmes and Joseph Stiglitz, *The Three Trillion Dollar War: The True Cost of the Iraq Conflict* (New York: W. W. Norton, 2008).

6. Goethe wrote: "Better to commit an injustice than to countenance disorder." In *Campagne in Frankreich 1792, 30 Goethes Werke*, 313–317. Also see Robert D. Kaplan: "Kissinger, Metternich, and Realism," *Atlantic Monthly* 283, no. 6 (June 1999): 73–82. Kaplan writes: "Disorder is worse than injustice. Injustice merely means the world is imperfect, but disorder implies that there is no justice for anyone."

WORKS CITED

Bakhtin, M. M. *The Dialogic Imagination: Four Essays*. Edited by M. Holquist. Translated by C. Emerson and M. Holquist. (Austin: University of Texas Press, 1981).

Bilmes, Linda and Joseph Stiglitz. *The Three Trillion Dollar War: The True Cost of the Iraq Conflict*. New York: W. W. Norton, 2008.

Burnham, Gilbert, et al. "Mortality After the 2003 Invasion of Iraq: A Cross-Sectional Cluster Sample Survey." *The Lancet*, 368 (2006): 1421–1428.

Ferguson, Charles A. "Diglossia." *Word* 15 (1959): 325–340.

"Baghdad drowning in sewage: Iraqi official (AFP)—Feb 3, 2008." Accessed September 12, 2010. *http://afp.google.com/article/ALeqM5jam-lrcdXuQLtrYRSz43-tYNO7fQ*

Goethe, Johan Wolfgang. *Campagne in Frankreich 1792, 30 Goethes Werke*, 313–317.

Kaplan, Robert D. "Kissinger, Metternich, and Realism," *Atlantic Monthly* 283, no. 6 (June 1999): 73–82.

9

The Politics and Poetics of Global Feminist Alliance, or Why I Teach Such Depressing Books

JENNIFER BROWDY DE HERNANDEZ

I. THE SHOCK: IS THE WORLD AN UGLY PLACE? AM I AN UGLY HUMAN BEING?

I'll never forget the first time I taught my "Women Writing Resistance in Latin America & the Caribbean" class. We were discussing a painfully angry passage in Jamaica Kincaid's book *A Small Place*, about how Western tourists appear to the natives of a small Caribbean island. "A tourist is an ugly human being," Kincaid declares. "You are not an ugly person all the time; you are not an ugly person ordinarily; you are not an ugly person day to day. From day to day, you are a nice person. From day to day, all the people who are supposed to love you on the whole do. ... An ugly thing, that is what you are when you become a tourist. ..." About half-way through the class, one of the students burst into tears and ran from the room crying. I gaped after her—I thought I had some idea of why she was upset (for one thing, I knew she had visited the Caribbean as a tourist over the winter vacation), but I had absolutely no idea how to respond to her, and to all the other students in my classes who often asked me curiously about midway through the semester, "Why do you teach such depressing books?"

For years I felt vaguely guilty and uncomfortable about asking students to confront such upsetting books, books that often unsettled their sense of comfort about their own place in the world. It wasn't until years after I had developed a "Women Writing Resistance" course series on contemporary women's literature from Latin America, the Caribbean, Africa and the Middle East, published two anthologies, *Women Writing Resistance: Essays on Latin America and the Caribbean* and *African Women Writing Resistance: Contemporary Voices*, and done a considerable amount of public speaking on the topic to various kinds of audiences, that I began to understand the kind of political engagement and self-questioning that these texts activate in students. Intuitively, I knew it was important to teach literature at the college level that jars students and challenges them to see themselves and the world differently, but it took a long time to discover ways to help to channel students' feelings of guilt, anger, fear and despair into more productive paths.

The books I include in my "Women Writing Resistance" course series[1] often wrestle with women's traumatic experiences—resistance is the other side of the coin of suffering, after all, and so naturally many of the women writers or testifiers that we read in these courses recount the wrenching stories of how they came to become activists around a given issue, whether it is female genital cutting, sweatshop or agri-business exploitation, or sexual abuse. As the student I mentioned above found out, though we ourselves, sitting in a comfortable college classroom, are seemingly removed from and innocent of the oppression against which these women writers are struggling, it is part of the work I undertake in these courses to make clearer the lines of connection that relate us to the women across the world whom we study. My aim is to move students beyond a naïve kind of feel-good multiculturalism—in which we "celebrate diversity" without implicating ourselves (whatever our own ethnic, racial, national and class background) or taking responsibility for the cultural landscape which we inhabit and which we create—into the far more complex terrain of dialogic cultural encounter.[2]

My "Women Writing Resistance" courses not only ask students to take in the often upsetting stories of women whose voices frequently remain unheard in mainstream American discourse, but also to question their own agency and responsibility in this encounter. Once having learned about the troubling reality of life for, say, an indigenous woman who has been treated inhumanely on a plantation in Guatemala or a Nicaraguan woman who has been raped and tortured in prison, what should we do with our knowledge? How can we bring our privilege to bear on the world, in order to manifest our heartfelt compassion for and possibly even solidarity with these women, whom we know only through their written words? One of the goals of my pedagogy, beyond simply introducing students to literature by women whose voices are often effaced and marginalized by mainstream academic discourse, is to help students move beyond the initial paralysis of guilt and depression over the difficult circumstances of many women in the Two-Thirds World,[3] towards a position of active engagement and solidarity.

As one student who took my "Women Writing Activism" class in her first year at Simon's Rock reported:

> the immediate impact of reading a variety of texts by women from different walks of life and from different countries on diverse issues was the shock of recognition of how many problems there were in the world and how many changes people were fighting to make. A secondary impact was how profoundly inspiring it was to read the writing of these passionate women who were actively working to create change, because I could relate. I could relate to Julia Butterfly Hill, since she wasn't that far removed from me in age. I felt like I could be her—I could be just as passionate or influential with very little resources or power to start with. I felt that I wanted to be like Naomi Klein and Arundhati Roy, who really pack a punch in their writing and have managed to get the world's attention. The primary linking factor amongst the authors we read wasn't their pedigree or how well-known they were in the world, but rather their passion for a cause. This led me to believe that I, too, could harness some of that energy and create change in my own community.[4]

II. COMING TO POLITICAL CONSCIOUSNESS: A JOURNEY OF SELF-EDUCATION

This is a journey that I had undertaken myself as a student, under the guidance of mentors I knew only through their writings. My own coming to political awareness had taken me many years. I had focused on literature in both my undergraduate and graduate education, completing a B.A. in English at Simon's Rock in 1982, and going on to earn an M.A. and Ph.D. in Comparative Literature at New York University. I entered graduate school during the heyday of poststructuralist literary analysis, and so my training taught me a lot about how to read a text, but discouraged me from inquiring too closely into the motivations of the author, who was presumed "dead." No one in my department was doing feminist literary analysis, and even the postcolonial approach to literary analysis was, I felt, jargonistic and abstract. I was frustrated by the lack of political engagement among my teachers and fellow graduate students, and began my own program of self-education, gravitating towards testimonial literature and political autobiographies. Hungry for models to spur my own ongoing political awakening, I was fascinated by women's narratives of coming to political consciousness. Especially powerful for me were the inspiring personal narratives by women who had suffered, struggled and overcome: I was blown away by the anthology *This Bridge Called My Back: Writings by Radical Women of Color*, and began reading everything I could get my hands on by Audre Lorde, Gloria Anzaldúa, Cherrie Moraga, Paula Gunn Allen and other women of color who were engaged in what I would come to call "writing resistance." Although our struggles were not entirely the same, I was deeply moved by their stories, and inspired to use my work in the academy to amplify their voices by sharing their books with my students. I took to heart Audre Lorde's clarion call to solidarity: "I am not free while any woman is unfree, even when her shackles are very different from my own," which was accompanied by an invitation to collaboration: "We welcome all women who can meet us, face to face, beyond objectification and beyond guilt" (*Sister Outsider,* 132–33).

My journey towards political awareness was also greatly informed by my travels in Mexico with my Mexican boyfriend, soon to become my husband. My upbringing in Manhattan had taught me well in the tactics of avoidance: I learned to avert my eyes when I saw homeless men and women camping out in packing boxes on the street and to keep my eyes fixed on the advertising billboards in the subway cars when a beggar staggered through the car shaking his cup. In New York, poverty was visible, but it wore the face of the mentally ill, the terminally lazy or the inept, and it was quite possible to ignore. In Mexico City, my habitual New York complacency and detachment was impossible to maintain. I saw whole families living on the streets, while wealthy men and women in Mercedes zoomed past them heedlessly. Crowds of children spent their days in choking traffic fumes washing car windshields frantically while the light was red, hoping to earn a few pennies. Outside the city, it was the same. Whether we were on the beach or in small towns, my blond hair was a magnet for children, who begged winsomely for a few cents or some crumbs from my plate. It was impossible to blame these children for their own misfortune. Their desperate, dirty faces were beacons on my long journey of political self-education. What were the root causes of the massive inequality and suffering I was witnessing, in New York as well as Latin America? What structural social changes could be made to improve the lives of impoverished people in both the One-Third and the Two-Thirds Worlds? Why were none of my professors talking about this or teaching the testimonials that documented it? How could I, with my vocation as a teacher of comparative literature, make a difference?

III. FROM *CONSCIENCIA* TO *CONOCIMIENTO*: MENCHÚ, ANZALDÚA AND THE POLITICS OF ALLIANCE

I found a kind of *ur*-text of political education, for myself and for my students, in the testimonial of Guatemalan Quiché Indian Rigoberta Menchú, which is titled in Spanish *Me llamo Rigoberta Menchú y así me nació la consciencia, My Name is Rigoberta Menchú and This Is How My Consciousness Was Born.* In her testimonial, which has become a contested classic in the field of non-Western personal narratives,[5] Menchú tells the story of how she was born in a hut on a remote mountainside, got caught up with her family in the disastrous Guatemalan civil war of the 1970s and 1980s, and became a revolutionary, fighting for the rights of her people to a life of peace, dignity and self-determination—something the indigenous peoples of Guatemala have not enjoyed since the European invasion of the region 500 years ago. Menchú won the Nobel Peace Prize in the symbolically important year of 1992, 500 years after the "discovery" of the Americas by Christopher Columbus. She says pointedly at the beginning of her narrative, "My story is the story of all poor Guatemalans. My personal experience is the reality of a whole people" (1). So when she tells the story of how her family used to go down from their mountain homestead in the *Altiplano* to the coastal plantation, or *finca*, in order to earn some money to sustain themselves, she is giving us a picture of what life is like for tens of thousands of Guatemalan children. I am going to quote at some length from Menchú's description of the journey—a description that often elicits tears of shock and anger from students reading the book for the first time:

> From when I was very tiny, my mother used to take me down to the *finca*, wrapped in a shawl on her back. She told me that when I was about two, I had to be carried screaming onto the lorry because I didn't want to go. I was so frightened I didn't stop crying until we were about half-way there. I remember the journey by lorry very well. I didn't even know what it was, but I knew I hated it because I hate all things that smell horrible. The lorry holds about forty people. But in with the people go the animals (dogs, cats, chickens) which the people from the *Altiplano* take with them while they are in the *finca*. We have to take our animals. It sometimes took two nights and a day from my village to the coast. During the trip the animals and the small children used to dirty the lorry and you'd get people vomiting and wetting themselves. By the end of the journey, the smell— the filth of people and animals—was unbearable.
>
> The lorry is covered with a tarpaulin so you can't see the country-side you're passing through. Most of the journey is spent sleeping because it's so tedious. The stuffiness inside the lorry with the cover on, and the smell of urine and vomit, make you want to be sick yourself just from being in there. . . . The drivers were sometimes drunk, boozed. They stopped a lot on the way but they didn't let us get out. This enraged us; we hated the drivers because they wouldn't let us get out although they used to drink on the way. (21–22; 24)

This is only the beginning of the story of the exploitation and repression under which Menchú's people are living. She goes on to talk about how workers on the plantation are fed with scant rations of moldy tortillas and rotten beans ("children who don't work don't earn, and so are not fed" [23]); how there are no latrines or sanitary facilities for the workers; how her brother is poisoned and dies from inhaling pesticides sprayed on the fields while the workers are harvesting cotton or coffee, a common occurrence; how her parents often get drunk at the *cantina* "out of despair," drinking away most of their wages (23); and how the landowners and overseers would casually rape the women and beat or even murder them if they dared to resist (150–51).

This is tough stuff to take in, and if anything the story gets even more grim as Menchú goes into the brutal civil war waged for years in her country between the revolutionary guerillas and the elite landowners, a war that frequently caught the native peoples in the crossfire.[6] When I teach *I, Rigoberta Menchú,* it is with a broadly interdisciplinary lens; we talk about the literary conventions employed by the text, but also about the history and economics of the region, politics, human rights, the women's perspective in the narrative, and the anthropological view of the indigenous Guatemalans. It's impossible for students to come away from our discussions without a greater understanding of the United States' role as the major buyer for the products grown and harvested on those inhumane *fincas,* as well as the major supplier of arms and military training for the soldiers who brutally murdered Rigoberta Menchú's mother and brother.[7] This leads to a deeper, more worrisome question: what is our own responsibility, as U.S. citizens (or at least, academics at an American college) for the exploitation and mistreatment of people like Rigoberta Menchú?

Questions like these do not make for easy discussions. Crucial to my own understanding of the process we undertake in working through these difficult questions in the classroom is Gloria Anzaldúa's essay "Now let us shift ... the path of *conocimiento* ... inner work, public acts," one of the last essays she published before her untimely death in 2002. In this essay, Anzaldúa describes *conocimiento* as a multi-stage process of coming to awareness, and then taking action based on that new awareness, in which the stages are not chronological or mutually exclusive, and where the process itself is more important than any given goal—in fact, it's a never-ending process, rather than a goal-oriented one. The seven stages of *conocimiento* are:[8]

1. The shock that jars you into openness to a new perspective
2. *Nepantla*, the in-between stage where you consider new perspectives
3. *Coatlicue*: doubt, despair, self-loathing, paralysis
4. A call to action sends you looking for ways to act productively in the world
5. Crafting a new personal narrative that reflects your new understanding of the world
6. Taking your new story out in public, testing it in dialogue with others
7. Forming holistic alliances with others based on your sense of commonality and compassion.

Anzaldúa emphasizes that "in a day's time you may go through all seven stages, though you may dwell in one for months" and "you're never only in one space, but partially in one, partially in another, with *nepantla* occurring most often as its own space and as the transition between each of the others" (546).

As I found out myself, and later saw demonstrated again and again in the classroom with my students, women's narratives of resistance have the power to send us on a journey through these seven stages of political coming to awareness, moving from the shock of learning about the suffering of others to the despair and self-loathing of inaction, to the passionate search for ways to initiate change. In my "Women Writing Resistance" classes I am looking not just to introduce students to a series of powerful, important and beautiful texts, with their accompanying political contexts, but also to find ways to use the power of the stories we read to understand ourselves and our place in the world more fully. Ultimately, I am searching for ways that my students and I can productively channel our knowledge and passions so as to have a positive impact in the world. Together we ask, how can we be the change we want to see, and enact a real politics of alliance with women of the Two-Thirds World?

IV. COMPASSIONATE WITNESSING: MOVING FROM TRAUMA TO ACTION

The beginning of an answer to this question comes in the first stage of *conocimiento,* the powerful emotional shock that comes from being exposed to a new and very different, unfamiliar view of reality. Such shocks, Anzaldúa says, are necessary to growth; they are moments of "awakening that cause you to question who you are, what the world is about" (547). The "depressing" moments in the books we read in my "Women Writing Resistance" series offer many opportunities for these kinds of productive shocks, which can take us further along the process of coming to awareness or *conocimiento.* Anzaldúa has observed that it is only by going through what she calls the "*Coatlicue* state" (*Coatlicue* being a reference to a dark, "hellish" Mesoamerican goddess who can drag one down to the underworld of "despair, self-loathing and hopelessness" [545]) that we can find an effective path of action. My own horror at the beautiful faces of Mexican children or the hysterical sobs that sent a student flying from my classroom years ago bear witness to the rapid movement from initial shock to the intense turmoil of the *Coatlicue* state. From my own experience, I can attest that emotional responses to the suffering we witness in these narratives are important stages in understanding and intellectual growth—it often takes powerful emotion to break through habits of complacency, detachment or silence. In the words of one of my students:

> The more books I read and the more I allowed myself to hear the voices of my classmates, the more I was forced to re-evaluate all the things that I had blindly accepted as truth. ... I was on a journey of self-discovery and rebirth. The willingness of the women writers we studied to share their oppression and humiliation forced to me to do the same. Through their testimonials these women provided for me a bridge from silence to voice, from victim to survivor. ... In the testimonies of these women mired in blood, death, hunger and unimaginable abuse, I found the greatest gift: myself.[9]

Such a journey, though challenging in every way, is ultimately healing and empowering. "Delving more fully into your pain, anger, despair, depression will move you through them to the other side," Anzaldúa says, "where you can use their energy to heal. Depression is useful—it signals that you need to make changes in your life, it challenges your tendency to withdraw, it reminds you to take action" (553).

And action is soon what students are looking for as the power of these narratives swells in the chorus of voices of "Women Writing Resistance." When we look at the reality of a Central American "banana republic" from the point of view of someone like Rigoberta Menchú—from the point of view, that is, of the indigenous female plantation worker, who is generally silenced and erased—we suddenly come up against the jarring awareness of our own responsibility, as members of the privileged One-Third World, for her suffering. We cannot help but question the obliviousness with which we, say, enjoy our morning cup of coffee or slip into a cheap imported cotton tee-shirt. Menchú's testimony forces us to acknowledge the undeniable reality of our own privilege in the world, first as Americans, and even more so as Americans with the luxury of peaceful time and space to sit in a college classroom and talk with a measure of academic detachment about the suffering of others. Understandably, students learning for the first time about the reality of life for most non-elite women of the Two-Thirds World find this information quite upsetting, and they don't want to just sit around and talk about it, they want to put themselves on the front lines of change—they want to *do something* to help the Rigobertas of the world. What can I, as their guide through these new waters, offer to help them process this information and make the cultural encounter I've initiated productive for both sides?

I always remind students that simply in choosing to listen to women like Kincaid and Menchú, they are *acting*—listening and striving to understand the other's point of view is the first step in any effective politics of engagement. By taking on the role of active, compassionate witness to the traumatic events narrated by these women writers, we are already going against the grain of our pervasively complacent and callous culture, which would prefer that violence, racism and injustice "be accepted as an immutable given in the fabric of [our] existence, like eveningtime or the common cold" (Lorde, *Sister Outsider,* 128).[10] Doing this difficult work of bearing witness to others' pain is genuinely healing for those who engage in it, as pioneering

Harvard psychologist Kaethe Weingarten has convincingly demonstrated. "During compassionate witnessing," Weingarten says, "states of resilience are activated, for both the witness and the person being witnessed" (states of resilience referring to the positive emotions of hope, purpose, community, agency). "Thus," Weingarten continues, "far from the experience of compassionate witnessing draining a person, it seems to replenish and restore" (232). The physiological and neurological research she has conducted shows that "compassionate witnessing can set off the brain's capacity to experience unity" or "flow," to feel at one with the person who is suffering. Compassionate witnessing thus contributes, she says, to "a perception of our common humanity" (234).

Narrators like Rigoberta Menchú, in placing us as readers into close imaginative proximity with the stories of their suffering, engage us in the process of compassionate witnessing, a relational act that humanizes both the victim and the witness. Menchú recreates history in order to overcome the residual trauma it has left behind, telling the story in order to move beyond it. In doing so, she lays to rest the ghosts of the past, and imparts a valuable lesson to the upcoming generations about the dangers of dehumanization and cruelty. As readers, we can participate in this process of history, for, as Weingarten says, "in each act of witnessing we give a gift: in effect we say, 'Your suffering mattered. Knowing about it changes me. Your pain is not in vain'" (234).

Writers like Rigoberta Menchú share their stories with us not to plunge us into horror at the misery of the world, but to bear witness to the tremendous strength and determination of the women who have survived such brutality and suffering and lived to tell the tale. Menchú invites us, as readers, to join her in the role of compassionate witnessing—witnessing that fosters hope, not despair. As Kaethe Weingarten says, "We create each other's hells, and we must create each other's hope." Weingarten sees hope as not just a feeling, but as an action, something that we *do*. "Hope happens when we see a pathway to effective action," she says. "Thus it is better understood as the responsibility of the community and something that we do together. . . . Compassionate witnessing is one of the ways I do hope with others. The effects of hope are profound, as are the effects of hopelessness. Just as food, water, and security must be equitably distributed, so too must hope. Compassionate witnessing is a way we can contribute to the equitable distribution of hope, and work for justice for all" (242).

V. WHAT CAN I *DO?* THE JOURNEY OF *CONOCIMIENTO* IN THE CLASSROOM

As practiced in my classroom, compassionate witnessing is not just an academic exercise—I am as eager as any of my students to find ways to *do something* to manifest my compassion for non-elite women of the Two-Thirds World, and perhaps even to make their lives a little more tolerable. What we *do* first is simply read carefully, and then use response journals to initiate a dialogic encounter in which we are able to talk with and question the texts we're reading. Students in my classes work on their response journals collaboratively, posting them online and commenting on each other's ideas, which allows for the discussion of the text to start even before we've entered the classroom. In the response journals, students engage in what Anzaldúa calls the work of the *nepantlera,* taking their ideas public and testing them out in dialogue with others. "*Nepantla*" is a Nahuatl[11] term meaning "the space in-between"; in Anzaldúa's usage, it is a "zone of possibility," a "liminal ... site of transformation, the place where different perspectives come into conflict and where you question basic ideas, tenets, and identities inherited from your family, your education and your different cultures" (548). Though by no means comfortable, *nepantla* is an ideal state for growth, exchange and dialogue; it is the kind of space I am always trying to create in my classroom, and it begins in a tangible way in the response journal exchanges, along with the many other discussions students have with each other, in the dorms or at home with their families and friends, in which they test out and refine new ideas.

This process of coming to voice may be the most important outcome of the kind of small-group class discussions that we typically stage at Simon's Rock. Some students enter my classroom with the impression that discussion and debate are one and the same—and for them, what's most important is to learn how to listen to others, and allow themselves to be changed and deepened by what they hear. Others come bearing the scars of years of silence, and need to learn to trust that they can express their ideas in this learning community without being shot down or dismissed. In many of my classes, no matter the topic, I include a reading of Audre Lorde's seminal essay "The Transformation of Silence into Language and Action," because her message forms the backbone of my pedagogical approach to reading literature. In this essay, first presented as a speech at the Modern Language Association annual convention in 1977, Lorde talks about how, after learning of her cancer diagnosis, what she "most regretted were [her] silences. Of what had I ever been afraid?" Muffling her own voice had not protected her, she realizes, and on the contrary may have actually caused her harm. "In the cause of silence, each of us draws the face of her own fear—fear of contempt, of censure, or some judgment, or recognition, of challenge, of annihilation," she says.

> But for every real word spoken, or every attempt I had ever made to speak those truths for which I am still seeking, I had made contact with other women while we examined the words to fit a world in which we all believed, bridging our differences. ... We have been socialized to respect fear more than our own needs for language ... and while we wait in silence for that final luxury of fearlessness, the weight of that silence will choke us.

> The fact that we are here and that I speak these words is an attempt to break that silence and bridge some of those differences between us, for it is not difference which immobilizes us, but silence. And there are so many silences to be broken. (*Sister Outsider*, 44)

This is a lesson that often hits home with students as we discuss testimonials that clearly demonstrate the power of speaking out. In her response to Lorde's essay, posted online for other students to read and respond to, one student wrote:

> Like everyone else it seems, I was most moved by this essay. Of course the issue of speaking out is important to me, because for the longest time I had no voice at all. I sometimes think I didn't even have an inner voice. And then suddenly I had a raging voice and it took me a long and painful time to learn how to express that. And I do know that we can learn to speak when we feel fear like when we're hungry, tired or frustrated. It's critical, in fact, that we learn to do this. How will you even find the words to express yourself if you have no voice with which to talk?[12]

In the classroom (as well as online), discussions of charged material like Rigoberta Menchú's narrative can sometimes become heated. One student may criticize the kind of old-school charitable benevolence she sees in the sympathetic response of another student to Menchú's story. She doesn't want to, say, raise money to donate to a humanitarian organization, she wants to go out and bomb the headquarters of the American corporation that owns the *finca*. Another student may remain detached and unmoved by the emotional content of Menchú's narrative, preferring to focus on the intellectual question of how her testimonial was constructed. In the classroom, all of these points of view have validity and are opportunities for exchange and growth. The important thing is to insist that students treat each other with the respect and attention they themselves would like to receive, and that no one voice or opinion dominates the discussion. My role as the facilitator of such a discussion is very much that of the Anzaldúan *nepantlera,* inhabiting the space in between the sometimes conflicting viewpoints of students, trying to hold them to a position of personal integrity and honesty that will eventually bring even the most skeptical to see the lines of connection and responsibility between herself and someone like Rigoberta Menchú. In doing so, I enact my own form of *conocimiento*, as the students' viewpoints inform my own, often leading me to see familiar material in a new and different light.[13]

All of my "Women Writing Resistance" courses include a major research project as the principal assignment, besides the primary readings and response journals. I ask students to start from a question they have about one of our primary texts, or about an issue that is at least tangentially related to a primary text, and to research this issue in depth, presenting their findings in class as well as writing them up as the final paper. To some students, this may not feel sufficiently like action, but again, I reiterate that informing oneself and one's community is an essential first step in the process of coming to awareness, which can culminate in one's becoming an agent of change. Students often find that my classes are the starting points of much more work around a given issue, which may become the topic of their senior thesis, or the focus of extracurricular activity, such as founding an Amnesty International chapter on campus, the publication of a zine related to social justice issues, or a campaign to pressure the campus food service to provide beverages produced by non-exploiting companies. The form of action is actually less important, at this point in students' lives, than the realization that they have the power to transform their passions and conviction into action.

An example of this process comes from Simon's Rock alumna Katharina Kempf, who recalled recently how her senior thesis topic grew out of her study of women activists in my "Women Writing Activism" class, which she took in her very first semester as a Simon's Rock student.

> My junior year, I decided to learn first-hand about some of the challenges people face in the world by studying abroad on a comparative politics program called International Honors Program: Rethinking Globalization. I traveled to England, Tanzania, India, New Zealand, and Mexico, living with host families ranging from the wealthy upper-crust to marginalized indigenous groups, and learning from field visits and lectures by scholars and activists in each country. I connected what I had read about in "Women Writing Activism" with first-hand experience, and when I came back to Simon's Rock, I helped organize a campaign to get the college to cut its contract with Coca-Cola because the company represented what was negative about neo-liberal economics: a disregard for worker's rights, the environment, and diversity. At the same time, I wrote my undergraduate thesis about a social movement in one of the places I studied while abroad: Oaxaca, Mexico. I felt that just like the women whose stories I had read three years ago, I too had a voice that I could use to share what I had learned and experienced. I was able to turn these lessons into something concrete and specific: Simon's Rock did eventually cut its contract with Coca-Cola, and I completed a 265-page thesis on the movement for a people's government in Oaxaca, my own version of the texts for change written by the women whose books I had read in "Women Writing Activism."[14]

Katharina represents the kind of seeker on the path of *conocimiento* described by Gloria Anzaldúa, who asks "How can I contribute?" Anzaldúa's advice is to listen to "your inner voice," which will "reveal your core passion" and "point you to your sense of purpose, urging you to seek a vision, devise a plan." Isn't this the motivation for all liberal arts college classes—helping to activate students' "core passions" and showing them productive paths in which to let those passions guide their life journeys? Once you've figured out what your passions are, says Anzaldúa, you will "discover resources within yourself and the world," and will begin "to take responsibility for consciously creating your life and becoming ... a contributing member of all your communities" (557).

VI. ENACTING THE POLITICS OF ALLIANCE

Thinking about communities as overlapping pluralities, rather than the hard-and-fast walls of self and identity, helps us to go beyond limiting categories of "ethnic and other labels" to "redefine what it means to be ... a citizen of the world," part of "an emerging planetary culture" (Anzaldúa, 561). It seems clichéd to say that in the twenty-first century we must become "global citizens," and yet there is a grain of truth in the cliché. Students today need to hear the stories of women of the Two-Thirds World, because more and more, our destinies are linked. This is a viewpoint eloquently expressed by Rigoberta Menchú, in her second book, *Crossing Borders,* which moves out of the harrowing terrain of the past into a discussion of Menchú's current role as an indigenous woman leader, as well as her vision for the future. Menchú's generous vision of how the native peoples of the Americas could co-exist with the descendants of the colonizers never fails to impress students.

> When the Spaniards arrived five hundred years ago, they raped our ancestors, our grandmothers, our mothers, to breed a race of mestizos. The result is the violence and cruelty that we are still living with today. The Spaniards used a vile method to create a mixed race, a race of children who doubted their own identity, with their heads on one side of the ocean and their feet on the other. That is what happened to our culture. ... The past cannot just be about myths. It must be a source of strength for the present and the future. ... We have to blend our two cultures, the ancient and the modern. We should not be trying to eradicate anything or anybody because we think one is better. We should be trying to find a way to living together, combining the ancient culture of our peoples with the culture of the colonizers. That is the strength of our American identity, the privilege of having roots that go back thousands of years. (Browdy de Hernandez, 132–33)

Menchú expresses her humanitarian vision in terms of what she calls "the indigenous cosmovision," which has much wisdom to offer global society today. "We indigenous Guatemalans think of ourselves as maize, as a cob of corn," she says. "If a grain is missing from the cob we notice that there is an empty space. ... When there is a wound in this beautiful K'iche' land of ours, I feel it as a pain in the heart of humanity, because El Quiché is like a grain in the cob of humanity" (*Crossing Borders*, 224).

Here is a beautiful vision of humanity not as separate races or separate worlds, but as profoundly interconnected—if one group of people is hurting, we all hurt, and conversely, if one group prospers, we all prosper. In the age of globalization, our interdependency is becoming ever more apparent, and yet still, very often, we fortunate denizens of the One-Third World are able to live complacently within our gated communities without even being aware of the suffering that might go into the cup of coffee we savor in the morning. The women writers that I share with students in my "Women Writing Resistance" series challenge this complacency and inspire students to dig deeply into the work of *conocimiento*: to "dedicate yourself, not to surface solutions that benefit only one group, but to a more informed service to humanity" (Anzaldúa, 574).

It is my hope that the non-elite women of the Two-Thirds World whose works we study will become catalysts for students, leading them to greater self-awareness, a deeper understanding of global social dynamics, and the desire to create and manifest transformative visions of positive social change locally, nationally, and worldwide. When students understand how much they have to learn from women of the Two-Thirds World, and also how much they have to offer these women, a circle of reciprocity is created, in which we are able to see that "we are the other, the other is us." From this knowledge we can enact the seventh and final stage of the journey of *conocimiento*, which Anzaldúa calls "spiritual activism," based in an affirmation of the importance of "mobilizing, organizing, sharing information, knowledge, insights and resources with other groups" (571). My "Women Writing Resistance" classes provide multiple openings for alliances with the women writers whose literary works "serve as gateways ... between worlds" (ibid.). Peering through these gateways, we can see for ourselves the truth of Alice Walker's perception, echoed by Kaethe Weingarten and many others, that "resistance is the secret of joy" (256).

NOTES

1. In addition to the courses already mentioned I am currently developing two more: "Women Writing Resistance in Asia," and "Indigenous Women Writing Resistance." I also teach a course called "Women Writing Activism," in which students read writing by women activists on a variety of issues, from all over the world, and try their hands at "writing activism" themselves, in a range of genres from a letter, to a manifesto, to a research paper. All of these courses are 200-level, open to any student, with no prerequisites.

2. My work in this area traces its beginning to a seminal passage in Gloria Anzaldúa's

Borderlands/La frontera: The New Mestiza (San Francisco: Spinsters/Aunt Lute, 1987) where she critiques the reactionary "counterstance" and argues instead for a *"mestiza* consciousness" that can "sustain contradictions" and "transcend duality." For Anzaldúa, "the answer to the problem between the white race and the colored, between males and females, lies in healing the split that originates in the very foundation of our lives, our culture, our languages, our thoughts. A massive uprooting of dualistic thinking in the individual and collective consciousness is the beginning of a long struggle, but one that could, in our best hopes, bring us to the end of rape, of violence, of war" (161–62). Uprooting dualistic thinking requires a recognition of the workings of privilege in cultural encounters; useful texts for thinking about the interplay of privilege and oppression would include Aida Hurtado, *The Color of Privilege: Three Blasphemies on Race and Feminism* (Ann Arbor: University of Michigan Press, 1996); Michael S. Kimmel and Abby L. Ferber, *Privilege: A Reader* (Boulder, CO: Westview, 2003); Frances Kendall, *Understanding White Privilege: Creating Pathways to Authentic Relationships Across Race* (New York: Routledge, 2006); and Wendy Brown, *Regulating Aversion: Tolerance in the Age of Identity and Empire* (Princeton, NJ: Princeton University Press, 2006).

3. I follow Chandra Talpade Mohanty in adopting the terminology proposed by postcolonial theorists Gustavo Esteva and Madhu Suri Prakash in *Grassroots Post-Modernism: Remaking the Soil of Cultures* (London: Zed Books, 1998): instead of First and Third Worlds, a terminological phrasing which privileges the First World, they suggest One-Third and Two-Thirds Worlds, which gives a more accurate sense of the relative size of these two broad constituencies. The Two-Thirds World encompasses Latin America, the Caribbean, Africa, Asia and the Middle East, although the boundaries are fluid: there are pockets of the one-third world among the elites of the two-thirds world, and pockets of two-thirds world poverty in the one-third world.

4. From a private communication by Simon's Rock 2007 B.A. alumna Katharina Kempf. Quoted with permission.

5. In the late 1990s, the veracity of Menchú's testimony was questioned by David Stoll, an anthropologist who interviewed some of Menchú's relatives and political enemies and produced a book, *Rigoberta Menchú and the Story of All Poor Guatemalans* (Boulder, CO: Westview, 2007), detailing his findings. The controversy that erupted is well-documented in the collection *The Rigoberta Menchú Controversy,* edited by Arturo Arias (Minneapolis: Minnesota University Press, 2001). While not glossing over the questions raised by Stoll when I teach Menchú's testimonial, I use the Arias volume to show students how the larger issues raised by Menchú can be lost in the back and forth of academic ping-pong, which too often takes place over the heads of the very people they are discussing. As Menchú says cuttingly in her second testimonial, published in English under the title *Crossing Borders,* (London: Verso, 1998): "I know people who think they know everything about indigenous people. People make careers out of us, people who think they can live by studying other human beings yet do not make the slightest effort to help them define themselves in society and history. We create defenses against these parasites. Getting to know another culture is wonderful, but it is ignoble when

certain irresponsible individuals try to put human dignity in a bottle and make a profit from selling it" (223).

6. Though there is no longer a "hot" civil war in Guatemala, the cold war of exploitation and neglect continues, with the majority population of indigenous peoples still enduring racism and disrespect from the minority elites, whose Spanish ancestors colonized the territory 500 years ago. After winning the Nobel Peace Prize in 1992, Rigoberta Menchú focused much of her energy on a campaign to gain international recognition of indigenous people's human rights in Guatemala and throughout the world. She successfully lobbied the United Nations to adopt a Resolution on the Rights of Indigenous Peoples (passed by the U.N. General Assembly in 2007 after years of struggle), and she also took the unprecedented step of mounting her own campaign for the Presidency of Guatemala in 2007. Although she lost, she galvanized the indigenous people of Guatemala to participate more actively in their country's political process, and to take themselves seriously as political actors, even if they, like her, had been born in a mud hut on a remote mountainside. Menchú remains an inspiring example of how much can be accomplished even from far outside the established circles of political influence, wealth and power.

7. In 1999, President Bill Clinton publicly apologized for the U.S. support of right-wing Guatemalan governments that killed more than 200,000 people, most of them civilians, during a protracted thirty-six-year civil war. As reported in the *New York Times* on March 11, 1999, Mr. Clinton "made the apology in his opening statement to an informal gathering of leaders from many sectors of Guatemalan society, including Indians, women, Government officials and representatives of a truth commission that issued a report last month on the war. The commission found that the United States gave money and training to Guatemalan forces that committed acts of genocide against Mayans and other extreme human rights abuses in the conflict, which began in 1960." Mr. Clinton said that "For the United States, it is important that I state clearly that support for military forces and intelligence units which engaged in violence and widespread repression was wrong, and the United States must not repeat that mistake" (John M. Broder, "Clinton Offers His Apologies to Guatemala," *The New York Times,* March 11, 2009.)

8. I am paraphrasing and condensing Anzaldúa's much lengthier description of the seven stages in her essay.

9. From a private communication by Simon's Rock alumna Simonette Swain (B.A., 2004); reprinted with permission.

10. A more recent iteration of Lorde's insight comes from Slavoj Žižek, who sees "systemic" or "objective" violence as just as destructive, if not more so, than typical violent actions such as war, rape, assault, etc., which he calls "subjective violence" (*Violence* [London: Picador, 2008], 11).

11. Nahuatl is an ancient Mesoamerican language still spoken by many indigenous people of central Mexico.

12. Response journal excerpt by sophomore Tiffany Albright (A.A., 2008), from "Women Writing Activism," Fall 2007. Reprinted with permission.

13. I recently received validation of my success in maintaining this delicate pedagogical balance from Simon's Rock 2003 B.A. alumna Simonette Swain: "I always felt that Jenny maintained a level of respect and was able to mediate heated discussions with grace. Had there not been this balance I might just have gone on the defensive and never truly allowed myself to examine and re-evaluate my beliefs. It is necessary that people change on their own terms; one should not force one's ideological beliefs on others, however passionately you might feel about a given position. One of the things that makes Jenny such a wonderful teacher is the fact that as a student, you never feel as if she judges you one way or the other, there is no pressure from her for to convert. Jenny recognizes that everyone has to evolve at his/her pace and this sentiment is always present in her classes. As a guide, she truly allowed students the freedom to explore and discover the power of the text. Therefore, whatever we took away from them was uniquely ours" (from a private communication; quoted with permission).

14. From a private communication by Simon's Rock 2007 B.A. alumna Katharina Kempf. Quoted with permission.

WORKS CITED

Anzaldúa, Gloria. "Now let us shift ... the path of *conocimiento* ... inner work, public acts." In *This Bridge We Call Home*. Edited by Gloria Anzaldúa and Analouise Keating, 540–578. New York: Routledge, 2001.

Browdy de Hernandez, Jennifer, ed. *Women Writing Resistance: Essays on Latin America & the Caribbean*. Boston: South End Press, 2004.

Esteva, Gustavo, and Madhu Suri Prakash. *Grassroots Post-Modernism: Remaking the Soil of Cultures*. London: Zed Books, 1998.

Kincaid, Jamaica. "From *A Small Place*." In *Women Writing Resistance: Essays on Latin America & the Caribbean*, edited by Jennifer Browdy de Hernandez, 147–156. Boston: South End Press, 2004.

Lorde, Audre. *Sister Outsider*. Freedom, CA: The Crossing Press, 1984.

Menchú, Rigoberta. *I, Rigoberta Menchú*. Edited by Elizabeth Burgos. London: Verso, 1984.

———. "The Quincentenary and the Earth Summit." In *Women Writing Resistance: Essays on Latin America & the Caribbean*, edited by Jennifer Browdy de Hernandez, 117–135. Boston: South End Press, 2004.

———. *Crossing Borders*. Edited and translated by Ann Wright. London: Verso, 1998.

Walker, Alice. *Possessing the Secret of Joy*. New York: Harcourt, 1992.

Weingarten, Kaethe. *Common Shock: Witnessing Violence Every Day—How We Are Harmed, How We Can Heal*. New York: Dutton, 2003.

10

Visual Learning

Female Students, Women Artists, and Mothers

JOAN DELPLATO

I. INTRODUCTION

As usual in New England on the first day of classes in late August, it is hot and humid in the classroom as ten students—all of them female—walk in and find their seats for the first time.[1] As is my custom, I open the course by asking students to introduce themselves by naming some of their academic and non-academic interests, the city from which they have just arrived, and what brought them into an art history course titled "Women Artists." As their identities begin to unfold, several of the young women claim that their mothers' serious interest in art and its history had helped draw them to the course material. My curiosity is piqued. Immediately I know there is something significant here that I want to think more about.

What happens when a female student looks at art? I will present some specific processes I have observed in my two decades of teaching at Simon's Rock. And I will address some considerations in my role as an art historian striving to facilitate visual learning. We are indeed midwives, to use Plato's very old metaphor for (mostly male) teachers, who assist with the birthing of ideas. To some extent we also take on a parenting role. I want to explore the more specific dynamics of females mentoring female students. In this role of mentor-professor I use my discipline to encourage students to develop both emotionally and intellectually. In part this happens through some of the core facets of my identity—female academic, scholar, and also mother.

In this article I draw upon my experiences in having taught several times my art history course, "Women Artists," along with comments written in summer and fall 2008 by some female students who had taken the course. I quote them throughout this article. These young women described their relationships to their mothers who are themselves either artists, art historians, art professionals or just visually creative, a fact that—by their own admission—contributes to their interest in art created by women.[2] I would like to explore how that occurs and the parallel between female students' mothers and their female professors.

I am posing a question that is unusual within the paradigms of college pedagogy: how can young women's burgeoning identities as art intellectuals be enhanced not only by the curricular study of past women artists but also by creative mothers and their curious parallel in women who are their art history professors? In thinking this through, I hope to illuminate several things. I ask some provocative questions that fall outside the realm of the usual focus in the liberal arts—but not the pedagogy of gender studies. And I will comment on how male teachers of female students can also play a prominent role in the gendered dynamics of their female students' visual learning processes.

Decades of scholars have convincingly argued that the process of a viewer's looking is deeply psychological. Some have critiqued the canonical history of art as a history of men's viewing of art works of the past in which they exercise their privileged masculine right of ownership and "overview."[3] Feminist scholars have examined some of the dynamics involved in contrasting male and female ways of seeing. I will extend these comments to inquire into some of the visual dynamics of adolescent females looking at art works reproduced as electronic images projected onto a screen in the classroom. Then I would like to use these observations to consider some of the psychological dimensions of classroom pleasure and learning. One of my main goals is to ask how I might trace stages in the development of students' love of looking and writing as they mature into *integrated* thinkers and writers about art, those who are capable of utilizing visceral, historical, and analytical wellsprings of information.

II. WOMEN ARTISTS:
WORKING THROUGH OUR AMBIVALENCES

In the past, I designed "Women Artists" as a survey of case studies of women artists in western art—working mostly with paintings and some photography, sculpture and printmaking—dating from the Renaissance to the present with an emphasis on nineteenth- and especially twentieth-century art. Reflecting the dramatic changes in the field of art history over the last two decades, I have blended material on African American, Chicano, Native American and lesbian women artists, and now I am working to meet the challenge of integrating analyses of art made by women in the global present. It is conducted as a seminar—small in size, interactive, discussion-based—in which students take turns reporting on scholarly readings. We look closely at images for nearly the entire class period. To some extent students can design their own course by selecting readings to closely analyze from an extensive list of choices. All students choose the subject of their final research paper. It is given much attention in the course as students are taken through the entire process of selecting a topic, researching, and writing the paper. This culminates with a reading of that paper by the entire class and a required revision of the first draft in response to the class's comments. They are given intensive practice in doing what art historians do.

In preparing to write this chapter, I sent a short questionnaire to students who had taken my course "Women Artists," including a few alumnae of the college, providing a forum which allowed them to comment on the course and its relationship to their mothers.[4] Nicole, quoted below, is very explicit about her motivation in taking the course as a way to understand her mother, who for some time has been an aspiring art curator:

> I saw it ["Women Artists"] as a way of understanding my mother, of finally finding a way into this world into which I had not yet been initiated, to have a stronger common ground with her, to learn about something she loved and maybe learn to love it too.

On the other hand, Roxann, now an alumna of Simon's Rock working full-time as an art administrator while designing and selling a jewelry line on the side, expresses ambivalence about creativity and the maternal even though she is fully aware that her mother's work as a glass cutter has directly affected her interest in the arts. Roxann, who is now applying to MFA programs in glass, writes:

> I see all kinds of associations between my art work and the maternal heritage of art. I see how my art work fits into the stereotypes of women's work. I go back and forth between accepting it and feeling trapped by it. I see how my work relates to quilting, collages, delicate bits and pieces, and fits into a "decorative" realm. (I had always known about these stereotypes, but the "Women Artists" class solidified my understanding of them.) I hate to think of the creative process as something maternal, because I would like to believe that the creative process is something elemental to the human experience.

Like Roxann, I have had to struggle with my ambivalence about writing a paper on this topic. I realize that this subject is unusual in that it concerns the intersections between motherhood and academia. Conventionally the two realms are kept separate in scholarly writing, even though female academics who have been mothers of small children know well the impossibilities in attempting to keep them distinct. Fast-track academia (located outside of Simon's Rock) hasn't looked favorably upon its professors being mothers, as the role of professor, like other "professionals," demands an apparent removal of the personal from the work it does. And to the extent that mothering is popularly understood as one's personal choice (far removed from one's professional life), the identities of an academic producing scholarly analysis and a mother aren't expected to converge. I believe there is great suspicion that acting "as a mother" in the classroom is even desirable and that it reflects an imbrication of gender stereotypes with educational hierarchies that see women as "fit" teachers for young children but still somewhat out of place in the higher realms of academia. In 1993 John Pease articulated how, in the large American university, teaching is considered "women's work," and research is thought of as "men's work."[5] This belief is regrettable. It undervalues motherhood on the one hand and restricts the range of learning techniques for how subjects can be academically analyzed on the other. The alternative classroom might draw upon the female professor's experience as having mothered as an enrichment of her teaching skills. And female students' focus on their relationships to their own mothers can open up new understandings of themselves and their academic interests.

Like Roxann, I had some real hesitation when as a beginning teacher, freshly minted from a major university, I considered teaching a course about women artists. I worried that it would be severed from a comprehensive history of art. And I feared I might have to surrender my familiarity with modern art history and the particular political approach I was schooled in. I wasn't sure that women artists—or women as a group—were inherently "different" in ways I could identify or would want to present to students or anyone else. Over time I learned that feminist scholars raised many of the same questions I had. And I was deeply impressed by the writing of feminists in my field like Griselda Pollock, whose *Vision and Difference* (1986) encouraged me to recognize that whether or not males and females are inherently different, the genders are *perceived* to be different and as a result they might well see differently—and produce different kinds of art. Thus I discovered that one could go into the experience of teaching "Women Artists" by being agnostic about what constituted the very concept "women artists."

Closer to home, I noted that my esteemed female colleagues at Simon's Rock mentored me as they taught courses in parallel fields such as "Women Writers," "Anthropology of Gender," "Psychology of Women," and "Women in Western Civilization." And in conversations with my art history students in the late 1980s and early 1990s, I heard their enthusiasm for such a course. Although I had always considered myself sensitive to gender inequality in my own life, I became an academic feminist only in the early years of my teaching.

Moreover, I retain some ambivalence about writing this chapter of the book on Simon's Rock. After all, the college is not a single-sex institution, and I do attempt to teach effectively both male and female students. Did I want to devote my contribution to this volume to the topic of female students' learning patterns to the exclusion of those of their male counterparts? Also I was somewhat familiar with the Carol Gilligan and Nancy Goldberger "women's ways of knowing" literature that was published in the 1980s. Today it appears to me to be an important set of questions to have asked, but one around which there is a dwindling consensus even among feminists. It appeared essentialist, too focused on the suspect premise of inherent differences that many of my intellectual generation distrusted in our counter-conviction about the "social construction" of gender. Moreover, I was concerned that a focus on "women's ways of learning" would discourage young women from pursuing certain subjects like advanced science and math and thus forfeit the opportunity to obtain the highest quality of education—too often seen as gender neutral but often masking boys' prerogative. Since then I have noted that Gilligan's writing in the last decade concerned the losses of expressiveness, of wider self-definition forced upon young boys in acquiring their masculine identities. Gender acquisition of all types requires a process of loss and limitation. Maybe Gilligan, like many recent critical scholars, has meandered from "women's studies" to "gender studies." In a related way, I hesitated teaching "Women Artists" because I want to be regarded as a scholar of more than only women's issues.

Nonetheless, I know that in both my undergraduate and graduate programs, I learned differently from my male professors than from female professors and that often the two genders approached teaching differently. And much as I may have admired and respected male professors, I formed distinctive bonds with my female professors. African American feminist bell hooks notes the value of having a course taught by a black rather than a white progressive teacher when she writes that the former would provide a distinctive "passion of experience, passion of remembrance"[6] in addressing like students.

I am aware that there are feminist art histories, or perhaps better, "feminist interventions into the histories of art."[7] But did I really want to presume that there was a feminine mode of teaching and learning art history? I know why asserting this—or even asking the question—might constitute the kiss of death for a younger female academic in a less hospitable environment. Inquiring into difference is tricky for an educational system that likes to consider itself gender-blind (and race- and class-blind too, for that matter). But as Leonard Sax retorts: "Twenty years of gender-blind education has not ameliorated gender differences in important educational outcomes; in some cases it has exacerbated them."[8] By erasing gender distinctions in the curriculum, he claims, gender socialization has intensified them, sexualizing children earlier (240). I don't want to endorse all of Sax's views, but I do wonder if there can really be a gender-blind system of education.

Might there be a way to carve out a system that positively reflects teachers' multidimensional identities, including their mothering skills, and which can draw from that set of experiences as an asset? And if we ask students to draw from the authority of their own experiences at Simon's Rock, beginning with the "Writing and Thinking Workshop" in their first week at the college, might we invite female students to think about the effect of what may be a major formative influence in their lives, namely, their relationships with their mothers?

One ongoing topic in the earlier periods discussed in the course on "Women Artists" was a focus on fathers' roles in the lives of Italian Renaissance women artists such as Lavinia Fontana (1552–1614) and Artemisia Gentileschi (1593–1651/1653). And throughout the class discussion of this theme is the historical question: why are the influences of mothers of women artists unrecorded?[9] Why indeed? As Anna, a former student who has recently earned her MFA in illustration, put it in thinking about her own artist-mother: "I also remember wishing that there were more examples in art history where a woman artist's mentor was her mother instead of her father."

Another fear of mine in teaching the course "Women Artists" was the extent to which I would find the course becoming a group therapy session, when I had been more comfortable with academic language and the principles of historical materialism. But as I quickly learned in preparing to teach the course, it wasn't necessary or even desirable to eschew academic techniques and vocabulary. Ironically, Roxann expressed a fear from the opposite end of the spectrum when she began her involvement with "Women Artists," namely, that intellectualized analyses of visual art would eclipse her own interest in art's crafting, the artist's delight in working sensual materials and colors. She entered Simon's Rock with this worry, but a video of a mother-daughter pair of artists at work (Betye and Alison Saar) helped assuage her concerns and indeed validated her relationship with her own artist-mother.

"Women Artists" was my first college level art history class. As an artist I was having personal frustration with the logistics of how art history works, such as taking a small component of an artwork and reading a huge narrative out of it. As an artist I understood that sometimes you just do things and there isn't that much meaning to it. One afternoon we watched a film about an African Ameri-

can mother and daughter who make assemblage. . . . It was a refreshing moment
to go from analyzing images . . . to actually watching the artist . . . talk about
how she just puts the red buttons along the outside because she likes the way
they look. Seeing the mother and daughter simply creating things in this film
reminded me of myself and my mother and our relationship to our art which is
completely different than a removed art historian's relationship to art.

Despite her fears, Roxann quickly became adept at scholarly language about aes-
thetics. In her senior year she produced a thesis on the topic of the simulacrum in
art, blending her interest in studio art with sophisticated art historical analyses. She
earned High Honors, the college's most prestigious grade for the year-long project.

My ambivalence about writing this article began to crumble, and I became
enthusiastic as I began to rethink the boundaries of "mentoring" and "mothering."
It is nearly impossible for me to describe moments in the classroom when I function "as a mother" as distinct from "as a teacher." I nurture my students; I support
them using a platform of concern for who they are; I also claim a particular kind of
love for them individually and as a group. As a female mentor to a class of young
women I have become aware that they might be *perceiving me* as motherly as well as
a professor and a particular kind of friend. As a mother to my own daughter (now
grown)—and as a teacher to female students—I am aware of the power imbalance
between us, but I strive to underplay its heavy-handed potential for how it can be a
tool for mutual exploration.

Now I struggle to clarify whether this study is really about some fundamental qualities that only female teachers have in their work with female students or
whether anyone can be a female-mentor in the ways I have been considering. I guess
I want it both ways: at times I believe teaching females is inherently different from
teaching males, requiring that I employ different ways of relating to them, and in
other situations I find the distinctions between the genders artificially rigid. Carol
Gilligan writes that her comments about "mothers" aren't limited to people who
are sexed female. And even Plato's definition of teaching as a kind of midwifery in
his *Symposium* addresses male teachers' assisting with the birthing of their students'
ideas. Thus I discovered the freedom for which I had been yearning in order to consider the topic. We can all function as midwives—male and female teachers alike.
Similarly, we can all be "female mentors" in the ways I describe. In the case of the
female teacher who is sexed female, there is a congruence between the "mother-
teacher" and her, but there needn't be in order for this chapter to have resonance for
a teacher who is sexed male. In other words, my interest is a mode of teaching that
is often gendered as female in our society but can in fact be practiced by anyone,
whether sexed as male or as female.

III. LOOKING AT THE ADOLESCENT FEMALE GAZE

[I]t is clear that mother-identification presents difficulties. A girl identifies
with and is expected to identify with her mother in order to attain her adult
feminine identification and learn her adult gender role. At the same time she
must be sufficiently differentiated to grow up and experience herself as a separate
individual—must overcome primary identification while maintaining and building
a secondary identification. Studies suggest that daughters in American society have
problems with differentiation from and identification with their mothers.
—NANCY J. CHODOROW, *Reproduction of Mothering* (1999 ed.), 177.

I begin class by lowering the lights and project onto the screen the provocative
photograph of Iranian-born Shirin Neshat, *Rebellious Silence*, 1994, from her *Women
of Allah* series (1993–97).[10] Students look intently as I ask what this artwork might
mean about the experience of being female. The room is warm and quiet as students' faces are bathed in the reflected light from the image.

When young women look at art, a rich set of experiences begins to occur that
take shape based on who they are—their background and interests—as well as the
art they observe.[11] I am particularly interested in the challenges I have encountered
in moving female students from experiencing visual pleasures silently to finding
their voice for its analysis. I would like to argue that girls oscillate between:

- an absorption with the image itself, a production of pleasure at a pre-verbal
  stage
- a sorting, a connection with some aspect of the image, and a recognition, one
  that evolves out of their own personal responses
- an articulation in a classroom discussion and ultimately a construction of a
  historically informed analysis.

While these may seem to be consecutive stages, I believe they are instead modes
of response that a student visits and revisits as she looks and thinks. I would like
to describe each of these in turn and then attend to the dynamics of the professor's
interaction with her female students.

1. Silent Absorption

My experience suggests that when an image is projected in the dark, students are
reacting often quite strongly–if wordlessly–to the images. The darkened classroom
grants the projected image a luminescent power that permits a physical absorption.
Film critic Laura Mulvey describes a similar physical-ocular phenomenon in the
movie theater: "the extreme contrast between the darkness in the auditorium (which

also isolates the spectators from one another) and the brilliance of the shifting patterns of light and shade on the screen." She writes that it "helps to promote the illusion of voyeuristic separation."[12] Students must work through this transition in which the physical reality of the classroom has been altered. Rather than a moment to be avoided, this silence can be valuable to their development as thinkers.

As teachers of interactive classes we might struggle to fill silences. Yet their silence can have several meanings. It can be an indicator of students' own fears about the possibility of failing to understand, of appearing un-smart or foolish or vulnerable in front of the teacher or their co-students. Or silence can have political dimensions. bell hooks writes that students of color may not feel safe in a classroom and that this contributes to their silence (39). Parker J. Palmer too notes the silence adopted by marginalized people "who have reason to fear those in power and have learned that there is safety in not speaking."[13] His claim has particular resonance for the work we do with female students who may have had to compete with male voices in the classroom or perhaps have stopped trying to compete with them, a major rationale for female education. These are real considerations for a teacher. Nonetheless, silence is also necessary for education. Palmer writes: "in authentic education, silence is treated as a trustworthy matrix for the inner work students must do, a medium for learning of the deepest sort" (80).

Similarly, I have found that girls' silence when viewing an artwork (or its simulacrum) can be a precious time in the process of bringing them to voice. At this stage young women are taking in the image, responding to its light and color, its design and texture, its composition and technical manipulation, in short, its beauty or its pathos. Art projected on a screen in a classroom can evoke visceral responses—feelings of horror and dread, bewilderment or anger, titillation or disgust. Responses might be non-verbal, and I want to argue that students return to them even as they begin to articulate what they see.

The French psychoanalyst Jacques Lacan and his followers have identified and developed the concept of the mirror stage, an early phase in human development involving seeing. Again feminist film theorist Mulvey describes briefly the business of the child in the mirror stage: "The mirror phase occurs at a time when children's physical ambitions outstrip their motor capacity, with the result that their recognition of themselves is joyous in that they imagine their mirror image to be more complete, more perfect than they experience in their own body" (17). Though strictly speaking this stage describes the child up to age eighteen months, current interpretations are that people continue to experience the mirror stage their entire lives. So it is reasonable to relate it to adolescent girls as the first pleasurable stage as they view artwork to find themselves. Following Mulvey and the significant body of visual theory she inspired, I argue that the mirror phase for girls differs from the mirror stage for boys. Important for the subject of this article is the assumption that the mother's face (or by extension the teacher's face or the image itself) can become that mirror and through her the child experiences a joyous recognition of herself.

But art need not depict faces in order to elicit the mirror stage in adolescent viewers. Abstract, figureless art too can meet a student's burgeoning identity to the extent that it is read as embodying emotion through color, line and composition. Still a human figure and particularly the female face—of a particular age, race and ethnicity—allow for more direct means of self-identification and positioning. Contemporary media, particularly advertising addressed principally to female consumers, are obsessed with the image of the female face—a historically specific phenomenon when considering the 40,000-year history of human art in which whole bodies are more typically what is represented.

In the case of the Shirin Neshat photograph there is much to fascinate pictorially. Neshat's photo combines a black and white image of an "eastern" female shown up close and wearing a *chador*. Her face is overwritten by Farsi script, and she holds a rifle whose shaft bifurcates her face. The photo is simply composed, but it is not easy to read. Students know it is a potentially explosive image that demands to be taken seriously.

2. Recognition

For an artwork to communicate to young women the visual field cannot remain a sea of inchoate forms. Young women read facets of themselves into an image projected onto a screen, an enormously complex process that is analyzable only in part. In order for young women to utilize art for their developmental needs, they must convert it, personalize it, and rework it to suit their own lives and emotional tensions. They must project themselves into it. The female student scans and rescans the picture in the classroom in search of a recognizable meaning for herself. Personalizing the material is an essential component of all successful pedagogy, but how it works is not totally mechanical, nor is it completely understood. No mere placeholder before getting on to real (read: historical) issues, student observations about what they are seeing are a crucial component of their move toward analysis.

For recognition to occur, several elements need to coalesce. In the processes suggested by the sentence "I see that," the student distinguishes herself from the subject she beholds. We know that in human development this is essential to the constituting of the self. In that short sentence, the first and last words refer to the two poles created by this binary viewing process, just as self and mother (and later "other") are created by the child as she grows. The "see" is the verb, the active process, the spark, the curiosity, or the desire that connects the viewer to the viewed.

In the case of the Shirin Neshat image, young women can project their own image and longings into the veiled face of a young woman. When they learn that the photographer was born in Iran in 1957, was educated in Los Angeles and San Francisco and that she now lives in New York City, they already share something with the artist—an American education as well as a female body. Though Neshat addresses Muslim traditions and is roughly the age of their mothers, her visual language is contemporary, as she comes in close on face and hands frontally presented to emphasize the eyes in high contrast. In part, because her face is partially hidden she can be any one of a number of women, the viewer's mother, sister, aunt, friend, cousin–or herself.

Backtracking in the lives of our students (and ourselves) to when they (and we) were very young children, we might draw from Chodorow, who describes the pleasure of a child in earliest communication with its mother (or other main caregiver), its first experience of visual pleasure and recognition. How does the fascination with looking at visual images parallel a nursing baby's fascination with her mother's face? Of course I am discussing a very different stage in human development when students are at the cusp and need to go beyond simply fulfilling parents' expectations and become more autonomous. In mid- to late-adolescence the challenge is to perceive the emotive apart from the mother's involvement, as Chodorow describes in the quotation with which I began this section. As psychotherapists, teachers, parents and some adolescents themselves are aware, there is a delicate balance between wanting to experience adult pleasures such as sex, humor, love, music as well as visual art–and their willingness to speak about or analyze them using the language of adults.

When one student offers a comment that the Shirin Neshat photo addresses both Iranian and American femininity, the class can recognize American femininity and can begin to consider similarities and differences between that and young Iranian women's lives. Projecting one's self into an artwork is a leap of faith that requires trust and safety. But without such a projection, or empathy, learning cannot take place.

3. Articulation/Analysis

Laura Mulvey claims to want to interrupt the absorptive pleasure that film-viewing affords by offering her readers another kind of pleasure—exchanging traditional definitions of visual delight for the power of reworking images in a non-sexist way. Similarly, I hope to supplement students' "pure" pleasure in looking with the pleasure of analyzing what they see. So in the sentence "I see that" another process can occur that is fundamental to art history: becoming aware of looking and articulating its dynamics. The development of students' love of looking *and* speaking is central to their development of ego and self-confidence.

Some students resist this phase of art historical analysis especially if they are more comfortable with intuitive uses of art, like the student who loves picking out tunes on a guitar but isn't interested in reading music, or the student who loves playing lacrosse but doesn't want to study exercise physiology. The discipline of art history requires that the student build upon that set of responses and articulate what she sees. Articulation of the effect of images allows for a "speaking back" to the power those images exert.

In the case of Shirin Neshat's photograph, students are very eager to discuss it. The class becomes lively, at first in the form of visual observations. We move to consider its ideological aspects. At the behest of the artist who insists that she is asking questions and not posing answers, we attempt to articulate the ambiguities in the photograph. Together we ask questions and propose tentative answers. Students want to know what life was like in Iran for young women after the revolution under Shah Ayatollah Khomenei–and now. They have heard of veiling. Some know quite a bit about it from direct experience, including students who voluntarily wear the chador on campus, which they have explained as a sign of their Muslim religious identity. This female figure has writing over her face like a veil—does the veil or the words silence her, or are they her words? Is the woman in the photo Neshat herself? Is she a feminist? What might Iranian-American feminism consist of? And is the photographer critical of Islam or supportive? Is she critical of her country or supportive? Why does a veiled woman in a photo have a rifle? What might the Iranian government think of her work? What was the U.S. position toward the Iranian Revolution? Why does the photographer not take a clearer stance about her political and religious views?

Neshat's visual language, like Barbara Kruger's thirty years before, bears resemblance to the language of fashion advertising. But Neshat focuses on a strikingly beautiful woman covered by Farsi language (the main language of Iran, spoken by about half of its population) often quoting from the poetry of Furugh Farrukhzad.[14] We move toward the conclusion that part of her work's appeal is that it borrows rhetorical conventions of contemporary fashion magazine advertising, adding global and political directions to this gendered representation that speak to some of the current interests of American students and scholars.

We consider the ambiguity of an art photo as compared to the often black-and-white positioning of politics. I encourage students to let ambiguity be, letting meaning totter between what can be known and what is unknowable. I ask them to use visual detail and historical fact to come to terms with contingency. Students grow to understand ambiguity as inherent in the complexities of history and ideology, as they move developmentally through the black and white thinking of their earlier adolescence.

The three modes of reaction that I have outlined do take place for both young men and young women. But how they are inflected for a young woman is distinctive, because silence, identification and public speaking are all fraught processes for female students. The process of young women's coming to voice is a political activity, and supporting this as their teacher is political work as well.

IV. LOOKING AT THE FEMALE PROFESSOR TEACHING GIRLS ART HISTORY

The "Women Artists" course was a small class with all female students, and our discussions were facilitated by a strong female professor who encouraged and challenged us to approach the material in ways that we could find personally and intellectually stimulating. So being in the "Women Artists" course was like being with family: my mother was the head of a four-daughter household, and she somehow managed to impart within each [of] us (all of us very different individuals) the skills needed to make meaning of our lives and chart our own paths (Lakita).

"Women Artists" was also the course that my mother enjoyed hearing about the most. Whenever I couldn't find my books for this class, I would ultimately find that my mother had stolen them for her own use (Lauren).

How do these looking and identificatory processes affect a female student's perspective on a female professor? To gain another perspective on this question I recall my own recent experience of being taught by a female teacher. I am in the campus athletic center well into my hour-long class in aerobics taught by Rebecca, a beautiful young woman whose body, I see, is strong and trim. I am one of seven middle-aged women students in the spacious, well-lit room surrounded by mirrors on three sides. She uses verbal cues to keep us unified as a group, and we watch her body lead. Well into the routine, I become aware that my eyes are glued to the instructor while I mimic her body movements. Mine are less clean and more faltering while I struggle to keep pace with her. At one point I see a curious sight: in the play of body imagery real and mirrored around me, my reflected face is transposed onto her strong and perfected body, the one I long to have as my own. Suddenly I understand. The tables are turned, and I am the female student with a deep desire to learn something personally meaningful from a female professional expert. I am stunned by the recognition of my students in myself.

It is well-known that all students long for meaningful connections with adults who are not their parents. Sax writes that research consistently shows that girls want to please teachers and follow the teacher's example, as compared with boys who are less likely to have either of these goals (80–81). He offers some conditions that encourage the bond between female teacher and female student:

> Girls are less likely [than boys] to think friendship with teachers equals geeki-
> ness. On the contrary, a girl student may actually raise her status in the eyes of
> her friends if she has a close relationship with a teacher—especially if the teacher
> is young, "cool" and female. (Sax, 85)

Meanwhile, in *The Birth of Pleasure* (2002), Carol Gilligan describes the process
by which adolescent girls develop a perspective on their mothers that involves a
split. The good mother encourages their freedom to grow and explore, indeed, to
love beyond her and beyond the family as they prioritize relationships with friends,
both romantic and platonic, in their lives. By her own example of glamour and
enjoying the pleasures of life, the good mother "allows freedom to love." The bad
mother on the other hand, curtails her daughter's freedom, warns and restrains her.
The mother's own freedom has been interrupted by the sacrifices involved with
managing marriage and family. She "embodies the cultural story: love leading to
loss, pleasure to death" (124). These two facets of adult femininity—opposing poles
constructed by the adolescent girl—are crucial, as one might expect, in the development of her own identity. Together they are the impulses necessary to "navigate" in
order to be "initiated [. . .] into being a woman in patriarchy" (124).

Thus an adolescent female's developmental needs include having interaction
with a range of feminine models beyond her mother. A female professor might
fulfill some of those needs. Extrapolating from Gilligan, I believe that a female
professor is by virtue of her position both a good female and a bad female. Although
they work together, it is the adult expert who allows girls the chance to exercise
their freedom, both personally and academically, and who sets the limits to it, as
she defines the nature of their common intellectual inquiry, and the ways in which
it will be conducted. In the end, in their interaction with a woman professor, students observe a living, breathing example of femininity that goes beyond the two
extremes of good girl-woman and bad girl-woman, leaving intact the complexity of
an identity that convention wants to reduce.

The female professor is a professional sanctioned by the mechanisms of academic power and thus serving as a representative of it. At the same time, she is
a female who permits a closer identification than a girl can establish with a male
teacher thus offering the young woman a chance to see in action several points on
the continuum of gender. A female professor can be seen as a border-crosser, someone who may wear makeup yet has achieved a measure of success in the male world
in the form of a Ph.D. and publications to her name. The professor can be seen as
a living disrupter of the very scholarly tradition she is expected to represent. More
pointedly, bell hooks writes of the ideal education that "enables transgressions—a
movement against and beyond boundaries," movement that allows education to
become "the practice of freedom."[15]

Authority is a suspect word for bright adolescents and for those who work to serve them, particularly when we are women who have had to learn to negotiate our way through the double-binds of male authority. But Palmer defines authority in an appealing way:

> Authority is granted to people who are perceived as authorizing their own words, their own actions, their own lives, rather than playing a scripted role at great remove from their own hearts. (34)

He further describes aspects of authority that are needed by students for their own growth as they allow for an exchange of personal experiences and a sharing of authority. He writes that female teachers' modeling of shared authority teaches young women to do the same:

> Authority comes as I reclaim my identity and integrity, remembering my self-hood and my sense of vocation. Then teaching can come from the depths of my own truth—and the truth of this within my students has a chance to respond in kind. (34)

Gilligan describes the trust that builds between mothers and their children, drawing from the work of her colleagues, Edward Tronick and Catherine Weinberg on babies and mothers. After a break or a separation of mother and child, trust grows when the two repair the breaks in their relationship; they are reunited and reconcile. So the female teacher or mentor can provide more opportunities for young women to reconnect not to their mothers *per se* but to another adult female who knows and cares about them. The female teacher can accompany young women into new intellectual places where their mothers may not. The greater opportunities for trust building can evolve over a semester, or over four years—and beyond. The result is that female teachers can contribute to the building of "a safe house for love" (Gilligan, 31)—or its parallel, a safe classroom for learning.

At issue here is not just trust in the classroom but trust among women over the topic of women artists, one which presumes a shared heritage that is to be understood, that is, both appreciated and critiqued. When the subject of the course is women artists one story of the course that students construct is the pathos in the struggle for female creative expression. Then the experience is even more powerful in "framing life," particularly as daughters of artists or art historians have seen these same stories, recorded in history and treasured by academia, played out in their homes as they grew up. Jackie's mother told me at Family Day her daughter's recent comments to her mother: "I am sorry, Mom. It must have been very hard for you trying to be a photographer when we were little and at home." Her mother saw that the course had encouraged in her daughter a recognition for her adult struggle, which her daughter sensed but had not yet articulated. The course helped bring Jackie to voice.

In my own life my focus on this topic could only happen now. Twenty years ago, as a single mother of a six-year-old daughter, I was still struggling with my mothering role for how it limited me from the level of achievement I felt I was capable of. I couldn't imagine ever writing about it. Instead I wanted to underplay my role as a mother in the eyes of my profession (and myself). That resentment has passed, and middle-age has brought a new appreciation and awe for the process of raising children—and educating young people. The appreciation seems to have gone both ways, as my daughter graciously wrote recently:

> My favorite part about my mom as mother and art historian is that I had the privilege to grow up with my own personal tour guide whenever I went to art museums. As a twenty-six-year-old who frequents art museums on my own now, I can still feel my mom's spirit behind me, with her hand resting reassuringly on my shoulder, whispering in my ear about the various details, dates, significances, and ways to look at different pieces. Our connection is certainly a blend of mother and daughter, nurturer and child, art educator and student, and female role model and apprentice.

In search of more spiritual values, I have watched my drive soften, the one that tyrannized me in my monomaniacal focus on critical politics (though I, like Jackie as a child, didn't recognize it then). My ebbing anger has made me a different, a calmer and more appreciative teacher. The classroom can become a place of healing of family relational conflicts for both student and teacher.

I write with new awareness of my great pleasure in my role as mother (and aunt) to young women (and young men)—pleasure in nurturing, playing, remembering and exploring together. I have deep empathy for their struggles of self-determination and financial independence, based on my own vivid experiences and informed by the newer, more complex twenty-first century stage on which this paramount work of adult identity-formation must play out.

V. TRANSFORMATIVE EDUCATION FOR TEACHERS

> Teaching always takes place at the crossroads of the personal
> and the public, and if I want to teach well, I must learn to
> stand where these opposites intersect. (Palmer, 66)

In reading over student responses to my questionnaire, I have gained insights into the ways the "Women Artists" course has affected them, insights that I hadn't had until now. The entire course is about the witnessing of bringing women of the past to voice, or perhaps more accurately, "to picturing," and often against intimidating odds. As Anastasia put it: "It was nice to learn about women in history who have made something with their lives despite the odds stacked against them." Such an orientation encourages students in the classroom to do the same—as both artists and scholars—to make their lives richly meaningful. Anna attests to this very point—that historical instances of women's creativity encourage the same in female students:

> I really wanted to learn more about women artists, because they are all too often absent from . . . art history textbooks. For me, there was also this feeling that, if a woman artist from the past was able to succeed when she was facing even worse odds than women face today, then I can certainly do my best to succeed in the art field as well.

For Anna the course about women artists of the past served to inform her own work as a visual creator in the present.

However, it is also the subject of the transformed teacher, which I want to address in this section. It's a truism in educational reform that teachers teach using multiple techniques in an attempt to reach a variety of learning styles. But the reform I am discussing goes further into being one's self more thoroughly in the classroom. Palmer writes of the necessity of focusing on the teacher in educational reform. He advocates that a teacher be an adult who is willing to use her skills in an integrated way—with intellect, of course, but also with spirit and emotion. He writes:

> [M]y ability to connect with my students, and to connect them with the subject, depends less on the methods I use than on the degree to which I know and trust my selfhood—and am willing to make it available and vulnerable [to "indifference, judgment, ridicule"] in the service of learning. (10–11; 18)

Having reached the end of this chapter I want to recall a curious aspect of the transformative education that has occurred in my years at Simon's Rock. Unlike my art historian colleagues who are to be found at larger institutions having more conventionally college-aged students and more conventional classrooms, I have watched myself evolve into a parallel figure to the mothers of my students, as they struggle to integrate their personal and academic identities in their college, family, and other communities, as I have already described. What's more, while I may be placed sociologically speaking in the role of a female mentor as well as professor to my students, I seem not to sustain a conscious awareness of that role. The model of both teaching and mothering I have experienced is perhaps an unusual one. I have rarely thought of my daughter as a baby or a child and more often as a person, granted, a younger one but a distinct person nonetheless. Similarly, for much of my in-class interaction with students, our roles, our ages, even our genders fall away. When a class is humming along in high gear, we grapple together in an absorbing, shared discussion about the fascinating process of understanding how specific pictures can elicit ideas, meaning, history and politics. When things go well, we are simply co-travelers on an exploration to figure out some questions to ask ourselves and think together about their possible answers.

I no longer fear being "motherly" in the classroom. But what exactly that means I am only beginning to grasp and in flashes. At the same time I am usually not aware of it. For the most part, I forget what age the students are, what age I am. To valorize female mentoring may be simply a means of setting up the conditions that precede the expression of our shared love of learning as we jettison from this imperfect world, in which there are inequities grounded in gender, race, and social class, to our utopian ideal.

I advocate for integrated teaching. Hearts must accompany heads in teaching as well as learning. If there are "women's ways of knowing," they are multiple and overlapping. Perhaps teachers—male and female alike—can help young women (and young men) learn by offering several alternatives. Faculty can help in the translation process for students who might need to see the value—and the power—of objective-based, factual information that is the more conventional curriculum. We can help equip students with skills to master established truths as part of the process of critiquing them. Lakita illustrates this last point admirably in her comments as she links the female body and its politics at three historical contexts—French Impressionism; American slave culture; and her own life and relationship with her mother that has evolved as she has become an adult:

> I remember a conversation with my mother that was started by the *Wet Nurse* imagery of Berthe Morisot—I was unnerved by the idea of a social hierarchy that depended on the bodies of working-class women to feed other women's children, potentially to the detriment of the families of these working-class women. I shared this feeling with my mom over the phone. For both of us, as black southern women, Morisot's work conjured up thoughts on the commodification of the bodies of black women in the Antebellum South. It also led to a really powerful insight into how my mother's decision to breastfeed me was not only out of my biological need but the need to strengthen the emotional attachment of our mother-daughter bond.

Knowing one's professional self seems to take time, decades even—perhaps an entire career. In the meantime, it has become a great life pleasure to participate in the growth of young people in body, intellect, and spirit. For me, this is female mentoring, this is mothering—and this is teaching. In response to my question-naire about art history, "Women Artists," and mothers Roxann writes:

> Sometimes I have dreams that I'm pregnant. In the dreams there is no father and I have no fears about societal issues (such as what will people think, how will I take care of this baby). I'll just know in the dream that I'm pregnant. I've been having these dreams on and off for years. My mother says these dreams are about potential, something growing inside of you until it's ready to be released.

Roxann's dream imagery suggests that young women, their mothers, and their teachers can share in the fascinating processes of birthing themselves and their creativity.

NOTES

1. This chapter is dedicated to the memory of UCLA Professor Albert Boime (1933–2008), inspiring mentor and committed activist. I want to thank my teaching colleagues at Simon's Rock who became my writing colleagues as this project developed, for their patient attentiveness to my process in thinking through this article, especially Philip Mabry, who encouraged me to follow my gut in pursuing this topic in its earliest stages. I am also grateful to our editor Nancy Yanoshak for her keen intelligence and limitless understanding in herding us cats.

2. Because our students are younger than the typical college student by a good two years, my focus on their having been mothered is perhaps less threatening to their identities as individuated people. Awareness that our students are younger means that faculty members are cognizant of their position *in loco parentis*. The college has a well-developed Student Life program. Academically, we provide more structure (and more structures) for our students than in most college programs most notably in the intensive academic advising and in the curricular supports we build into the classroom.

3. John Berger, *Ways of Seeing* (London: Penguin and BBC, 1973), chapter 3.

4. Six students responded to my questionnaire, which consisted of the following questions: 1) How have you expressed your interest in visual art and/or art history until now? 2) How was your interest in the course "Women Artists" informed by your relationship with your mother? 3) As you were growing up, how did your mother express her interest in art or art history? 4) Describe a vivid memory you have as the daughter of a female artist or art historian. Provide as much detail as you can. 5) Think back to the classroom in which you took "Women Artists." What aspects of that classroom experience evoked associations to your mother? 6) What are the associations you have between your experience of art or art history and the maternal? 7) What are your education goals and/or career thoughts? 8) What are some of your mother's attitudes

toward those goals? Your father's attitudes toward them? 9) How did the "Women Artists" course address or call out to you? 10) Other comments you might have. All of these students have given me permission via e-mail to quote or paraphrase their responses. In order to protect their privacy, I use their actual first names, but no surnames, when I refer to them. Likewise, later in the piece, I quote with permission, the mother of one of my students, and my daughter.

5. John Pease, "Professor Mom: Woman's Work in a Man's World," *Sociological Forum* 8, no. 1 (March 1993): 133–39, accessed October 22, 2010, *http://www.jstor.org/stable/684288.*

6. bell hooks, *Teaching to Transgress: Education as the Practice of Freedom* (London: Routledge, 1994), 90.

7. This is a hallmark phrase of Griselda Pollock. *Vision and Difference* (London and New York: Routledge, 1988), 1–17.

8. Leonard Sax, *Why Gender Matters: What Parents and Teachers Need to Know about the Emerging Science of Sex Differences* (New York: Broadway, 2006), 119.

9. This is an intriguing issue about which there is little information. The case of German botanical painter Maria Sibylla Merian (1647–1717) suggests that mothers might not always have been supportive (but silenced) by the nature of the writing of conventional histories. Following the death of her father and her mother's remarriage to still-life painter Jakob Marrel (1614–81), her stepfather encouraged her in her art studies "against her mother's will." Whether her mother's disapproval of her daughter's profession was a way to protect her daughter against impropriety is unclear. Merian went on to become an artist and an entomologist, entrepreneur, and traveler to the Dutch colony of Suriname in South America, who encouraged her two daughters in art. Her illustrations helped disprove the theory that insects are produced from spontaneous generation. ("Maria Sibylla Merian & Daughters: Women of Art and Science," accessed February 18, 2011, *http://www.getty.edu/art/exhibitions/merian/.*)

10. See *http://www.metmuseum.org/toah/ho/11/wai/ho_1997.129.8.htm.* Accessed October 22, 2010.

11. Art history is popularly understood to be a smooth fit with female adolescence. It isn't math, after all, and, like the other arts, it is thought to be feelings-based. In fact, the science of art history (*Kunstgeschichte*) is not grounded in feeling but in German scientific positivism. Nonetheless the field does ask for a reading of signs and symbols that utilizes skills that girls especially are encouraged to develop.

12. In contrast to "the adolescent female gaze" now under consideration, "the male gaze" is the topic of feminist film critic Laura Mulvey's 1973 essay, "Visual Pleasure and Narrative Cinema" a fascinating, now classic account of the way the human subject watches a 1940s film. She considers the gendered nature of the interaction between desiring members in the audience and fictionalized characters on the screen (Mulvey, "Visual Pleasure," in *Visual and Other Pleasures* [Bloomington: Indiana University Press, 1989], 17).

13. Parker J. Palmer, *The Courage to Teach, Exploring the Inner Landscape of a Teacher's Life* (San Francisco: John Wiley and Sons, 2007), 45.

14. Heilbrunn Timeline of Art History, Metropolitan Museum of Art, accessed October 22, 2010, *http://www.metmuseum.org/toah/ho/11/wai/ho_1997.129.8.htm*.

15. hooks, *Teaching to Transgress*, 12.

WORKS CITED

Belenky, Mary Field, Nancy Rule Goldberger, eds. *Women's Ways of Knowing*. New York: Basic Books, 1986.

Chodorow, Nancy J. *The Reproduction of Mothering*. Berkeley: University of California Press, 1979 and 1999.

Gilligan, Carol. *In a Different Voice: Psychological Theory and Women's Development*. Cambridge, MA: Harvard University Press, 1982.

———. *Birth of Pleasure*. New York: Alfred A. Knopf, 2002.

Goldberger, Nancy, et al., eds. *Knowledge, Difference and Power: Essays Inspired by Women's Ways of Knowing*. New York: Basic Books, c.1996.

hooks, bell. *Teaching to Transgress: Education as the Practice of Freedom*. London and New York: Routledge, 1994.

Mulvey, Laura. "Visual Pleasure and Narrative Cinema." In *Visual and Other Pleasures*, 13–26. Bloomington: Indiana University Press, 1989.

Palmer, Parker J. *The Courage to Teach: Exploring the Inner Landscape of a Teacher's Life*. San Francisco: John Wiley and Sons, 2007.

Pease, John. "Women's Work: Professor Mom: Woman's Work in a Man's World. *Sociological Forum* 8, no. 1 (March 1993): 133–39. Accessed October 22, 2010. *http://www.jstor.org/stable/684288*.

Pollock, Griselda. *Vision and Difference*. London and New York: Routledge, 1988.

Sax, Leonard. *Why Gender Matters: What Parents and Teachers Need to Know about the Emerging Science of Sex Differences*. New York: Broadway, 2006.

11

The Simon's Rock Dance Concert

Reflecting, Defining, and Creating Community

WENDY SHIFRIN

Simon's Rock is not merely an educational institution, it is a community. Administrators, faculty, staff and students are very aware that we bill ourselves as the nation's only residential four-year liberal arts college designed specifically for "younger scholars." This defines us as being exceptional in both the "different" and "special" connotations of that word. In addition, we are a small school in a rural area, resulting in an insulation that further contributes to our sense of being in a separate world. But our sense of self also comes from internal markers that we deem "SO Simon's Rock." These range from a unique pedagogical philosophy, to standards for interacting with each other, to reoccurring campus events that express and reinforce who we are and the values we hold dear.

One such regularly scheduled event is the dance concert which I have directed since 1984. For more than a quarter of a century, it has been an end-of-semester tradition which probably elicits the greatest amount of voluntary involvement (usually fifty to sixty students, faculty, and staff within a campus community of about 650), and as such is a mirror of how we see ourselves. The relationship established between dancers and audience is a performance of a community in which shared learning and supportive, egalitarian interactions occur. It is a mark of Simon's Rock citizenship to attend and/or participate.

> Dance has always been a big part of my life. I attended the concerts before
> I was employed here or even knew what Simon's Rock was. They are full of

imagination—originality with energetic talent. Coming to Simon's Rock was supposed to be temporary, but instead it grew on me, and part of the reason I stayed was because I could continue my love for dance and music with classes open to faculty and staff. I participated in a dance class the first year I was here. In nineteen years I have been in dance concerts and asked to be in special productions, so I feel very fortunate to be here and be included in our little community. To be in performances and have my choreographic ideas recognized and used is a wonderful thing.

—EVELYN DOUGLAS, Housekeeping Staff[1]

Neither enrollment in a dance class or having prior dance training is a prerequisite for dance concert participation. Some students do receive credit but performing is never a dance course requirement. Choreographers, comprised of faculty and staff but mainly students, recruit friends or announce their need for dancers via e-mail and posters. Participants have included faculty in math and Chinese, the registrar, women from the housekeeping staff, members of student life and counseling, and students from all disciplines and class levels. Anyone who volunteers can get involved. The concert offers the opportunity to choreograph and dance for the first time onstage, learn different styles of dance, or to continue prior dance training. The May 2008 concert, for example, included students who learned classical solos from the ballet faculty member, a group which identified itself as "science geeks" who made their own elaborate costumes and props, and three sophomores and one junior who bravely performed their modern dance in silence. Dance styles other than the Western ballet, modern, jazz and hip-hop have always made an appearance. Choreographers—often international students—have contributed Maori, Native American, African, Flamenco, Korean, Indonesian, Indian, and belly dancing, sometimes teaching neophytes these movement forms.

The concerts also involve the participation of non-dancers whose contributions are crucial to the enterprise. Student musicians accompany their peers and theater technicians get a chance to experiment with the knowledge gained in classes. Art students design the announcements and program cover. Singers, instrumentalists, lighting designers, sound and light board operators, stage managers, electricians, and videographers have the opportunity to participate in an important community event and to receive gratitude for their efforts.

The dance concert audience, consisting mainly of Simon's Rock community members, is personally acquainted with many if not most of the performers. In addition to the large number of students, attendees include parents, families, and alumni, as well as administrators, faculty, and staff. All the dances are received with applause—of varying intensity, to be sure, but always supportive in nature. Some dances elicit active audience responses in the form of loud laughter and calling out of encouragement, while others receive hushed attention. The connection between watchers and dancers is palpable.

During the week following the performance the concert is a subject of many conversations. Sometimes a dance will become part of the community lore, a story to be recounted and passed on to future generations. For example, a dance performed quite a few years ago by a male science student wearing a fluorescent skeleton costume has become legend, as has a piece in which a male student majoring in dance assembled a sandwich on stage. Another male student, renowned on campus for his juggling skills, was a popular concert participant remembered many years after he left. There have been a number of belly dancers over the years who hear the story of the first time that genre was performed by a student studying not dance, but politics and art history. These collective memories cement the notion of a community existing over time and create a culture with an ancestry.

The dance performance is also important to alumni who tend to be very loyal to Simon's Rock after they leave. Former students often come to watch and sometimes even to participate again. This allows them to sustain their identity as Rockers, a definition of which they are proud.

> As an alumna, I love returning to see dance concerts. For one, it is a way to access old friends and professors in one space. Secondly, it allows me to gaze into the ever-evolving community, seeing new people and interests of that group while not feeling like an outsider. Dance concerts have always centered around accepting any desire in the community to dance and encouraging everyone to create works of movement and music that are directly reflective of personal and group energy and interests.
>
> —JAIME SOPER, A.A., 2006

> I am really glad that I ended up being able to participate in a dance concert during my last semester at Simon's Rock. I will definitely come back to visit next semester just to see the dance concert. It is my favorite performance the school puts on.
>
> —DALE SIMMONS, A.A., 2008

Events recognized by a society to be essential and/or fundamental to its identity reflect values the group deems important. Because dance concerts at Simon's Rock present a potpourri of styles and are open to all members of the community, each performance is both a symbol and representation of one of our core beliefs: diversity is enriching and stimulating. All participants feel equally validated in a context in which difference is encouraged.

I was impressed by the variety of dances in this semester's dance concert. There was hip-hop, Latin, ballet, tango, belly dancing, flamenco, Native American and much more. It is great that each student has an opportunity to participate in the dance concert. That is what I love about the size of our school.

—DALE SIMMONS, A.A., 2008

The notion that we can all learn from each other is another cornerstone of our pedagogy and our community life. We heartily support the idea that each individual has something to contribute. It is obvious that the dancers vary in technical ability, but everyone's participation is honored. People come to the concerts in part to see what others in the community have to say.

This egalitarian philosophy creates an atmosphere of mutual respect and nurturing. Because the dance concert unifies people from various campus strata, it allows for interactions that rarely occur at larger colleges. Backstage, help is offered with hair pins and costume changes, support is given after one's piece is performed, and in the bow everyone takes together at the end, there is a sense that together something of value has been created for the community. The presence of a staff or faculty member in a dance thrills students and pleases adults because they understand roles and identities are being re-imagined. When faculty, administrators, and staff witness kids excited by what they are doing, the adults come away with positive feelings about students. Someone who may be quiet in class can be a dynamo onstage.

I started attending dance concerts because it was a good way to get a glimpse of what some of my students did when they weren't studying mathematics. Each time, I could count on seeing a couple of performances which gave me something to think about, either something very personal or something which reflected on community social life. After awhile I was recruited to participate in one dance, and since then I've come up with ideas for two others.

—WILLIAM DUNBAR, Faculty in Mathematics

[The dance concert encourages] everyone to create works of movement and music that are directly reflective of personal and group energy and interests.

—JAIME SOPER, A.A., 2006

In a supportive atmosphere it is easier to take risks and try new things. Simon's Rock encourages students to be intellectually daring. The dance concert is a venue in which innovation and experimentation are rewarded. To perform in front of an audience, particularly when the art form is as self-presentational as dance, takes and nurtures courage. In developing approaches to creative problem solving, dancers are practicing a methodology and attitude transferable to other learning situations. People taking risks onstage underscore our identity as a community dedicated to developing students who value the exploration that leads to personal growth.

Central to our educational mission is the idea that intellectual development occurs through interactive, cooperative educational experiences. In the context of our close college community, the Simon's Rock dance concerts are particularly enriching opportunities for group learning. The dancers, usually rehearsing without adult supervision, must develop an effective approach to working with others. The choreographers gain insight into teaching and leadership. The value of discipline, hard work, responsibility, and organization are made evident by the nature of the enterprise. Students experience what it is like to practice for and actualize a performance, thereby gaining insight into a real-world experience and the need to act cooperatively in order to accomplish a joint goal. Camaraderie is created between people who may not have been friends before, while inevitable interactions between people who may not like each other very much must be navigated. Frictions can arise, necessitating student negotiations and compromise. Observing the achievements and foibles of others in the same situation as oneself can teach important lessons.

The audience also experiences interactive, engaged learning and the challenges posed by intimacy with other people. The community expectation that everyone will be supportive usually results in a response geared towards appreciation rather than judgment. Learning to validate and endorse others develops abilities necessary to becoming an effective classroom discussant. There have been a number of occasions when someone screamed out a friend's name, distracting the dancers and annoying others sitting nearby. This led to discussions after the concert about appropriate behavior and the individual's responsibility to the group.

Though no official surveys have been conducted, anecdotal evidence indicates that the dance concert raises awareness of aesthetic issues:

> I found out a lot about what's involved in creating a dance performance. There's a lot of freedom to imagine movement, but constraints are introduced by the abilities of each dancer.
>
> —WILLIAM DUNBAR, Faculty in Mathematics

> Oh, the Pokemon dance! It is forever ingrained in the hearts and minds of all who witnessed such an illustrious masterpiece. This dance exemplifies what you were saying about a "bad" way of doing silly things and an amazing way of doing silly things. The Pokemon dance would definitely lie in the category of amazing.
>
> —NICOLE MYLES, A.A., 2009

For choreographers and dancers, the concert offers an experience with art that can only be achieved in its execution. The opportunity to observe talented dancers and choreographers enriches everyone's sense of the art form. Because all dance forms are given equal status in the concert, the audience encounters a variety of aesthetic approaches which it might not otherwise choose or have the opportunity to see. The frequently asked question "What WAS that dance about?" invites conversation about the relationship between form and content and teaches about personal interpretation of art.

The dance concert is not an exercise in automatic, unquestioning approval: rather it encourages critical thinking—a cornerstone of our pedagogy. Discussions often arise about dance as entertainment and dance as art. Differences of opinion about particular pieces are often aired, leading to the need to articulate and defend one's opinions. For example, some members of the community have objected to the sexualized representation of women onstage, while others are most entertained by the female as well as male music-video dances.

> I liked the dance concert this semester better than last semester's, probably because there weren't so many dances which resembled rap music videos and were offensive/objectifying. This semester there were two questionable ones: the one with a lot of dancers wearing white T-shirts, and the weird sexually explicit one. But I think the white T-shirt dance wasn't so offensive because it seemed as though the dancers were dancing with one another to have fun rather than for an audience. They didn't seem like they were showing off or trying to gain someone's approval; they seemed more playful.
>
> —MIRIAM GRIFFIN, A.A., 2009

Some adults and students have complained about obscenities in the song lyrics while others are not at all bothered by them. One year there was a verbal altercation during a performance in which a student in the audience loudly voiced a criticism about white people using African-American music. This led to a fierce discussion amongst students after the concert, and multiple campus conversations about what constitutes offensiveness, cultural ownership, and freedom of choice. Just recently, a wheelchair-bound student known as the campus poet performed a piece originally created for an academic class, "First Year Seminar," which ended with him intentionally falling to the floor as he reached for an elusive female dancer. Some in the community felt this was too painful to watch, while others argued that it was an incredibly brave performance.

Though it sometimes gives rise to conflicts of opinion, the dance concert also plays a therapeutic role on campus. It is scheduled at the end of the semester to allow for maximum rehearsal time. Thus it occurs when finals loom and papers need to be written and graded. However, rather than contributing to people's stress levels, it tends to function as an emotional outlet and a morale booster for everyone involved. It offers a welcomed relief from an intense academic focus and the pressure of finals. Even if just for a few hours, the concert creates an atmosphere of appreciation for one's presence in a community that can produce such energy and inventiveness.

> [The dance concert] is a forum for creative expression and different styles of dance, but more importantly it is a time for everyone to have a ridiculously fun experience. It is a time for everyone to emerge from social microcosm and come together as a community.
>
> —ALEXA WEISS, A.A., 2009

> [The dance concert] is extremely charismatic and endearing and amazing, and I think everyone, the people who are in it and the people who watch, really, really need something like this at this point of the semester.
>
> —NICOLE MYLES, A.A., 2009

While the ongoing existence of the dance concert is a cornerstone of community continuity, it is also a forum for reflecting changes in the world at large. Ten years ago, all of the choreography was original, whereas today students often replicate dances they have seen on music videos. The Pokemon dance, mentioned above, was performed by seniors who assumed an audience familiarity with this element of youth culture. A dance based on "The Lion King" with a Resident Dorm Director playing the Lion was another reflection of the context in which students grew up. Popular culture is also reflected, of course, in the choice of music and the development in dance styles. Dances with political themes are less common, but they do occur. For example, one student who would go on in her senior year to write a thesis on sustainable agriculture did a dance as a sophomore about garbage and waste. Thus the dance concert connects the community to the outside world and helps us to feel we are informed about the latest fads and events.

There are many reasons people participate in or attend dance concerts at Simon's Rock. For performers it can be a way to share themselves with others, seek approval, entertain, learn something new, earn class credit, do something non-academic, engage in the creative process, or explore their personal artistic voice. The audience comes to see people they know and to have fun, but also because it is an important event on campus that is not to be missed. But whether or not performers and audience are consciously aware of it, the dance concert is an institution which helps to define, inspire, and reflect Simon's Rock as a community.

In many ways the Simon's Rock dance concert captures the overall spirit and energy of the college. The institution is marked by this large impact event; because of this the concert is as funny as it is a true marker of students' interests and initiative. Every semester the dance concert begins as an exercise of individual confidence and ends with a community. There is no comparable space on campus that allows for the open-ended showing of commitment.

—JAIME SOPER, A.A., 2006

NOTE

1. Comments were solicited from community members and alumni in the spring of 2008. They responded via e-mail, all giving me permission to quote them by name. Students identified by name in Figures 1–6, also e-mailed me permission to include photographs of their dance concert participation. I thank all of these people for their help. I am grateful as well to the parent of one student who was under eighteen, who also gave her consent to use the image of her son. All photographs were taken by my husband, Steven Moritz, and are reproduced with his permission.

IMAGES FROM RECENT DANCE CONCERTS

FIGURE 1. "Annie" (Annie Macrae-Rosenberg). Property of Steven Moritz. 12/2009. Reproduced with permission.

FIGURE 2. "Tatiana" (Tatiana Kaptan). Propery of Steven Moritz. 12/2009, Reproduced with permission.

FIGURE 3. "Christian" (Christian Hopkins). Property of Steven Moritz. 12/2009. Reproduced with permission.

FIGURE 4. "Mel and Kevin" (Melissa Chavarria and Kevin Hu). Property of Steven Moritz. 12/2009. Reproduced with permission.

FIGURE 5. "Sam and Ekiwah" (Sam Scott and Ekiwah Adler-Belendez). Property of Steven Moritz. 5/2007. Reproduced with permission.

FIGURE 6. "Trio in Silhouette." Property of Steven Moritz. 5/2007. Reproduced with permission.

12

At Home with Uncanny Labors

A Case of Working and Thinking the Social Sciences

Collaborators: ASMA ABBAS, NUOLA AKINDE,
NOAH APPELBAUM, ELS BAUM, LAURA CHEUNG,
BRENDAN FLYNN, DARA LEVY-BERNSTEIN, DYLAN NEELY,
ANASTASIA RODIONOVA, EMANUEL STULTS

INTRODUCTION

This essay was written by the faculty and students of the Proseminar in Social Scientific Inquiry over the course of several months, beginning in December 2008, in an effort to emblematise and examine the experience of participating in a social science classroom at Simon's Rock, with special reference to the Proseminar theme of "Home and the Haunts of Modernity."[1] This collaboration between students and professor—a fellowship that serves (and not without difficulty) at once as the zero-level production of this article while also influencing and, indeed, orienting our discussion of the politics and pedagogy of a classroom in the social sciences—is the central motif of this piece. This motif is rendered experientially rather than in a functional or analytic manner, in an effort to channel the commingling of form and content, process and product. We have avoided serving the experience up as fodder for the kind of social scientific inquiry that is too quick to separate its epistemic goals from its ontic material. The Proseminar's emphasis on form and method comes from the wish to attune us to the unspoken cruelties of misrecognition and invisibility that prevail in an academic, social, and political world too focused on the correctness and, worse, righteousness of its boundaries, content, and commitments. This pertains to our enterprises of knowledge as well as to our experience of belonging, cohabiting, laboring, *with* others; we attempt here to speak to the overlaps and intersections of these worlds.

The essay recollects how this program allowed for the collaborative consideration and examination of community, home, relationships, and foundations as crucial tenets of the Simon's Rock experience itself. We are possibly hopelessly self-indulgent here: in not compiling the disciplinary lessons we learned about social science inquiry, the essay focuses on our everyday interactions and endeavors that prioritized the aesthetic, ethical, and political integrity of our work as worldly social scientists over an instrumental accumulation of knowledge via utilitarian encounters. Thus, we hope that in witnessing, working with, and perhaps being baffled by, our performance of a peculiar set of relations to the spaces and acts of knowing in this narrative, the reader will thwart old lines of questioning where they are most tempting, suspend tried and tested forms in which to fit the content of our musings, and, for some time, be, feel and wonder—*with* us.

Sections of text in italics indicate quotations from the students and faculty in the pilot year that begged to be separated from the rest of the coauthored text. However, since all of us are coauthors, we have decided not to identify individual voices. The multivocal effect—both in the sense of multiple distinct "italicized" voices where needed (the quote will make clear if the voice is a student's or a professor's), as well as the harmonic voices that are not parsed out for the reader in normal text—is intentional, and hopefully indexes a facet of the collaboration that we enact here. The decision not to attribute quotes to specific individuals reflects the aspirational spirit of the class as it worked to speak together, however successful (or not) that voice may be. Our efforts to rethink authorial presence are connected to our overtures to intellectual intimacy and community, their fates connected in our collaborative authorship. We seek experimentally to document the labors and processes of creating and existing in a democratic intellectual community that we have found cannot be presumed or postulated in advance but can only be achieved by working to articulate its very meaning. What follows is product and process of that labor.

HOMECOMINGS: MEET THE PROSEMINAR AND THE COLLABORATORS

The ideal of a collaborative learning community is certainly not a new one, and not one limited to those of us who commit to it at Simon's Rock. However, attention to the constitutive elements of "the collaborative"—to "presence" as both a condition of and a quest for these labors—may illuminate how this concept is not a distant inspiration but one that is struggled with every day in this and every community. When we speak of working together, then, it is important to investigate the nature of this work, the relations within which these labors happen and the relations this work enables. With this in mind, then, any analysis of pedagogy, inquiry, and learning has to contend with collaboration as a premise of these rather than a consequence or accoutrement.

This essay narrates our experience in the Proseminar in Social Scientific Inquiry, the academic component of the Junior Fellows Program, a Signature Program designed for pre-thesis juniors by combining two conceits that have long defined Simon's Rock: engaging younger scholars in social issues and generating new kinds of educational experiences. Housed in the Social Sciences and directed in its pilot year by a faculty member in Politics and Philosophy, the program attempted a collaborative undertaking by re-imagining and re-tooling a social science classroom: focusing on the close connection between modes of inquiry and knowledge and the modes of relating to others in a shared space that could ultimately contribute to rethinking the social scientific enterprise. Through intellectual exchanges with social scientists and interdisciplinary scholars in a variety of settings, Junior Fellows became acquainted with professional standards for scholarly work as practiced by their own teachers and by an array of guest lecturers and workshop leaders.

A two-semester sequence, the Junior Fellows Program was designed to consist of a series of regular class meetings of the Proseminar, engagements with invited scholars, working dinners, symposia, trips to regional events and institutes, independent scholarship, student colloquia, and collaborative work. Throughout, participants would think and write collaboratively, expansively, and rigorously, honing their methodological and research skills, as they also contemplated post-baccalaureate life: working through the year to find their own voice for public scholarship and engagement and to appreciate (and in some cases rehearse for) professional demands of their aspirational academic disciplines.

In its first semester, the Program hosted seven guests, and in the rest of its sessions, worked in-house on students' own projects and attended an academic conference in Boston. In the second semester, the students themselves became the guests, with every class dedicated to a single student sharing her work in a colloquium. The pages that follow give a brief outline of the Proseminar, detail some of its key mechanics, and reminisce on important moments from its first year, with observations on how we attempted to work and think the social sciences together, where we took important risks, where we failed and succeeded in the goals of collaboration, and what ethical and political questions were inspired. This essay is co-authored by the Junior Fellows who were in residence for both semesters of the 2008–09 Proseminar, and the Program Director (who also corralled and navigated this production).

With the pilot theme, "Home and the Haunts of Modernity," as our locus, we trace how this theme and its material unfolding throughout the year—in the spaces it was able to carve out and the interactions with thought and writing it enabled—reflect an uncanny convergence of topic, method and quest that involved students and faculty alike in uniquely intimate and risky, furtive and trusting, public yet particular, permissive yet responsible, generous yet guarded, moments of learning and relating. Collectively and collaboratively, we constructed a space as fraught and as welcoming as home. At the same time we grappled with the very idea and work of home. We questioned home's comforts and tyrannies, and interrogated the complex notions of safety, domesticity, nurturance, hospitality, and territoriality that come with it. Both inside and outside the classroom, the Proseminar enacted a form of engagement and an intimate navigation of relations and spaces, of power and sentiment, which illuminated the problematic of "home" in its many manifestations at many levels, and especially as it crystallizes the defining challenges and aspirations of a learning community like Simon's Rock.

WHAT DOES IT MEAN TO STUDY ONE'S HOME?

The theme for our first Junior Fellows Program was "home" as trope, element, and object of social scientific inquiry. Whether in its resonance with notions of origins, dwelling, foundations, constructions, stability, etc., metaphors and valences of home are numerous, and inhabit some of the most basic presumptions of, and most visceral challenges to, our desires and our struggles in this world.

"Home" is a canny and, in many ways, an organic concept that figures at once in the epistemological and ontological concerns of our disciplines. It was chosen as the inaugural theme for its merits as a topic to which we could reach out from our diverse pedagogical and scholarly habitats. To excerpt from the Proseminar brochure:

> Home lingers overtly or covertly in the quests of scholars and students all across the humanities and the social sciences. Home is the *oikos* that forms the root of the words economics and ecology, and is in the *nostos* that infects literary, philosophical, artistic, political endeavors. It is the *heimat* that can be home only to some, and the real or imagined community—or nation—for which we fight. Is home something we are of or something we are from, is it our source or our origin, is it something we came from or something we are going to? Do we build the homes others live in or do we live in homes others build? Does the state determine who lives with me in my home, and do I decide when I can leave it? Is home a right or a privilege and how must it be distributed? Home is the walls I want to break down, and then at the same time is the room of my own I want. Home is the locale in local politics, and it is in nature in its purity or its

construction. When we want a house that can include everyone, and when we want to destroy the master's house in which we have been forced inhabitants; when what we call "home" sometimes threatens us to seek refuge and when home is what cannot contain our madness and banishes us to an asylum; as we seek foundations and justifications for truth and as we commit to questioning the foundations of truth; as we fight for privacy and as we resist domestication; as we make domestic violence political and as we struggle to keep "politics" out of our bedrooms; we are addressing the myriad spirits of home.

Fellows were invited to bring their own pursuits, interests and proclivities to bear on it in direct or indirect ways, collaboratively articulating and responding to questions in engagement with speakers and with texts.[2] We responded to this invitation to dwell with each other in these plural yet integrated haunts. In our work throughout the year, we pushed this promise further. We considered not only *what* home is, but also *how* it is insinuated in our methodological and formal investments, at work and in everyday life, as part of broader trajectories of thought and practice or as dissidents from them.

We came to the topic of home as object of critical inquiry, both personal and distant, and sought to explore explicit and implicit attachments to it as a notion and an actual place, as a part of our intellectual and experiential comportments. Home provided an arena of inquiry as well as a sort of common point of entry, regardless of the specific tools each of us had from our own peculiar academic enclaves at Simon's Rock. For us, home became a method for exploring the relation between where we come from, how we engage with the world, and where we can find ourselves in it. It is difficult to explain what the trope of home became for us other than to say that we began to unsettle our own selves, pushing back against the concept that we had never before critically examined in any deep way. Somehow, rather than render us all suddenly homeless, this allowed for a different kind of space to be opened up in the classroom, which we want to try to characterize in this essay. *The knowledge that we were all working on our own separate projects (which were somewhat related to the theme of the class but not dependent on it) worked with the theme itself to foster an atmosphere in which we felt that we could relate to each other not just as fellow students, but as those calling to each other in different ways.*[3]

THE STORY GOES …

Coming into the class, I had no idea what to expect from the Proseminar. I knew that there would presumably be some outside speakers, that presumably we would each have an individual research project to work on; and I knew the people who were going to be in the class (many of whom I was already on good terms with). Beyond that, my guess was as good as anyone's. How could I have known that Proseminar would become something more than an average class at Simon's Rock, even beyond the fact that it was "edgy" to allow students to conduct class with esteemed professors from other universities? My goals for the semester started off relatively simple: as I wrote in my letter of application, "I hope to achieve a kind of synergy of understanding through the process of the Proseminar, bringing together different points of view to more thoroughly understand the seminar theme of "Home and the Haunts of Modernity." I quickly discovered, however, that "Home" was not so easily teased out of obscurity, and that my original plan of interdisciplinarity alone was going nowhere fast. It seemed like every class our guest for the day would ask us what we each meant by home, and each class everyone had a different answer. I think the Proseminar itself, more than any one text we read or speaker we heard, complicated the issue of home for us, as Proseminar became a sort of home to us all, complete with "family dinners" and the fact that we all behaved differently when there was a "guest" in our home. I think we all felt this to some degree or another during class, but to what extent we articulated it then leaves some conversation to be desired.

Haunting proved to be an apt trope, both for study, and for representing the Proseminar, for home seems to be, by its very nature, haunting and haunted. When at home, we can usually not speak of it in a critical and reflexive way. When not at home, it is an abstract and distant mixture of images and impressions. In common understanding, home as a place of origin or comfort seems inarguable; most of us associate it with childhood, safety, comfort, and fixity. However, the moment home becomes a "haunt"—metaphorically, politically, philosophically—it is a much more elusive location and reality, asking for a different locution that revisits the very notions of comfort, origin, desire and destination. This haunting of home begins the moment we realize that perhaps it is not what it has seemed or what we have wanted it to be. At that moment and from then on, we are both haunted by our homes, individual and shared, and haunted by our difficulty in grasping home.

In the Proseminar, this haunting prevailed, exposing how so much of the enterprise of knowing and being that carries the social as at least a nominal ontological and methodological commitment, tackles the perpetual intermingling of presence and absence, the familiar and unfamiliar, self and other, attachment and repulsion, and possessing and yielding.

Throughout the class, we were haunted by haunting itself; by our inability to grasp or make present things that hovered with this newly unsettled relationship with home. By literally dwelling in "home" as a subject and an object, we dislocated our sense of home even as we tried to examine it. But haunting as a subject as well as object provided no such home either. However, the two notions together, haunting coupled with home, opened a space of inquiry that home alone could not.

We began away from home, at the American Political Science Association conference in Boston, in order to connect us with and incorporate us into a larger academic community before creating our own space. Students travelled and lived together and negotiated with the complexities of a professional convention. We got the chance to interact closely with a group of thinkers from myriad disciplines, levels of intellectual radicalism, theoretical or pragmatic focuses, and both formal and informal demeanors.

After we returned to campus from APSA, we met in our assigned classroom, a wide room with many wicker chairs, two green chalkboards, oddly-angled ceilings, and views of our library and the surrounding woods of our campus. Most social science classes at Simon's Rock take place in rooms of this design. Since we had envisioned a different incubating space for our Proseminar, we romped around campus in search of a more inviting environment; however, a space with the personality of a home and the unsettled feeling we hoped to explore in it was not quick in coming. We whirled through discussion spaces, administrative spaces, cramped and stuffy spaces, inviting spaces, and house-like spaces, before we together made the decision to use the original classroom for our default meeting space and the dining room at Blodgett House[4] for meals. We wanted to occupy comfortable spaces— pleasant, conducive to discussion, uplifting—places to bring us together, to ground us. At times we were haunted by sterile spaces, dim and discouraging, that disrupted whatever cohesiveness we managed to muster as the Proseminar class. One of our favorite moments came one day when a chance meeting in the College Centre brought us to a Kafkaesque encounter with so many doors that led us to believe that more than exposed, insulated, attic spaces lay behind them.[5]

Our first class meeting was devoted explicitly to haunts and haunting in our individual academic inquiries. We each shared a scholarly text that we admired, and another text, of any genre, that we felt haunted by. *The admired text was required to encourage students to think about things that they do like instead of things that they don't, because our students (and to be honest, we faculty as well) spend so much of our time at Simon's Rock in a mode of negation, criticism, and objection as a mark of creativity and independence. The haunting text was assigned with the aim of collectively setting up the premises of our work to come: by working with something as elusive and so lexically unspecific as haunting, we might push the boundaries on the possibilities of material knowledge.* Our experiences of the word itself, and of objects associated with that sentiment, created a fairly intimate starting point; instead of working from a definition clearly specified and shared, these more diverse experiences were expected to lead us to a sense of haunting itself that would be collectively iterated through this exercise. Among the haunting texts were excerpts from Alan Moore's *Watchmen*, Edwidge Danticat's *Krik? Krak!* Aleksander Hemon's *Nowhere Man*, Gadi Taub's *The Dispirited Rebellion*, Tennessee Williams's *The Glass Menagerie*, and *The Anarchist Yearbook*. This exercise allowed us to find ways of relating to texts without feeling obligated to possess them in any way. This distance allowed for a different perspective on "text" from the usual need to summarize, analyze, and consume for the sake of reproduction. We determined that haunting creates a home in the text itself; freeing us up to really soak in it and walk around in it without rushing to a particular kind of instrumental momentum or consequential action. By imagining these texts as haunting, we found a different mode in which to frame our projects.

Every class was documented so that students were free to be in the moment with the knowledge that they would be able to go back to those moments for clarification, something I had tried in many of my other courses; here it seemed particularly pertinent, given the degree to which a "shared text" was to be produced in the interactions rather than posited as their premise. We decided we would record ourselves in discussion on tape, with the audio files available to us all, because it became important for us to witness someone articulating her own work to others and being in the moment rather than dividing our attention between our notes and our classmates. This made the start auspicious: anticipating five seniors and six juniors sharing their sense of their own processes and progress with different things to learn.

In the first semester, we met once a week for a three-hour afternoon session. The speakers brought to campus in conjunction with the Proseminar directed seven of our classes. For the fall 2008 semester, the speakers were professors David Adams, Adolph Reed, Chris Russill, June Nash, Anaele Iroh, Susan Jones, and Leela Gandhi. As we discuss our guests below, we try to illuminate those aspects of our interactions with them that inspired us to ask questions about the purpose and method of intellectual inquiry "as if our hearts and lives were at stake!" rather than see them as objects of cold analysis or sources of conventional knowledge to fill old containers. To prepare for their visits, we read selections from the guest scholars' work. In class we had a chance to question them about their writing, certain intricacies or intriguing aspects of their work, their careers, their inspirations, and even their experience of Simon's Rock. Each speaker was hosted by one or two Fellows. The host(s) were given the responsibility of publicizing the lecture, eating lunch with the guest in the Dining Hall, and generally taking care of the guest and his or her needs for the time spent on campus, though in practice, a number of the class's members were always happy and excited to eat lunch with the guest and everyone was available to help if need be, making the hosting duties largely symbolic.

Before the class began, some of us were worried about the speakers—would there be pretensions and intellectual formalities? Would we be looked down upon for being younger scholars? With David Adams as our first speaker we were given a really good start to the semester. His openness and willingness to listen, his lack of judgment coupled with amity towards us, as students and as youngsters, was encouraging and we simply gave him what we expected back in terms of conversation and openness. His work on colonial literature and its metaphysical preoccupations offers to frame the Western search for God and knowledge, for science and conquest, as a search for home inscribed within colonialism. Adams' work is replete with his own sense of haunting and home, particularly as regards the ways in which literature contains, complicates, and tries to resolve both.

Our second speaker of the semester was Adolph Reed, an active leader of the United States Labor Party and a prominent progressive voice. Reed engaged with the legacy of W. E. B. Du Bois to shed light on the conundrums of theory and practice faced by African-American politics in contemporary America. It was this week that the value of the Proseminar participants eating a casual dinner with the speaker asserted itself; only during the more casual dinner were students able to really ask questions of Adolph and the casual nature of the conversation gave him license to indulge in much more interesting and controversial thought than that of the class period. Not only was the "family dinner" portion of the Proseminar useful time for getting guests to open up with us and relax in a setting dissociated from the professorial obligations of the classroom, it actually taught us something about what goes into making something home: the material accoutrements, the literal and edible provisions, the time, the accommodation, the looking out for each others' needs and ticks that fill the spaces that are so easily assumed or taken for granted.

Our next guest was Christopher Russill, whose studies are centered around the fields of Environmental Communications and the Media. The discussion was wide-ranging, focusing on the question of home with regards to how we treat our environment. In terms of the reified relation the West, and especially the United States, has to the spatial and proprietary notion of home, a turn to government policies and procedures was really eye-opening for more concretely locating the conversation about home. Especially in the context of disasters, which Russill has studied, we talked about "bad" neighborhoods and "broken windows," the charge of cleaning up unsafe neighborhoods and being done with those distraught spaces ridden with crime and poverty, reminiscent of Reed's caution against the contrived superficialities of urban life and demands of security: where home, so to speak, is only skin deep!

Our fourth speaker, June Nash, lives in the Berkshire region and is a renowned anthropologist. She spoke to us about where we live, about the history of what she calls her own home, and the homes of others she has inhabited as an "activist-anthropologist." This led us into an experience with an "artist-anthropologist," Anaele (Adis) Iroh, whose work on immigrant communities and their everyday practices of building homes in situations of virtual internment brought in a necessarily global view on the dynamic of homebuilding for refugees, synchronising contemporary theory and installation art. Dealing with similar issues of home and displacement, although dealing with them in an opposite way, was Susan Jones, a practicing lawyer and advocate. Her work with microfinance and social entrepreneurship read its subjects in a very different way from Adis, giving us an insight into the pragmatic challenges of giving people homes they can live in.

The final speaker of the semester was Leela Gandhi. To end a seminar on haunting and home with someone so unquestionably present and available was quite a treat, almost soothing, bringing us to a different home than we had imagined having left. From the moment she arrived, while eating lunch, walking to take a smoke break, in class, at dinner, during her lecture, all of these moments felt equally privileged to her being herself, which made each part of the day feel a lot more meaningful to some of us. This offered a contiguous learning experience that added up to more than the sum of its parts, emphatically making a statement that one's way of moving in the world is inseparable from claiming it as home (something we had dealt with earlier in the term in confronting Descartes, Susan Bordo, and our own Samuel Ruhmkorff[6] as an in-house guest lecturer).

Outside guests continually reaffirmed the Proseminar goal: to connect us with and incorporate us into a larger academic community. In those moments where the limited time kept us wanting for more, we had to contend with yet another quirk of home—that this was always a place someone could return to! However, such revelations were not always available, especially in those moments where we were left wanting something more self-reflexive and almost more vulnerable on the part of our guests. Maybe we wanted them to become our friends right away, and to be "honest." *We now wonder how brutal that demand could have been, and how completely rooted in our experience at Simon's Rock it was—given how secure we seem in unrelenting exposure to ourselves and each other, whether or not we want it to be that way. This has not been a small realization, given how taxing this burden of constant giving of oneself is to many of us. Ultimately, it was beneficial for us to be checked in our ceaseless demands for more of oneself and the other, and at the same time to be goaded into new forms of engagement, sharing and relationships.*

This ethos was honed further during our semester of student colloquia, where students were required to present their works at different stages of completion and seek others' input. For many students whose independent projects were struggling with completions and containments, it provided a certain way of thinking about integrity in the process that allowed for the product to be more easily completed, parted with, and shared.

I think the most important form of development for me was coming to terms with the ways in which a topic makes itself clear to you. This project of mine now looks incredibly different from how it once did. Before, I was incapable of writing anything other than fractured sections, all of which use different narrative voices and which seemed irreconcilable. Only recently have I realized how I can stitch them together; using the theme of home I can use an exploration of the trope of home in history: what is it to remove something from its historical home?

WHAT SOCIAL SCIENCE CLASSROOM?

So what is the role of a social science classroom, particularly one devoted to the methodology of social sciences, given the reality of our education system? Our concerns, in attempting to create a truly radical educational space, should be the same as those of our discipline—questions of power, social organization and authority. The point of the class should not only be to examine these terms in relevant worldly contexts, but to look at what happens at home, the ways in which, for instance, the class itself sculpts authority and power. *It is quite a different undertaking to examine questions about authority and power in a conventional classroom where the asymmetry of visible authority and power is deemed to be on the teacher's side (even if it may not be), than it is to study them from the lens of a presumably democratic one (where many visible modes of authority are given up by the teacher, but where many acknowledged and unacknowledged forms of power asymmetries swirl around, not always privileging the teacher).* In a sense what needs to be done is to turn the social sciences in on themselves; we must not only point out power structures, and discuss ideas of equality and democracy, but also see how inexhaustive many of these analytics are, and how much harder it is to acknowledge unseen power enacted within a learning environment, let alone make it part of social inquiry. This endeavor requires a level of complexity and collaboration that is rarely present in a classroom even at Simon's Rock.

I see our time together in Proseminar as an experiment in this kind of learning and studying, the beginning of a journey, of figuring out together how to build a space such as the one we have described. We were without pretenses that this was some ideal endeavor, untainted by the power dynamics—in our college and by the unkemptness of the world of which it is part—that continually bring into relief the tension between liberal claims to equality and liberty on the one hand, and democratic notions of self-governance and community on the other. *The classroom became a space in which to cope. We became a community, not in the sense that we needed some deep-seeded emotional support (although many of us play that part in each other's lives, and being a part of Proseminar has brought some of us closer together) but rather that in light of all of the difficulties ahead of us we needed a space in which to work together. We did not assume that we had, a priori, some beautiful and idealized classroom space, but we actually needed to create it, to make a place for ourselves in which we could do the kind of work we wanted. What has felt remarkable for me about our time together this semester is how productive it has been. When discussing texts we almost always seemed to be engaging with each other, not simply with what we had read. While not every class with the visiting professors went as we had expected or wished, the overall feeling was that we had invited in collaborators, people who would work with us on our project of examining ideas of home, and of creating a kind of intellectual home for ourselves.* The role of the professor departed from what might be expected in a classroom with a greater emphasis on content rather than method. Even so, her role was not as navigator, facilitator, or mediator within known or unknown territory, but as perhaps a conductor of our peculiar ensemble of impulses, capacities and interests with gestures, ruptures, and inflections that refreshed our pursuits. In a way, these directorial interventions, as haunting as they were in their figurality (their suggestive sensory materiality, their expressive potential), were firmly beholden to relations that brought an intellectual community into being through the coexistence of desire and lack, image and matter, tactic and feeling, certainty and suspension, in our work as social scientists. As someone herself engaged in an intellectual enterprise that also begged to be translated into the tropes the Proseminar was built around, the professor ceased to be merely a director on the outside of the dynamics that shaped our own work in the classroom—she, like the students, was an actor and contributor. This insiderness was certainly complicated by her institutional role, rendering her absence and presence much more interwoven, perhaps enabling a valuably different embodiment as a social science professor.

Straddling the line between the outside and the inside of our shared space, she spoke, whenever appropriate, with the same voice as the students or as a voice that reflected and deflected ours en route to deeper engagement; the teacher ceased to be solely a figure of judgment or the lone locus of knowledge, obviating her role as someone whom students would need to impress or tread carefully around.

A catalyzing moment for us was when {the professor} had to leave the country at the last minute, and was gone for two weeks. It seemed natural to us that we would need to meet—there were logistical matters to deal with, related to our guests and to our work, and we couldn't just neglect these things. Ultimately we decided to use much of our time together to bring our work to each other for peer input and review (what goes by the verb "workshop" around here), since our course schedule had been rearranged. The space that we created, in the absence of any immediate authority figure (as much as the professor had positioned herself as a very different kind of non-authoritative figure), was by far the most productive workshopping environment I have ever been a part of. For once, it felt as though I was having an actual conversation with other students about their work, that they were genuinely sharing, and that the rest of us were seriously engaging with their thinking and writing. Having this conversation about my own thesis work was pretty incredible. There was something very natural and unforced about our interactions.

We met several times while our professor was away, mostly working on our own. One of these times another student walked by our classroom, looked around, and did a double take. It was clear that he had noticed the lack of professor in the classroom. He looked a little confused. It was not until that moment that it occurred to us that we had been up to something unusual, when it was really only an extension of our normal practice. We had become a community, a group of people focused on one another and on the space that we were working to create. With our primary focus on collectivity, the absence of the professor left us lacking a collaborator, perhaps a conductor, but not a point of reference. So when she was gone we were still able to continue our work, and to be a functional intellectual community.

The Proseminar felt, with its flaws and inconsistencies, like a purposeful community with a strong support system in place. Everything we did together, the way that we incorporated these personal everyday activities into our work as a class, made it feel like a home. We did routine, mundane things together. It demonstrated for us that learning does not happen in isolated classrooms but rather between people who have relationships with one another.

Openness in the classroom is something we frequently talk about at Simon's Rock, but this has in all these years helped me become closer to nothing other than myself in a conversation. *This year, I know that in my personal life I tried harder to assume nothing, to not project myself further than was necessary, and I know that this desire was also present in the attitude in the classroom. At the moment, this seems to me to be a better step in my personal development (academic or otherwise—the more these things are intertwined the more I think I grow—if I can respect people the same way throughout all areas of my life and that is surely better) although I suppose it is hard to know really when one is doing "better."*

Looking back at this class, what strikes us the most is how we spoke to each other. *In no other class did I feel as respected or listened to as I did in the Proseminar, but it was not just about whether or not I was heard; I also participated more than I have elsewhere. For me Proseminar was home in as much as it was a genuine space. It felt to me like we had left our pretensions behind and were functioning in the space not just as ourselves but also relative to each other, by which I mean that we were aware of each other in different ways than in any other class. There was no sense of competition or need to impress, and I think the fact that the class focused on a theme and was not about a specific subject as it is in a normal classroom, meant we could all approach it more openly. While in other classes we do attempt to acknowledge that we do not know everything about the subject at hand, it is in the Proseminar that I felt most comfortable admitting a lack in knowledge and having that be part of the process of learning.*

CENTRIFUGAL HOMES

How do we build, enrich, enact, and problematize this community without legislating behavior in it, in accordance with mutually shared and assumed notions of morality and politics? One way for teachers and students to broach this question is through allowing our idiosyncratic intellectual pursuits to translate into our desires for the kind of community that perhaps lies at the core of all inquiry. *Or perhaps that is a conceit only those of us committed to the social (human!) sciences—asking in different ways the age-old question of the possibility, wonder, form, perplexity, possibility of the human community—have to deal with on a regular basis, as we attend to our own relations to disciplinary and subtler powers, finding Simon's Rock the place that compels with the possibility of having a role in building and determining the community we live in, the spaces we fill, the relations we labor on, and ultimately the homes we inhabit, sometimes successfully, sometimes not so much.*

There were things we learned that went beyond studying home as part of our method rather than only as an object of inquiry. This involved conceiving of the space constructed in the Proseminar classroom as one not limited to it. Once the classroom is thought of as a space of comfort that does not quell questions and presumptions about community, but instead raises, and, hopefully, confronts them, we are invited to think about the problems with and the demands of home at many levels. There is no sure-fire way of telling who answered this invitation and in what way. However, we examined—sometimes not with the most comforting and reassuring results—mechanics of relationships, questions of obligations, the labors that collaboration consists of and how these are divided, where the reaches and the desires for home are at odds with those who are in it, and how questions of power and authority almost never take the paths one sees them limited to, even in a conventional classroom.

Not every student took unquestioningly and positively to this kind of critical humanistic inquiry into our own selves, privileges and assumptions. While some were led to regret the distractions from the concrete goals of the course caused by my investments and attachments as a teacher that wanted us to confront the unspoken power dynamics, entitlements, and hierarchies of labor in the classroom, others found a different strength and optimism in those same sorts of humanity and fragility, whether it came from me or fellow students. The aim, in some ways, was to expose that the act of working together, if indulged to its fullness, will, after managing some of the hurdles, raise more, harder, questions. What options and choices do we have when it comes to wanting to build together with someone? How do the communities we build extend beyond questions of tolerating dissent to addressing the irreconcilable differences in depth and investment?

Are any deeper reconciliations possible on the basis of something other than the scripted demands of contemporary education? How do we confront the human and the personal at the same time? We feel that questions of visibility and invisibility cannot be limited to just the ability and right to speak and hear as homogeneous beings—as this is a foregone assumption at least in a space as consciously liberal and progressive as Simon's Rock—but raise issues of obligation: of whom and what we are obligated to, and of how we are obligated, when education is an emotional labor that some will shirk, and others will embrace.

EPILOGUE

Home became the perfectly available and polymorphous concept through which to encounter the weight and the multiplicity of the charge of the social sciences. Our experiences were able to poke at key challenges at the heart of normatively oriented human and social sciences: (1) when we tried to bring the political and the ethical explicitly into the functionings of the classroom, by looking at relations, expectations, power and labor, and when the intrusion of the moral into the normative led to many performative learning moments; (2) when students worked on their projects untethered to conventional disciplines but by capaciously allowing method and topic to illuminate each other to push them to multidisciplinary rigor; (3) when we were charged with producing space that would serve as home for the intellectual work of students and teachers alike—especially in the context of wanting to be a space of thought and substantiation for a broader campus politics of inclusion and diversity.

The experience of the Proseminar offered the possibility of alternative ways of thinking and acting in relation to people and texts. These alternative modes of interaction made themselves accessible to the extent that we as a class operated from a different point of departure than the one traditionally assumed within the classroom. By this we mean simply that rather than assume the gap between ourselves and positive objects of possible knowledge, we worked to allow the themes of each other's work and of the Proseminar—signified and haunting in its monosyllabic gesture—to ask questions of us.

We labored to imagine a pedagogical experience that locates itself in contrast to Enlightenment presumptions of the individual in relation to knowledge and truth, in which there is a (ritualized and closed) movement from an impoverished knowledge to a glutted one.

Whereas this paradigm, which arguably still maintains quiet ascendancy, assumes a generally stable subject moving to a fixed field of objects, our classroom attempted to probe the desire for epistemic comfort and to push a self-reflexive openness in regard to how one relates to and interprets possible knowledge. Our work brought us to imagine intellectual intimacy as a space in which to share gestating ideas. It is in this way that such a space within academic experience becomes personal, a context in which enrichment and fulfilment are the operative desires. These spaces are not realms of comfort; rather they push us to imagine selves and be accountable for and to them, without positing a future of greater clarity or certainty. This feeling of facilitating the growth of another is the nature of a Simon's Rock education.

However flawed, our willingness to aid in the development of the other, and in turn ourselves, defines us. Whether in the rides to the local Cumberland Farms, bumming cigarettes, or showing up to an event even though we should be studying, Simon's Rock culture is largely one of the shared need to communicate oneself through acts of love and kindness. The space of intimacy is complicated, however, when we begin to re-imagine ourselves not as an intellectual utopia for misfits but as much part of our nation's narrative—with all its history and burdens—as any other institution of learning. It is because a school like ours would not be possible without tremendous privilege and economic mobility. Is this what makes us a home? But, there is often a stifling sense of too much closeness, of not enough distance between oneself and the other, hence conflict and friction—no less homely attributes. In these ways we still grow. The challenge is to articulate the intimacy of Simon's Rock and claim its role in progressive education in this country, without insinuating ourselves into the legacy of self-congratulatory liberal multiculturalists.

Perhaps that requires a pedagogy of love, for which this legacy may not be the correct, only, or final, abode.

NOTES

1. Special thanks to Jocelyn McElroy (A.A., 2009) and Katherine Willkens (B.A., 2010), whose experience as members of the Proseminar in fall 2008 has impacted this piece, and who were missed as we planned, wrote, and revised this essay over the course of 2009 and 2010—*The Authors.*

2. The Proseminar had an application process in which students were required to submit materials including a curriculum vitae and a short essay that explained how the year's theme—"Home and the Haunts of Modernity"—tugged at their intellectual hearts and practice. This application could be seen as a pedagogical tool of its own. For the students, the application process provided an opportunity to look back over their academic accomplishments and shortcomings and gave them practice in crafting their academic resumes. Applicants were expected to say what they wanted the fellowship experience to deliver not only in relation to their respective projects but also in relation to their intellectual life after Simon's Rock, with a special emphasis on scholarly activity outside of Simon's Rock in the form of publications, conference presentations, or other public fora.

3. Reminder: Sections of text in italics indicate quotations from co-authors where the separation of voice, but not the identification of the speaker, seemed relevant. Where necessary—and we believe, where it really matters—the quotation itself will make clear whether the author is in role as a student or professor.

4. Blodgett House is the old home of our College's founder, Elizabeth Blodgett Hall, and now repurposed for use by college offices except for the charming Oak Room where various fora are held, and the pink dining room adorned with the Blodgett-Hall family paintings and photos, where we gathered for Proseminar meals every Thursday.

5. Since all students were familiar with Kafka's *The Trial* from their "Sophomore Seminar" reading list, our journeys through our home at the Rock allowed us some imaginative license when eyeing these familiar spaces, such as the College Center, more purposively—to judge them on their homeliness. The plethora of doors in the Hall College Center triggered a naughty reaction on the part of this group—assessing this space as the perfect setting for a theatrical interpretation of *The Trial*. Of course, that hasn't happened (yet), but this wisdom has probably been appropriately sent down the Simon's Rock grapevine.

6. Sam, who returned to the faculty in 2010, was our Academic Dean at the time of the Proseminar. He is also the author of one of the chapters in the present collection.

13

Bringing Our "Best Selves" to the Table

Awakening Critical Compassion in the Classroom

LINDA ANDERSON *and* ANNE O'DWYER

> One's reality rather than being fixed and predefined, is a perpetual
> emergent, becoming increasingly multiplex, as more perspectives
> are taken, more texts are opened, more friendships made.
> —MAXINE GREENE, *The Dialectic of Freedom*

> Reason's last step is recognizing that an infinity of things surpass it.
> —BLAISE PASCAL

The importance of compassion has somehow been lost in most contemporary discussions about education. This absence occurs across the educational spectrum, but is particularly pronounced in the discourse on post-secondary education. This chapter will examine pedagogies of compassion in light of various psychological and pedagogical models, and propose a new way of thinking about these pedagogies in college and university classrooms—that of critical compassion.

This chapter is consistent with our book's overall theme about the unique combination of challenge and nurture that supports students as they move toward taking responsibility for their own education. Bard College at Simon's Rock was deliberately poised from its inception as a liberal arts college for younger students to challenge traditional pedagogies that reinforced professional distance and hierarchies as well as professed objectified knowledge. As such, perhaps compassion is and has been more salient in the education we offer here at Simon's Rock (although such pedagogies are by no means unique to Simon's Rock in practice or in potential). In this chapter we will explore an alternative understanding of teaching and education that is not merely based on information-transfer and skill-building, but is also affective and transformational. We will draw on literature from psychology and education, as well as our own experiences in the classroom and what our students have shared with us over the years about their educational experiences.

WHY COMPASSION?

There is a popular theme in higher education today that college faculty need "new tricks" to sustain our students' interest and focus in education. Given contemporary advances in technology, "virtual" learning communities are viewed as the wave of the future, and immediate classroom response technologies (e.g., clickers) are seen as necessities. Moreover, colleges and universities respond to mounting pressures to increase revenue in order to respond to market-driven trends and students feel the pressure to earn increased credentials in order to more effectively compete for scarce employment. Evidence of these latter trends can be seen in the growth of for-profit institutions of higher education.[1] Under these conditions students are increasingly becoming anonymous consumers at the educational marketplace and teachers merely the vendors of education. How often does one hear from students the likes of: "I don't really care about this course. I just need it for my degree." Or "Just tell me what I need to do to get the grade, and I'll do it." Given the current national obsession with standardized testing, measurable educational outcomes and performance-driven learning that is conveniently localized within an evidence-based culture, it is no wonder that students and faculty can fall prey to becoming dispassionate consumers and service providers.

But, ultimately, if our colleges and universities (and high schools, for that matter) are to transform the adolescents and young adults of today—if we are to use education to better the condition not only of our students but of our societies overall—then we must do more than offer our students a new product or fill them up with new skills or talents. Of course, we must teach our students information and "critical thinking skills." All agree that students need to be able to analyze, evaluate and judge the many ideas, opinions, and proposals that they will encounter when they leave the educational setting, and that they should be encouraged and challenged to create even better ones.

Bard College at Simon's Rock is a residential early college experience. Teaching college students during their middle adolescence is a challenging joint venture, as we draw upon their energy, enthusiasm, and oftentimes outrage at social injustices. Within our pedagogical practices our students are encouraged to connect levels of analysis with deeper levels of self-understanding en route to imagining new worlds and new ways of living.

There are different ways in which compassion can be viewed. It is often associated with a capacity for empathy and caring for self and others. For example, the Buddhist tradition emphasizes compassion in terms of insight, that is, by being aware of one's own imperfections as well as one's capacity for joy, the individual finds compassionate comfort in joining the universally shared experiences. The Judeo-Christian perspective focuses on the capacity to feel the pain of others as well as administering healing to relieve the suffering.

The emphasis on compassion across a variety of cultural traditions implies that it has been a core value in our lives in the past, and, we argue, will be essential to making the world a better place in the decades to come. Without the consideration of compassion, how will our students be able to respond when there is—and there no doubt will be—injustice and suffering in the world? Will they be able to face life as it really is without falling into the trap of cynicism, escapism and dehumanization? If we can't help our students to respond to the suffering to which they are exposed—in their own lives as well as the lives of their friends and family, in their communities and in their classrooms—how can we ask them to ultimately respond to the many challenges which they are yet to witness?

Of course, as teachers, we wonder why and when compassion fell so out of favor in the discourse and prescriptive writing on post-secondary education. Popular images of the truly transformative college experience—inspiring students to go beyond what is expected—are often associated with compassion from a professor, mentor or peer. Similarly, when college graduates describe the most transformative educational event in their careers, they often talk about the impact of a course that introduced them to deepening awareness of themselves and connection with others whose experience often contrasts dramatically with their own. However, despite these grassroots understandings of the importance of caring, compassion has, at best, been ignored in most contemporary scholarly and academic discussions on education and, even worse, it has come to be seen as something that does not belong in and is even harmful to achieving excellence in post-secondary education.

It is clear that in the Western educational tradition this move away from highlighting the role of compassion and other affect-based dispositions occurred early on and on a broad intellectual scale. The importance of reason and rationality in the mind of American—and most Western—scholars, scientists, and educators has, of course, been growing since before the Enlightenment, and more recently via the schools of rational positivism, among others. Emotions in the scientific literature have generally been viewed as irrational and distracting from one's ability to think and reason. As Mayer, Salovey, and Caruso[2] summarize, "Throughout history, philosophers and pundits alike have argued about whether to follow one's 'head' or one's 'heart.' Through much of this time, the 'heads' have had the upper hand, so to speak. The Stoic tradition that thought trumps emotions is well embedded in Western philosophy."

As psychologists, we can't help but speculate that over the past half century, education has also been profoundly influenced by the cognitive revolution that has transformed psychology. The rise of cognitive theories has led to a focus (in both psychology and education) on the place of reason and information-processing in all aspects of human experience—from the cognitive milestones of childhood development to the disorders of cognition and cognitive-based psychotherapies. Too many contemporary programs in training educators value their graduates' understanding of children's cognitive development at the expense of social-emotional learning.

To many still today, "great professors" are assumed to be those who are brilliant, regardless of their ability to connect with and have an emotional impact on their students. Even the growing psychological literature supporting the role of emotional intelligence as a "third intelligence" outside the verbal and perceptual intellectual domains emphasizes the cognitive conception that "includes the ability to engage in sophisticated information processing about one's own and others' emotions and the ability to use this information as a guide to thinking and behavior."[3]

However, there have always been voices reminding us of the importance of compassion, and it could be that educators are beginning to recognize (or re-recognize) the importance of compassion in education—and beyond. For example, the negative effects of the declining presence of compassion among physicians, especially those in "non core" specializations, on treatment outcomes are beginning to be acknowledged. Redden reports that intuitive or more emotion-based "vicarious empathy" is declining, replaced by a more "imaginative empathy" involving one's cognitive ability to role-play; this shift she attributes to the heightened emphasis on medical technology, growing cultural differences between patients and doctors, as well as to the lack of available clinical role models.[4]

The legacy of the American educational reformer John Dewey asks us to examine the meaning of the institution of education as well as the teacher's role within the complexity of our democratic society. In reference to classroom practices, Dewey initiated "the concept of 'reflective experience' into educational discourse to refer to the process by which the personal and social meanings of experience interact and become one."[5]

Philosophers have, of course, long debated the role of compassion in critical thinking—indeed in debate itself. Even the mathematician Pascal recognized the importance of emotion, stating, "Reason's last step is recognizing that an infinity of things surpass it." Contemporary philosophers, likewise, are beginning to see its value. For example, in a 2004 convocation address at Knox College, Martha Nussbaum argues that emotions inform our appraisals, with compassion forming "a psychological link between our own self-interest and the reality of another person's good or ill," and further describes the importance of compassion in educating young adults in this era of globalization:

> Young people, especially when they are at the crucial time when they are on the verge of adulthood, should learn to be tragic spectators, and to understand with increasing subtlety and responsiveness the predicaments to which human life is prone. ... [Through] studies of many kinds, they should get the habit of decoding the suffering of another, and this decoding should deliberately lead them into lives both near and far.[6]

In his recent re-issue of *The Culture of Education*, the classic text on education, developmental psychologist Jerome Bruner suggests,

> What we need is a school reform movement with a better sense of where we are going, with deeper conviction about the kind of people we want to be. Then we can mount the kind of community effort that can truly address the future of our educational process—an effort in which all of the resources of *intellect and compassion* that we can muster, whatever the price, are placed at the disposal of the schools.[7]

Similarly, Maurianne Adams agrees, proposing that, "Culturally relevant teachers are also 'caring teachers' and dare to use the language of love in their writing."[8] Maxine Greene likewise, reminds us that one of the main goals of teaching—in addition to fostering critical thinking in our students—is to help us all "overcome carelessness, thoughtlessness, and indifference to the best of our abilities."[9]

By all accounts, if we teach young people with and for compassion, the potential impact is real. As Goodlad aptly describes it, "Make no mistake, teaching is high stakes work. What happens in our classrooms matters. Futures are born, dreams emboldened, passions ignited—or not. Because it matters, we need to be alive in this work."[10] Similarly, Waghid describes the challenges of South African educational reform in the post-Apartheid era in the following manner:

> There is more to nation-building ... than equipping pupils with practical-reasoning skills in critical judgment and rational, intersubjective discussion. ... [It] also requires that pupils be taught to have respect for human suffering and to take the suffering of others seriously. ... Compassion is not a virtue that can be cultivated through practical reasoning alone.[11]

WHAT ARE PEDAGOGIES OF COMPASSION?

The traditional view, thus, in much—although not all—of American higher education is that the best professors will present information in a dispassionate and objective manner and judge their students similarly; and their students, in turn, will
reason their way through an argument without considering their own feelings—or
those of others. According to this viewpoint, emotions—any emotions—threaten
both teachers' and students' ability to see the "truth." These contemporary expectations belie the fact that excellent teaching comes from one's core, and that this
"core" is made up of more than one's rational faculty. As educators we communicate our concern for the everyday lives of our students by inviting them to engage
in conversations about their authentic concerns, creating spaces for transformative
learning and even sometimes, healing; calling attention to the underlying dialogue
that highlights the complexity of difficult and often contradictory feelings that
hallmark adolescent development.

Many scholars and educators have used a variety of terms to refer to pedagogies
that create spaces where students can experience and develop a sense of appreciation
and respect for themselves as well as for others, what we are calling pedagogies of
compassion. What such pedagogies—i.e., Freire's pedagogies of liberation and critical dialogue[12] and his concept of critical consciousness,[13] and Rose's empathic affiliation,[14] receptive rationality,[15] bell hooks' transformative pedagogy,[16] temporary
affiliation and experiential analysis,[17] and connected teaching and midwife-teach-
ers[18]—share in common is that they create a setting that is nurturing, personal, and
facilitates feelings of growth, connection and emancipation. Carson and Johnson
describe "a pedagogy of compassion" thus:

> A responsible pedagogy in the face of ethical dilemmas that inevitably arise
> when stories of oppression are told in the classroom might be termed "a peda-
> gogy of compassion." Compassion is a response to suffering. Racism has visited
> suffering upon both its victims and those who must now bear the responsibility
> for the "sins of the past." ... Faced with this suffering, it is the obligation of
> the teacher to notice this and to respond compassionately. Compassion does not
> mean ignoring or forgetting, it means recognition of the demand that is there in
> the suffering face of the Other.[19]

So, what does it mean to be compassionate or to have compassion and how does
it impact learning? Compassion is, we argue, not about liking; one can feel compassion for an individual whom one dislikes. It is also not about altruism or uncondi-
tional acceptance: one can feel compassion for the distress of a person whose behavior one finds offensive or harmful. Compassion involves recognition, respect, and

caring—recognition of the suffering and struggles of another, respect for his or her own experiences and the subjective meaning of the personal biography surrounding those experiences, and caring enough to wish to alleviate the pain (or increase the joy). Aragno describes empathy in much the same way we view compassion:

> Empathy in psychoanalytic practice is described as that aspect of a specialized attentional stance that opens channels of interaction facilitating the formation of a trusting bond and enabling one to gain access to the emotional qualities of another's experience.[20]

Belenky et al. cite philosopher Nel Noddings: "In the intellectual domain our caring represents a quest for understanding."[21] In pedagogies of compassion, techniques to enhance self-reflection are used to increase self-knowledge as well as understanding of others. In doing so, pedagogies of compassion do not seek to understand phenomena in impersonal terms devoid of their impact on and implications for the social context out of which these phenomena arose. Compassionate teaching may pose such questions as, Why do you think that way? What is your thought process that directs your reasoning in this way?

Professors can apply the pedagogies of compassion in myriad ways. The real question is how we move beyond this impasse—of devaluing compassion—in education into a more impassioned learning community? First, compassion can be fostered in response to a text or narrative. Increasingly, scholars and educators—e.g., Jerome Bruner and Martha Nussbaum—cite the value of literature to foster compassion, and Nussbaum argues in fact that this is one of the key reasons it should be included in a college curriculum.[22]

Compassion can also occur through the conversations among students in a class—conversations about injustice, about suffering, about different life experiences and perspectives. These are not easy conversations, and faculty may feel awkward at first having them.

Pedagogies in this sense—pedagogies of compassion—are often criticized, even misunderstood, as valuing "connected knowing" and "experiential analysis" over "separate knowing" (logical sequential thinking, critical thinking, analytic ability). This is why we prefer to describe such pedagogies as those of "critical compassion" in order to highlight both the cognitive and affective domains of teaching and learning.

hooks reminds us that, "To build community requires vigilant awareness of the work we must continually do to undermine all the socialization that leads us to behave in ways that perpetuate domination."[23] And "One of the dangers we face in our educational systems is the loss of a feeling of community, not just the loss of closeness among those with whom we work and with our students, but also the loss of a feeling of connection and closeness with the world beyond the academy."[24] In the same text, hooks also reflects on her own role as an educator,

> My hope emerges from those places of struggle where I witness individuals positively transforming their lives and the world around them. Educating is always a vocation rooted in hopefulness. As teachers we believe that learning is possible, that nothing can keep an open mind from seeking after knowledge and finding a way to know.[25]

WHAT IS CRITICAL COMPASSION?

In highlighting the importance of compassion—and not just feelings—in teaching, we have chosen to use the term "critical compassion" to articulate the mode of teaching we are proposing. In using this term, we are searching for more creative ways to frame compassion and prompt a new generation to think about ways of reawakening our humanity in a world of learning systems and measured educational outcomes.

Erik Erikson described the relevance of education to emerging adolescent identities—a focus perhaps particularly relevant to us at Simon's Rock as we seek to educate our "younger scholars"—"It is the ideological potential of a society which speaks most clearly to the adolescent who is so eager to be affirmed by his peers, to be confirmed by teachers, and to be inspired by worth-while 'ways of life.'"[26] Or, as some of our students have described it, they want to be challenged to integrate all levels of experience—emotions, thoughts, and opinions—in developing an understanding of ideas and events. We have both heard from students who reflect on the "I hear you saying ... but/and ..." exercise from the "Writing and Thinking Workshop" (see Chapter 2 of this collection) who now realize how they had to *learn* to listen, respond, and agree or disagree effectively with others.

So what is critical compassion? What are pedagogies of critical compassion and how may they lead to transformative teaching and learning? How we come to understand and reflect on other's perspectives is as important as the actual content we are taking in. Empathic affiliation emphasizes the learner's process toward understanding perspectives of difference. In so doing, self-reflection and engaged dialogue within a motivated learning environment propel the shared ownership and rate of learning forward. However, it is important to note that one need not lose sight of critical thinking when one places value on emotions such as compassion. Critical compassion is more than just "feeling with" another—perhaps this is what differentiates it from empathy; it involves important cognitive and normative elements, as well.

Critical compassion highlights the strengths of students rather than addressing their errors too quickly. As we know, the fear of making mistakes contributes to the passive avoidance of intellectual risk taking; in contrast, recognizing students' contribution to the discussion reminds them of what they already know and they can then be challenged further to expand their thinking and problem-solving ability, the core of what the developmental psychologist Lev Vygotsky viewed as learning,[27] giving shape to a higher level of learning and commitment to exploring an issue more in depth. This drawing-out process gives permission to think on one's own, thus inviting students' agency without directing it.

All of these transformative pedagogies of compassion emphasize the synthesis of content with process while keeping in mind that knowledge production is socially constructed and interdependent. In the teaching of our discipline-based content whether in the arts or sciences, we are striving to be mindful of the differential impact of personal ways of knowing and connecting to others while filtering in a critical compassion that inspires students to critique, challenge, and create new ways of problem solving.

hooks observes,

> Women of all races and non-white men have been the students that I see most often paralyzed by fears that their work will not be excellent. In such cases I always think it important to be less of a perfectionist and more concerned about completing the work on time. ... Every caring teacher knows that our ideas are always in process. Unlike other professions we have the opportunity to return to our written work and make it better. Sadly, students from marginalized groups who have not had a long history in the academy (they are often the first generation in their family to attend college) are often devastated when the work they do is good but not excellent. Perfectionist thinking, reinforced by professors, prevents them from seeing that none of us is excellent all of the time.[28]

Critical compassion embodies a respectful awareness of matters of social justice that affects not only our personal joys and pathos, but also seeks to understand others outside our familiar intellectual and cultural orbits. In so doing, it provides a structural framework by which to acknowledge how our emotions and feelings are influenced by both intrapsychic and social forces.

Our emphasis on critical compassion highlights that normative unconscious developmental processes such as the formation of identification, capacity for empathy, and establishment of preferences are also influenced by social organization. Critical compassion as a route toward transformative learning (both inside and outside the classroom) challenges us to maintain an awareness of those stabilizing defensive systems that channel our emotions in certain directions over others while keeping in mind that we are apt to close down certain forms of empathy with some while opening up our ability to empathize with others.

For example, students become increasingly aware of the effects of power hierarchies and social stratification. Sometimes those in the dominant group become cognizant that their own recognition and openness for the feelings for those most like themselves can be viewed as closed off and perceived as undesirable by students representing more marginalized groups.

Critical compassion can occur at the curricular level. For example, a course was developed at the college to promote awareness and deeper inquiry into the significance of Hurricane Katrina. The students and faculty examined and deconstructed both the sociological impact of Katrina as well as the environmental implications. Students and faculty collectively organized a service-based spring break trip to the lower ninth ward that involved working on a project related to drainage in a local area. The scholar–activist model, and its connection to critical compassion, is well represented in this example.

On a more interpersonal level, students of ours commented on compassionate learning practices in the social sciences and humanities by observing the value of connecting with the texts and materials on a personal level. In so doing, they recognize that they must act with compassion and empathy because, in order to share their thoughts in an open environment, they must create and support a positive atmosphere for others as well.

CHALLENGES OF CRITICAL COMPASSION

The place of compassion in contemporary higher education can be problematic and misunderstood. In many halls of learning, it is seen as inappropriate and scary to encourage faculty to come to care about, or even know, their students beyond the academic realm—to invest themselves in their lives, interests, hopes and personal struggles beyond the classroom. Schools today are faced with challenges of liability and perceived risk, often involving the hovering anxiety of violence and untreated psychopathology among our youth.

Also, in practice we are not always successful regardless of our best intentions. While critical compassion in the classroom involves bringing one's "best self" to the table, it also requires the ability to be self critical and aware, keeping in mind that what may be meaningful and supportive to one student can as easily unravel with another.

Additional roles associated with teaching can include mentoring, mediating conflict, advising theses and counseling, to name only a few. As a result, some of the risks of teaching from a critical compassion framework can include the "compassion fatigue" and role strain that are often associated with wearing multiple professional hats and managing the pressures of publishing and active participation in other forms of expected professional development and collegial interactions. Critical compassion is more subterranean—rarely explicit in contemporary educational contexts; it is not intended to ease our minds or responsibility; rather it helps to create an affiliative space that localizes ourselves to grow and problem-solve, along with our colleagues and students. Ideally, it creates relational spaces that enable us to hold the emotional tension that is necessary to understand complexity. Similarly, knowing when or when not to tolerate the irresponsible, and sadly, at times disrespectful, statements and behaviors of our students is not something taught in doctoral programs.

Knowing the boundaries of compassion is essential to our self-care. We may be called upon to help a student reflect on difficult or burdensome ideas, giving her space to truly recognize her experiences. This may mean making detours. In our experiences, at times one student in a class finds a particular topic or reading quite inspiring or troubling; the task of the teacher is to help the student communicate his/her developing or potential epiphany to the class—to make it meaningful and educational for all, not merely a therapeutic moment for the student.

Moreover, the risks associated with critical compassion can involve tendencies toward over-identification with students with whom there is an affinity that overlook other aspects of students as whole human beings. We risk something too in the teaching process, sometimes making a presumptive move in thinking we know what is in the best interests of our students. This may risk us losing key connections with students who defy or distance themselves from our agendas without our being able to grapple with and understand the often complex silences that result. Intrator and Scribner describe this feeling as,

> When we are scared, ground down, and lonely, we cannot do and be our best. Teachers know fear. Standing before a classroom of students is a daily exercise in vulnerability. Our students can defy us, disregard us, or reject what we offer. When we feel vulnerable and fearful, we either hunker down in isolation or strike out against that which threatens us. Neither approach imbues the world with beauty and heart.[29]

Students also don't necessarily experience "compassionate" teachers in the way in which we intend. Rather, students as well as teachers unconsciously carry experiential "baggage" that may significantly alter our perceptions of ourselves and each other in the classroom.

> Any experienced teacher, if being honest, will tell you how much it can hurt to confront student resistance, distrust, or hostility after devoting hours, days, or

even weeks to the preparation of the perfect lesson that was supposed to thrill a grateful classroom. While it is common for teachers to exalt the power they possess to shape their students' self-understandings, the reverse is equally true. Students shape teachers' self-understandings as well.[30]

Moreover, we all come to the table with preferred learning and teaching styles as well as students with whom we more easily connect. These differences often correspond to our personality, life experience, prior academic training and teaching experience. While some of us may be more comfortable responding to students who find safety in a performance-based dialogue actively seeking external criteria for validation, others of us may be more invested in nondirective methods that speak to students who are more process oriented and/or willing to take the risks of making mistakes en route to creative problem solving.

Still other students may question or reject the pursuit of intellectual inquiry altogether, sometimes challenging educational ideals that foster a culture of exceptionalism and intellectualization on a campus of "gifted" students. In similar fashion others express a yearning for more harmony in life within a competitive landscape of emerging younger scholars. At times, some of our students have expressed how "back home," where families may have to focus on day-to-day struggles, compassion actually feels more prevalent. Students from families new to American higher education, with its emphasis so often on achieving some sort of intellectual objectivity, may experience a dichotomy of mind and emotion that in the moment renders them feeling lost from friends and family and struggling to restore an earlier sense of agency.

We are often challenged to deal with the existential crises among those who identify as outsider as well as those who are vulnerable to the spectrum of risky behavior during adolescence. We attempt to be aware of and decode the heightened challenges and risks of working with young people who are trying on new ways of being, seeking authentic connection to others and themselves, and becoming more aware of themselves as individuals differentiated from their families of origin.

Knowing that, students give us signs all along the way that point to their need for safety, connection, acceptance, and trust from their peers and learning community. They come to our faculty office hours under the auspices of talking about the class, but it may be about a lot more. They may be looking for acceptance without being judged and may actively choose to seek out a trusted adult in the community for counseling, crisis intervention, advisement or an informal conversation that satisfies a nagging question. The impact of some of these interactions may be life changing, yet in these often fleeting moments this relational connection is usually unspoken. The student in his or her quest to discover freedom and independence returns toward relying on self-understanding and then moves on, seeking other guides as needed to decipher more of the mysteries, challenges, and dangerous intersections within and outside of her- or himself.

One student in a recent "Psychology of Women" course described his experience of critical compassion by highlighting the value of learning in a context of connection with others, understanding, and acceptance. Another noted that a compassionate classroom can at times feel like a separate world—where one can discuss and analyze difficult and controversial topics—leaving the time outside of class for further personal contemplation and examination of the relevance of these discussions for understanding one's own life and experiences.

CONCLUSION

We believe that the importance of critical compassion—as both the cause and effect in our pedagogies of change—will yield wider change requiring not only higher order thinking and creativity, but responsible imagination and commitment to actively contributing to the common good—something we profoundly need today. Stanton-Salazar and Spina, drawing on Freire, describe the implications of such a pedagogy as,

> being able to understand, analyze, question, seek one's own meaning, recognize one's right and responsibility to take actions that have impact on the explicit and implicit sociopolitical and economic realities of our lives. ... [This pedagogical approach] facilitates mobility across multiple and often conflicted borders without sacrificing psychological well-being. Perhaps more important, critical consciousness goes beyond the affective and cognitive. It requires more than good intentions. It requires actions. It must be emancipatory and empowering, not only transforming consciousness but changing lives.[31]

From long traditions in both psychology and higher education, there are those who believe that higher-order thinking is not independent of the affect realm. Thinking cannot—and should not—be separated from emotion. As Aragno suggests,

> Mature and psychoanalytic empathy depend on the ability to formulate an *idea* of what the other's experience is like, and on having come to this understanding by way of a synthesis of perceptual, sensory-emotive, and ideational referents generated *in oneself* by the *other*. The bidirectionality of this process is contingent on the unimpeded flow of emotional (and unconscious) information passing

through less differentiated channels of communication and, where blockages or defensive obstructions arise, on making these impediments the very targets of interpretive understanding.[32]

This analysis can apply to other emotions in the classroom as well—anger, self-doubt, cynicism, intolerance, to name a few. The goal for both teachers and students is to allow the awareness of these feelings, but to not get overwhelmed by one's emotions to the point of losing a critical stance. The task is to connect emotions to analysis, and then to process this in a way that allows others to engage and reflect more critically on their own experiences. Such engagement allows students at various levels of expertise and verbal ability to participate and benefit. The experiences, feelings, and observations that others share in class discussions can have a great impact and promote deeper thinking, especially as students' responses to readings and each other are often remarkably honest and open. Moreover, in such contexts, the act of listening to those whose stories or opinions are different from one's own promotes deeper analysis, while recognizing that others have similar experiences can be liberating.

As a result, the strength of critical compassion is not about servicing, tolerating or "tending to" student needs. It does not become the solution in and unto itself. It considers what learning threshold students can cross as well as understanding its impact upon them. It involves creating an affiliative space and/or a space of safety that allows students to proactively problem-solve and take the risks necessary to expanding their learning curve as well as their connection to humanity.

NOTES

1. Rebecca Clay, "The Corporatization of Higher Education," *Monitor on Psychology* 39, no. 11 (2008): 50.

2. John D. Mayer, Peter Salovey, and David R. Caruso, "Emotional Intelligence: New Ability or Eclectic Traits?" *American Psychologist* 63, no. 6 (2008): 513.

3. Mayer, Salovey, and Caruso, "Emotional Intelligence: New Ability or Eclectic Traits?" 503.

4. Elizabeth Redden, "Tomorrow's Doctors: Less Empathetic Tomorrow Than Today," *Inside Higher Ed*, February 29, 2008.

5. Maurianne Adams, "Pedagogical Frameworks for Social Justice Education," in *Teaching for Diversity and Social Justice: A Sourcebook*, 2nd Edition, ed. Maurianne Adams, Pat Griffin, and Lee Anne Bell (London: Routledge, 1997), 26.

6. Martha C. Nussbaum, "Liberal Education in a Time of Global Tension," *Knox College News*, accessed September 14, 2008, http://www.knox.edu/x8053.xml.

7. Jerome Seymour Bruner, *The Culture of Education* (Cambridge, MA: Harvard University Press, 1997), 118.

8. Adams, "Pedagogical Frameworks for Social Justice Education," 23.

9. Maxine Greene, "Countering Indifference—The Role of the Arts," The Maxine Greene Foundation, accessed January 24, 2009, http://www.maxinegreene.org/articles.php.

10. John I. Goodlad, "On the Edge," in *Teaching with Fire: Poetry That Sustains the Courage to Teach,* ed. Sam M. Intrator and Megan Scribner (New York: Jossey-Bass, 2003), 47.

11. Yusef Waghid, "Compassion, Citizenship and Education in South Africa: An Opportunity for Transformation?" *International Review of Education* 50, no. 5/6 (2004): 535–536.

12. Paulo Freire, *Pedagogy of the Oppressed* (New York: Seabury Press, 1970), 48.

13. Paulo Freire, *Education for Critical Consciousness* (New York: Continuum Press, 1993), 19.

14. A term used by Patricia Rose at a panel presentation at the Dalton School, New York City in 2004.

15. Nel Noddings, *Caring: A Feminine Approach to Ethics and Moral Education* (Berkeley: University of California Press, 1984), 1.

16. bell hooks, *Teaching to Transgress: Education as the Practice of Freedom* (New York: Routledge, 1994), 36.

17. Shulamit Reinharz, *On Becoming a Social Scientist: From Survey Research and Participant Observation to Experiential Analysis* (New Brunswick, NJ: Transaction Publishers, 1984), 356.

18. Mary F. Belenky, Blythe M. Clinchy, Nancy R. Goldberger, and Jill M. Tarule, *Women's Ways of Knowing: The Development of Self, Voice, and Mind* (New York: Basic Books, 1986), 214.

19. Terry Carson and Ingrid Johnston, "The Difficulty with Difference in Teacher Education: Toward a Pedagogy of Compassion," *Alberta Journal of Educational Research* 46, no. 1 (2000): 81–82.

20. Anna Aragno, "The Language of Empathy: An Analysis of Its Constitution, Development, and Role in Psychoanalytic Listening," *Journal of the American Psychoanalytic Association* 56, no. 3 (2008): 713.

21. Belenky et al., *Women's Ways of Knowing,* 102.

22. Martha C. Nussbaum, "Liberal Education in a Time of Global Tension," accessed September 14, 2008, http://www.knox.edu/x8053.xml.

23. bell hooks, *Teaching Community: A Pedagogy of Hope* (New York: Routledge, 2003), 36.

24. hooks, *Teaching Community,* xv.

25. hooks, *Teaching Community,* xiv.

26. Erik H. Erikson, *Identity: Youth and Crisis* (New York: W. W. Norton, 1968), 130.

27. Lev Vygotsky, "Interaction between Learning and Development," in *Mind in Society: The*

Development of Higher Psychological Processes, ed. Michael Cole, et al. (Cambridge, MA: Harvard University Press, 1978), 87.

28. hooks, *Teaching Community*, 90–91.

29. Sam M. Intrator and Megan Scribner, *Teaching with Fire: Poetry That Sustains the Courage to Teach* (San Francisco: Jossey-Bass, 2003), xx.

30. Michael. J. Nakkula and Eric Toshalis, *Understanding Youth: Adolescent Development for Educators* (Cambridge, MA: Harvard Education Press, 2006), 13.

31. Ricardo Stanton-Salazar and Stephanie Urso Spina, "Adolescent Peer Networks as a Context for Social and Emotional Support," *Youth & Society* 36, no. 4 (2005): 251–252.

32. Anna Aragno, "The Language of Empathy," 733.

WORKS CITED

Adams, Maurianne. "Pedagogical Frameworks for Social Justice Education." In *Teaching for Diversity and Social Justice: A Sourcebook,* 2nd Edition, edited by Maurianne Adams, Pat Griffin, and Lee Anne Bell. London: Routledge, 1997.

Aragno, Anna. "The Language of Empathy: An Analysis of Its Constitution, Development, and Role in Psychoanalytic Listening." *Journal of the American Psychoanalytic Association* 56, no. 3 (2008): 713–740.

Belenky, Mary F., Blythe M. Clinchy, Nancy R. Goldberger, and Jill M. Tarule. *Women's Ways of Knowing: The Development of Self, Voice, and Mind*. New York: Basic Books, 1986.

Bruner, Jerome Seymour. *The Culture of Education*. Cambridge, MA: Harvard University Press, 1997.

Carson, Terry, and Ingrid Johnston. "The Difficulty with Difference in Teacher Education: Toward a Pedagogy of Compassion." *Alberta Journal of Educational Research* 46, no. 1 (2000): 75–83.

Clay, Rebecca. "The Corporatization of Higher Education." *Monitor on Psychology* 39, no. 11 (2008): 50.

Erikson, Erik H. *Identity: Youth and Crisis*. New York: W. W. Norton, 1968.

Freire, Paulo. *Pedagogy of the Oppressed*. New York: Seabury Press, 1970.

———. *Education for Critical Consciousness*. New York: Continuum Press, 1993.

Gladwell, Malcolm. "Most Likely to Succeed." *New Yorker,* December 15, 2008.

Goodlad, John I. "On the Edge." In *Teaching with Fire: Poetry That Sustains the Courage to Teach,* edited by Sam M. Intrator and Megan Scribner. New York: Jossey-Bass, 2003.

Greene, Maxine. *The Dialectic of Freedom*. New York: Teachers College Press, 1988.

———. "Countering Indifference—The Role of the Arts." The Maxine Greene Foundation. Accessed January 24, 2009. *http://www.maxinegreene.org/articles.php*.

hooks, bell. *Teaching to Transgress: Education as the Practice of Freedom*. New York: Routledge, 1994.

———. *Teaching Community: A Pedagogy of Hope*. New York: Routledge, 2003.

Intrator, Sam M., and Megan Scribner. *Teaching with Fire: Poetry That Sustains the Courage to Teach*. San Francisco: Jossey-Bass, 2003.

Mayer, John D., Peter Salovey, and David R. Caruso. "Emotional Intelligence: New Ability or Eclectic Traits?" *American Psychologist* 63, no. 6 (2008): 503–517.

Nakkula, Michael. J., and Eric Toshalis. *Understanding Youth: Adolescent Development for Educators*. Cambridge, MA: Harvard Education Press, 2006.

Noddings, Nel. *Caring: A Feminine Approach to Ethics and Moral Education*. Berkeley: University of California Press, 1984.

Nussbaum, Martha C. "Liberal Education in a Time of Global Tension" *Knox College News*. Accessed September 14, 2008. *http://www.knox.edu/x8053.xml*.

Redden, Elizabeth. "Tomorrow's Doctors: Less Empathetic Tomorrow Than Today." *Inside Higher Ed*, February 29, 2008.

Reinharz, Shulamit. *On Becoming a Social Scientist: From Survey Research and Participant Observation to Experiential Analysis*. New Brunswick, NJ: Transaction Publishers, 1984.

Shor, Ira. *Empowering Education: Critical Teaching for Social Change*. Chicago: University of Chicago Press, 1992.

Stanton-Salazar, Ricardo, and Stephanie Urso Spina. "Adolescent Peer Networks as a Context for Social and Emotional Support." *Youth & Society* 36, no. 4 (2005): 379–417.

Waghid, Yusef. "Compassion, Citizenship and Education in South Africa: An Opportunity for Transformation?" *International Review of Education* 50, no. 5/6 (2004): 525–542.

Vygotsky, Lev. "Interaction between Learning and Development." In *Mind in Society: The Development of Higher Psychological Processes*, edited by Michael Cole, Vera John-Steiner, Sylvia Scribner, and Ellen Souberman. Cambridge, MA: Harvard University Press, 1978.

V

EARLY COLLEGE FROM MARGIN TO CENTER

Transforming Higher Education by Rethinking "The Spaces In-Between"

14

Early College

What and Why?

PATRICIA SHARPE

As I write today in 2010, an initiative is under way to revolutionize the education of American adolescents. Challenging the notion that college learning is most appropriate for students eighteen and up, the early college movement holds that young people between the ages of fifteen and twenty are not only capable of doing college work, but are ideally suited for the intellectual and personal exploration as well as the critical thinking essential to undergraduate study.

In 2002, the Bill and Melinda Gates Foundation launched the Early College High School Initiative with support from Carnegie Corporation of New York, the Ford Foundation, and the W. K. Kellogg Foundation. The plan was to establish 150 Early College High Schools across the country by 2011, enrolling 60,000 students. That initial goal proved insufficiently ambitious: more than 200 have already been created by 2010, according to "Early College High School: A Portrait in Numbers."[1] These small, autonomous schools are designed to enable all students to achieve as much as two years of college credit at the same time as they are earning a high school diploma (within four to five years of entering ninth grade). The design and theme of the schools vary; some emphasize science or technology; some are charter schools, while others are regular public schools; some partner with community colleges, while others collaborate with a public state university, or a private liberal arts college.

Two existing models directly inspired this initiative: Bard High School Early College, established in 2001, and Middle College High School at LaGuardia Community College, established in 1973-74. Both schools were visited in fall 2001 by Tom Vander Ark and other representatives of the Gates Foundation. Already deeply committed to high school reform and support for small schools, the Gates Foundation became convinced that creating early college opportunities would enhance their efforts to increase the college attendance and completion rates of traditionally underserved students. Interestingly, these two schools that recently served as direct models for the Gates initiative, both urban public institutions, themselves took their inspiration from Simon's Rock College, the rural private college founded by Elizabeth Blodgett Hall in 1966.[2]

This chapter will focus on the philosophy of early college that underlies the current initiative, how it has evolved and developed over forty-five years at Simon's Rock College, and how it was adapted at Bard High School Early College in 2001, and subsequently at Bard High School Early College II in 2008, the three institutions I know well. I joined the Simon's Rock faculty in Languages and Literature in 1983, and became Dean of Academic Affairs of the college in 1993. Because of that experience with early college, I was one of three people with ties to Bard College asked to work with representatives of the New York City Board of Education to found the first Bard High School Early College. As a strong believer in both the early college idea and in public education, I was delighted to have this opportunity to work with an inner-city population and to help them discover how much they could accomplish when challenged.

These two schools—Bard High School Early College and Simon's Rock College—differ in structure, population, and funding, demonstrating the reach of the underlying early college conception which is my primary topic, and validating the commitment of the Gates foundation to support variety in the models, school designs, and themes by which the core principles of early college are achieved. Mrs. Hall founded Simon's Rock because, as headmistress of the private preparatory school, Concord Academy, she had become increasingly aware of the redundancy her graduates faced in their first two years of college.

Eager to improve and rationalize the education of students in the crucial years between fifteen and twenty, eliminating the disjunction she observed as students moved on from high school, she established what soon became known as Simon's Rock Early College without the intention of accelerating students. She envisioned it as spanning the last two years of high school and the first two of college. Between 1972 and 1974, through the leadership of the college's second president, Dr. Baird W. Whitlock, the curriculum leading to the Associate's degree was restructured, eliminating high school components and establishing the pattern by which all students entering Simon's Rock after the tenth or eleventh grade become first-year college students. By 1974, through support from the National Science Foundation and the Carnegie Foundation, the college developed its interdisciplinary Bachelor's degree program and became a four-year college of liberal arts and sciences for younger scholars.

Mrs. Hall was also motivated by the growing alienation of youth in the sixties, and her conviction that it arose from young people being denied an outlet for their idealism in effective action. Young people completing tenth grade, she believed, were physically mature human beings eager to be treated as adults and intellectually ready to undertake college work. High school, she believed, too often caters to the competition for admission to college, rather than offering students the opportunity to search for a full understanding of themselves and others at the moment when they are most open to such questions. By age fifteen or sixteen, she argued, students should begin the process of discovery of their particular interests and abilities, free of the invidious comparisons of rankings and test scores which beset the student in competition with his fellow in a preparatory track.

While her experience was primarily with students of privilege, this insight underlies the appeal of the early college idea for Janet Lieberman, founder of the Middle College High School movement, as well as for the Gates initiative. Even more than the private school students of the sixties who pioneered the Simon's Rock experiment, students who have grown up in poverty, whether in the inner city or in rural isolation, are liable to be eager to begin their lives as productive adults and impatient with the controls, limitations, and stratification of traditional high school. Too often this impatience results in students cutting their education short, thereby denying themselves access to other opportunities. An approach that stresses remediation is only likely to increase such students' frustration and temptation to drop out.

Our standard K-12 education system is based on the assumption of a clear delineation of levels that is seldom, in fact, the case. Nevertheless, confronted with the idea of early college, many parents ask anxiously about the material that will be "missed." They are interested to learn that attending college at fifteen or sixteen was, in fact, the norm in the nineteenth century and that our current model of twelve years of schooling was only established during the 1930s and 1940s. In part a response to the Depression, it delayed young people entering the job market; it also helped assimilate the large numbers of immigrants in that period.

Almost immediately, the new norm was challenged, most notably by Robert Maynard Hutchins who established an early entrance program at the University of Chicago in the 1940s. In subsequent years, the development of a variety of options including advanced placement programs in high schools, governor's schools, dual enrollment opportunities, middle college high schools, and a few other early entrance programs all testify to students' impatience and readiness to take on college work while still high school age.

What, one may well wonder, is the difference between a rigorous high school course and a college course? According to Jack Meiland, philosophy professor and former director of the Honors Program at The University of Michigan, it is the approach that makes the difference. While it is the norm in high school to present material as information to be accepted and learned,

> material is presented in college not as something to be believed on the basis of authority, but as something to be believed because such belief is rationally justified and can be rationally defended. Thus, much work in college—and, I would say, the work that is characteristic of college—deals with the rational justification of belief.[3]

Fifteen- and sixteen-year-olds are not merely capable of responding to such an approach; they are ideally suited to it. Questioning authority and the status quo is the work of middle adolescence. An approach which encourages critical thinking, skepticism, and the rational justification of belief can engage students who would be discouraged and alienated by material presented "with an air of being absolutely and unchangingly true."[4]

College thinking, as described by Meiland, opens a space for the student's critical and creative intelligence. It treats material that in high school would be regarded as "eternal and unchangeable fact that human beings have discovered in their continual and relentless progress toward total knowledge" as theory, as "belief that may perhaps be well supported at the present but that could turn out to be wrong."[5]

It is at fifteen and sixteen, before vocational or professional training, indeed before students have found a clear direction, that they are most open to such an approach. They are ready to become acquainted with the range of human inquiry, to test their perceptions, abilities, limits and interests. They need to discover their own views and to be expected to take adult responsibility for the views they hold in an atmosphere that fosters their capacity for considered judgment. Taking young people's ideas seriously, asking students to defend and see the consequences of their suggestions and positions and interpretations in an atmosphere of rational interchange is the essence of the early college idea.

The connection to the small schools movement, also supported by the Gates foundation, should be evident. Relationships are crucial to the early college experience, and are vital for the success of all small schools, which are usually limited to no more than 400 students. They are structured so that the adults at the school should be able to know all the students by name, each student is actively involved in an advisory group, and instruction can be individually tailored to a student's talents and interests. In early college, it is not simply the closeness, but also the nature of these relationships with adults that is crucial. To rise to the challenge of college work, students of this age must be expected and encouraged to enter into active and thoughtful interchange with their teachers as well as with their classmates.

In their research on adolescent preparation for the world of work, Csikszent-mihalyi and Schneider discovered that optimal learning experiences occurred most frequently when students were confronted with high levels of challenge and when they perceived the activities they were asked to perform as not mere busywork but meaningfully related to their future goals.[6] One reason for the greater potential effectiveness of early college programs versus early admission programs, whereby able younger students enroll at regular colleges, is that lecture is an ineffective mode of instruction for high-school-age students. While more mature students, committed to a career path and engaged in professional training might find lectures beneficial, younger students had difficulty experiencing lectures as challenging, engaging, or meaningful.[7]

Recent research on the development of the brain in adolescence offers further justification for creating early colleges rather than simply integrating younger students into pre-existing structures and institutions. While fifteen- and sixteen-year-olds may be intellectually prepared for the challenge, the ability to make responsible and well-reasoned decisions centers in areas of the brain which are not fully developed until age twenty. Teachers and administrators working with younger college students need to create structures in which they are offered freedom of choice in a context that is safe, one that encourages them to deepen their awareness of possible consequences and impacts on others of their actions.

While high schools often feel bound to regulate students' choices and behavior, in early college the aim is to help students develop self-restraint. Through developing competence and responsibility, students recognize that the freedom of maturity comes from having won the trust and respect of others. This involves cultivating each student's awareness of the effect of his individual actions on himself and on others. "Respect and responsibility among students, among faculty, and between students and faculty," is one of the core attributes of small schools and of early college high schools.[8]

To bring about such growth, an early college must encourage students to integrate their learning in the classroom with their lives outside. Too often in high school, students feel social pressure to hide their engagement with ideas even in the classroom. At Simon's Rock, by contrast, they are invited to bring their observations and concerns about their own growth and development, about society, politics, and the environment to bear on classroom assignments.

The early college initiative stands in direct contrast to what Diane Ravitch has called "A Century of Failed School Reforms," and her criticism of all the forces that have conspired to deny students rigorous academic challenge.[9] In his review of Ravitch's book, Alan Wolfe argues that the "dumbing-down" of American education has costs not only for individual students too poor to opt out of the public school system, but also for our democracy. As Mrs. Hall did in the sixties, he believes that

> schools that make demands on students, and hold them responsible for their actions ... will form individuals capable of rebelling against illegitimate authority. ... Political freedom and educational discipline go hand in hand, as do educational freedom and political apathy. It is a great and urgent paradox; and to appreciate it our schools need to teach a greater respect for the complexities of the world than they do now.[10]

Early colleges, of necessity, embrace this complexity. At a 1994 conference on "Adolescence, Acceleration, and National Excellence" which brought together all the early entrance and several early college programs extant at that time, William Durden, Director of Johns Hopkins' Center for Talented Youth criticized the "either/or" of American education, for example, the perceived opposition of excellence and equality, or of content and pedagogy.[11]

By contrast, Simons' Rock College endorses competing values: it accelerates talented students, yet de-emphasizes competition and ranking in favor of collaboration, drawing all students together into required core seminars which stress the value of engaging diverse opinions. Working with younger, and often underprepared students, early college faculty use a delicate interplay of affirmation and critique, enticing students to stretch their vision of true accomplishment without allowing them to be discouraged about their current achievements.

The affirmation of individualism is balanced with a strong sense of intellectual community; open engagement with all ideas and the willingness to entertain criticism do not preclude assiduous attention to core requirements and rules, including a college-wide attendance policy, weekly advisor meetings for first-year students, and strict policies on drug and alcohol use. Helping students learn to negotiate for themselves within a system of rules and deadlines, to write a petition for exception or an appeal of an infraction notice, to make a case for what they want, to understand and address the principles that guide the rules, are all important aspects of their maturing process.

Even today, however, acceleration is viewed as a by-product rather than a goal at Simon's Rock. The primary intention still is to offer students college work when they are most prepared to absorb and be moved by it. Students attracted to early college are usually active and inquisitive, prepared to question other taken-for-granted ideas and structures. They readily respond to an approach that values skepticism, critical analysis, and argument from evidence rather than from authority.

This approach, introduced in the week-long "Writing and Thinking Workshop" (described by John B. Weinstein in Chapter 2, above), serves as an orientation for all new students. It is designed to give students the chance to learn by speaking aloud in a small supportive group and to write in response to a wide variety of texts, thereby developing their awareness of some of the many kinds and uses of language. The workshop introduces new students to some of the values of the college: textual sensitivity; active learning; and group discussion as intellectual and personal discovery. Two other important values include re-thinking of the role of faculty as sole authority and encouraging students to take responsibility for their own learning. This week-long experience conveys the message that writing and critical analysis skills are fundamental to success in college, and it invites students to extend their attention span and their patience working with ideas where there is no clear answer. Though its goals are serious, the tenor of the workshop is often playful and exciting. Workshop is taught by faculty from all disciplines of the college and new faculty are invited to participate in the training, and to offer a section of it as part of their orientation to the college. At both Bard High School Early College campuses, students in all grades participate in "Writing and Thinking Workshop" each year and virtually all faculty act as Workshop facilitators.

Simon's Rock, as a residential college, extends the culture of growing responsibility and respect to include adult advisors in the dormitories, developing processes for student participation in the judicial process and decision making about community living. In 1967, Mrs. Hall anticipated that "giving young people between the ages of fifteen and twenty a chance to practice adult responsibility should result in earlier maturity."[12] That prediction was born out by research conducted on the development of maturity of students at Simon's Rock in the early 1970s, using stage theory of ego development as described by Jane Loevinger and the conceptual framework of William Perry for understanding the intellectual and philosophical changes students undergo during college. The results, as described by Nancy R. Goldberger showed that

> change in the early college years at Simon's Rock is comparable to, if not more rapid than, change at other colleges. Developmentally lower stage students, even after one year, catch up with their 18 to 19 year old counterparts, and a significant proportion of the mid-stage students shift into the Post-Conformist stage by the sophomore year. ... Simon's Rock seniors are developmentally on a par with seniors at other colleges.[13]

Crucial to this student development is the particular character of early college faculty. Teachers in this setting develop remarkable skills; they have genuine and deep commitment to their fields and at the same time must be able to consider student challenges to their authority that rattle the basic assumptions of their discipline with a wise and patient appreciation for the underlying spirit of questioning that motivates the student. Early college teachers develop the willingness and ability to articulate and explain underlying disciplinary assumptions that too often, in traditional college settings, go unacknowledged and have to be intuited or picked up over time. They model intellectual engagement, enthusiasm, and dedication; they balance rigor with informality and help students find ways to speak and write an academic prose that is at once informed and direct, and imbued with individual voice.

The "Writing and Thinking Workshop," taken by all new students, plays a central role in building this learning culture among students and faculty. Like the general education seminars, mentioned above, and a year-long required senior thesis, this workshop was adopted at Simon's Rock in 1979 when it became a unit of Bard College. Bard's president, Dr. Leon Botstein had himself experienced early college in the Hutchins program at the University of Chicago, and he believed that Bard and Simon's Rock had much in common, including commitments to innovation, to rigorous learning, to a curriculum that brings together the best of traditional and progressive education, and to the reform of American secondary education.

In his book, *Jefferson's Children: Education and the Promise of American Culture* (1997), President Botstein engaged in a spirited critique of the American high school, advocating a curriculum that would develop basic competencies which students would accomplish by the end of the tenth grade. At that point, he recommends that students desiring to go to college do so, whether remaining home and attending community college or by going away to a four-year college directly. For students electing to continue their education past this demonstrated basic competency, he advocates the development of vocational education programs, internships, or work for the community.[14] This view was echoed in 2001 by Richard Clark in a report on dual credit for the Pew Charitable Trust where he recognizes two significant trends in K-16 education: "today's secondary school students increasingly engage in postsecondary schooling (technical or pre-baccalaureate), and a number of states view the tenth grade as the point by which acquisition of basic skills and knowledge should be completed."[15] His report goes on to describe a reconfigured educational sequence in which students would move on after tenth grade to what he calls "People's College" for grades 11–14, then on to College or University for grades 15–18, ending in a Bachelor's or Master's degree.

Bard High School Early College, LaGuardia Middle College High School, and the other middle college high schools took a different approach, beginning at ninth grade and incorporating postsecondary learning into the school's structure and curriculum It is this model that the Gates early college high school initiative has adopted. This is, in part, because their mission is not only to make higher education more accessible, affordable, and achievable by bridging the divide between high school and college, but also to encourage collegiate ambitions in traditionally underserved students. To that end, they instill awareness of the demands and rewards of college in students just beginning high school. An additional ambition of the Early College High School Initiative is to reach out to middle schools, providing extensive support and preparation for undertaking college work.

Bard High School Early College had its origins when Harold O. Levy, then Chancellor of the New York City Board of Education read Leon Botstein's *Jefferson's Children,* and became excited about putting its idea into practice and offering New York City students the early college opportunity as part of their public school education. Given the size of the city system and its commitment to high school choice among a wide range of options, it seemed an ideal situation for recruiting students eager for such an opportunity. And indeed, although the foundation of BHSEC was only approved on June 20, 2001, after students had made their high school choices and after most middle schools holding their records had closed for the year, it was able to recruit the initial intended population of 250 students. For fall 2004, several thousand students indicated it as a preference on their high school selection forms and 400 were interviewed as candidates for the 125 seats in the ninth grade class.

From the start, the early college program at BHSEC was informed by the Simon's Rock experience; the new challenge was to determine what curriculum and practices in ninth and tenth grade would most effectively prepare students for early college work. Unlike the middle college high schools which simply enabled students to take individual community college classes as they became capable of succeeding in them, BHSEC"s ambition was to have all students move on from tenth grade to become first-year college students, taking a full program of college courses and completing requirements for the Associate's degree in an additional two years.

A significant feature of the memorandum of understanding establishing BHSEC was the agreement that the faculty would be made up of both high school and college teachers, selected by a team of interviewers representing Bard College, the Department of Education, and the United Federation of Teachers, all of whom would become employees of the Department of Education. With remarkable unanimity, this committee selected the initial faculty of twenty teachers, several experienced and tenured in New York public schools, two of whom held the Ph.D., three coming from senior faculty positions at public and private colleges, a number coming fresh from graduate school after completing either the Ph.D. or a master's degree in teaching. It immediately became clear that the designation of high school and college teachers anticipated in the memorandum of understanding was naïve, and the success of the school depended upon the whole faculty understanding and embracing the full four-year curriculum.

Teachers in the college program who came to that work from teaching older college students in traditional higher education settings needed to appreciate the particular challenges of working with this age group, something where the high school teachers were experienced. The college teachers also needed to have input into the approaches and material covered in the two high school years, helping to determine how best to raise students' appreciation of the work to be accomplished and their expectations for themselves. Increasingly, all faculty members at BHSEC were asked to teach both high school and college classes as part of their ongoing participation in the design of an integrated four-year curriculum. The program meets the state high school graduation requirements, but does not allow them to determine or limit the ambitions and emphasis of the classes. By the end of tenth grade, students have studied the material covered in the five required state Regents exams. Their work and Associate's degree requirements in the two college years assure that they have also met minimum course requirements for the high school diploma.

The challenge we were expecting of our faculty was at once to teach in new ways to new populations in a situation where all structures and expectations were undefined and to reflect constantly on the experience, planning and adjusting in response to their observations. Eager to understand and share this challenge, I undertook, as Dean of Studies at BHSEC, to teach a ninth-grade English class after thirty years of experience exclusively in higher education. I was eager to discover what would engage the students and bring them along most effectively. What were the skills and habits of mind we count on being instilled—or at least not destroyed—before students come to early college?

I found that ninth graders like to write ... on the blackboard, that is. They like to sit next to their best friends and talk to their best friends; asked to focus for too long, they squiggle. My ninth graders, confronted with something to read, either got it in a snap and were ready to move on, or ... didn't get it at all, and were just as ready to move on. It was wonderful over the course of the year, to see them gradually develop patience with not understanding, skills for taking sentences apart, for sharing ideas and insights, and drawing connections.

The theme of my course was "Growing Up in a Time and Place." In part that evolved from the terrible fact that the World Trade Center towers fell, in full view of every window in our school, in the first week that our brand new school was in session. We felt blessed, in some ways, to have no set curriculum in place, so that the social studies teacher could open the year with a unit on the Middle East, and in conjunction with that, I could work in-depth with a memoir of growing up in a Muslim household in Morocco in the 1930s, *Dreams of Trespass: Tales of a Harem Girlhood* (1995). In conjunction with that text, we also worked on numerous articles from the public press about the world situation, as well as other accounts of growing up in particular circumstances. My hope was to encourage the students to develop perspective on their own process of development as an Egyptian American in Queens, or a Nigerian American or Palestinian American in Brooklyn.

That was my theme, but the students said it was really "how is everything we read connected to everything else?" And it is true that I found encouraging students to draw connections—intellectual, historical, stylistic, or even accidental—was my way of fostering greater reflectiveness and of encouraging them to move back and forth creatively between particular and abstraction, between generalization and example. This setting of a work in a larger context, and drawing for your reading of one work on a whole pattern of relationships and frameworks seemed to me an essential skill usually developed in college, but one I could see these younger students learning to use and take pride in.

Another issue for the early college high school has to do with how to schedule the day and how to help students develop the independent work habits expected in college. Course delivery is different in the usual high school and college. High school students typically spend as much or more time in class as they do on homework; in college, the opposite is true. At BHSEC we needed to organize class time so that students who have to commute to lower Manhattan from all of the boroughs have concentrated class schedules and that the college students have sufficient out-of-class time available for research and out-of-class learning.

At Simon's Rock we have learned that much of the first semester, and sometimes the first year, is devoted to helping the students understand and adjust to this type of collegiate expectations. We have structured our programs and policies accordingly. For example, at Bard College all regular courses earn four credits; many meet only once a week. At Simon's Rock, most courses for first- and second-year students earn three credits and meet twice or three times per week. It is only courses at the 300 level and above that earn four credits and are permitted to meet once per week. This reflects our sense that it is only over the course of their time in the A.A. program that the majority of our younger students come to appreciate fully all that they can and should be accomplishing outside of class and gain the maturity and self-discipline necessary to make it happen with only infrequent supervision. At Simon's Rock, this maturation process is fostered not simply in class, but also by the Student Life Staff and the larger academic culture of the residential campus.

Our challenge at BHSEC was to figure out how to foster such maturation in a non-residential setting and to adapt the lessons of Simon's Rock to an urban school where many students commute over an hour. In our first year, the difficulty of making this adjustment was intensified by our setting on one floor of a junior high school in a fairly remote location with minimal library facilities. Also, we had no upper-class college students to serve as role models and a new faculty who had not faced exactly this challenge before.

In terms of class schedules, our solution was a compromise that seems to have worked fairly well. The standard class period is fifty-five minutes at BHSEC, as it is at Simon's Rock. However, most required college classes meet four periods per week at BHSEC, rather than the three that are standard at Simon's Rock. The idea was that some in-class time could be devoted to modeling a variety of activities and approaches that students would be expected to carry forward on their own. It also assured students some more time for access to the faculty, given that they do not have the luxury of hanging around in the late afternoon or running into their teachers at evening events as students do at a residential college. This did entail some rethinking on the part of faculty about the structuring of class time.

We believe it is consonant with the larger rethinking of classroom practice and assignments that should be part of learning to teach early college. Many teachers who come from the large lecture halls of research universities to early college teaching find that smaller classes with inquisitive and challenging students requires renewed attention to, and willingness to explain and even rethink, underlying assumptions. The orientation of new teachers that precedes the "Writing and Thinking Workshop" at Simon's Rock initiates this process, but then most faculty also learn from their experienced colleagues during their probationary two-year contract.

Since BHSEC would not have faculty already seasoned at early college teaching, we did expand the initial training workshop, which was held at the Great Barrington campus, and did include time for meetings with experienced Simon's Rock faculty in each person's field, as well as time to observe Simon's Rock colleagues conducting Workshop classes.

Elective classes at BHSEC meet on a more typical college schedule. There are several reasons for this. One is logistical: several of these electives have been taught by faculty from Simon's Rock or Bard who commute to the school, or by a distinguished writer who also teaches at the CUNY graduate center, a post doctoral student doing research at Columbia University Hospital, or a scholar who also teaches at NYU. We felt these were important opportunities for the students, enabling them to take courses in such fields as Neuroscience, African History, Economics, Abnormal Psychology, and Philosophy of Law and to benefit from our ties to other colleges. In cases where the visiting professor could meet them only one day per week, we arranged a second recitation session where students could ask questions and do a variety of related assignments. Second, these are courses the students select based on their interests and direction. It seems likely that they will be more motivated to work outside the classroom in these areas.

Finally, this fits into our larger plan of gradually building students' readiness for college. Students in the ninth grade have only two or three free periods for study in the building per week. Those in tenth grade have a bit more flexibility, notably in their Doing Art selection. First-year college students take four required classes and one elective each semester. They are no longer meeting the state physical education requirement, which means that most days they have at least one period free. They are allowed to leave the building during the day for lunch and once their classes are over to pursue research or internships.

Second-year college students usually take primarily elective courses, and thus have a greater proportion of their work to be completed outside of class and even greater flexibility in their schedules. Most seem ready to take on this responsibility and, we feel, will be able to adjust to a typical college schedule when they transfer.

"Do students at BHSEC experience learning at the college level that is similar to what students experience at Simon's Rock?" is a question we were frequently asked in our first two years of operation. Certainly, this is our goal. In our first year, we had a good deal of evidence that they are. When a Simon's Rock faculty member came to BHSEC to give the lecture on Dante to the "First Year Seminar" class, which he frequently gives to a similar group at Simon's Rock, he was deeply impressed with BHSEC students' familiarity and obvious engagement with *The Inferno*, as well as with the quality of their observations and questions. This was gratifying, since several of the seminar teachers were working with this text for the first time.

The BHSEC faculty who have significant experience in other post-secondary settings all observe that the quality and sophistication of the work expected and achieved is comparable to what they have received from college students elsewhere. Simon's Rock faculty members who have guest lectured in BHSEC classes have found them as lively and prepared to engage with ideas as their students in Great Barrington. We are using the same, or similar level, books in many courses, notably "First Year Seminar," "Introduction to Psychology," "Physics with Calculus," and "Chinese."

Areas of concern were mathematics and languages. We began with the observation that college language courses progress at a pace and with a seriousness that is simply not the norm in most high schools, as evidenced by how many students who have taken years of language study still place into introductory courses when they get to college. This is one of the redundancies in the articulation between high school and college that our school was designed to address and we were determined to do so.

The problem was intensified in our first year because of our numbers. With only 114 students in the first-year college class and 130 ninth graders, it made the most sense to divide students taking each of our three languages by ability level rather than by grade. However, we observed that most ninth graders did not have the study skills and maturity to work at the college pace we aspired to. Many students at both levels also lacked basic grammatical information that is often assumed in language classes.

Accordingly, we devised an innovative foreign language curriculum designed to get students working at a college pace by the second semester of the tenth grade, with the goal that they enter the college program prepared for an intermediate-level (second-year) college course. In their first semester as ninth graders, they take an introduction to language study, which includes modules in Chinese, Latin, and Spanish—the three foreign languages offered at the school—as well as in English. This gives them some sense of the grammatical features of language and how they work, as well as practice in and techniques for mastering vocabulary and pronunciation. This led to stronger enrollments in Chinese and Latin and to much greater commitment to gaining mastery.

Early college is particularly suitable for students gifted in mathematics, given the sequential nature of the subject. Consequently, the curriculum for ninth and tenth grade has to be carefully designed to enable strong students to go on to calculus as first-year college students and to assure that the weakest students have a solid enough foundation to undertake more basic college mathematics courses.

The first class of students who began at BHSEC as ninth graders in September 2001, and graduated with their A.A. degrees in June 2004, have now graduated from four-year institutions, and a number are in graduate or professional schools. The first ninety-seven graduates, those who entered the early college program after completing tenth grade at other schools, all successfully went on to four-year colleges, many of them with junior status. And now the similar first class at BHSEC II has also graduated and moved on to four-year schools. Both groups have reported finding themselves well prepared, particularly as writers and independent learners, for the expectations of the colleges to which they transferred, whether one of the SUNY campuses or a private college like Haverford or Bard College. The students in both of these classes were the courageous risk-takers who decided to take a chance on a brand-new school that did not yet have books, a defined curriculum, or even a building, but only an idea. As the faculty has grown in their confidence and experience in preparing students for early college work, as laboratories have been built and traditions established, the school must also continue to treasure that spirit of experimentation that motivated these students, as it did Mrs. Hall and the generations of students who have moved through Simon's Rock. Although early college has become a national movement, it must not lose the sense of intellectual adventure that is essential to its appeal.[16]

NOTES

1. Jobs for the Future, "Early College High Schools: A Portrait in Numbers," accessed July 3, 2010. *http://www.jff.org/publications/education/portrait-numbers/741*.
2. Janet Lieberman, Personal oral communication, 2002.
3. Jack Meiland, *College Thinking* (New York: Penguin Books, 1982), 13.
4. Ibid., 11.
5. Ibid., 14.
6. Mihaly Csikszentmihalyi and Barbara Schneider, *Becoming Adult: How Teenagers Prepare for the World of Work* (New York: Basic Books, 2000), 148–149.
7. Ibid., 146.

8. "Early College High School Initiative,"accessed October 31, 2010, *http://www.earlycolleges.org/*.

9. Diane Ravitch, *Left Back: A Century of Failed School Reforms* (New York: Simon and Schuster, 2000).

10. Alan Wolfe, "Subject Matter Matters," review of *Left Back: A Century of Failed School Reforms*, by Diane Ravitch, *The New Republic*, December 11, 2000, 41.

11. William Durden, speech at the conference, *Adolescence, Acceleration, and National Excellence*, Simon's Rock College, Great Barrington, MA, June, 1994.

12. Elizabeth Blodgett Hall, *The House of Education Needs Overhaul: The Theory Behind Simon's Rock* (National Association of Independent Schools, 1967; reprint, Great Barrington, MA: Simon's Rock College, 1973, 1994), 3.

13. Nancy R. Goldberger, "Breaking the Educational Lockstep: The Simon's Rock Experience," in *The Early College in Theory and Practice*, ed. Paul E. Kaylor (Great Barrington, MA: Simon's Rock Early College, 1978).

14. Leon Botstein, *Jefferson's Children: Education and the Promise of American Culture* (New York: Doubleday, 1997), *passim*.

15. Richard Clark, "Report on Dual Credit for the Pew Charitable Trust," June, 2001, 46.

16. This text is an updated version of an article originally published in *Time for Change: New Visions for High School*, ed. Robert W. Smith (Cresskill, NJ: Hampton Press Inc., 2006), 121–134.

WORKS CITED

Botstein, Leon. *Jefferson's Children: Education and the Promise of American Culture*. New York: Doubleday, 1997.

Clark, Richard. "Report on Dual Credit for the Pew Charitable Trust." June, 2001

Csikszentmihalyi, Mihaly and Barbara Schneider. *Becoming Adult: How Teenagers Prepare for the World of Work*. New York: Basic Books, 2000.

Goldberger, Nancy R. "Breaking the Educational Lockstep: The Simon's Rock Experience." In *The Early College in Theory and Practice*, edited by Paul E. Kaylor. Great Barrington, MA: Simon's Rock Early College, 1978

Hall, Elizabeth Blodgett. "The House of Education Needs Overhaul: The Theory Behind Simon's Rock." National Association of Independent Schools, 1967. Reprinted by Simon's Rock College, Great Barrington, MA, 1973 and 1994.

Meiland, Jack. *College Thinking*. New York: Penguin Books, 1981.

Mernissi, Fatima. *Dreams of Trespass: Tales of a Harem Girlhood*. Philadelphia: Perseus Books, 1995.

Ravitch, Diane. *Left Back: A Century of Failed School Reforms*. New York: Simon and Schuster, 2000.

Wolfe, Alan. "Subject Matter Matters." Review of *Left Back: A Century of Failed School Reforms*, by Diane Ravitch. *The New Republic*, December 11, 2000: 38–41.

15

Early Ever After

Alumni Reflect on Life after Simon's Rock

MICHAEL LAWRENCE *and* LOREN L. ALIKHAN

What does it mean to be a Simon's Rocker after leaving Simon's Rock? What does it mean to have been a "younger scholar," as students at Simon's Rock are sometimes called, once one is no longer very young? When we leave the Rock, what of the Rock stays in us? Many alumni share the conviction that their early college experience was life changing—be it subtle or pronounced, some indelible trace of our time there remains. And so it should: the school is committed to fostering lifelong habits of mind, and as students we are invited to subject ourselves profoundly to its influence, spending our most impressionable years immersed in Simon's Rock culture and pedagogy. Thus, to say that Simon's Rock has a lasting transformative effect on its students' lives is no mere nostalgic platitude; rather, it is simply to say that Simon's Rock delivers on its promise. And yet, what do we really know about that long-lasting influence?

A comprehensive study of life after Simon's Rock would be fascinating, but our goals here are considerably more modest: as a first gesture toward understanding what it means to have been a Simon's Rocker, what it means to have achieved the sort of transformation we were promised, we distributed a series of writing prompts to a number of our fellow alumni, inviting them to reflect on how their experiences as younger scholars continue to shape their lives as adults. The thoughts and stories we collected are of course anecdotal, and the pool of respondents skews towards our own cohort, most of whom have been away from the college for almost a decade at the time of this writing. The responses we received ranged from gushing to clinical. Many were quite eloquent. Most were wonderfully thoughtful and heartfelt. To preserve the plurality of distinct voices, we've quilted together extended quotations rather than attempting to forge from them a singular message. We couldn't include all of the great material we received, so we've presented a selection that we feel best characterizes the range of perspectives reported.

The school we attended has evolved—there are new faculty, new leadership, a new name, and perhaps most notably, the early college path is less of an anomaly today than it was when we took the risk of following it. Given the complexity of the forces that influence our lives, any conclusion about how our time at Simon's Rock has shaped the people we have become risks a kind of *post Rock, ergo propter Rock* fallacy. Nevertheless, we believe that the comments collected here represent an honest—and we hope illuminating—sketch of how Simon's Rock has been written into the narratives of our lives.

INCITEMENT TO DISCOURSE: THE GIFT AND CHALLENGE OF TALKING ABOUT SIMON'S ROCK

Simon's Rock prides itself on offering an educational experience that truly challenges its students—and its students take pride in meeting those challenges. Many of those challenges are the same that any college might offer. Students are asked to understand difficult material and to form thoughts about its strengths and limitations. We are asked to pose serious questions to our teachers, to our peers, and to ourselves, and to take the risk of discovering meaningful, if provisional, answers. We are asked to produce strong scholarly and creative work and then asked to make our work even better. In addition to these, there are challenges we face that are more distinctly Simon's Rock. There's the challenge of leaving home at sixteen and straying from the educational path we'd been expected to follow, be that finishing high school or going to a "big name" university. Soon after making the bold decision to go to Simon's Rock, there's the challenge of deciding whether to stay for the B.A. degree or to transfer after earning the A.A. And finally, after leaving, one of the unique challenges that alumni confront for years afterward is that of having to explain the school and the choice to go there.

Alumni often end up talking about Simon's Rock an awful lot. Because it is small and unique, we have to be prepared to talk about it every time we apply to jobs or to other schools, or really any time we meet new people. It can be exhausting, but it is also an opportunity. That little cocktail question, "Where did you go to college," invites a story as much about our school as about ourselves, and we develop strategies for deploying that story to different ends. We can use it to show how qualified we are for a job, as proof of our ambition or risk-taking or casual relationship with convention. We've heard the story used to explain an alumna's refusal to defer blindly to authority. Another offers it as an apologia for a lack of social graces. The story can serve as a litmus test too: we learn to read our interlocutor's reaction as a hint of how we'd fit in at the company or school he or she represents. We've also had to find ways to *avoid* telling the story, especially to avoid telling it in ways that make us sound like we're bragging about having been dorky little over-achievers. Perhaps, then, one of the hallmarks of Simon's Rock graduates is not so much that we're always talking about our alma mater, but that we understand the choice of when, whether, and how to talk about it as another challenge, one we can continue to work through in useful and meaningful ways for the rest of our lives.

We asked fellow alumni how they talk about Simon's Rock to people unfamiliar with the institution. We wondered if and when they "out" themselves as having gone to college early and just how they explain it. Has the way they talk about the college and their choice to go there changed over time? Here's just some of what they had to say:

> Over the years I have found myself less and less inclined to get into the whole story of Simon's Rock in casual conversation, mostly because I get tired of deflecting the "Wow, you must be really brilliant if you skipped two years of school!" line of questioning. I'm proud of my college experience and of the education I received, and if the person asking seems genuinely interested I'm happy to elaborate. But if it comes up in passing, very often I'll just give the name of the school and explain that it's a small liberal arts college in the Berkshires that most people haven't heard of and leave it at that.
>
> I don't feel sheepish about it or embarrassed, and I'm not trying to blend in. It's just that it's very hard to get people to understand not just that the Rock is unique, but why. The common assumption when you explain the early college model is that the students must be freakishly smart, that we had to "test out" of two years of school, or walk through the door with a genius IQ.
>
> —DAVID COLLINS

> I don't tell many people about Simon's Rock. It's an omission for convenience's sake—people I care about know of my past as a younger scholar, and if I'm talking to someone who wants to know about my academic credentials, I usually don't feel like going into the whole explanation. I want to protect it from their opinions. ... It's not enough to call it an early college and leave it at that; to paint it as a school of overachievers is to write it off, to simplify it beyond repair, ignoring the spirit and missing the point. Perhaps it's not convenience then, but laziness—the ease of naming my more widely known transfer school is luxurious in its brevity. No one will believe me if I say it's

not out of preference for said school's name, even though that is the truth. It was a good little school that I went to after Simon's Rock—I maybe could have loved it if I hadn't previously fallen for another—but during the two years I spent there I missed Simon's Rock terribly for the first, and was too busy preparing to leave it for the second.

—CYNTHIA GUNADI

There was a time, closer to when I was in school, that I had to justify my choice to go to SRC to others. It took a lot longer for me to have to stop justifying it to *myself.* Many people, my parents included, had expected me to go make my mark at a big-name school. My guidance counselor told me I was "throwing away my future" by dropping out and going to SRC. As my friends and peers headed off to schools people had heard of and respected, I wondered if I had made a mistake. I thought about transferring. A lot. I left for a term, and then went back, realizing that there was really only one place I wanted to learn. Just after graduation, writing résumés and grad school applications, I wondered again if I had made the wrong decision. It wasn't until much later that I gained enough confidence in my own abilities and intellect, and experience at life and work, to realize that a big-name degree would have made no difference at all. Furthermore, to have missed out on SRC because of my own vanity would have been a tragedy indeed.

—SIMONE

I do indeed feel like I have to justify it, and I spend a reasonable amount of time soft-shoeing around the notion of being a younger scholar in an effort to avoid awkward conversation about my child genius status or lack thereof. But justify it I do! ... I spend my fair share of time proselytizing on its behalf. I describe it as the option for students who feel that they are wasting their time in high school, and are ready to move forward with their lives, whether academically or socially, but usually both.

—ELI ROOD

Since I left the Rock for graduate school, I have been uncomfortable being younger than everyone else. My first year of law school, when I was still under legal drinking age, was particularly awkward because drinking in bars and at parties seems to be a huge part of law school social life. One benefit of the "head start" is that it allowed me to finish a J.D. and a Ph.D. and still be within the normal age range for a Ph.D. recipient. ... When I started teaching in graduate school, I was very self-conscious about trying to put a distance between my students and myself. I was especially nervous about this when I started my current job at a campus that attracts a lot of non-traditional students who are older than I. Just this year (at thirty-one), I finally feel comfortable being the age I am and not feeling like I'm too young or inexperienced to be taken seriously. ...

—PETRA

I had to learn some delicate ways of talking about Simon's Rock when I was in graduate school, mostly because I noticed that I lost a bit of authority when some people realized how young I was. It was never an issue when talking with classmates or teachers who had more than a few years on me; it was only ever mentioned by colleagues who were just a year or two older, that is, folks who were themselves a little uneasy about being among the younger members of the cohort. It was definitely something I avoided mentioning to my students. They knew I was young of course, and they'd note on my evaluations that they liked having an instructor they could "relate to," but I knew it was better not to let them know just how young. This, too, was less of an issue when I had so-called "non-traditional students" who were ten or fifteen years my senior. They respected my position and what I had to teach them, and they didn't care about my age. In fact, I found I was more at ease than were some of my colleagues when it came to teaching older students.

One of the things I've learned we have to be prepared for when talking about Simon's Rock is the "I wish I'd known about that" reaction. There are plenty of people who, hearing about Simon's Rock, volunteer all kinds of intimate details about how unhappy they were in high school and how desperately they could have used an alternative. They understand right away that all kinds of young people could use something different.

—MICHAEL LAWRENCE

I proudly let people know I never graduated high school. Heading off to college after tenth grade is an accomplishment to be proud of. No apologies needed. It does not come up much now, but when I was recently graduated I needed to do a lot more explaining. The "early college movement" did not exist. ...

Now no one is really interested if I went to high school, so I need to figure out other ways to work it into the conversation. I do get to talk about it a lot in regards to my daughter. She is a junior at the Rock. When I talk about the Simon's Rock she attends I tend to focus on how Simon's Rock is a college for scholars, people, who happen to be younger than other college students, who are very interested in scholarly academic pursuits. I talk about the small classroom size and intimate learning experience, the first-name basis with professors.

—KEITH BRIERLEY-BOWERS

INTERSECTING MODES OF ALTERNATIVE:
YOUNGER, BUT NOT ONLY

Throughout its relatively short history, Simon's Rock has been unmistakably *alternative*. As students, we had a sense not just that we were doing something cool, but that we were doing something *different*. It wasn't just about taking great classes, it was about taking those great seminars *instead of* sitting in some required class with the high school classmates we'd left behind. We had made a choice, exercising a degree of agency over our education that many first-year college students don't feel like they have. More traditional students may have a say about *where* they go, but many feel they have no choice about *when* or *whether* they go. When I [Michael] asked my students at a big state university why they decided to go to college, many of them had trouble making sense of the question; they felt like they hadn't "decided" anything at all. As access to higher education has expanded, so too has the thinking that a college degree is not so much an accomplishment as it is an expectation. And when students understand college as compulsory, the dreaded "I'm just here for the piece of paper" mentality flourishes. By contrast, many Simon's Rockers give up on the "piece of paper" mentality when they shrug off their high school diploma, and do so once again by choosing Simon's Rock over that big-name university.

When we consider what makes Simon's Rock work, it becomes important to make a few distinctions. Yes, Simon's Rock is different, and part of that difference, though certainly not all of it, is rooted in the fact that it is an early college. But there are other characteristics. Simon's Rock is tiny. It is geographically isolated. It is expensive. It is largely residential. It has no fraternities or sororities or major sports programs. It has a core curriculum built around a "First-Year" and "Sophomore Seminar" program. It has a senior thesis requirement, but it also has an expectation that only a fraction of the students will choose to stay for their bachelor's degree. To try to learn about "early college" broadly by examining Simon's Rock in particular is to risk privileging just one of the school's distinguishing features above all the others. It also risks overlooking the fact that for most Simon's Rock students to date, early college has been an unusual choice—and this rarity as such has shaped the community's understanding of itself.

Simon's Rock alumni are inevitably talking about more than just the idea of early college when we reflect on our experience. We're talking about small liberal arts education. We're talking through the haze of nostalgia about having been a part of an experiment in the Berkshires. We're talking about having made a bold choice and about having surrounded ourselves with others who had done the same. Given all these factors, we've got to consider just how and to what extent the "early" part of "early college" matters; we cannot assume that it is the one feature that makes all the difference. To begin to understand this, we asked alumni to consider how "earliness" shaped their Simon's Rock education. How did the fact that we were younger make a difference? Are the distinguishing features of that experience bound up with the early college mission? Would it have been the same if early college had been a more widely available option, or was it important that Simon's Rock was doing something unconventional? We found that, yes, the "earliness" figures prominently in our stories, but not always for the reasons that might be expected.

> I think that starting at a younger age meant I was more idealistic, more willing to embrace new ideas and dive headlong into intellectual pursuits. Maybe it has to do with skipping over the "senior slump"—not spending an entire year going through the motions academically, having already checked out of that environment. The cynic in me would say I had two fewer years of damage inflicted on me by the mainstream educational system than the typical student. From a strictly developmental standpoint, most teens are still in more of an exploratory stage at sixteen as opposed to eighteen. I definitely liked the increased freedom of living away from home and the chance to get away from the daily routine of high school.
>
> The unconventional aspect was certainly a selling point for me; my sense is that I would have still embraced the process if it were more widely available, but perhaps not as fully and enthusiastically. At the time, its weirdness was appealing to me, but looking back I think the small college atmosphere, the collegial environment, the sense of intimacy and community that were integral to the learning process—all those were of much greater importance to my sense of belonging, even if I might not have put my finger on it while I was there.
>
> —DAVID COLLINS

> I spent a semester at an experimental college, founded about the same time as SR, on the main campus of a larger university. Those students have a lot in common with Rockers, and I would imagine that many of them could or would have been Rockers if given the opportunity. Having seen a small community of intelligent, free-thinking individuals in action on a mainstream campus, I am not sure that it is age that makes the biggest difference at the Rock. That said, though, the energy coming from so many, so young, with so much to prove, cannot be overstated.
>
> —SIMONE

> The earliness certainly mattered at the time. Getting out of high school two years early was a pretty big motivator for getting an application together. I think it was important to sixteen- and seventeen-year-old me to feel smart

and advanced. Twenty-nine-year-old me, however, has a more nuanced perspective: intelligence is more than just cleverness—it requires practice and effort to develop. Simon's Rock pushed me to understand and develop that side of my intellectual life, even if that wasn't what seemed most important at the time.

—DANIEL NEILSON

I see myself at sixteen as naive and a little bit dopey—the product of a small town, Catholic high school, and a loving but rather apolitical family. ... My high school left me suffocating in its apathy. When I imagine myself back in my first year at Simon's Rock, I remember a feeling of exhalation and homecoming. Here were the people whom I wanted to learn with and from.

It is such a daunting task to try to unpack what those years meant to me. How do you pare down something so seminal and complicated? Not only were they formative at the time, but when I now try to distill the narratives of my life I usually find a way to connect them—directly or tangentially—back to the decision of leaving high school early to attend Simon's Rock. Whether or not it's true I tend to bind much of my identity and my successes (or failures) to that decision.

For this reason it feels intensely personal to reveal my inner younger scholar. I shyly take great pride in that leap we all made. Whether or not they loved the school, every student was there because she or he chose it. It was an active decision, not something merely happened across and not something done for convention's sake. This active seeking bloomed in the classrooms and the dorm rooms. That adolescent earnestness, the indie cool, the hippie joy. Reason says I could have been happy in many places, along other paths not chosen, but of course I don't really want to believe that. What would my life be if I never met the friends or professors who so strongly influenced me?

—CYNTHIA GUNADI

I was not at all interested in pursuing the few options of being an accelerated student amongst a crowd of conventional college students. I wanted to be amongst my peers, but until that postcard from SRC showed up, I just didn't know where to find them. Had there been other colleges doing the same thing as SRC, I might have explored them, but it was very important to me to go to a place where everyone was on the same track, and where everyone had taken the time to examine his or her options and pursue an unconventional path.

[Then Bard Vice President and Simon's Rock Dean] Bernie Rodgers used to talk about SR as a community of kindred spirits, and that has always resonated very strongly with me. One of the best parts of an early college experience, I always thought, is that we all chose to be there—we didn't get swept along to college by the tide of family/friends/public opinion. We had to consciously take ourselves off the usual path and onto this one, and I think it makes for a more engaged and committed academic atmosphere.

—ELI ROOD

The sense that one has had a fabulous, unexpected, and possibly undeserved stroke of luck in finding Simon's Rock is tremendously motivating. It was a lot to live up to. Also, I think teenagers are less cautious than older students, not having experienced much responsibility. They will say anything, they don't shy away from being shocking, and they live moment to moment. ... It made things visceral and exciting.

There was something very special about SRC that came from the fact that we were the age we were, but ultimately, that was only one of many of the special things about the place and the education I got there. Features such as the size and setting may have been more crucial. Interacting constantly with people I found deeply intimidating (our faculty, whose experiences made them giants in my eyes), being treated with respect by those people, and developing ideas about the world side-by-side with peers—those things made me a thinking adult.

—SARAH PARADY

As a Simon's Rocker who was a couple of years older than my classmates, I didn't feel like I was dealing with younger kids. In a way age didn't matter anymore; I was not "older," they were not "younger". ... We were connected as fellow Simon's Rockers and as friends. Since I was coming from a different country with a distinct culture, ... I felt that every experience was new, all the clichés were new ideas to me.

—PAULA JUNN

I am not sure the early part shaped my education per se, at least not the classroom education. ... The fact that I went to college after tenth grade, debated with professors who took me seriously as a person, as a scholar, those aspects of the school imparted a great sense of self worth and imbued me with confidence to take risks.

The very nature of going to college early served to reinforce my proclivity for taking risks, and the way thinking is taught at the Rock furthered my tendency toward unconventional thinking. Companies pay me a lot of money because I will take on projects no one else thinks can work and I come up with solutions that stump others. Risk and creative thinking are how I make my livelihood.

—KEITH BRIERLEY-BOWERS

NOT JUST YOUNGER, BUT ALSO SCHOLARS

Taking the risk of doing something different on our educational path forces all Simon's Rockers to think a lot about things other college students may take for granted. We're asked to think not only about *where* to go, but also *when* to go. If we stay for the B.A., the Moderation process[1] requires us to think carefully about our academic plans and to justify them to others. In short, Simon's Rockers don't get to follow a course of study, we get to create one.

For many of us, our formal education doesn't end when we leave Simon's Rock. Very many of us go on to all kinds of other institutions, be they large state schools, small liberal arts colleges, or elite private universities. Some of us pursue graduate education. Simon's Rockers go on to law schools, art schools, massage schools, divinity schools, military training, conservatories, medical schools, culinary schools. ... It is the norm rather than the exception for Simon's Rock to figure as only one piece of its students' higher education experience. Just as we were always quick to compare Simon's Rock to the high schools we'd left behind, it becomes a standard against which we measure the other learning communities we join. Quite a few alumni go on to do some teaching of their own, in which case our early college experience may shape our own pedagogy, influencing our notion of just what is possible in the classroom.

With this in mind, we asked alumni to reflect on Simon's Rock's unique brand of pedagogy and compare it with their experience at other educational institutions. Did the SR experience continue to shape their learning? Did it make them a different kind of scholar or teacher? Which of the hallmarks of learning and teaching at Simon's Rock—"Writing and Thinking Workshop," all those free-writes and response journals, "First-Year Seminar," Moderation, B.A. Thesis—have stayed with them, continuing to shape their work and their habits of mind?

> I found many of my undergraduate courses at Simon's Rock quite a bit more challenging and engaging than those in my Ivy League graduate program. I also found myself far better prepared for graduate level work than many of my peers, and the strengths I gained from areas of emphasis at Simon's Rock—critical thinking, writing and the discussion format, to be precise— were often what separated me from the pack. Being able to attack difficult or complicated issues in a clear, purposeful fashion, and being able to commit

my thoughts to writing effectively, have been absolutely invaluable skills to me ever since I left the Rock, although I never could have predicted exactly how they would come in handy. At the time I thought I was preparing to write beautiful prose and political philosophy; it turned out, however, that the process prepared me just as well to debate social welfare policies and submit program proposals, which sounds entirely unromantic but has actually been a fulfilling experience.

Writing and Thinking and the Seminars prepared me to express ideas clearly, to read with attention to detail and a critical eye, and to take nuanced positions and deal comfortably with ambiguity and uncertainty. The B.A. thesis gave me experience tackling an enormous project and seeing it through to completion.

—David Collins

I found graduate school enormously frustrating, which I attribute to having grown up academically at SR. After choosing and planning my own course of study at Simon's Rock, the prescriptive syllabus of my well-respected English grad school was stifling. Classmates of mine were thrilled with the freedom to choose between writing on Reading A or Reading B. It sounds trite to say so, but I thought I would die of boredom. The whole experience made me reconsider if I would be able to work in the mainstream academy at all. By the end of the year, I was so frustrated that I gave up on the idea of continuing from my Master's to a Ph.D. (a plan I had always held dear) and went on to other things.

—Simone

I noticed the difference most clearly during my first year in graduate school. There was a profound unwillingness among my cohort to critically engage and question the professors; they were much more about absorption of information. Working in the following semesters as a teaching assistant, I saw how these students came to see their education in this way—the undergraduates I taught, even at a "good" school, were all about mastering a fixed set of ideas for the exam. Having now also taught at Simon's Rock, there is no comparison—anything the SR students might lack in preparation, advanced math, whatever, they make up in willingness to discuss, to debate, to question.

Being a professor at Simon's Rock brings it all home. The effort is always in getting everyone engaged; a successful class is one in which everyone has contributed and the discussion has felt productive. I love having to be ready to moderate a discussion that may differ markedly from what I imagined when preparing. And when this happens, I feel like I have succeeded as a professor—I have created a space where my students and I challenged each other to ask and answer new questions. This experience is fundamentally at odds with the idea of learning as absorption.

—DANIEL NEILSON

I've heard from many non-Rocker friends that my tales of the Rock remind them a lot of their own small liberal arts college experience, and that some of what I attribute to SR's culture is really more ubiquitous as "tiny liberal arts college" culture. But I think the stakes are higher for Rockers, since we're younger, and it means more to us to be taken so seriously so quickly. I cannot overestimate the value of the confidence that I gained from my time at the Rock. I can only hope it doesn't make me tend towards overconfidence!

—ELI ROOD

The graduate program I am in now seems to value the same ideals as SRC did during my time there: writing, questioning, teacher/student interaction that is not hierarchical, individual responsibility, genuine thinking, whole to part teaching, and constant self-reflection. ... The ingrained habits of inquiry and self-reflection that I developed at SRC have not only served me well in my own life, but have become my most valuable tools as I begin to view myself as a teacher.

—ELICIA CÁRDENAS

GROWING UP AND MOVING ON:
YOUNGER, BUT NOT ALWAYS

When we graduated from Simon's Rock with our A.A. or B.A. degrees and went on to join other institutions and communities, the feature that perhaps most readily distinguished us from our new colleagues was that we were eighteen or twenty while our peers were at least in their twenties. But the significance of this age gap fades over time, both because we grow older and because individuals are not as closely tracked and grouped by age in the workforce and graduate programs as they are in secondary school and college. As this age gap closes, we wondered, what do Simon's Rock alumni see as the defining characteristics of their early college education? Is their status of having been a sixteen-year-old college freshman the most salient feature, or is there some other aspect of the early college experience that persists? Did they feel different from their colleagues who followed more traditional paths? What were the advantages or disadvantages of this unique position? We asked alumni to reflect on the aspects of the "younger scholar" identity that have stayed with them. What ways of thinking, ways of being, ways of approaching risks or challenges, remain? What has fallen away? Is there a point at which Rockers stop thinking of themselves as younger than everybody else? As a part of a rather small community at SR, one of the skills we had to perfect was just being a member of that particular community, with all its idiosyncrasies. What happens as we transition to other communities? In what ways are we prepared, and in what ways is it a challenge?

     I am a plaintiffs' lawyer who has owned my own firm since passing the bar exam. The success of my firm depends upon the connections I make outside of the practice of law, especially in volunteer work and the roles I am able to take on in my state's trial lawyer organization. In the four short years of my law practice, I have managed to climb to the very top of the pyramid in my state organization. In fact, I am the youngest attorney to ever be appointed to their board of directors. How did I do that? I'm not more skilled, more successful, or more socially connected than other young trial attorneys in Kansas. I believe my success in networking (and just plain working) with more senior attorneys can be directly attributed to the non-hierarchical learning structure at Simon's Rock. My non-Simon's Rock peers have bought into the idea that if you're young, your opinions and ideas matter less. It's just like that wise Eleanor Roosevelt quote: "No one can make you feel inferior without your consent." Young people have consented to the idea that their opinions and their abilities are inferior to their elders. Young attorneys have also fallen victim to this related saying: If you act like a child, you will be treated like a child. By showing unnecessary deference in their social interactions with older attorneys, and by hesitating to challenge the ideas put forth by the same, young attorneys have a hard time garnering respect or recognition, let alone client referrals.

     This is where I differ from my peers. At Simon's Rock, not only was I encouraged to share my opinions and ideas with all and sundry, my grade depended upon it. Simon's Rock equates success with a young person's ability to reject our culture's insistence that we should be seen and not heard. Success at Simon's Rock means rejecting the notion that the way I see the world is somehow inferior to those who have been in it longer. From the beginning I have always treated older and more successful colleagues as equals, and like any good Rocker, it physically hurts me to not share my ideas with them. In turn they have accorded me the respect they give to their peers. It was not a conscious strategy of mine at the time. I only realized the difference when reflecting on how I had managed to move further and faster than other young attorneys. It turns out that it's not magic—it's just Simon's Rock.

While a student at Simon's Rock, if you had asked me what the deal was with discussion-based classes and the professors and the administration going by their first names, I would have told you it's just some gimmick left over from the hippies who founded the school. Now, I will tell you that the teaching methods employed at Simon's Rock establish a rock-solid framework for the empowerment and success of young people, the benefits of which I am still reaping a decade later.

—RACHEL MONGER

On a social level, I have stayed largely within small, idiosyncratic communities, so I feel exceptionally well prepared by my time at the Rock! Professionally and academically, I was underprepared for how difficult it would be to form meaningful connections. Being cooped up at the Rock where all professional relationships are also personal gave me perhaps a blurred sense of boundaries, and I worry that sometimes I come across as too forward, too eager to make a personal connection. . . .

Having been sixteen (or fifteen, in my case!) when I arrived at college remains the most unusual feature, but I don't believe it is forever the most pertinent. Though it's not unrelated to what may be the most salient, which is the maturity and confidence that I gained, as an academic, as an artist, just as a person. I do believe that being respected and given responsibility, and having an opportunity to be a fully functioning member of a community, gave me an early sense of my self and my abilities. In addition, I have always felt the luxury of having plenty of time to find my career and my life path. I have felt the two years that I skipped in high school to be a buffer—I feel like I have time to explore options, and reverse course, because I am two years younger.

—ELI ROOD

For me, one of the unanticipated perks of finishing college early is the luxury of having a few extra years to play with before the pressure sets in to "grow up" and set about achieving major personal and professional milestones. It's as though SRC alumni have two "bonus" years in our twenties to explore—personally, professionally, or geographically. Many of my fellow alumni spent those years in the Peace Corps or Teach for America. I went to law school after Simon's Rock and graduated at twenty-two. Completing law school at an age when many are just finishing college enabled me to explore different aspects of the law through clerkships and fellowships without ever feeling like I was in a rush to settle into a particular practice area or job.

—LOREN L. ALIKHAN

The expectation of women to be mothers and keepers of households, with no congruent added expectation for men, is very real and very hard to face. And this has been the most unexpected reason I'm grateful to SRC: that two-year head start really means something; something especially valuable to women. Because of Simon's Rock, at twenty-seven I'm professionally established to a degree that will make it easier for me to negotiate everything I want from life in the next few years.

I have noticed that I have a deep-seated resistance to formalities and symbols of status, which we largely disposed of at Simon's Rock. I embarrassed myself during my first year of law school by blurting out a professor's first name in a discussion, but I was also angry to have been embarrassed: I will always believe that enforced use of titles does harm by reinforcing the divide between people who have them and people who don't. I try very hard to hold onto that sense in my day-to-day life as a member of a formalistic and status-respecting profession.

—SARAH PARADY

For me the age gap hasn't closed, but I'm happy about that; Simon's Rock made me believe that I didn't have to wait in line for anything, whether it be a college education or a job that I know I can handle. We are often told, growing up, that motivation and merit conquer all obstacles; that if you're good enough, you will find a way to get the things you want. But nothing about the American educational system made me *believe* that; it seemed like I spent most of my time waiting to get something over with or wishing I was somewhere else, no matter how well I did. Simon's Rock was the first place where I really saw that practical connection between my level of ability, effort, and the outcome of my work. Despite being told my whole life that the world is full of endless possibilities, I never believed it until I got to Great Barrington.

—DAVID COLLINS

[In graduate school] I have consistently been praised for having a broad and original approach to my research. The interdisciplinary social science education I received [at Simon's Rock] also informs my teaching to help me bring in a broad variety of aspects of world political and social experience, rather than just straight political science. On the negative side, I don't always do enough to ground my writing in the established literature, a must in academic writing.

As much as I enjoyed the education that I received at the Rock, there are some drawbacks to it. There is a tendency for Rockers to be a little too pleased with their ideas and to ignore criticism. (I would apply this to myself as well, at times.) I think there was too little emphasis on logic and reasoning and too much on expression and emotion. This emphasis made for a great experience (and probably made us better people!), but wasn't necessarily the best preparation for graduate school. As a professor, I am still struggling to strike my own balance between these two concerns.

—PETRA

ONE OF A KIND, OR A MODEL TO EMULATE?

Recently, a broad national debate has ignited about whether the last two years of high school really matter. Should everyone be encouraged to go to college (or learn a trade, or pursue other options) after tenth grade? That's an idea that Simon's Rock has been thinking about for forty years. Part of the motivation behind this chapter (and this book) is the thought that Simon's Rock can serve as an instructive point of inspiration, maybe even a model, for new programs developing across the country. Indeed, the school is already doing just that, perhaps most directly through the two Bard High School Early College campuses in New York City, where a Simon's Rock–style education is made available as an option through the public school system. BHSEC continues the emphasis on smaller seminar-style classes, the development of writing and thinking skills, and a full load of college courses beginning after tenth grade. But are there aspects of the Simon's Rock experience that can't be replicated? With that in mind, we posed these final prompts to our alumni respondents: How does your experience as a Rocker inform the way you view the expansion of early college programs across the country? What elements of your early college experience do you think would be translatable to another institution? What parts are unique to Simon's Rock?

> Simon's Rock is a combination of several unique and progressive ideas, and for that reason I think it will always be one of a kind, or close to it. (Also in no small part because it can be prohibitively expensive and the economies of scale enjoyed by larger schools just aren't present). But the broader principles underlying each of those ideas—the flexible, individualized approach to learning, the emphasis on skills and ideas rather than standardized testing, the availability of a broader range of options as students enter late adolescence—these are all applicable in a much wider context and I think we will continue to see innovation in each of these areas.

—DAVID COLLINS

Perhaps the one key realization inherent in SR is that your education is what you make of it. This is what changed the moment I learned that I could leave high school and go to college. I think that everyone should have such an opportunity. Not all will choose a liberal arts education, to be sure. Many might even choose four years of high school. But having the chance to define what we fill our minds with—with some guidelines perhaps—is tremendous.

—DANIEL NEILSON

Just as "regular" colleges have different focuses, so too can early colleges. . . . I am sure there are students who, as [Simon's Rock founder] Betty Hall used to say, find the last two years of high school a waste, but who are not scholars. They may be students interested in a more applied college education. They may be people interested in learning complex trades.

The Simon's Rock experience needs to be taken as a whole, not in its components. There was and is a synergistic effect of the school's approach to students, pedagogy, the student's self-selection and the uniqueness of the experience. From what I have seen over the years, Simon's Rockers tend to bend the world to their own twist on living. We may not be the biggest movers and shakers, but we seem to consistently make life *work* for us by pursing our interests and passions, not just careers: Nat makes a living writing comic books; Peter keeps mastering new branches of engineering so he can play with new toys; Kim researches winter ecology because she like playing outside in winter; Alanna writes role-playing books and games because she likes traveling and role-playing. . . . [The] list goes on. They all seem to make it work.

—KEITH BRIERLEY-BOWERS

CONCLUSION

If this chapter demonstrates anything, it is that there are plenty of Simon's Rock alumni willing to speak and write enthusiastically about their experience of early college. But more than that, these reflections illustrate the many ways in which the experience has become written into the narratives of its students' lives. Simon's Rock is the name we give to a formative chapter of our youth, but it is also a name for the risks we have taken, a name for a whole way of thinking, a name for a worldview we hold dear.

Our hope is that this chapter contributes to a broader conversation about the rich possibilities of early college and that we might provide some insight into what it is that Simon's Rock is doing right. We conclude with a few brief thoughts on what the comments collected here have to teach.

Something about the Simon's Rock experience stays with its students long after they've left the college, but this *something* is not the same for everyone. Some alumni understand the enduring impact of Simon's Rock in terms of the particular writing and thinking skills they sharpened there. Others emphasize the attitudes cultivated, crediting Simon's Rock with fostering their commitment to risk-taking, to critical reflection, to community, and to being heard. Some express gratitude for the two "extra years" after graduation that create time for growth and exploration, making room for living a bit more fully while also advancing professionally. Each comment demonstrates that Simon's Rock is something we talk about, and we talk about it with purpose. When a mention of Simon's Rock invites explanation, we find an opportunity to explain something about our own character, revealing the ways in which we might fit in or stand out, hinting at the ideals we value.

Like all stories worth telling, our accounts of early college involve challenges and complications. Notably, many of the difficulties we felt when we were students do not figure prominently in our retrospective accounts. It may have been hard leaving home at a young age, for example, but no one mentioned that here; all of our respondents recalled more vividly the welcome academic challenges. Some respondents described discomfort when starting graduate programs or a first job and being a little younger than their new peers, but this was generally experienced as a problem with other people's perceptions, not our own limitations. Many of the difficulties reported might be characterized as cultural, in that they are symptoms of the values of living and learning at Simon's Rock conflicting with the values of other communities and institutions. A commitment to egalitarianism, a sense of self-confidence and the importance of sharing our own insights might be read as a lack of deference to authority, but it might just as well be the secret of some alumni's success. A commitment to interdisciplinary inquiry that emphasized creative thinking over immersion in a particular field's canon has led some Rockers to feel a little unsteady when beginning graduate programs. And yet, everyone who mentioned this reported that after a semester or two, they had not only caught up, but had distinguished themselves as innovative and able scholars. With remarkable consistency, they did not find fault in their Simon's Rock training, but instead identified possible limitations in the style of thinking and learning expected of first-year graduate students.

There are many things that set Simon's Rock apart from other institutions, the most obvious being the age of its students. This matters a great deal, and what becomes evident from the comments collected here is that it matters in different ways; earliness fuels many of the school's other distinctive qualities. Early college means challenge and acceleration, but it also means a community composed of people who, in part because of their age, may be more willing to take risks and to think creatively. Respondents mentioned that this might also mean Simon's Rock-ers see themselves as having something to prove: as students we've got to prove we can handle the rigor, and as graduates we work to prove that we're just as quali-fied as colleagues who are a bit older or who graduated from schools with more name recognition. Being younger, we were perhaps a bit more impressionable, but alumni reflect positively on having come of age someplace other than high schools where popularity and athletic stardom were core values. Starting early meant we skipped the "senior slump," beginning college without having spent time internal-izing the notion that scholarly pursuits were mere formality, something grownups made young people do in exchange for letting them have a prom. Going to col-lege early also meant going to college deliberately—exercising agency, being part of a self-selecting community of individuals grateful to have escaped something that wasn't working for them. Everyone at Simon's Rock chooses to be there. It is nobody's "safety school," nor did anyone apply because she grew up lusting after its brand name or rooting for its sports teams. Getting us early meant getting us before we could consider many other colleges, so Simon's Rock can attract the attention of some students who, having distinguished themselves academically, might other-wise have felt pressure to consider nothing but the Ivies. More generally, we might say that earliness is bound up with the weirdness of the place, the feeling that it is something different, special, alternative.

Can Simon's Rock serve as a model to emulate, an inspiration for other pro-grams, elite or otherwise? Yes, of course. It already has, and we know there's more to come. But as the reflections included here make clear, one of the most important aspects of our Simon's Rock experience is that it meant flexibility. It provided an option, an alternative where one was badly needed. The school takes seriously the notion that students should be forging a path, not merely following one—so if there is a lesson other institutions might learn from Simon's Rock, that lesson can never take the form of a cookie-cutter template to be borrowed from one setting and installed in another. One of the most important things we learned by going to college early is that age does not matter the way our culture often insists that it should. Looking back, we remember having gone to college early as less a matter of having gone to college *younger* and more about having gone to college *deliberately* and having gone to college *differently*.

NOTE

1. During the sophomore year, any Simon's Rock student considering staying on for the B.A. goes through "Moderation." This consists of a meeting with a "Moderation Com-mittee" (the student's advisor and other faculty familiar with the student's achievements at Simon's Rock, and with the fields in which the student wishes to concentrate). At the

meeting, the student's academic record, statement of educational goals, writing samples, etc. are discussed, and a plan for the next two years is tentatively formulated. Formal acceptance into the B.A. program is confirmed by a letter from the student's advisor summarizing the course of study that the student and committee have outlined for the junior and senior years.

CONTRIBUTORS

LOREN L. ALIKHAN, B.A., 2003 (Politics, Law, and Society; Philosophy; Cultural Studies). J.D., Georgetown University.

KEITH W. BRIERLEY-BOWERS, B.A., 1984 (Social Science). M.A., West Chester University (Industrial Organizational Psychology). M.B.A., Johns Hopkins University. Independent Management consultant focusing on advising and guiding organizations through major transactions.

ELICIA CÁRDENAS, A.A., 1994. B.F.A., Boston University. M.A.T., Lewis and Clark College.

DAVID COLLINS, B.A., 2003 (Politics, Law, and Society; Music; Creative Writing). M.S.W., Columbia University. Assistant Director for Adoption & Foster Care at The Children's Village, a leading multi-service child welfare agency in New York City.

CYNTHIA GUNADI, A.A., 2000. A.B., Brown University (Art-Semiotics). M.Arch I, Harvard Graduate School of Design. Architect in Cambridge, MA.

PAULA JUNN, A.A., 2004. B.A., Expressive Arts Therapy, Lesley University. M.A., Expressive Therapies, Mental Health Counseling.

MICHAEL LAWRENCE, B.A., 2002 (Cultural Studies; Drawing, Painting and Printmaking). Ph.D., University of Iowa (Rhetorical Studies). After Simon's Rock, Michael worked as a program assistant at Bard High School Early College in Manhattan. He now teaches "First-Year Seminar" at Columbia College Chicago.

RACHEL MONGER, B.A., 2002 (Gender Studies). J.D., University of Kansas School of Law.

DANIEL H. NEILSON, B.A., 2001 (Mathematics; Music). Ph.D., Columbia University (Economics). Economist, AJA Risk Management Consultants; Visiting Assistant Professor, BCSR.

SARAH PARADY, B.A., 2003 (Politics, Law, and Society). J.D., NYU Law. Staff Attorney, Colorado Legal Services.

ELI ROOD, B.A., 2005 (Linguistics). Assistant Registrar, Franklin Pierce University in Rindge, NH.

PETRA and SIMONE are pseudonyms for respondents who asked to remain anonymous.

16

"We Work the Black Seam Together"

Ritual Politics and the Educative Ethic
of Tending Delirium

PHILIP MABRY *and* CHRIS COGGINS

We matter more than pounds and pence
Your economic theory makes no sense
–STING, *We Work the Black Seam (Together)*

THE (UNCONSCIOUS) RITUAL STRUCTURE
OF THE LIBERAL ARTS

It's an annual rite involving thousands of first-time college students and their families across North America. Planes, trains, and automobiles are loaded for the trek to an isolated retreat of higher learning. Parents' tearful goodbyes are tolerated by offspring who eagerly embark on a new adventure to discover the possibilities of adulthood, a new life, and the people they can become. Much the same happens here at Simon's Rock but with one crucial difference: not only do students come here earlier than most of their counterparts across the nation, they have made a uniquely affirmative choice to do so. Not infrequently, upon learning about Simon's Rock, prospective students must lobby their parents for permission to apply, quietly hoping that this college with a funny name represents a means to escape what had become an uninspiring or painful high school experience. In different ways, Rockers often must do battle with the adult figures in their lives for the opportunity to accelerate the course of their education, to leave high school without a diploma, and to rob their families of what are presumed to be their final years at home before beginning their lives as independent adults.

The decision to matriculate at Simon's Rock, in other words, is weighted in ways that are fundamentally different than for most college-bound students for whom the first year away from home is a long-anticipated milestone in their life-trajectory. And with this weighty decision to interrupt life-as-usual comes a number of important consequences, both disruptive and exhilarating. We will argue that this experience can be seen as analogous to the initial phase of the ritual process as described by anthropologist and comparative symbologist Victor Turner.[1] Like other ritual subjects, our students are invited to make the passage, or transition, from the structural conditions that define one phase of their lives—in this case, childhood and early adolescence—into their college years, a period of profound personal transformation, in this case on the outskirts of a small New England town, and finally (with some good fortune and plenty of fortitude) to return to life beyond the halls of academia, as young adults possessed of college degrees and student loans to pay off, but also fundamentally transformed.

Departures and Beginnings

Strangely—or perhaps not—the journey to a North American liberal arts college environment frequently involves a "removal" from the everyday world with which students have become familiar, a departure from what has defined their home and their belonging, marked by entry into a new and different place. It is worth stating the obvious here: liberal arts colleges in the United States are notorious for being a world unto themselves, socially and often spatially separate from their environs. So isolated are many such colleges—"in the middle of nowhere," as some students complain—that many towns bear the same name as the institution itself, having no (appellative) "identity" other than the institution that calls it home.[2]

If many small, private liberal arts colleges in the United States are so removed from urban life, this has much to do with the decisions by early founders to locate these institutions in pastoral places, far from the madding crowd, likely a historical (and cultural) precipitate of the era during which many of the nation's liberal arts colleges were founded, when education was unabashedly infused with a variety of heroic missions, both religious and secular.[3] And while a multiplicity of functions were ascribed to North American colleges and universities between the seventeenth and nineteenth centuries, many were implanted in the midst of nature where the immensity and purpose of the divine (or sublime) could be contemplated uninterrupted and uncorrupted by the doings of man, a purpose for which removal from the overwhelming distraction and pollution of urban living was an imperative.

Clearly, this is no longer the overarching narrative that frames the work of higher education—although, at key moments, echoes of it can still be heard—and so, as a result, this physical isolation is, at best, viewed as a recreational and natural amenity and, at worst, a condemnation and banishment from the "real" world.

It is worth noting, however, that such spatial separation and removal is what students of religion have taken to be one of the hallmark signs of the sacred, insofar as it designates that which sits in contrast to the profane.[4] Lest it be forgotten, the idyllic—and distant—setting of many of the nation's liberal arts colleges recalls the notion of "retreat," a term commonly paired with the goal of "renewal." In this sense, North American liberal arts institutions draw on symbols of a monastic tradition premised on the value of withdrawing from public life for the purpose of seeking truth and transformation. In this light, it is no coincidence that U.S. liberal arts colleges of the eighteenth and nineteenth centuries were established by various Protestant denominations, and that their presidents were predominantly members of the clergy.[5] Retreat and spatial sequestration bearing strong traces of spiritual eremitism mark the North American reworking and domestication of the medieval European university, an institution that bred tremendous social conflict and contestation and helped give rise to the very possibility of a secular-religious divide.[6]

The persistence of symbolic retreat and sequestration is most evident in that annual ceremony we call Commencement, a term that clearly delineates the end of a period of incubation, and which has its formal origins in the medieval rites of "educational passage," such as those marking the ranks of those qualified to teach.[7] As with any ritual, ceremonies of completion denote a change in status, publicly marking a turning point in identity.[8] While students enter the institution uninitiated, upon graduation they are presumed to have been transformed by a disciplined experience, bearing the right to wear cap-and-gown and obligated to reenter the world to make a contribution among the living. Since "commencement" points to the passage from one world to another, mirrored by such a shift in status, it marks the culmination and fruition of a preceding period of gestation.

Beyond this, annual graduations are one of the few moments in calendrical time when liberal arts institutions embrace high ceremony. Informality in dress and address are exchanged for ornate phrases and foreign tongues, in addition to cap-and-gown. Rank-and-file solemnized to the tune of *Pomp and Circumstance* replaces the unremarkable and mundane rituals of college life—syllabi, lectures, seminars, exams, and papers. The compulsion to seriousness and study is replaced with noisy celebration and unabashed emotional display. A public—family and friends—is invited for the show, as students, faculty and administrators don the colors that define their especial status, marking the distribution of social honor that defines the institution and the scale against which the passage the initiates have just completed should be measured. Invited guests of honor are recruited to speak to the gravity of the moment, to commemorate the achievements of the past and invoke the obligations of the future. Parchment exchanges hands. Tassels are flipped.

Procession. Recession. Benediction.

These remnants from a previous age epitomize the completion of a ritual process. As such, commencement can be seen as a contemporary analogue to the rites of passage that, in other contexts, marked the achievement of adulthood in the eyes of the community. It stands among those time-honored religious occasions that highlight pivotal moments that punctuate the course of life: naming ceremonies that bless the newly arrived, rituals publicizing full membership in the (adult) community, celebrations that sanctify the joining of two lives, somber rites marking the completion of one's earthly existence.

Rather than seek to "explain" this apparently anachronistic vestige of the religious in the heart of institutions dedicated to the rational and secular pursuit of knowledge—and, it should be said, also implicated in the logic of certification and the reproduction of inequality—at this point, we would like to (merely) assert its largely unconscious existence. Commencement ceremonies supersede in grandeur and transitionary power the everyday ritual work that defines the institution and the mundane lives of its members. They are moments that stand in marked contrast to the other logics and imperatives of academia, although they also seek to provide a grand summation for the very different micro-rituals of educative practice that mark incremental advancement through an undergraduate program of study. This contrast can be taken as a measure of the two separate "rhythms" that define a liberal arts education, each shadowing the other, each only barely cognizant of the other. And each is premised on different answers to the question about the nature of truth, for "truth" is but one of the operative keywords that signals the academy's uneasy "religious" inheritance.

For, in a different age, truth was less about the apprehension of the objective world than gaining access to that other domain veiled by reality, for it is precisely the awareness of our doubled existence—and the mystery of living—that is captured and celebrated in the ritual process. One can, in other words, consider the ceremonial remnants that continue to define the academy as a form of haunting that is consequent to the (re)definition of knowledge as rationality, crowding out the transcendent function that, until recently, always attended centers of higher learning.

This ghostly presence is evident in the etymology of the terms used to describe the actors on this academic stage, where one witnesses an analogous "doubling" in relation to the pursuit of knowledge and truth. (For what is etymology if not a method of discerning the accretion of meaning—of tapping the historical unconscious—made available through language?) According to the *Oxford English Diction-ary*, the term *professor* denotes not only an "academic or other professional function or status" but "the declaration of faith, principles, etc.," as well. The *OED Online* itemizes this second—and older, less familiar—sense as:

1. A person who proclaims or publicly declares something. ...
2. a. A person who makes open declaration of his or her feelings or beliefs, or of allegiance to some principle; one who professes ...

The term *student* carries similarly doubled connotations. First, it signifies "a per-son undergoing a course of study and instruction at a university or other place of higher education or technical training." Beyond this, however, *student* also connotes a certain degree of eagerness and zeal, affection, friendliness, devotion to another's welfare, partisan sympathy, and desire.[9]

In other words: passion and compassion.

This, of course, stands in stark contrast to the keyword associated with the work of Michel Foucault—i.e., discipline[10] (a theme to which we will return)—that focuses on the mundane labor characteristic of higher education, in which syllabi and lesson plans, lectures and seminars, papers and examinations are the relatively standardized tools, the rituals of accumulation and certification, through which learning is framed and measured, and whereby students are expected to absorb and assimilate the (dispassionate) techniques and apperceptions made available through their interactions with teachers and texts.

It is precisely during ceremonial moments such as Commencement, that ele-ments suggesting the impassioned and transformational power of truth emerge from behind the shadows, bringing to the fore other connotations of enlightenment. Not insignificantly, this is also what characterizes many students' interest in the liberal arts—especially for an institution like Simon's Rock, where an affirmative choice is made to leave high school and family for another world of possibility—in which notions of learning exceed the accumulation of knowledge, technical skills, and the acquisition of academic credentials, emphasizing instead a different set of promises: the desire for insight and growth, and the yearning for inspiration. For this reason, it is to the period following matriculation, of involvement in the material practices of learning, and to the question of how the sequestered space of college—and the classroom—forms the heart of the educative process, that we now turn our atten-tion.

The Space In-Between

It is at this point that we can begin to identify how the aspirations of incoming students map onto the largely unconscious ritual structure of the liberal arts institution, how the desire for "something more" translates into a commitment (or willingness to submit) to the seclusion and challenges of an undergraduate education, a commitment that necessarily entails severing many of the worldly ties that defined their lives prior to enrollment. Most undergraduates expect that the period of seclusion will be limited (rather than indefinite) and that their persistence will somehow be rewarded, and this can be understood as easing their voluntary withdrawal from the world beyond.

The expectations of the younger scholar—and their confluence with the structure of beginnings and endings—constitute the focus of our exploration of the relevance of Victor Turner's conception of the ritual process,[11] and its utility for thinking more deliberately about the possibility and promise of a liberal arts college education such as that provided at Simon's Rock and elsewhere. We suggest that this model of the ritual process provides a useful frame for (re)asserting the value and purpose of the liberal arts that side-steps the vapid rhetoric that equates students with computer technology (as consumers or managers of information) or the empirically (and politically) empty conception of democracy that couches education as (magically) fostering and enabling engaged citizenship.[12] Instead, in envisioning a liberal arts education as analogous in form to a rite of passage, this model turns our attention to matters of transformation, and puts us in the position of asking what kind of transformation matters? It also allows us to reflect on our own positions as teachers to ask how our everyday practices enable or work toward such transformation or, alternatively, how they—however dimly or distantly—are animated by such aspirations.

Drawing upon Arnold van Gennep's *Rites of Passage*, Turner describes the basic structure of the ritual process as follows:

> The first phase, separation, comprises symbolic behavior signifying the detachment of the individual or the group either from an earlier fixed point in the social structure or from a set of cultural conditions (a "state"). During the intervening "liminal" period, the state of the ritual subject (the "passenger," or "liminar") becomes ambiguous; he passes through a symbolic domain that has few or none of the attributes of his past or coming state. In the third phase the passage is consummated and the ritual subject, the neophyte or initiand reenters the social structure, often but not always at a higher status level.[13]

In his examination of the ritual process, Turner was most interested in the middle phase. It is also what interests us here. It is, after all, the in-between space—framed by ritual departures (separation), on the one hand, and beginnings (commencement), on the other—within which the ordinariness of the college life of teaching and learning (and eating, sleeping, and playing) unfolds.

In using the language of passage, Turner suggests that this middle space bears little resemblance to the before and the after. And whether we conceive of students' passage in terms of travel (movement through space) or birth (emergence in time, as from a womb), the intermediary domain is set apart, separated and segregated from the "normal" world. Instead, during this phase, the initiate is "betwixt and between the positions assigned and arrayed by law, custom, convention, and ceremonial."[14] As a result, and by virtue of the very structure and rhythm of the ritual process, liminal persons, things, and places come to be associated with existential states that defy easy categorization or full explication except as "transitional"—defined precisely in terms of passage—often associated with death, the fetus in the womb, the invisible, the obscure, the bisexual, the wilderness, and eclipses of the sun and moon. Furthermore, Turner adds that

> [N]eophytes in initiation or puberty rites ... may be represented as possessing nothing. They may be disguised as monsters, wear only a strip of clothing, or even go naked, to demonstrate that as liminal beings they have no status, property, insignia, secular clothing indicating rank or role, position in a kinship system—in short, nothing that may distinguish them from their fellow neophytes or initiands ... they must obey their instructors implicitly ... it is as though they are being reduced or ground down to a uniform condition to be fashioned anew and endowed with additional powers to enable them to cope with their new station in life.[15]

While this certainly does not correspond to the image of the prototypical college student, it underscores the functionality of geographic and symbolic "removal" as laying the existential and material foundation for transformation and renewal. It is also worth noting that many of these terms and images are not far removed from what could generally be considered the (painful) liminality of teenaged existence in societies where rites of passage (to adulthood) no longer punctuate and define the life-course. In many ways, being a teenager—particularly the age at which most students arrive at Simon's Rock—is to be "betwixt and between," no longer beneficiaries of the "freedoms" accorded to children and not yet bearers of the rights, responsibilities, and dignities associated with adulthood. Not surprisingly, then, many of the methods used by teens to assert themselves and establish their sense of worth are seen as "monstrous."

However, rather than relegating liminal subjects to the status of the abject—as shunned and unspeakable—Turner argues that this phase of the ritual process comprises a social space with infinite transformative potential, precisely because it is a space that maintains a tenuous relationship with the "normal" social order. "The novices are, in fact, temporarily undefined, beyond the normative social structure. This weakens them, since they have no rights over others. But it also liberates them from structural obligations."[16] Thus, while this space of passage affords a certain degree of liberty (from normal rules and demands), it also leaves the initiate in a state of suspension, bereft of the social and cultural coordinates most taken for granted in creating and sustaining a secure sense of one's place and purpose in the world. It is no wonder, then, that

> Liminality may be the scene of ... *anomie*, alienation, *angst*, the three fatal *alpha* sisters of many modern myths. ... Liminality is both more creative and more destructive than the structural norm. In either case it raises basic problems for social structural man, invites him to speculation and criticism.[17]

The "freedom" associated with this ritual sequestration, in other words, is shot through with ambivalence. Shorn (or "freed") of the unquestioned normative order, initiates are isolated, left alone in the company of each other, denied markers of identity and structures for action that would otherwise channel and organize their activity. This loss—this freedom (for freedom is also an absence)—is what lays the foundation for the generative capacity of the ritual process, since it is a space that allows for critical reflection, both on oneself, and on the environments from which one comes.

> Sociocultural systems drive so steadily towards consistency that human individuals only get off the normative hooks in rare situations ... [T]here has to be an interfacial region or, to change the metaphor, an interval, however brief, of *margin* or *limen*, when the past is momentarily negated, suspended, or abrogated, and the future has not yet begun, an instant of pure potentiality when everything, as it were, trembles in the balance.[18]

Rather than embodying a collective state of denigration, then, this liminal period of the ritual process can best be understood in terms of its generative promise—"pure potentiality"—precisely because the rest of the world is held in temporary abeyance. Furthermore, Turner argues, because of the incessant (normative) demands that define and organize existence beyond the margins of the ritual process, this (protected) space of passage can be held as the fount and origin of all structures and, simultaneously, their critique. As with the Daoist notion of the "uncarved block" (*pu*), the primordial bonds that develop among initiates place in stark relief socially authorized lineaments of power, calling them into question and, according to Turner, suggesting other possibilities of collective arrangement.

For, "everything ... trembles in the balance."

WORKING THE SEAM(S), CONSCIOUSLY

It is to this idea of "pure potentiality" that we must return in order to understand how certain structural and practical features of an undergraduate education do (or do not) engender a specific kind of educational culture. In examining our own environment here at Simon's Rock, it is clearly evident that there are a number of practices and traditions that seek to foster the generative and transformative capacities of educative practice. And to the extent that Simon's Rock can be considered exceptional, it is because its formal institutional history and shared experience—evident in folklore, anecdote, and everyday praxis—have produced an ethos in which the space between matriculation and graduation is consciously organized to enhance the liminal properties within the social space of the classroom. A potentially radical sociality, in which "normal" delimitations between "professor" and "student" are intentionally altered, provides a setting within which rituals of classroom interaction privilege forms of communication that disrupt conventional norms of educative practice and require extraordinarily high levels of student investment in their learning and intellectual growth.

As has been noted more than once in this collection, all members of the campus community—students, faculty, staff, and administrators, alike—address one another on a first-name basis, recasting (although certainly not ignoring or eliminating) the social hierarchies that define and organize our social worlds, including those beyond the college campus. Students are encouraged and expected to see their professors as individuals, like themselves, albeit occupying very different occupational niches. Much of this ethos is learned (or absorbed) when incoming students arrive at Simon's Rock in the late summer and are immediately immersed in the "Writing and Thinking Workshop," an intensive period in which small groups of students are led through various reading, writing, and discussion exercises involving playful exploration of techniques for literary and oral expression. As a matriculating rite of passage, the Workshop introduces students to a culture of informal, yet rigorous and communal, intellectual exploration. It also begins the process by which they are primed for a college experience in which the classroom becomes the ritual space for collective efforts to make sense of the world beyond the classroom, and beyond the college.

We must, however, fight the tendency to treat any practice, including those enumerated here, as holding the key to educative success. For the tension between the liminal and the normative cannot be displaced; neither can the thoroughly ambivalent "freedom" of passage be fully institutionalized. "The spontaneity and immediacy of [this experience]—as opposed to the jural-political character of (social) structure—can seldom be sustained for long. [It] soon develops a (protective social) structure, in which free relationships between individuals become converted into norm-governed relationships between social personae."[19]

If there are any "laws" in the social sciences, this is surely one of them: that the emergence of the spontaneous, of that which unexpectedly inspires, delights, invigorates, and transforms, whether individually or en masse, will eventually dissipate. All other things being equal, successful movements of protest will find their objectives absorbed (and diluted) into the mainstream. Inspired forms of religious revolt will generate their own orthodoxies. No matter how hard we might try, lightening cannot be captured in a bottle. But rather than attempt to "fix" the ineffable or stabilize the transitory, to sustain their generative capacities, we see the pressing task as one of sustaining an understanding of our mission as educators, its promises as well as its challenges.

Teaching Euphoria, Tending Delirium

If transformation is what we pursue as teachers and students, then education cannot—and should not—be reduced to a process of acquisition and accumulation. Knowledge, if it is to be generative, cannot—and should not—be shrunken to bits and bytes of information to be digested and assimilated into pre-existing modes of apprehension and frames of cogitation. It is—and should be—something else, an Other to normal (and normative) existence, incubated and nurtured in the womb-like space that defines the teacher-student encounter. The capacity of transformation relies upon and requires an emptiness—a capaciousness—that can hold the passing of the old as it conjoins with the promise of the new.

As nice as this may sound, we should not fool ourselves about the nature of this process. It is not easy. It is often painfully difficult. Even violent.

For, as Turner points out, "liminal" is derived from the Latin word (*limen*) meaning "threshold." And threshold, in addition to signifying a point or moment of transition, harkens back to the Germanic base from which it is derived, "which means 'thrash' or 'thresh,' a place where grain is beaten out from its husk, where what has been hidden is thus manifested."[20] The connecting link between "threshold" and "thresh," then, can be found in the original definition of the latter: "to tread, trample." Processes of transformation, in other words, require a trampling of the old—including its certainties and securities—as a prelude to what is to come. To the extent to which the "old" is the ground upon which personal identities and life-paths have been built, the process of trampling can also signify a form of (social) death.[21]

The structure and function of the ritual process is intimately bound-up with this tension between the old and the new, the known and the unknown—the seams of life—where the un/known exceeds our cognitive capacities but which nevertheless speaks to the very material—and mundane—modes of being that capture and define existence with ourselves and among others. Social scientists tend to describe these normative modes of being using the metaphor of (social) structure, in large part to underscore the relative permanence, and seeming immutability, of the regularities that coordinate the rhythms and dilemmas of living: the roles that shape relations both professional and intimate, the networks that bind us to others, often against our very wishes and desires, the imperatives that define (and often compel) acceptable forms of behavior, and the frontiers that mark and protect the taboo. But since these constraints are held in temporary suspension during the ritual process, the identities and certitudes that acquire their substance and coherence from the normative order of things are also suspended. As a consequence, they also lose their normal ability to motivate and organize.

The kind of (social) death that accompanies the ritual process can, therefore, be seen as the necessary and enabling condition for the kind of ("trampled") transformation that follows and, in the context of the educative process, it is precisely the condition of possibility for learning. Due to the liminality that envelops both students and teachers in ritual separation, it is also the basis for a certain kind of *euphoria*: the classroom—and, more broadly, the college experience, itself—can be considered a space (relatively) unhindered by the roles, statuses, obligations, etc., that structure "normal" experiences and perceptions of the world or, alternatively, a threshold where normativity can be thrashed and separated from the forms that assert its legitimacy. This liminal space acquires a capacity—*in potentio*—that constitutes the ideal condition for (ritual) transformation, a capacity that can be transferred to its occupants (its passengers): As a space apart, it allows initiates to think, feel, and see otherwise, and to do so with each other. It provides the basis for a different kind of public, another kind of sociality—euphoria.

It is for this reason that Victor Turner associates the liminal phase of the ritual process with what he calls *anti-structure*:

> I meant by it [the term anti-structure] not a structured reversal, a mirror-imaging of "profane," workaday socioeconomic structure, or a fantasy-rejection of structural "necessities," but *the liberation of human capacities of cognition, affect, volition, creativity, etc., from the normative constraints* incumbent upon occupying a sequence of social statuses, enacting a multiplicity of social roles, and being acutely conscious of membership in some corporate group.[22]

This "anti-structure," in other words, provides the space—and generates the capacity—to articulate differently, to speak other-wise. It is a generative space that allows for a different existence of that which is suppressed in the social structural world. According to this formulation, the ability to not only speak but to speak "freely" cannot be reduced to the mere capacity to express oneself, to give voice to some (pre-formed) opinion or belief. For these are already circumscribed by the normative order of things and inscribed in the "social structural (hu)man." The task, instead, is to liberate those capacities from such constraint.

This "anti-structure" is both structural and experiential. It is co-produced and sustained in communion with others—fellow passengers—who are similarly displaced from the normal and structurally obligatory. The "impossible" becomes possible, due precisely to this co-presence while the usual and the normative, the con-solation of the regularities of life outside ritual time, are suspended. What we are calling the "euphoric" is the impossible freedom found in the fumbling attempts to articulate what normally remains unspoken and repressed, of glimpsing and grasp-ing at that which exists beyond the veil, and the delight and wonder such a shared experience provides. As such, this notion of the euphoric shares a certain kinship with what Turner describes as *communitas*.

> Communitas ... may be said to exist more in contrast than in active opposition to social structure, as an alternative and more "liberated" way of being socially human, a way both of being detached from social structure—and hence poten-tially of periodically *evaluating* its performance—and also of a "distanced" or "marginal" person's being more attached to *other* disengaged persons—and hence, sometimes of evaluating a social structure's historical performance in common with them. Here we may have a loving union of the structurally damned pro-nouncing judgment on normative structure and providing alternative models for structure.[23]

There is an intimate relation between this experience of being *socially* human, on the one hand, and the form of (ambivalent) detachment that defines the liminal condition, on the other. As such, an experience that might otherwise be reduced to alienation, anomie, and angst, serves as a point of a different kind of origin, from which emerges a complex—but liberating and euphoric—sense of communality that asserts the right of judgment (on normative structures) while simultaneously celebrating the promise of an other (possibility).[24] Turner quotes Brian Sutton-Smith to underscore this point:

> The normative structure represents the working equilibrium, the "anti-structure" represents the latent system of potential alternatives from which novelty will arise when contingencies in the normative structure require it. We might more correctly call this second system the *proto-structural* system [he says] because it is the precursor of innovative normative forms. It is the source of new culture.[25]

In this sense, the liminal can best be understood as the space "in which new models, symbols, paradigms, etc., arise—as the seedbeds of cultural creativity."[26]

This conception of euphoric space puts the lie to the notion that a college lec-ture or seminar can take place in a "pure" space, sanitized and sterilized of worldly concerns, particularly those considered political or normative. For in a group pos-sessed of some degree of *communitas*, the experience of power—and release from its normatively obligatory character—is also a lesson about fundamental questions concerning the nature and operation of culture, interpersonal communication, and the promise of transformation. As Renato Rosaldo rightly points out, ritual is best understood "as a busy intersection,"[27] where emotional energies and individual experiences are determinative forces, where "culture" is composed of polyvocal socialities, and where we all are active constituters of the world through our interactions with others, whether they be heroic or unremarkable. Despite being linked with liminal (ritually suspended) space and time, the euphoric both presumes and requires delving into the messiness of the profane, for it is the ultimate object of the ritual process. It is the "other side" of social life to which the initiates must return following their seclusion.

Our experiences at Simon's Rock demonstrate to us how the euphoria of *communitas* in the classroom, on field trips, and in other settings is the unspeakable and unspoken link—often only dimly understood—between members of the learning community, its sacred quality often emerging precisely from an engagement with the messiness of the profane (see textbox accompanying this chapter, below). Structural definitions dividing student and teacher can, in the liminal space of passion and compassion captured in the moment, lose their normativity and dissolve in the face of revelation and transfiguration.

There are, of course, competing theaters for staging the euphoric that proliferate under the contemporary conditions that define the global consumer marketplace. In our view, many of these[28] come closer to *delirium*, insofar as what is being offered is an experience divorced from the generative and transformative experience we have described above.[29] We should add, however, that these consumptive "alternatives" are not so different from the signal danger of higher education itself, a danger conveyed by the pejorative use of the term "academic" and accusations of an "ivory tower" existence. This is the seductive danger of withdrawal—the autistic pleasure found in the worship of the Word or the Idea—whereby ascetic seclusion becomes the site and source of pleasure itself, rather than a (temporary and transitional) moment that is deliberately, yet ambivalently, defined in relation to the "outer" world. For that is where students must return, even if their teachers do not.

"Working the seams," then, requires vigilance against such forms of isolated pleasure, insisting that our speechifying be mindful of its rightful targets that reside outside of ritual time. It requires avoiding the delirious temptation to attribute transcendent qualities to the object (of study, discourse, teaching, speaking). Equally, it requires avoiding seductive entrancement to what we take to be absolute, unchanging, and essential, thereby leaving us blind to the ever-emerging real. We must be humbled by the challenge and the responsibility of this task, for it requires paying attention to and making serious and critical inquiry into the very conditions that make a liberal arts education possible. It means examining the seams—the contours and the limits, the joints and the folds—that delimit and protect the privileged space of "hallowed" seclusion from the world beyond and, particularly for our students, from the experience that is yet to come.

Battling the Afflictions of Enlightenment

In tracing the trajectory we have described, and in reflecting how it does (or does not) conform to our experience, we should not allow ourselves to believe that the tempo and rhythm of the ritual process is preordained merely because it is made conscious. Like any practice, it is dependent upon conditions that support and enable, as well as generous quantities of discipline, intention, and goodwill among all participants in the educative process.

There are, in addition, other demons with which to do battle, spirits that—while often sharing in the structure of feeling of the ritual process—belie and sometimes resist the kind of transformation advocated here. Two of these demons spring from the condition of being unmoored, swallowed in their solitariness, insofar as the immediacy of experience is taken as a complete measure of (collective) existence itself. In different ways, each is enthralled by a quasi-autistic experience which is transposed onto the social world, hoping—sometimes demanding—that this internal "reality" will constitute the basis of a different kind of sociality. A world in one's own image. On the one hand, unfettered optimism shares the solipsistic character of the dysphoric, whereby the experience of (disconnected) pleasure is translated and projected outwards, and emerges in the absence of the kind of labored *sociality* that is the product of the ritual process. Unmitigated despair, on the other hand, yearns for the *communitas* that is characteristic of the euphoric but is paralyzed by its absence, obsessed about normative structures that seem to constrain and drain the lifeblood out of existence, unable to make the leap from detached criticality and alienation to shared experience.

The ritual structure of the educative process is well-suited to address the challenges of the former, unfettered optimism, to the extent that it involves—even requires—a certain form of symbolic death, a certain degree of thrashing, whereby the college experience acts as the container within which new modes of responsible personhood can be experimented with and, eventually, taken on as one's own. This is, after all, the defining feature of rites of passage that Turner also describes as life-crisis rituals, insofar as they involve "the transition from one phase of life or social status to another ... [following] a long and often painful learning process."[30]

It is less clear how well this ritual process addresses the problem of unmitigated despair, since isolation and "thrashing" would seem to only reinforce and exacerbate an alienated state of existence, already suffused by angst and anomie. Like unfettered optimism, however, it can be said that unmitigated despair is fostered by the larger (social, cultural, political, ecological) environments that house our normatively-structured lives. In other words, both demons represent more than personal failings or character defects. Instead, each is a form of affliction that has deep roots in the modes of collective organization that shape life for "social structural man." As such, they speak directly to the educative mission of a liberal arts education, particularly one that seeks to address the urgencies characteristic of contemporary realities beyond the protected liminal space many of us call home.

For, in many ways, the liberal arts college of the twenty-first century lives in the shadow of the dual imperatives that fueled the hearths of medieval higher education: we have inherited the strictures and structures of an educational ritual complex, on the one hand, and a set of economic imperatives that gave rise to what we now call global capitalism, on the other. The two share an intimate and intertwined history that continues to define the present. Nowadays, college graduates are not only required to be smarter and wiser than when they first matriculated, they are also expected to succeed within the network of contemporary guilds—the modern professions—with their long training programs and high capital costs (and benefits). These requirements and expectations form a patchwork of systems of indoctrination that have deep historical precedents and considerable structural weight, fixity, even path dependency and yet, oddly, we still remain largely unconscious of the logic that binds these together and implicates the work of teachers and students at all levels of the educational complex. Today, it seems as if the most "profound" public dialogues that North American education pundits can muster concern whether there is room for politics in the classroom and whether American students are sufficiently competitive with their peers in a globalizing world.

More concretely, the increasingly high cost of private education, combined with economic recession, national militarization, and the diffuse, lingering, and fundamentally xenophobic anxiety concerning "terrorist activity" have done much to collapse the mission of higher education, reducing educative aspirations to the preparation of students for lives of financial and psychological security. While these tendencies are certainly not new, even the concern with moral virtue that defined certain corners of public dialogue and debate appears to have faded into what seems to have been an "idyllic" prelude to national dysphoria. Could it be that we who have borne witness to the fiery collapse of the twin towers, the retaliatory invasions and mutually destructive occupations of Afghanistan and Iraq, the horror of Abu Ghraib, the making of "Katrina refugees" through systemic and systematic national neglect, and the failure to forge coherent national policies addressing global warming and a looming energy crisis (of world historical proportions) are no longer capable of speaking publicly about what compels and binds us, one to another? Under these circumstances, can anyone who questions the moral or political efficacy of a liberal arts education be held in contempt? Indeed, is it wise for students and their families to take on a financial burden of more than $40,000 a year in order to gain an education in the liberal arts? We are thankful, even if only from a narrow sense of self-interest, that there are students and families who believe the answer is "yes." But we are humbled, as well. Have we actually earned that trust? Are we up to the task? Are we even cognizant of what it requires?

Given the world from which our students come, and to which we belong, it is no surprise that the aspirations they bring to their education are frequently infused with a desire that has found few—if any—channels for self-renewal and inspiration. Neither is it a surprise for educators to recognize that their work takes on the qualities of that larger world, whether by way of the bureaucratization of the life-world, the managerialism of decision-making, or the flattening of affect in the face of the ceaseless onslaught of obligation. It would be a mistake, therefore, to allow ourselves to believe that the mere desire for an impassioned education and the lingering remnants of ceremonial celebration in themselves are sufficient conditions for making it so. For there are other contingencies that have molded the landscape of higher education and, because of this, the liminal promise of the liberal arts college is largely an untapped potential.

Prime among these contingencies is the (potential) enslavement to *another* kind of ritualized activity that, for the purposes of this essay, we can call "disciplinary" (it could, just as well be called ideological or alternatively, in the language of the sacred, illusory) in which the "reality" of academic life is continually recreated. Louis Althusser has described this process as one that operates through ritual, albeit of a very different kind than the rituals of transformation described by Turner:

> we are subjects ... [that] function in the practical rituals of the most elementary everyday life (the hand-shake, the fact of calling you by your name, the fact of knowing, even if I do not know what it is, that you "have" a name of your own, which means that you are recognized as a unique subject, etc.)—[to recognize this] gives us the "consciousness" of our incessant (eternal) practice of ideological recognition—its consciousness, i.e., its *recognition*.[31]

In place of the handshake, etc., we can substitute the other kinds of (practical, everyday) rituals that define academic life, including regimented meeting times, habitual seating arrangements and modes of address, the routines of assigning texts and methods for discussing them, the compulsion to write, and the imperative to assess. The ultimate result of this kind of disciplined and disciplinary activity is the constitution of subjects, and their ability to "recognize" each other—as students and professors—thereby giving and reinforcing (particular) meaning to the worlds they inhabit. If this is indeed the case, we are compelled to ask: of the definitions cited at the beginning of this chapter, which "student" and which "professor" acts on this stage?

To restate our argument: what is being described here—the practical rituals of academic discipline—belongs to a very different category of ritual than those analyzed by Victor Turner and advocated here. It refers to the nature of academic routines, the habitual practices that define our everyday work as students and teachers. In addressing *this* kind of ritual, Althusser identifies a peculiar speculary structure, one staked on an organizing principle that confers identities through the promise of "recognition."[32] We suggest that in the context of the static rituals of academic practice—as opposed to the transformative practice of education—"enlightened" Knowledge operates as that principle, where the professor serves as the descendant of the priest, proxy and stand-in for the Absolute Subject, in which established routines conspire to constitute students (and teachers) as subjects of and for secular knowledge.

And what is wrong with that, we may ask?

It is with this concern (among others) that Michel Foucault analyzed the rise to prominence of the "analytic of finitude" as the secular foundation and (ironic) source of knowledge, in which (empirical) discovery displaced earlier understandings of revelation and transformation.[33] This had important consequences, particularly given our interest in the mission of the educative endeavor:

> I think the modern age of the history of truth begins when knowledge itself and knowledge alone gives access to the truth. That is to say, it is when the philosopher (or the scientist, or simply someone who seeks the truth) can recognize the truth and have access to it in himself and solely through his activity of knowing, *without anything else being demanded of him and without him having to change or alter his being as subject.*[34]

Furthermore, he adds that

> We ... no longer think that access to the truth will complete in the subject, like a crowning or a reward, the work or the sacrifice, the price paid to arrive at it. Knowledge will simply open out onto the indefinite dimension of progress, the end of which is unknown and the advantage of which will only ever be realized in the course of history by the institutional accumulation of bodies of knowledge, or the psychological or social benefits to be had from having discovered the truth after having taken such pains to do so. As such, henceforth the truth cannot save the subject.[35]

The relation between the subject and truth, in other words, becomes a mode of accumulation, whereby knowledge is understood as a possession rather than something of which we are possessed. Thus are the (new) fruits of our labor.

In turning our attention to this shadow of Enlightenment rationality, we are not advocating a return to some "idyllic" religious past. Instead, we are asking what "knowledge" and "truth" mean in the context of our everyday activities as educators, and what we can learn from the largely unconscious ritual elements that continue to define the margins of this academic existence, moments of departure (separation) and commencement (return). In light of our investigation, one theme becomes quite clear, which is: the competing definitions and purposes of knowledge—one premised on the self-contained and self-transparent "knowing subject," the other premised on the promise of that subject's destruction, via the expectation of enlightenment and transfiguration—and the gulf that separates them.

It is within *this* context that the high ceremony of Commencement gains its significance, but also remains profoundly ambivalent. On the one hand, it points to another domain, an Other to our normal, everyday activities that haunts our work as intellectual (and emotional) laborers, that speaks to and through us as we seek insight. On the other hand, it consolidates and stabilizes modes of being that, ironically, deny these very yearnings for illumination insofar as they are premised on a certain kind of domestication of knowledge, conquering the unknown by naming it and taking those appellations as truth.

EPILOGUE: RECONCEIVING THE MONASTIC TRADITION

> [M]onsters are manufactured precisely to … startle neophytes into thinking about objects, persons, relationships, and features of their environment they have hitherto taken for granted. … Put a man's head on a lion's body and you think about the human head in the abstract. … Liminality here breaks, as it were, the cake of custom and enfranchises speculation.
>
> —VICTOR TURNER, *The Forest of Symbols*

According to Turner, the subject of the ritual process—the "passenger"—is generally "invisible," both structurally (by virtue of isolation and segregation) and metaphorically (since the passage does not conform to the structural logic of the living).[36] This in/visibility does not reside in the faulty capacity of the senses but, rather, in the inherited frames that organize our individual and collective existence.

> As members of society, most of us see only what we expect to see, and what we expect to see is what we are conditioned to see when we have learned the definitions and classifications of our culture. A society's secular definitions do not allow for the experience of a not-boy-not-man, which is what a novice in a male puberty rite is (if he can be said to be anything).[37]

The question for us is what one apprehends in "student" (or "professor," for that matter), since the meaning—and significance—of the term will most likely reflect (structurally normative) investments, whether one be a student, parent, teacher, administrator, or interested observer. We have been advocating a model of education that conceives of the liberal arts college as a site of transformation *in potentio*. But given the weight of the Enlightenment inheritance, we wonder about the comprehensibility—the legibility and the desirability—of such an enterprise from the point of view of that which exists outside the liminal space of education.

And yet, we are convinced that the ritual structure of academia already manifests the doubling of the "secular" investment in knowledge, in which ceremony and other reminders of an older monastic tradition give evidence of other, often unspoken, aspirations and desires. Following Slavoj Žižek, we may consider this an "external" form of the unconscious, one evident in our objective practices and routines of which we normally remain unaware.[38] In this sense, the (academic) unconscious is always already there in our everyday activities, pervasive and ritualized, visibly and repeatedly reenacted in the presence of others. Hope lies in the shadow of our regularized doings and the unending obligations that drag us, frenetically, through the routines and rhythms of our bureaucratized existence.

Teaching at Simon's Rock has helped us find hope, even amid the chaos, betrayal, and lingering dysphorias of everyday (structural) life. For, this is the fruit of working the black seams that circumscribe, exclude, and repress, but also establish the basis for privilege, sanctuary, and withdrawal. Thus, we close with the words of W. E. B. Du Bois, whose vision of the relationship between higher education and the greater social world remains unsurpassed, particularly as it speaks to the promise of attending to the oppressed—and repressed—as the necessary threshold for the transformation of the human spirit:

> "[T]here must come a loftier respect for the sovereign human soul that seeks to know itself and the world about it; that seeks a freedom for expansion and self-development; that will love and hate and labor in its own way, untrammeled alike by old and new. Such souls aforetime have inspired and guided worlds, and if we be not wholly bewitched by our Rhine-gold, they shall again. Herein the longing of black men must have respect: the rich and bitter depth of their experience, the unknown treasures of their inner life, the strange rendings of nature they have seen, may give the world new points of view and make their loving, living, and doing precious to all human hearts. And to themselves in these the days that try their souls, the chance to soar in the dim blue air above the smoke is to their finer spirits boon and guerdon for what they lose on earth by being black."[39]

LIMINALITY ON THE ROAD:
ENGAGING WITH THE MESSINESS OF THE PROFANE

In the fall of 2007, we co-taught a course on the historical geography of New Orleans, focusing on the social dimensions of "natural disaster" and trauma, and the spatial dimensions of racial and ethnic marginalization before and after Hurricane Katrina. The course included a service-learning project in one of the city's hardest-hit and most ethnically diverse neighborhoods—Broadmoor—which lies in "the bowl" near the center of the metropolis. We also analyzed a broad array of recovery initiatives and the contentious cultural politics of post-Katrina rebuilding efforts, and assessed the conflicts over space and place that tend to defy the best-laid plans of national and municipal planning agencies alike. Readings included works by W. E. B. Du Bois, Slavoj Žižek, Derek Gregory, David Harvey, Henry Giroux, Pierre Bourdieu, and James C. Scott. The course also included presentations by specialists in the city's historical ethnic geography, flood control measures, local art scene, and community-led recovery efforts. Final projects were based on semester-long research, on-the-spot work experience, field observation, and data collection.

Twenty-two hours of driving (one way), camping out in the Blue Ridge Mountains, "crashing" on the basement floor of a renovated shotgun house in Broadmoor, constructing the neighborhood's first bioswale (a human-made wetland for flood absorption and water purification) (Figure 7), and visiting with the professors' parents in Virginia and Alabama were all part of the field trip. And what, one may fairly ask, does this have to do with liminality, euphoria, and the reworking of intersubjective spaces in higher education?

To begin with, all rituals have their place(s), and to remove the liminars from the mundane space-time of the classroom and its micro-rituals of texts, talks, tests, and clock-time, is to open up new and diverse forms of structure and anti-structure. While we maintain that the Simon's Rock classroom is structured for anti-structure in the dialogic sense, field trips and service projects foster *communitas* and demand even more extensive social engagement than is offered in the classroom or even that suggested by Turner himself. For his assertion that *communitas* stands "... as an alternative and more 'liberated' way of being socially human, a way both of being detached from social structure—and hence potentially of periodically *evaluating* its performance. ..."[40] begs the geographic question of *where* students and faculty find themselves in relation to networks of hegemonic social structures, and the sociological question of *how* they participate with other human and non-human actors/actants in these structures.[41] Answers, tentative as they may be, help uncover forms of agency through which to enact structural change.

In theoretical terms, we addressed the following kinds of questions through Du Boisian historical sociology, Foucauldian *biopolitics*, and Actor-Network-Theory *inter alia*: What roles have African Americans and Euro-Americans played in ante-bellum social ecology and post-bellum attempts to "reconstruct democracy" in the Gulf Coast region, particularly in New Orleans?[42] What did the widely broadcast (re)presentation of black bodies in post-Katrina media reports suggest about race and class and the (bio)politics of "disposability,"[43] and why were living black males—the survivors—*"supposed* to loot and rape"?[44] How are levees "authoritative and unquestioned stand-ins for a set of racial politics in New Orleans," and what would a "black politics of technology" look like?[45] In this class our students hailed from Namibia, Guinea, Mexico, and many parts of the United States *except* for the South, where both professors have familial roots. As a whole, they did not represent the "structurally damned," nor did all represent the structurally privileged, but all were faced with these questions, that stemmed from an initiatory assignment during the first week of class: to analyze the official White House report on Katrina, which begins with the statements: "Terrorists still plot their evil deeds, and nature's unyielding power will continue. We know with certainty that there will be tragedies in our future."[46]

Engaging in hard but gratifying physical labor brought students and professors together within a realm less mediated by textual and other forms of symbolic intervention, and students eagerly engaged in documenting their work both on the bioswale (on the grounds of the Broadmoor community library) and within the residential section of the Broadmoor neighborhood, where they handed out fliers for the Broadmoor Improvement Association (BIA), the organization that helped facilitate our service project. Several students made a video documentary and others made interpretive brochures about the bioswale. All took part in dialogue with leaders of the BIA in order to gain a stronger understanding of the strengths and weaknesses of their strategies for grassroots community organization. In summary, this project—a course within a course—was a reassertion of the value and purpose of the liberal arts as a means of transformation of self and other. Like the city of New Orleans itself, such educative initiatives contain tremendous generative promise, bringing into play the old and the new, the known and the unknown, and some degree of certainty that novelty is arising as contingencies in the normative structure require it. Is it too much to suggest that these are proto-structural systems, new sources of culture? In any case, there is a wealth of experience in the messiness of the profane, where teachers and students alike are challenged to rethink themselves as they encounter the everyday joys and hardships of others. One student, struck by the stark disparities of experience and understanding, drew upon the language of Marx in writing-up her reflections about the trip:[47]

I cannot stand to even describe the people I met in Broadmoor as "research subjects," [quotation marks added] but they very much were. Not limited to [that], but certainly [this constitutes] a real relationship where I must face my social agency as a student. It brings up so many heavy insecurities of mine about being a student, its inherent circle always back to the "I." But then again, with responsibility to where I am from and what abilities I have, my scholarship does not have to privilege the bourgeoisie. The inherent asymmetry can actually be seen as positing privilege to its rightful meritor, the oppressed; the intellectual as the very literal surface of the proletariat, relying and resting upon it. It privileges the working oppressed because without their knowledge of social theory, it is meaningless to our interests. My interests as a student are hard for me to justify though. I have such a fear of failing somewhere, of gaining knowledge only to sell it back; of maintaining my luxuries under capitalism and perpetuating the evils of bourgeois intellectualism. I can place New Orleans in the framework of capitalism all I want and critique the shit out of it, and will still be speaking in abstractions. While people are sick, displaced and suffering, neglected, I fancy myself fussing about late-night thinking and political hubbub. I yearn for the manifestation of my efforts to go beyond my own self.

–JOCELYN MCELROY, A.A., 2009

Another student used poetry to express her sense of the suffering and disavowal that had taken place in New Orleans:

A Poem

When I die,
Don't bury me.
I'd like to be left
for all to see.

Please,
be disgusted.
Please,
distort my image.
Please,
make me into a spectacle.

I'd like to be left
out in the open.
No casket please,
save for the vines which will someday cover me entirely.

I would like to be full of toxic waste.
I would like for people to steal my valuables.
I would like for no one to visit.

More than anything,
I would like to be ignored.

Please, oh please,
have a parade around me, not for me.

Please,
make me into a joke.
Please,
pretend like I never existed.

I understand,
It's easier for you to forget about
my death and my life
than to give me proper acknowledgment now.

I will become
a part of the background.
           White Noise.

Maybe you'll put me in a textbook one day.

        —STUDENT IN "New Orleans/Katrina/
        New Orleans(?)"

FIGURE 7. Students taking a break from work on the bioswale in the Broadmoor neighborhood of New Orleans. October 2007. Property of the authors.

NOTES

1. See Victor Turner, "Passages, Margins, and Poverty: Religious Symbols of Communitas," in *Dramas, Fields and Metaphors: Symbolic Action in Human Society* (Ithaca, NY: Cornell University Press, 1974), 231–271, and Victor Turner, *The Ritual Process: Structure and Anti-Structure* (Ithaca, NY: Cornell University Press, 1977).

2. Although it bears different connotations, even urban colleges and universities have tended to maintain a certain social insularity, reflected in the perennial problem of town-gown relations.

3. Christina Elliott Sorum, "The Problem of Mission: A Brief Survey of the Changing Mission of the Liberal Arts," in *Liberal Arts Colleges in American Higher Education: Challenges and Opportunities* (American Council of Learned Societies. ACLS Occasional Paper, No. 59, 2005). As Sorum notes regarding the establishment of Harvard in 1636, "if the Puritans who came to Massachusetts were going to carry forward their founding mission, they would need a learned clergy and literate people who could become the governing elite."

4. On this point, see Emile Durkheim, *The Elementary Forms of the Religious Life* (New York: Free Press, 1965) and Mircea Eliade, *The Sacred and the Profane* (New York: Harcourt, Brace & World, 1957).

5. Sam Speers, "Secularity, Spirituality, and Liberal Arts Education," *Social Science Research Council* (2007), accessed 15 July, 2008. http://religion.ssrc.org/reforum/.

6. For a discussion of the European university's rise during a period of economic, social, and intellectual transformation, during which it occupied a peculiarly marginal or hybrid status between the sacred and the secular, which may have subsequently changed in form, but perhaps not in essence, see Hastings Rashdall, *The Universities of Europe* (Oxford: Oxford University Press, 1936). Wallerstein provides a useful overview of the line of evolution—from *studium*, cathedral school, to university—that marked the stirring of secularism in Europe, when truth gradually began to lose its soteriological dimensions. See Immanuel Wallerstein, *The Modern World-System*, vol. 1: *Capitalist Agriculture and the Origins of the European World-Economy in the Sixteenth Century* (New York/London: Academic Press, 1974). For a discussion of the monastic roots of medieval institutions of higher learning and their successors—the cathedral schools of the eleventh century—which soon became corporate guilds, see Charles Homer Haskins, *The Rise of Universities* (Ithaca, NY: Cornell University Press, 1957); Rashdall, *The Universities of Europe*; and Helene Wieruszowski, *The Medieval University* (New York: Van Nostrand, 1966).

   For a more general discussion of the secular, see Talal Asad, *Formations of the Secular* (Stanford, CA: Stanford University Press, 2003).

7. See Lowrie John Daly, *The Medieval University: 1200–1400* (New York: John Wiley, 1961).

8. Anselm Strauss, *Mirrors and Masks: The Search for Identity* (New Brunswick, NJ: Transaction Publishers, 1959), 91–133.

9. According to the *Oxford English Dictionary Online*, the etymology of student includes the Latin "*studium*, zeal, affection, painstaking study, related to *studēre* to be zealous, seek to be helpful." Accessed 11/1/10, http://www.oed.com/.

10. Michel Foucault, *Discipline and Punish: The Birth of the Prison* (New York: Pantheon Books, 1977).

11. See Turner, "Passages, Margins, and Poverty" and Turner, *The Ritual Process*.

12. Regarding the latter, we believe that claims made about "engaged citizenship" appeal to so vast a range of political positions as to render them meaningless, i.e., it is a rhetoric equally available to those who advocate terrorist violence as well as those that defend eviscerated understandings of ("informed") electoral politics. Hopefully, our discussion clarifies the notion of citizenship that motivates the concerns we address here.

13. Victor Turner, *Dramas, Fields, and Metaphors: Symbolic Action in Human Society* (Ithaca, NY: Cornell University Press), 232.

14. Turner, *The Ritual Process*, 95.

15. Turner, *The Ritual Process*, 95.

16. Victor Turner, *From Ritual to Theater: The Human Seriousness of Play* (New York: PAJ Publications, 1982), 27.

17. Turner, *From Ritual to Theater*, 46–47, emphasis in the original.

18. Turner, *From Ritual to Theater*, 44, emphasis in the original.

19. Turner, *From Ritual to Theater*, 47.

20. Victor Turner, *The Anthropology of Performance* (New York: PAJ Publications, 1987), 92.

21. This bears a great deal of similarity to what Goffman describes as the mortification of the self, a kind of symbolic or social death he associates with "total institutions," a broad category that—quite significantly, given our discussion—includes monasteries and boarding schools. See Erving Goffman, *Asylums: Essays on the Social Situation of Mental Patients and Other Inmates* (Garden City, NY: Anchor Books, 1961), 1–124.

22. Turner, *From Ritual to Theater*, 44, emphasis added.

23. Turner, *From Ritual to Theater*, 50–51.

24. Julia Kristeva's distinction between rebellion and revolt is especially relevant on this point. See Julia Kristeva, *The Sense and Non-Sense of Revolt: The Powers and Limits of Psychoanalysis*, Vol. 1 (New York: Columbia University Press, 2000); Julia Kristeva, *Intimate Revolt: The Powers and Limits of Psychoanalysis*, Vol. 2 (New York: Columbia University Press, 2002); and Julia Kristeva, *Revolt, She Said* (New York: Semiotext(e), 2002).

25. Turner, *From Ritual to Theater*, 28.

26. Turner, *From Ritual to Theater*, 28.

27. Renato Rosaldo, *Culture and Truth: The Remaking of Social Analysis* (Boston: Beacon Press, 1989), 17.

28. . . . . although certainly not all: To the extent that they share in these qualities of critical

evaluation and communal celebration—to the extent that they also involve experimental enactments of the socially human—Turner applied the term "liminoid," describing a mode of organization and experience he finds more characteristic of post-industrial societies no longer beholden to the ritual process. See Turner, *From Ritual to Theater.*

29. The distinction we are making here—in terms of the (non)relation between pleasure and transformation—is not dissimilar from that made by Barthes, concerning the difference between "pleasure" and "bliss." See Roland Barthes, *The Pleasure of the Text* (New York: Hill and Wang, 1974), 14, emphasis in the original.

30. Victor Turner, *The Forest of Symbols: Aspects of Ndembu Ritual* (Ithaca, NY: Cornell University Press, 1967), 7.

31. Louis Althusser, "Ideology and Ideological State Apparatuses," in *Lenin and Philosophy and Other Essays* (New York: Monthly Review Press, 1971), 173, emphasis in the original.

32. In asserting that this process of (ideological) recognition operates through a speculary structure, Althusser writes:

> [This] means that all ideology is centered, that the Absolute Subject occupies the unique place of the Centre, and interpellates around it the infinity of individuals into subjects in a double mirror-connexion such that it subjects the subjects to the Subject, while giving them in the Subject in which each subject can contemplate its own image (present and future) ... the absolute guarantee that everything really is so, and that on condition that the subjects recognize what they are and behave accordingly, everything will be all right: Amen—"So be it." (Althusser, 180–81, emphasis in the original)

33. Michel Foucault, *The Archeology of Knowledge and The Discourse on Language* (New York: Pantheon Books, 1982). For a succinct overview of this argument, see Hubert L. Dreyfus and Paul Rabinow, "The Archeology of the Human Sciences" in *Michel Foucault: Beyond Structuralism and Hermeneutics*, 2nd edition (Chicago: University of Chicago Press, 1983), 16–43.

34. Michel Foucault, *The Hermeneutics of the Subject: Lectures at the Collège de France*, 1981–82 (New York: Palgrave, 2005), 17, emphasis added.

35. Foucault, *The Hermeneutics of the Subject*, 18–19.

36. Turner, *The Forest of Symbols*, 93–111.

37. Turner, *The Forest of Symbols*, 95.

38. Slavoj Žižek, "How Did Marx Invent the Symptom?" in *The Sublime Object of Ideology* (New York: Verso Books, 1989), 11–53.

> Here we have one of the possible definitions of the unconscious: the form of thought whose ontological status is not that of thought, that is to say, the form of thought external to the thought itself—in short, some Other Scene external to the thought whereby the form of the thought is already articulated in advance. (19)

The "interiorized" notion of the unconscious challenged here is precisely the conceit of a certain form of Enlightenment rationality that presumes that the "unknown" must reside elsewhere, outside of consciousness, but nevertheless adjacent to it and within its grasp (i.e., the subconscious). In contrast to such an interiority, Žižek argues, much like Althusser before him, that the "order" of our everyday existence can be apprehended as the Unconscious: "The symbolic order is precisely such a formal order which supplements and/or disrupts the dual relationship of 'external' factual reality and 'internal' subjective experience." (19) What we take to be real and what we think we are achieving may, in fact, be quite different from what is actually accomplished. To the extent that this is the case, we can thank our (Unconscious) everyday, academic, ritual practices.

39. W. E. B. Du Bois, *The Souls of Black Folk: Authoritative Text, Contexts, Criticism*, ed. Henry Louis Gates Jr. and Terri Hume Oliver (New York and London: W. W. Norton and Company, 1999), 73.

40. Turner, *From Ritual to Theater*, 50–51.

41. See Bruno Latour, *Politics of Nature: How to Bring the Sciences into Democracy* (Cambridge, MA: Harvard University Press, 2004).

42. W. E. B. Du Bois, *Black Reconstruction in America: An Essay Toward a History of the Part Which Black Folk Played in the Attempt to Reconstruct Democracy in America, 1860* (New York: Atheneum, 1983).

43. Henry A. Giroux, "Reading Hurricane Katrina," *College Literature* 33, no. 3 (2006): 171–196.

44. Slavoj Žižek, "The Subject Supposed to Loot and Rape: Reality and Fantasy in New Orleans," *In These Times* (October 20, 2005), accessed July 15, 2008. http://www.inthesetimes.com/article/2361. emphasis added.

45. Rayvon Fouché, "The Wretched of the Gulf: Racism, Technological Dramas, and Black Politics of Technology," *The Black Scholar* 36, no. 4 (2006): 7–12.

46. The White House, *The Federal Response to Hurricane Katrina: Lessons Learned*, 2006, accessed January 15, 2008. http://www.whitehouse.gov/reports/katrina-lessons-learned/.

47. Student work is cited with permission. Likewise, students and teachers in Figure 7 all granted permission to use their images. We would also like to express our thanks to Laura Conant (B.A., 2006), who provided a thoughtful response to our work.

WORKS CITED

Althusser, Louis. "Ideology and Ideological State Apparatuses." In *Lenin and Philosophy and Other Essays,* 127–186. New York: Monthly Review Press, 1971.

Asad, Talal. *Formations of the Secular: Christianity, Islam, Modernity.* Stanford, CA: Stanford University Press, 2003.

Barthes, Roland. *The Pleasure of the Text.* New York: Hill and Wang, 1974.

Daly, Lowrie John. *The Medieval University, 1200–1400.* New York: John Wiley, 1961.

Dreyfus, Hubert L., and Paul Rabinow. "The Archeology of the Human Sciences." In *Michel Foucault: Beyond Structuralism and Hermeneutics*, 2nd edition, 16–43. Chicago: University of Chicago Press, 1983.

Du Bois, W. E. B. *The Souls of Black Folk: Authoritative Text, Contexts, Criticism.* Edited by Henry Louis Gates Jr. and Terri Hume Oliver. New York and London: W. W. Norton and Company, 1999.

———. *Black Reconstruction in America: An Essay Toward a History of the Part Which Black Folk Played in the Attempt to Reconstruct Democracy in America, 1860.* New York: Atheneum, 1983.

Durkheim, Emile. *The Elementary Forms of the Religious Life.* Translated by Joseph Ward Swain. New York: Free Press, 1965.

Eliade, Mircea. *The Sacred and the Profane: The Nature of Religion.* New York: Harcourt, Brace & World, 1957.

Foucault, Michel. *Discipline and Punish: The Birth of the Prison.* New York: Pantheon Books, 1977.

———. *The Archeology of Knowledge & The Discourse on Language.* New York: Pantheon Books, 1982.

———. *The Hermeneutics of the Subject: Lectures at the Collège de France, 1981–82.* New York: Palgrave Macmillan, 2005.

Fouché, Rayvon. "The Wretched of the Gulf: Racism, Technological Dramas, and Black Politics of Technology." *The Black Scholar* 36, no. 4 (2006): 7–12.

Gennep, Arnold van. *The Rites of Passage.* Chicago: University of Chicago Press, 1960.

Giroux, Henry A. "Reading Hurricane Katrina: Race, Class, and the Biopolitics of Disposability." *College Literature* 33, no.3 (2006): 171–196.

Goffman, Erving. *Asylums: Essays on the Social Situation of Mental Patients and Other Inmates.* Garden City, NY: Anchor Books, 1961.

Haskins, Charles Homer. *The Rise of Universities.* Ithaca, NY: Cornell University Press, 1957.

Kristeva, Julia. *The Sense and Non-Sense of Revolt: The Powers and Limits of Psychoanalysis*, Vol. 1. New York: Columbia University Press, 2000.

———. *Revolt, She Said.* New York: Semiotext(e), 2002.

———. *Intimate Revolt: The Powers and Limits of Psychoanalysis*, Vol. 2. New York: Columbia University Press, 2002.

Latour, Bruno. *Politics of Nature: How to Bring the Sciences into Democracy.* Cambridge, MA: Harvard University Press, 2004.

Rashdall, Hastings. *The Universities of Europe in the Middle Ages.* Oxford: Oxford University Press, 1936.

Rosaldo, Renato. *Culture and Truth: The Remaking of Social Analysis.* Boston: Beacon Press, 1989.

Rudolph, Frederick. *The American College and University: A History.* New York: Knopf, 1962.

Sorum, Christina Elliot. "The Problem of Mission: A Brief Survey of the Changing Mission of the Liberal Arts." In *Liberal Arts Colleges in American Higher Education: Challenges and Opportunities.* American Council of Learned Societies. ACLS Occasional Paper, No. 59, 2005.

Speers, Sam. "Secularity, Spirituality, and Liberal Arts Education." *Social Science Research Council* (2007), accessed 15 July, 2008. http://religion.ssrc.org/reforum/.

Strauss, Anselm. *Mirrors & Masks: The Search for Identity.* New Brunswick, NJ: Transaction Publishers, 1959.

Turner, Victor. *The Forest of Symbols: Aspects of Ndembu Ritual.* Ithaca, NY: Cornell University Press, 1967.

———. *Dramas, Fields and Metaphors: Symbolic Action in Human Society.* Ithaca, NY: Cornell University Press, 1974.

———. "Passages, Margins, and Poverty: Religious Symbols of Communitas." In *Dramas, Fields and Metaphors: Symbolic Action in Human Society*, 231–271. Ithaca, NY: Cornell University Press, 1974.

———. *The Ritual Process: Structure and Anti-Structure.* Ithaca, NY: Cornell University Press, 1977.

———. *From Ritual to Theater: The Human Seriousness of Play*. New York: PAJ Publications, 1982.

———. *The Anthropology of Performance*. New York: PAJ Publications, 1987.

Wallerstein, Immanuel. *The Modern World-System*. Vol. 1, *Capitalist Agriculture and the Origins of the European World-Economy in the Sixteenth Century*. New York/London: Academic Press, 1974.

The White House. *The Federal Response to Hurricane Katrina: Lessons Learned*, 2006, accessed January 15, 2008. http://www.whitehouse.gov/reports/katrina-lessons-learned/.

Wieruszowski, Helene. *The Medieval University*. New York: Van Nostrand, 1966.

Žižek, Slavoj. "How Did Marx Invent the Symptom?" In *The Sublime Object of Ideology*, 11–53. New York: Verso Books, 1989.

———. "The Subject Supposed to Loot and Rape: Reality and Fantasy in New Orleans." *In These Times* (October 20, 2005), accessed July 15, 2008. *http://www.inthesetimes.com/article/2361*.

VI

CONCLUSION

17

Mentors, Centaurs, and Tutors

The Old "New Pedagogy" of Simon's Rock[1]

NANCY YANOSHAK

BACK TO SIMON'S ROCK

In the preceding pages we have discussed our experiences teaching and learning at Simon's Rock in a number of disciplines and interdisciplinary areas across the liberal arts curriculum. Our contributions have been oriented toward demonstrating how "younger scholars" (our first-year students and sophomores) and students of traditional college age (our juniors and seniors) can be engaged in the work of a demanding Baccalaureate program. We trust that some of what we have said will resonate with the practices at other institutions, and hope that we have provided some ideas worth considering to colleagues interested in the teaching areas we have covered.

Beyond the specifics of classroom experiences and pedagogical strategies, we have wanted to convey something of the ethos and the spirit of the learning culture at Simon's Rock. Animating all of the works presented here, and underlying what we hope to accomplish in our day-to-day activities, is what we have termed a "new pedagogy." Neither teacher-centered (as it had been for much of the past in the West) nor even student-centered (as oft described in contemporary literature on education), this idea is grounded in a pedagogical relationship that is genuinely a two-way street, involving students and teachers in a joint enterprise that is important and meaningful to both. We understand that for the most part, what we have presented are our "success stories" about this joint enterprise, and we want to acknowledge here that we are not in fact asserting that Simon's Rock is an educational utopia. Like all other schools, we have had our times of struggle, and as I note in the introduction to this collection, some of these times have been almost unbearably tragic. On a more mundane level, like all relationships, the "pedagogical relationship" that defines us, regularly has its rocky moments. These are the times when the coziness of a place where "everybody knows your name" can turn claustrophobic, and when it appears to us that what we mainly have in common is not a delight in each other's commitment and creativity, but the foul weather of a late winter in New England, and the "campus cold."[2]

Life, then, at Simon's Rock has its conflicts, stresses, misunderstandings, and frustrations. We frequently assert egalitarianism as an educational ideal, but the pedagogical relationship that is at our core is inevitably inflected with power, and it must always be clear who bears the responsibilities of the teacher, and who those of the student. Nevertheless, it is in the end a fluid, flexible and rewarding connection. Teachers move with students (sometimes forward, and occasionally the reverse) as they traverse the complicated path to intellectual and personal maturity; students are encouraged, nurtured, and challenged to take this path, and their success at doing so is most impressive. Idealistic though it may sound, what most of us feel about what we do here as students, faculty, administrators, and staff, is gratitude for the opportunities we have had to know each other, and a deep satisfaction in what we have been able to accomplish together.

BACK TO THE FUTURE

The ancestors of our "new pedagogy" are found in Classical Greece in what came to be called the "Socratic Method," and in images of the wise and kind centaur Chiron as the tutor of Achilles and other Greek heroes.[3] They can be seen in the medieval era before higher education became fully institutionalized, when "the teacher was the school," i.e., when students, normally aged fifteen or sixteen, sought out particular scholars in order to study with them.[4] Other antecedents are the tutorial systems of Oxford and of Cambridge, discernable in outline roughly by the seventeenth century.[5] Closer to home, are the adaptations of this "don system" at Sarah Lawrence and then Bard in the 1930s, as part of their commitment to bringing the ideas of educational progressivism to higher education. Crucial too, was the birth of the progressive education movement itself in the 1890s, which sought to prepare our children for active participation in a democracy, and to rescue them from the stultifying disciplinary regimes of public secondary and primary schools, where, as the pioneer thinker on progressive education Francis W. Parker put it, subjugated pupils merely "stood up, recited, and sat down as if moved by strings controlled by electric wires."[6] Finally, there were the egalitarian and iconoclastic impulses of the sixties that formed backdrop of Mrs. Hall's vision of an education that genuinely matched the capabilities and desires of the adolescents of her time. Given this lineage, it would seem that the "new pedagogy" of Simon's Rock is also an "old pedagogy."

Simon's Rock has on occasion puzzled outside observers who did not quite know what to make of a college designed for sixteen-year-olds. Interestingly an appreciative story that aired on National Public Radio in 2009 described it as "enduring experiment that's tough to replicate."[7] Well aware of the unique aspects of our institution, we note, nevertheless, that the pedagogical relationship that characterizes it has been born and re-born many times, and in many places, whenever student and teacher could be brought together in productive ways. The most important lesson that our experiences at a "teaching-intensive" institution which is both "early college" and "college," have taught us is that students of all abilities and levels of preparation develop intellectual maturity if they are challenged to do so by knowledgeable and sympathetic adults who take them seriously. In this volume we offer our thoughts on the ways that we have attempted to do so, to all those who share our conviction that one of the greatest impediments young people face in realizing their full potential may in fact be their elders' underestimation of what this potential is.

NOTES

1. My thanks to Joan DelPlato and Sandra Smith for their helpful comments on earlier drafts of this chapter. Particular thanks are due to Pat Sharpe for seeing it through its final, and most challenging, stages.

2. These sorts of feelings, which we suspect occur in other small college communities, do call to mind one very difficult moment in our history of a far different order from the mundane frustrations of working and living in an intimate campus setting. Indeed in this particular case, the kinds of relationships between student and teacher that are the norm here were sorely tested. In 1990 a group of students who named themselves the "Defense Guard" surrounded, in turn, several professors and a student, and accused them of sexual harassment in a series of rehearsed chants. The students were suspended for their confrontational behavior, and then reinstated, and the instances of alleged harassment were investigated by the school. The incident raised questions for all of us about what led to these events, about what they meant for the school's mission of educating younger students, and about how to assess the responsibilities of the institution, and of particular individuals, for what occurred. For an analysis of the ways community members discussed the event, see Patricia Sharpe, and Frances E. Mascia-Lees, " 'Always Believe the Victim,' 'Innocent Until Proven Guilty,' 'There Is No Truth': The Competing Claims of Feminism, Humanism, and Postmodernism in Interpreting Charges of Harassment in the Academy," *Anthropological Quarterly* 66, no. 2, Constructing Mean-

ingful Dialogue on Difference: Feminism and Postmodernism in Anthropology and the Academy, Part 1 (April 1993): 87–98.

3. "Kheiron," Theoi Project Copyright © 2000–2008, Aaron J. Atsma, New Zealand, accessed September 30, 2010, *http://www.theoi.com/Georgikos/KentaurosKheiron.html*. The webpage cites passages from the works of classical authors such as Homer, Pindar, and Philostratus the Elder which refer to Chiron the Centaur as a wise, just, gentle, and/or inspiring teacher for Achilles, Jason, Asclepius, etc. Leon Botstein's *Jefferson's Children* first brought Chiron to my attention as an early representation of a mentorial figure in Western civilization. (*Jefferson's Children: Education and the Promise of American Culture* [New York: Doubleday, 1997], 100–101.)

4. Lowrie John Daly, SJ., *The Medieval University* (New York: Sheed and Ward, 1961), 5. Daly's italics removed in the quote above. Also on the connection between teacher and student as key in the formative period of European higher education, see Daly, pp. 18, 122, and Helene Wierusowski, *The Medieval University* (Princeton, NJ: D. Van Nostrand Company Inc., 1966), 16. Daly (p. 126) puts the age of matriculation at fifteen to sixteen; Wierusowski (p. 106), indicates that a student could be fourteen or even younger.

5. Merry E. Wiesner, review of *The History of the University of Oxford*, Volume III: *The Collegiate University*, by James McConica, *The Sixteenth Century Journal* 18, no. 2 (summer 1987): 302; *The Cambridge History of English and American Literature in 18 Volumes (1907–21)*. Volume IX. *From Steele and Addison to Pope and Swift.*, XV. Education., § 24. The Oxford Tutorial System, Accessed on line, December 3, 2010, http://www.bartleby.com/219/1524.html.

6. Francis W. Parker, *Talks on Pedagogics: An Outline of the Theory of Concentration* (New York and Chicago: E. L. Kellogg and Co., 1894), 364, accessed and downloaded October 3, 2010, *http://www.archive.org/details/talksonpedagogic01park*.

7. Larry Abramson, "Starting College While Still in School," National Public Radio, January 6, 2009, Transcript accessed October 3, 2010, *http://www.npr.org/templates/story/story.php?storyId=99056483*.

WORKS CITED

Abramson, Larry. "Starting College While Still in School." National Public Radio, January 6, 2009, Transcript accessed October 3, 2010. *http://www.npr.org/templates/story/story.php?storyId=99056483*.

Daly, Lowrie John, SJ. *The Medieval University*. New York: Sheed and Ward, 1961.

Botstein, Leon. *Jefferson's Children: Education and the Promise of American Culture*. New York: Doubleday, 1997.

Parker, Francis W. *Talks on Pedagogics: An Outline of the Theory of Concentration*. New York and Chicago: E. L. Kellogg and Co., 1894. Accessed and downloaded October 3, 2010, *http://www.archive.org/details/talksonpedagogic01park*.

Sharpe, Patricia, and Frances E. Mascia-Lees. "'Always Believe the Victim,' 'Innocent Until Proven Guilty,' 'There Is No Truth': The Competing Claims of Feminism, Humanism, and Postmodernism in Interpreting Charges of Harassment in the Academy." *Anthropological Quarterly* 66, no. 2. Constructing Meaningful Dialogue on Difference: Feminism and Postmodernism in Anthropology and the Academy. Part 1 (April 1993): 87–98.

The Cambridge History of English and American Literature in 18 Volumes (1907–21). Volume IX. *From Steele and Addison to Pope and Swift*. XV. Education. § 24. The Oxford Tutorial System. Accessed December 3, 2010, http://www.bartleby.com/219/1524.html.

Theoi Project Copyright © 2000–2008, Aaron J. Atsma, New Zealand. "Kheiron." Accessed September 30, 2010. *http://www.theoi.com/Georgikos/KentaurosKheiron.html*.

Wieruszowski, Helene. *The Medieval University*. Princeton, NJ: D. Van Nostrand Company, Inc., 1966.

Wiesner, Merry E. Review of *The History of the University of Oxford*, Volume III: *The Collegiate University*, by James McConica. *The Sixteenth Century Journal* 18, no. 2 (summer 1987): 302–304.

List of Contributors

(Teaching areas of faculty at Simon's Rock listed in parentheses)

Asma Abbas (Politics, Philosophy, 2005–) B.B.A. (Hons.) 1997, M.B.A., Institute of Business Administration, Karachi, Pakistan, 1998; M.A., New School for Social Research, 2001; Ph.D., The Pennsylvania State University, 2005.

Nuola Akinde, B.A., Bard College at Simon's Rock, 2009.

Loren L. AliKhan, B.A., *summa cum laude*, Bard College at Simon's Rock, 2003; J.D, *magna cum laude*, Georgetown University, 2006.

Allen B. Altman (Mathematics, 1986–2008, Faculty Emeritus) B.A., Stanford University, Phi Beta Kappa, 1964; M.A., Columbia University, 1965; Ph.D., Columbia University, 1968.

Linda Anderson (Psychology, Visiting Professor, 2007–2009) A.B., Boston University, 1976; M.S.,Teachers College, Columbia University, 1979; M.Phil., Columbia University, 1983, Ph.D., Columbia University, 1983. Tenured Professor within the City University of New York (CUNY).

Noah Appelbaum, B.A., *magna cum laude*, Bard College at Simon's Rock, 2009.

Gabriel V. Asfar (French, Arabic, 1983–) B.A., Phi Beta Kappa, Hamilton College, 1966; M.A., Princeton University, 1968; Ph.D., Princeton University, 1972.

Els Baum, B.A., *summa cum laude*, Bard College at Simon's Rock, 2010.

Jennifer Browdy de Hernandez (Literature, Gender Studies, 1994–) B.A. *magna cum laude*, Bard College at Simon's Rock, 1982; M.A., New York University, 1987; Ph.D., New York University, 1994.

Laura Cheung, B.A., *summa cum laude*, Bard College at Simon's Rock, 2009.

Chris Coggins (Geography, Asian Studies, 1998–) B.A., Wesleyan University, 1985, M.S., Louisiana State University, 1991; Ph.D., Louisiana State University, 1998.

Joan DelPlato (Art History, 1987–) B.A., *magna cum laude*, Phi Beta Kappa, University of Buffalo, 1975; M.A., University of California Los Angeles, 1980; Ph.D., University of California Los Angeles, 1987.

Rebecca Fiske (Literature 1986–; Dean of New Students 1994–2010) B.A., Bennington College, 1980; M.A.T., Smith College, 1986; Ph.D., State University of New York, Albany, 1999.

Brendan Flynn, B.A., Bard College at Simon's Rock, 2009.

Michael Lawrence, B.A., *summa cum laude*, Bard College at Simon's Rock, 2002; M.A., University of Iowa, 2005; Ph.D., University of Iowa, 2009.

Dara Levy-Bernstein, B.A., *cum laude*, Bard College at Simon's Rock, 2009.

Philip Mabry, (Sociology, 2003–2009) B.S., *cum laude*, Alpha Epsilon Delta, University of Pittsburgh, 1987, Ph.D., University of Pittsburgh, 1996.

Mary B. Marcy (Political Science; Provost and Vice-President, 2004–) B.A. with honors, University of Nebraska, 1987; M.Phil., University of Oxford, 1989; D.Phil., University of Oxford, 1992.

John E. Myers (Music, Interactive Arts, Asian Studies, 1987–) B.A., Towson State University, 1977; M.M., Howard University, 1979; Ph.D., University of Maryland, 1987.

Dylan Neely, B.A., *magna cum laude*, Bard College at Simon's Rock, 2010; Fulbright Grant, Belgrade, Serbia, 2010-11.

Anne O'Dwyer (Psychology, 1996–; Associate Dean of Academic Affairs, 2008–2010; Dean of Academic Affairs, 2010–) B.A., *summa cum laude*, Phi Beta Kappa, Boston College, 1987; Ph.D. Boston College, 1996.

Anastasia Rodionova, B.A., Bard College at Simon's Rock, 2010.

Samuel Ruhmkorff (Philosophy 2001–; Dean of Academic Affairs, 2005–2010) A.B., *summa cum laude*, Washington University in St. Louis, 1993; M.A., The University of Michigan, 1996; Ph.D., The University of Michigan, 2001.

Patricia Sharpe (Literature, Women's Studies, 1983–; Dean of Academic Affairs, 1993–2005; Elizabeth Blodgett Hall Chair in Literature, 2005–; Dean of Studies, Bard High School Early College, 2001–2003; 2007–) B.A., Barnard College, 1964; Ph.D., University of Texas at Austin, 1975.

Wendy Shifrin (Dance, Women's Studies, 1984–) B.A., University of Michigan, 1972; M.A., New York University, 1980.

Emanuel Stults, B.A., Bard College at Simon's Rock, 2010.

Laurence D. Wallach (Music, 1972–; Livingston Hall Chair in Music, 2005–) A.B., Columbia University, 1965, M.A., Columbia University, 1968, Ph.D., Columbia University. 1973.

John B. Weinstein (Chinese, Asian Studies 2001–; Emily H. Fisher Faculty Fellow, 2009– 2011) A.B., *summa cum laude*, Phi Beta Kappa, Harvard College, 1993; M.A., Columbia University, 1996, Ph.D., Columbia University, 2002.

Nancy Yanoshak, (History, Women's Studies, 1982–; Emily H. Fisher Faculty Fellow 2007–2009) B.A., with high distinction, Phi Beta Kappa, Phi Alpha Theta, Phi Kappa Phi, The Pennsylvania State University, 1970; M.A., The Pennsylvania State University, 1973; Ph.D., Georgetown University, 1981.

Index